EXERCISES

IN

LATIN COMPOSITION,

ADAPTED TO

BULLIONS' LATIN GRAMMAR;

WITH

VOCABULARIES,

LATIN AND ENGLISH,—ENGLISH AND LATIN.

BY

REV. PETER BULLIONS, D. D.

LATE PROFESSOR OF LANGUAGES IN THE ALBANY ACADEMY; AUTHOR OF THE SERIES OF GRAMMARS, GREEK, LATIN, AND ENGLISH, ON THE SAME PLAN; CLASSICAL SERIES, ETC.

NEW YORK:
PRATT, OAKLEY AND COMPANY,
NO. 21 MURRAY STREET.
1858.

JOHN F. TROW,
STEREOTYPER.

PREFACE.

THIS work completes the series of elementary works in Latin, originally proposed, and is intended to furnish a collection of exercises in illustration of the principles and idioms of the Latin language, as they are exhibited in the Latin Grammar. No pains have been spared to make the work as simple, and, at the same time, as complete as possible.

The first part is a mere grammatical exercise on the several parts of speech, with only so much of Syntax as is necessary to form simple sentences and phrases, and may be gone through orally, without any difficulty, when the pupil has gone through the Grammar. The second part contains illustrations of all the Rules of Syntax, and of the leading principles and idioms exhibited in the notes and observations under each rule, in the order in which they occur in the Grammar, to which reference is constantly made. At the end of each rule, and sometimes at intermediate places, an English exercise, without Latin, is furnished, for which the Latin words will be found in the English and Latin vocabulary at the end. This in general may be found too difficult for the beginner, and may be deferred till he goes through the book a second time.

All the examples in the second part, and most of those in the first, are strictly classical; and for the most part reference is made to the work from which they are taken. They have been selected for this work chiefly from Turner's Grammatical Exercises, a work long used in the Albany Academy—from Kenrick's Exercises adapted to his edition of Zumpt's Grammar—from Ellis's collection of exercises translated from Cicero—Carson's rules for the subjunctive mood,—and not a few have been taken from the classic authors themselves.

In using this work, every judicious teacher will of course adopt that plan which he may judge best adapted to the age, capacity, and attainments of his pupils. With those more advanced, the exercises may be gone through orally. In general, however, it may be best to have them written out by the pupils, and then, after the necessary corrections are made, they may be drilled in the principles the examples are intended to illustrate. This process should be continued orally, or by writing, or both, till the learner has become so familiar with the Latin construction and forms of expression, as to be prepared for original composition in Latin, or to retranslate into Latin, English translations from Latin Authors, which may then be compared with the original. Of the latter, a few examples are given as exercises at the end, and these may be increased to any extent by the teacher, as he may judge proper; or other exercises may be devised in the manner suggested at the end of the Latin Reader, p. 325.

TROY, N. Y., *August* 15, 1854.

EXPLANATIONS.

1. In Part I., the paragraphs are marked by a series of numbers from 1 to 75, for the sake of convenient reference. In Part II., this series is not continued.

2. In the English part, words in parentheses, ( ), are intended for explanation, or to give the literal form of the Latin expression. Words in brackets, [ ], are to be supplied, having no corresponding term usually expressed in Latin.

3. The numbers from 1 to 6, before nouns and pronouns, indicate the cases in their order: those from 1 to 10, before verbs, indicate the tenses in order from the present indicative, to the pluperfect subjunctive. The numbers from 11 to 14, indicate the tenses of the infinitive mood in their order.

4. The numbers from 1 to 75, in parentheses, ( ), indicate the paragraph marked by that number in Part I. Numbers with Gr. before them, and all numbers above 75, whether in parentheses or not, refer to the paragraph in the Latin Grammar marked by that number.

GRAMMATICAL EXERCISES.

PART I.

1.—The Exercises in Part I. are intended only as a *praxis* on the parts of speech, with just so much of syntax as may be necessary to form phrases and propositions of the simplest character. They may be used either orally, or written out as a stated exercise.

The verb *sum*, used occasionally here to form a simple sentence (Gr. 753), is inflected at length in the Grammar (187).

Exercises on the Declension of Nouns and Adjectives.

2.—In the Exercises on nouns and adjectives, the following things must be carefully attended to:

1. The English articles *a* or *an* and *the* have no corresponding words in Latin: thus, *cura* means "care," "a care," or, "the care;" *hasta*, "a spear," or, "the spear;" *hastæ*, "spears," or, "the spears."

2. In the following examples, the oblique cases of the Latin noun, without a preposition before it, are indicated by the English case-signs; viz., *of* for the genitive; *to* or *for*, for the dative; and *with*, *from*, *in*, *by*, for the ablative (Gr. 52). But a preposition before a noun determines its case, and requires the case-sign to be omitted (Gr. 235, 1, 2, 3). The possessive case in English is expressed by the genitive in Latin.

3. A noun or pronoun being the subject of a finite verb, must be in the nominative (Gr. 304).

4. An adjective must be in the same gender, number, and case, with the substantive which it qualifies (Gr. 263), or of which it is the predicate (Gr. 322). Also a noun in the predicate, after a finite verb, must be in the nominative case (Gr. 319).

N. B. In all the Exercises in this work in which the Latin words are given, nouns, adjectives, pronouns, and participles are put in the nominative case, and verbs in the infinitive; and they are to be made to correspond to the English in the first column.

English.	*Latin to be Changed.*
In the Forum.—From the love of country.—The tree of life.—The sound of the harp,—of many harps.—To the end of time.	Forum.—Amor patria.—Arbor vita.—Sonitus cithara,—multus cithara.—Ad finis tempus.
The goddess of the woods.—By the counsels of wisdom.—From the slaughter of wild beasts.—The prows of the ships.—With all the ships of Carthage.	Dea silva.—Consilium sapientia.—Cædis fera.—Prora navis.—Omnis navis Carthago.
The cares of men.—With many cares of many men.—To the armies of the Roman people.—By the liberality of friends.—Abundance of fodder.	Cura homo.—Multus cura multus homo.—Exercitus Romanus populus.—Liberalitas amicus.—Copia pabulum.
The way of life.—From many dangers.—On the bank of the river.—From the shore of the sea.—From the beginning to the end of time.	Via vita.—Multus periculum.—Ripa fluvius.—Littus mare.—Ab initium ad finis tempus.
The investigation of truth is appropriate to man.—Life is short.—The fear of death is common to all (men).—A conspiracy of the nobles was dangerous to the state.	Investigatio verum esse proprius homo.—Vita esse brevis.—Timor mors esse communis omnis (homo.)—Conjuratio nobilis esse periculosus civitas.
Cæsar's Commentaries.—Milo's house.—Cicero's letters.—Catiline's wickedness was great.	Cæsar Commentarium.—Milo domus.—Cicero epistola.—Catilina scelus esse magnus.
Antony was equal to Catiline in wickedness.—The wickedness of Antony was equal to the wickedness of Catiline.—Death is the end of life.	Antonius esse par Catilina scelus.—Scelus Antonius esse par scelus Catilina.—Mors esse finis vita.

3.—VOCABULARY.

Always, semper.
Are, is, was, sum, esse, fui (Gr. 187).
Black, niger, gra, grum.
Crow, corvus, i, 2.
Dangerous, periculosus, a, um.
Eternal, sempiternus, a, um, adj.
Feather, pluma, æ, 1.
Forest, silva, æ, 1.
Friend, amīcus, i, 2.
Future, futūrus, a, um.
Good, bonus, a, um.
Happiness, felicitas, atis, 3.
Knowledge, scientia, æ, 1.
Liberty, libertas, atis, 3.
Man, homo, homĭnis, 3.
Miltiades, Miltiades, is, 3
Not, non.
Reward, præmium, i, 2.
Swan, cycnus, i, 2.
Thing, res, rei, 5.
Tree, arbor, ŏris, 3.
Useful, utilis, e.
Virtue, virtus, ūtis, 3.
White, albus, a, um.
Wild beast, fera, æ, 1.

Translate the following phrases into Latin—the words will be found in the preceding vocabulary.

Virtue's reward.—The trees of the forest.—A crow's feathers are black, a swan's feathers are white.—The happiness of good men is eternal.—Men are useful to men.—The knowledge of future things is not always useful.—Miltiades was a friend to the liberty of all [men].—Happiness is the reward of the good.—The wild beasts in the forest are dangerous to men.—The rewards of virtue.—Trees are in the forest.—Trees are useful.—Happiness is the reward of virtue to good men.

EXERCISES ON VERBS.

4.—In the Exercises on the Latin verb, the following things should be carefully noticed, viz.:

1. The noun or pronoun, coming before a finite verb, is its subject or nominative, and must be in the nominative case (Gr. 304).

2. The noun or pronoun following a transitive-active or deponent verb, without any case-sign, is its object, and must be put in the accusative (Gr. 436, 437).

3. The same idea is expressed passively, by making the object of the verb in the active voice the subject in the passive, and putting the doer in the ablative governed by *a*, *ab*, *abs*, "by" (Gr. 136-1 and 530).

4. The finite verb must be made to agree with its subject-nominative in number and person (Gr. 303), and, in the com-

pound tenses of the passive form, the participle must agree with it in gender, number, and case (Gr. 263, 264). The subject of the verb, when a pronoun of the *first* or *second* person, is commonly omitted; also *ille* frequently when the subject of the verb is the third person (Gr. 305).

5. The introductory word *there* in English (An. & Pr. Gr. 529) has no corresponding word in Latin: thus, *est* means "is," or, "there is;" *sunt*, "are," or, "there are."

6. *Interrogative Sentences.*—A question is made in Latin in four different ways, as follows:

1st. By an interrogative pronoun; as, *Quis vĕnit?* "Who comes?" *Quem misit?* "Whom did he send?"

2d. By an interrogative adverb; as, *Unde venit?* "Whence came he?" *Cur venit?* "Why did he come?"

3d. By the interrogative particles *num*, *an*, or the enclitic *ne*, which, in direct questions, have no corresponding English word in the translation; as, *Num venit?* or, *an vēnit?* or, *venitne?* "Has he come?" Negative interrogations are made by *annon* or *nonne;* as, *Annon* (or *nonne*) *venit?* "Has he not come?"

4th. By simply placing an interrogation mark at the end of the question; as, *Vis me hoc facere?* "Do you wish me to do this?"

INDICATIVE MOOD.

PRESENT TENSE.

5.—The present tense expresses what is going on at the present time (Gr. 157).

I praise thee; Thou art praised by me.	Ego *laudare* tu; Tu *laudari* a ego.
Thou desirest wisdom; Wisdom is desired by thee.	Tu *expĕtĕre* sapientia; Sapientia *expĕti* a tu.
God governs the world; The world is governed by God.	Deus *gubernare* mundus; Mundus *gubernari* a Deus.
We write letters; Letters are written by us.	Ego *scribĕre* litera; Litera *scribi* a ego.

You get riches; Riches are gotten by you.	Tu *parare* divitiæ; Divitiæ *parari* a tu.
All [men] blame ungrateful [persons]; The ungrateful are blamed by all.	Omnis *culpare* ingratus; Ingratus *culpari* ab omnis.

Deponent Verbs.

I confess.	Ego *fatēri.*
Thou deservest praise.	Tu *merēri* laus.
The sun rises.	Sol *oriri.*
We agree to thee.	Ego *assentiri* tu.
You forget injuries.	Tu *oblivisci* injuria.
Men die.	Homo *mori.*

Interrogations.

When a question is asked, the nominative case in English is placed after the verb, or the sign of the verb (An. & Pr. Gr. 502).

Dost thou praise me? (4–6).	An tu (tune) *laudare* ego?
Am I praised by thee?	An ego (egone) *laudari* a tu?
Do I not praise thee? Art thou not praised by me?	Annon (nonne) *laudare* tu? Annon (nonne) *laudari* a ego?
Dost thou desire wisdom? Is wisdom desired by thee?	An tu (tune) *expetĕre* sapientia? An sapientia *expĕti* a tu?
Dost thou not desire wisdom? Is not wisdom desired by thee?	Annon *expĕtĕre* sapientia? Nonne (annon) sapientia *expĕti* a tu?
Does God govern the world? Is the world governed by God?	An Deus *gubernare* mundus? An mundus *gubernari* a Deus?
Does not God govern the world? Is not the world governed by God? By whom is the world governed?	Nonne Deus *gubernare* mundus? Annon mundus *gubernari* a Deus? A quis *gubernari* mundus?

Note.—In this way may all the other sentences be made interrogatively, if thought proper.

Deponent Verbs.

Dost thou confess? Dost thou not confess?	Num tu *fatēri?* Annon tu *fatēri?*

Do I deserve praise? Do I not deserve praise?	An ego (egone) *merēri* laus? Annon ego *merēri* laus?
Does the sun rise? Does not the sun rise? &c.	An sol *oriri?* Nonne sol *oriri?* &c.

6.—VOCABULARY.

Accuse, accuso, are, avi, atum, v. tr. 1.
All, omnis, is, e, adj.
Appoint (create), creo, are, avi, atum, v. tr. 1.
Approve, probo, are, avi, atum, v. tr. 1.
Deed, factum, i, n. 2.
Do, facio, facĕre, feci, factum, v. tr. 3:—pass. fio, fieri, factus.
Find out, comperio, ire, perui, pertum, v. tr. 4.
Formerly, antea, adv.
From, a, ab, abs, prep.
Good, bonus, a, um, adj.
Greatly, valde, adv.
Hear, audio, īre, īvi, ītum, v. tr. 4.
If, si, conj.
Letter (an epistle), literæ, arum, fem. pl. 1, and epistola, æ, f. 1.
Love, diligo, ĕre, lexi, lectum, v. tr. 3:—pass. *loved*, *beloved*.
Madness, amentia, æ, f. 1.
Magistrate, magistratus, us, m. 4.
Man, homo, homĭnis, m. or f. 3.
Many, multus, a, um, adj.
Name, nomino, are, avi, atum, v. tr. 1.
No, nullus, a, um, adj.
Nobody (no one), nemo, ĭnis, c. 3.
Now, nunc, adv.
Overcome (to conquer), vinco, ĕre, vici, victum, v. tr. 3.
Reason, ratio, onis, f. 3.
Receive, recipio, ĕre, cepi, ceptum, v. tr. 3.
Send, mitto, ĕre, misi, missum, v. tr. 3.
Sulla (pr. n.) Sulla, æ, m. 1.
That, ille, illa, illud, -is, &c. adj. pr.
Then, tunc, adv.; tunc temporis.
Thing, negotium, i, n. 2 (commonly understood), and res, rei, f. 5.
This, hic, hæc, hoc, adj. pr.
To-day, hodie, adv. i. e. hoc die.
Well, bene, adv.
When, quum, cum, conj.
Yearly, annuus, a, um, adj.

Translate the following into Latin, observing carefully the directions, No. 4.—The words will be found in the preceding vocabulary. —The pronouns *I*, *thou*, *he*, *she*, *it*; *we*, *you*, *they*, when the subject of a verb, are commonly understood, being sufficiently indicated by the person and number of the verb itself. See Gr. § 28.

English Examples to be turned into Latin.

I name no one—no one is named by me. Madness overcomes reason—reason is overcome by madness. He finds out all these *things*—all these *things* are finding out by him (An. & Pr. Gr. 456 and Appendix V.). Nobody accuses Sulla—Sulla is accused by nobody. They appoint magistrates—magistrates are appointed by them. Sulla approves the deed—the deed is approved by

Sulla. Do you hear these good men (4–6)? I love the man greatly—the men are greatly beloved by all.

Note.—Change such of the preceding sentences as will make sense into the negative form by inserting *non*:—change into the interrogative form, as directed, 4–6.

IMPERFECT TENSE.

7.—The imperfect tense represents an action or event as passing and still unfinished at a certain time past, expressed or implied (Gr. 159).

I wrote (did write) letters then; Letters were then written by me.	Ego tunc *scribĕre* litera; Litera tunc *scribi* a ego.
At what time thou soughtest for* me; I was sought for by thee.	Quis tempus (Gr. 565) tu *quærĕre* ego; Ego *quæri* a tu.
When Numa held the kingdom; When the kingdom was held by Numa.	Ubi Numa *obtinēre* regnum; Ubi regnum *obtinēri* a Numa.
At that age we gave our minds (endeavour) to learning; you always gave your minds (endeavour) to play.	Ego isthuc ætas (Gr. 592) *dare* opera literæ; tu semper *dare* opera lusus.
While the fields did flourish.	Dum arvum *florēre.*

Deponent Verbs.

I was glad so long as thou didst follow virtue, and so long as he reverenced his parents.	Ego *lætari*, donec tu *sectari* virtus, et donec ille *reverēri* parens suus.
Whilst we hunted hares, you followed, they talked in the mean time.	Dum ego *venari* lepus, tu *sequi*, ille *fabulari* interea.
In the golden age, men observed fidelity and integrity of their own accord, without law, nor did they fear a judge; ditches did not yet surround towns; the earth gave	In ætas aureus homo, spontis suus (Gr. 542), sine lex, fides rectumque *colĕre*, nec *timēre* judex; nondum *cingĕre* oppidum fossa; per sui

* *Querĕre* means "to seek," or, "to seek for;" so that *for* here is not the sign of the dative.

all [things] of itself, and bore corn (fruits), not being ploughed (unploughed). — *dare* omnis tellus *f.* et frugis, inaratus, *ferre.*—Ov. *Met.* 1.

Interrogatively (4–6).

Didst thou write letters then? Were letters writing by thee then? — An tu (tune) tunc *scribĕre* litera? An tunc *scribi* (*scribi*ne) litera a tu?

Did I not write letters? Were not letters writing by me? — Annon (nonne) *scribĕre* litera? Annon litera *scribi* a ego?

Didst thou seek for me? Was I sought for by thee? — Tune *quærĕre* ego? An ego (egone) *quæri* a tu?

Did I not seek for thee? Wert not thou sought for by me? — Nonne *quærĕre* tu? Annon tu *quæri* a ego?

Did Numa then hold the kingdom? Was the kingdom held by Numa? By whom was the kingdom held then? &c. — An Numa tunc *obtinēre* regnum? An regnum *obtinēri* a Numa? A quis tunc *obtinēri* regnum? &c.

8.—The present tense may often be rendered into English by the participle in *ing*, with *am*, *art*, *is*, *are*, prefixed as auxiliaries, and likewise the imperfect, with *was*, *wert*, *were*, as auxiliaries. This form in many cases has also a passive sense. An. & Pr. Gr. 506, and 456 with reference, and 457.

EXAMPLES.

PRESENT TENSE.

I am writing letters; Letters are writing. — Ego *scribĕre* litera; Litera *scribi.*

What art thou doing? What is doing there? — Quis tu *agĕre?* Quis illic *agi?*

He is building a house; A house is building. — Ille *ædificare* domus; Domus *ædificari.*

We are getting (are learning by heart) our lesson. — Ego *ediscĕre* prælectio.

You are talking. — Tu *fabulari.*

They are making (composing) verses. — Ille *componĕre* versus.

IMPERFECT TENSE.

I was writing letters then; Letters were writing.	*Scribĕre* litera tunc; Litera *scribi*.
What wast thou doing? What was doing there?	Quis *agĕre?* Quis istic *agi?*
He was building a house; A house was building.	Ille *ædificare* domus; Domus *ædificari*.
We were reading.	Ego *legĕre*.
You were playing in the mean time.	Tu *ludĕre* interea.
They were setting trees; Trees were setting at that time.	Ille *serĕre* arbor; Tunc tempus (Gr. 592) arbor *seri*.

English Examples to be turned into Latin.

The words in the following Examples will be found in Vocabulary, No. 6, p. 10.

They accused us.—Nobody accused them.—We were accused by them.—Did they not accuse us?—We were not accused by the magistrates.—Were we not accused by them?—No one approved those deeds.—That deed was approved by no one then.—Were those deeds then approved by many (men)?—Did you receive a letter from me?—We received letters from them.—They did not receive letters from us.—Did not he receive a letter from them?—They named Sulla.—Sulla was named by them.—Were they not named by Sulla?—We loved the men greatly.—The men were loved greatly by all.—Did not they love us?

PERFECT TENSE.

9.—The perfect tense is used in two different senses—*definite* and *indefinite*.

Note.—In the compound tenses of the passive voice, or in deponent verbs, the participle must be made to agree with the subject in gender, number, and case. (Gr. 164. Note, and 263, 264.)

1. *The Perfect Definite.*

10.—The PERFECT DEFINITE represents an action or event as completed at the present time, or in a period of time of which the present forms a part—and is translated by the English present-perfect (An. & Pr. Gr. 407); as, *scripsi*, "I have written;" *scriptum est*, "It has been written." (Gr. 162.)

EXAMPLES.

I have often sought for thee. Thou hast often been sought for by me.	Sæpe *quærĕre* tu. Tu sæpe *quæsītus esse* a ego.
Thou hast spoken well, and hast deserved praise.	Tu *locūtus esse* bene, et *merĭtus esse* laus.
She has found [her] parents.	Ille *reperīre* parens.
We have made trial. Trial has been made by us.	*Facĕre* periculum. Periculum *factus esse* a ego.
You have kept [your] promise. [Your] promise has been kept by you.	Tu *solvĕre* fides. Fides *solūtus esse* a tu.
All [men] have sinned, and have deserved punishment.	Omnis *peccare*, et *merĭtus esse* pœna.

Interrogatively.

Hast thou often sought for me? Have I often been sought for by thee? Have I not often sought for thee? Hast thou not often been sought for by me? &c.

2. *The Perfect Indefinite.*

11.—The perfect indefinite represents an action or event simply as past, and is translated by the English past tense (An. & Pr. Gr. 415); as, *scripsi*, "I wrote;" *scriptum est*, "it was written." (Gr. 163.)

EXAMPLES.

I sought (did seek) for thee yesterday. Thou wast sought for by me yesterday.	Ego *quærĕre* tu heri. Tu *quæsītus esse* a ego heri.
Thou didst well. It was well done by thee.	*Benefacĕre*. *Benefactum esse* a tu.
God created the world. The world was created by God out of nothing.	Deus *creare* mundus. Mundus *creatus esse* a Deus ex nihilum.

Pompey got great praise.	Pompeius *adeptus esse* laus magnus.
We went away presently.	Ego statim *abire.*
You saw it.	Tu *vidēre.*
They did not believe these things. These things were not credited by them.	Ille non *credĕre* hic. Hic non *credĭtus esse* ab ille.

Interrogatively.

Didst thou seek for me?	Num *quærĕre* ego?
Didst thou not seek for me?	Annon (nonne) *quærĕre* ego?
Was I sought for by thee? Was I not sought for by thee? &c.	Num *quæsītus esse* a tu? Nonne *quæsītus esse* a tu? &c.

And so in the rest.

This tense, after *antequam, postquam, ubi,* or *ut* for *postquam,* may be translated as the pluperfect (Gr. 164–3).

English Examples to be turned into Latin.

(See Vocabulary, No. 6.)

I have named no one.—Did they name Sulla?—Has nobody been named?—They have found out all these *things.*—Have these *things* been found out?—Did they not find out that?—Has Sulla been accused?—They have not accused Sulla.—All *men* have approved these things.—Have not these things been approved by all?—Did you hear that good man?—Have you all heard him?—They received letters then.—They have received letters to-day.—Were letters received formerly?—Have letters been received to-day?—An epistle was sent to Sulla.—He did these things well.—All the letters were sent by us to the magistrates.

PLUPERFECT TENSE.

12.—The pluperfect tense represents an action as completed at or before a certain past time expressed or implied; as, *scripseram,* "I had written;" *scriptum erat,* "it had been written." (Gr. 165, 166.)

EXAMPLES.

I had sought for thee before. Thou hadst been sought for by me before.	*Quærĕre* tu antea. Tu *quæsĭtus esse* a ego antea.
Thou hadst promised the day before.	Tu *promittĕre* pridie.
The master had often forbidden that. That had often been forbidden by the master.	Magister sæpe *prohibēre* is. Is sæpe *prohibĭtus esse* a magister.
We had dined long (much) before.	*Prandēre* multo ante.
You had asked.	Tu *rogare*.
[Their] fathers had taken care of* that. That had been taken care of* by [their] fathers.	Pater *curare* is. Is *curatus esse* a pater.

Interrogatively.

Hadst thou sought for me? Hadst thou not sought for me before? Had I been sought for by thee? Had I not been sought for by thee? &c.

English Examples to be turned into Latin.

(See Vocabulary, No. 6.)

I had named no one.—Had nobody been named?—They had found out all these *things*.—Had these *things* been found out?—Had they not found out that *thing?*—Had they accused this man?—This man had not been accused by them.—They had appointed a magistrate.—Had magistrates been appointed by them?—All things had been approved.—Had the men heard these *things?*—Had the magistrates been appointed then?—No one had been named.

13.—In the compound tenses of the passive voice, the participle is sometimes regarded nearly in the sense of an adjective. In that case, the auxiliary *sum* becomes the verb, and is translated in its own tense; thus, perfect, *scriptum est*, "it is writ-

* *Curo* signifies "to take care of," and governs the accusative.

ten," instead of "it was written," or "it has been written;" pluperfect, *scriptum erat*, "it was written," instead of "it has been written." (An. & Pr. Gr. App. V. II. Gr. 182–3.)

EXAMPLES.

I am reduced to poverty.	*Redactus esse* ad paupertas.
The work is finished.	Opus *fīnītus esse.*
The city is taken.	Urbs *captus esse.*
We are conquered.	Ego *victus esse.*
Her parents (the parents of her) are found.	Ejus parens *repertus esse.*
The times are changed.	Tempus *n. mutatus esse.*

So in the pluperfect,

I was reduced to poverty.	*Redactus esse* ad paupertas.
The work was finished, &c.	Opus *fīnītus esse*, &c.

14.—A few intransitive verbs, both active and deponent, in the perfect and pluperfect, have the English verb *to be* instead of *have* as an auxiliary in the translation (An. & Pr. Gr. 374). Thus, *veni*, "I *am* come," for, "I have come;" *abiit*, "he *is* gone," for, "he has gone."—Pres. *moritur*, "he dies,"—"is dying."—Perf. *mortuus est*, "he *is* dead," for, "he has died."—Plup. *mortuus erat*, "he *was* dead," for, "he had died," &c. (An. & Pr. Gr. 374).

EXAMPLES.

PERFECT TENSE.

Thou art come quickly.	*Advenīre* citò.
He is gone away.	*Abīre.*
He is entered into the city.	*Ingressus esse* (in) urbs.
The sun is set.	Sol *occidĕre.*
The moon is risen.	Luna *ortus esse.*
The time is past.	Tempus *prœterīre.*
The labour is lost.	Opera *perīre.*
We are set together on the soft grass.	In mollis *considĕre* herba. VIRG. (Gr. 608).
The twenty pounds are lost.	Viginti minæ *perīre.*—TER.

PLUPERFECT TENSE.

The summer was come then.	Tunc *venīre* æstas.
He was gone away before.	Ille *abīre* antea.

The time was past.	Tempus *præterīre.*
The labour was lost.	Opera *perīre.*
The sun was set.	Sol *occidĕre.*
The morning star was risen.	Lucifer *ortus esse.*—Ov.
We were set together on the grass.	*Considĕre* in herba. (Gr. 608.)

FUTURE TENSE.

1. Expressing *will*, *purpose*, or *resolution*.

15.—*Will*, as an auxiliary, in English, expresses the will, purpose, or resolution of a person with respect to his own actions or state; *shall*, his will, purpose, or resolution with respect to the actions or state of another under his control (An. & Pr. Gr. 336). Hence, ordinarily, without a preceding clause, in order to express *will*, *purpose*, or *resolution*—*will* is used in the first person, and *shall*, in the second and third.

EXAMPLES.

I will write letters. Letters shall be written by me.	*Scribĕre* litera. Litera *scribi* a ego.
Thou shalt hear the whole matter.	*Audīre* res omnis.
He shall suffer punishment. Punishment shall be suffered by him.	Ille *dăre* pœnæ. Pœnæ *dări* ab ille.
We will do our endeavour. Endeavour shall be used by us.	Ego *dăre* opera. Opera *dări* a ego.
You shall know.	Tu *scire.*
The boys shall play.	Puer *ludĕre.*

Imperatively.

Thou shalt worship God, reverence thy parents, and imitate the good.	*Venerari* Deus, *reverēri* parens, et *imitari* bonus.
Thou shalt beware of* passionateness, govern thy tongue, and	*Cavēre* iracundia, *moderari* (Gr. 405–3d) lingua, et

* *Of* is here part of the English to the verb *cavēre*, which signifies *to beware of*, and governs an accusative case.

follow (practise) peace; neither* shalt thou do injury to any one. — *colĕre* pax; neque *facĕre* injuria quisquam.

16.—Exc. An absolute promise, or purpose, or resolution, so fixed as to divest ourselves in some measure of *will*, and put ourselves at the disposal of another, is better expressed, in the first person in English, by the sign *shall* (An. & Pr. Gr. 338). Thus,

(Since it is proper) we shall labor chiefly in these things. — *In hic potissimum* elaborāre.—Cic. Off. 1. 31.

(At your command) we shall use diligence. — Adhibēre *diligentia.*

Interrogatively.

17.—In asking questions, the reference obviously is to the will, purpose, &c., of the person addressed. Hence, in interrogative sentences of this kind, *will* is used in English in the second person, and *shall*, in the first and third.

EXAMPLES.

Wilt thou write letters? Shall he write letters? Shall I write letters? Shall letters be written by thee?—by me?—by him? Shall I hear the whole matter? Wilt thou hear, &c. (as in the preceding sentences.)

2. Expressing *simple futurity.*

18.—The use of *shall* and *will*, in English, expressing simple futurity, or, that an event will happen, is directly the reverse of what it is when they express will, purpose, or resolution; that is to say, without a preceding clause, *shall* is used in the first person, and *will* in the second and third (An. & Pr. Gr. 340).

EXAMPLES.

I shall see. — Ego *vidēre.*

Thou wilt oblige him (wilt do an agreeable thing to him). — *Facĕre* 3 ille gratus.

* After *neither* and *nor*, the nominative case, in English, must be put after the verb, or the sign of the verb (An. & Pr. Gr. 767).

He will give thanks to thee. Thanks will be given to thee by him.	*Agĕre* gratia tu. Gratia *agi* tu ab ille.
We shall obtain leave. Leave will be obtained by us.	*Impetrare* venia. Venia *impetrari* a ego.
You will get (make) an estate.	Tu *facĕre* res.
They will get (find) friends. Friends will be gotten (found) by them.	Ille *invenīre* amīcus. Amīcus *invenīri* ab ille.

Interrogatively.

19.—In interrogative sentences having respect to simple futurity, the second person also is translated by *shall* (An. & Pr. Gr. 342); thus,

Shall I oblige him? Shall I not oblige him? Will he oblige us? Shalt thou see? Shalt thou not see? Will he see, &c.

Note.—After *adverbs, conjunctions*, and the relative *who* for *whosoever*, the sign is SHALL in all persons; as, *Scribes aliquid, si vacabis*, CIC. "You will write something, if you shall be at leisure."

In the prophetic style, both the second and the third person have the sign SHALL; as, *Et tu spectabĕre serpens*, OVID. *Met.* 3. "You also shall be looked upon being a serpent." *Puero, quo ferrea primum desinet, ac toto surget gens aurea mundo.* "The youth, under whom (in whose reign) the iron age shall first cease, and the golden age shall commence over all the world," VIRG. *Ecl.* 4.

Note.—These distinctions, however, respecting the use of *shall* and *will*, are more important in translating from Latin into English, than in translating from English into Latin; because in the latter case, whether *shall* or *will* is used, the tense in Latin is the future. Also, the future tense in Latin may sometimes be translated by the present in English, and consequently without either *shall* or *will* (An. & Pr. Gr. 406 & 436).

The Periphrastic future in RUS.

20.—The periphrastic future in *rus* (Gr. 214–8), used to intimate that a thing is about to be done, is sometimes rendered as the future tense in the manner stated above.

I shall see.	Ego *visurus esse.*
Thou wilt oblige him (wilt do an agreeable thing to him).	*Facturus esse* gratus 3 ille.

He will give thanks to thee.	Ille *acturus esse* gratia tu.
We shall obtain leave.	Ego *impetraturus esse* venia.
You will get (make) an estate.	Tu *facturus esse* res.
They will get (find) friends.	Ille *inventurus esse* amīcus.
Wilt thou (*fem.*) not tell (me) plainly?	Non *dictura esse* aperte? —TER. *Eun.* 5. 1.

English Examples to be turned into Latin.

(See Vocabulary, No. 6.)

[In the following English sentences, state whether the future is used to express *will, purpose, resolution;* or only *simple futurity.* This distinction will make no difference as to form in the Latin word, though the difference in sense will be the same as in English.]

I will accuse no one.—I shall accuse no one.—He shall be accused.—They will not be accused.—Will he not be accused (4–6, 3d)?—Shalt thou be accused?—Shall he accuse us?—Shall Sulla be accused by them?—Wilt thou name him?—Shalt thou not name them?—They will appoint magistrates.—They shall appoint magistrates.—Will they appoint magistrates?—Shall they not appoint magistrates?—Shall magistrates be appointed?—Will he receive the letter?—Shall I receive the letter?—Will the magistrates approve the deed?—Shall the magistrates approve the deed?—They shall approve.—They will approve.—Wilt thou approve these deeds?—He will hear.—These good men shall be heard.—Will they not hear?—They shall hear.—They will hear.

FUTURE-PERFECT TENSE.

21.—The future-perfect tense intimates that an action or event will be completed at or before a certain time yet future; as, *scripsĕro,* "I shall have written;" viz. at or before some future time.

1. Though this tense is properly rendered by the auxiliaries *shall have,* or *will have;* yet frequently, after conjunctions, &c., the *have,* or the *shall* or *will,* and sometimes both the auxiliaries are omitted (Gr. 168–2. An. & Pr. Gr. 412).

EXAMPLES.

When I (shall) have determined, I shall write.	Quum *constituĕre,* scribĕre.

When you (shall) have said all.	Quum *dicĕre* omnia.
After he has spoken with Cæsar.	Postquam *convenīre* Cæsarem.
When we (shall) have written letters. When letters (shall) have been written by us.	Ubi *scribĕre* litera. Ubi litera *scriptus esse* a ego.
When you (shall) have performed your promises. When promises (shall) have been (are) performed by you.	Quum *præstare* promissum. Quum promissum *præstātus esse* a tu.
As soon as (when first) they (shall) have heard.	Quum primum (Simul ac) *audīre.*
If I (shall) ask.	Si *rogare.*
If thou shalt obtain.	Si *impetrare.*
If any one (shall) discover.	Si quis *indicare.*
If we (shall) do that.	Si is *facĕre.*
If you (shall) make me Consul.	Si *facĕre* ego Consul.
Unless they (shall) come tomorrow.	Nisi cras *venīre.*

Come, gone, set, &c., have, in this case, the sign SHALL BE, or else only the same as in the perfect tense (14).

EXAMPLES.

When thou shalt be (art) once gone out.	Quum semel *exīre.*
When the time shall be (is) past.	Quum tempus *præterīre.*
When summer shall be (is) come.	Quum *venīre* æstas.
As soon as (when first) the sun shall be (is) set.	Quum primùm sol *occidĕre.*
As soon as he shall be (is) grown up.	Simul atque *adolescĕre.*
As soon as thou shalt be (art) come thither.	Simul ac *pervenīre illuc.*

2. Without conjunctions, &c. the sign of the first person is commonly SHALL, of the rest WILL—the *have* being omitted (Gr. 168–2).

EXAMPLES.

I shall see.	Ego *vidēre.*
Thou wilt do kindly, if thou wilt come.	*Facĕre* benigne, si venīre.

A covetous [man] will always want.	Avarus semper *egēre.*
We shall obtain.	*Impetrare.*
You will conquer.	*Vincĕre.*
They will get (find) friends.	Ille *invenire* amicus.

22.—Sometimes it is rendered by *shall have;* as, *Quum tu hæc leges, ego illum fortasse convenero,* I shall have spoken with him perhaps, when thou shalt read these things. Cic. *Att.* 9, 15. *Tibi Roma subegerit orbem,* Rome will have subdued the world for you. Lucan, 1. *Troja arserit igni? Dardanium toties sudârit sanguine litus?* Shall Troy have been burnt? &c. Virg. *Æn.* 2, 581.

English Examples to be turned into Latin.

(See Vocabulary, No. 6.)

When he has accused us, we shall hear.—When you (shall) have heard that.—If we (shall) do this.—If the magistrates (shall) have been appointed.—When the deeds (shall) have been approved.—When we (shall) have received the letter.—Thou wilt hear, if the magistrate (shall) be appointed.—If you (shall) have been appointed, we shall hear, &c.

IMPERATIVE MOOD.

23.—The imperative mood commands, exhorts, entreats, or permits; as, *scribe,* "write thou," (Gr. 149).

24.—The imperative mood in English has the subject or nominative placed after the verb. It is, however, generally understood; as, "come (thou) forth." The imperative of the third person is rendered into English by "let," in the second person, and the infinitive without "to" prefixed; as, *ito,* "let (thou) him go" (An. & Pr. Gr. 467, 468).

EXAMPLES.

PRESENT TENSE.

Learn thou good arts. Let good arts be learned by thee.	*Discĕre* bonus ars, f. Bonus ars *disci* a tu.
Shun thou sloth.	*Fugĕre* segnities.—Cat.

Let the victor have a horse.	Victor *habēre* equus.
Beware thou of passionateness.	Tu *cavēre* iracundia.
Call ye me.	*Vocare* ego.—PLAUT.
Let scholars obey their masters.	Discipulus magister *parēre*. (Gr. 405–3d.)
Let them suffer themselves to be taught.	Docēri sui *pati*.—CIC.

25.—The present subjunctive is often used instead of this mood, especially in forbidding, after *ne*, *nemo*, *nullus*, &c. (Gr. 150).

EXAMPLES.

Try that which thou canst [do].	Qui posse, is *tentare*.—CATO.
Love a parent, if he is kind; if otherwise, bear [him].	*Amare* parens, si æquus esse; si aliter, *ferre*.—PUBL.
Covet not other men's goods.	Ne *concupiscĕre* alienus.
Do not thou injury to any one.	Ne *facĕre* injuria quisquam.
Do not hurt any one.	Ne quis *nocēre*. (Gr. 405–1st.)
Give not up thyself to laziness.	Ne *tradĕre* tu socordia.
Give not yourselves wholly to pleasures; but rather give yourselves to learning.	Ne *dedĕre* tu totus voluptas; quin potius doctrina tu *dedĕre*.

26.—*Note.*—The conjunction *ut*, and some former verb, are here understood, and may be supplied; as, *fac, vide, cura, moneo, velim,* (*ut*) *tentes. Cave, vide, moneo,* (*ut*) *ne facias injuriam* (Gr. 144, 145).

27.—The future-perfect is also used instead of the imperative mood (Gr. 168–3).

EXAMPLES.

Remember thou.	Tu *meminisse*.
See thou to it.	Tu *vidēre*.
Do not say it.	Ne *dicĕre*.
Do not thou do injury.	Ne *facĕre* injuria.
Make not haste to speak.	Ne *festīnare* loqui.
Deride nobody.	Nemo *irridēre*.
Give not up thyself to idleness.	Ne *tradĕre* tu ignavia.
Let him look to it.	Ille *vidēre*.

28.—The future indicative (15) and the perfect subjunctive are sometimes used in a concessive or imperative sense; as, *liques vina*, "filtrate the wine;" *parta sit pecunia*, "suppose the money were obtained;" *hæc dicta sint patribus*, "let these things be told quickly to the fathers," (Gr. 173–4).

SUBJUNCTIVE MOOD.

29.—The indicative and the imperative are the only moods of the verb in Latin used in propositions strictly independent (Gr. 145). The subjunctive mood is used to restrict or modify the thought expressed by other parts of the verb with which it is connected. That connection is usually made by conjunctive particles expressed or understood, or by the relative; and the subjunctive so connected is rendered in a great variety of ways in English, according to the nature of the relation expressed—sometimes by the auxiliaries *may, can, might, could, would*, &c., as in the paradigms of the verb (Gr. 189); very often by the indicative after such connectives as *though, that, as*, &c.; not unfrequently by the infinitive; sometimes by the participle in *ing*, preceded by a preposition; and also in other ways to which the connection only can direct.

The following Exercises furnish examples of the various ways in which this mood is rendered; but the full consideration of the subject must be referred to its place in syntax, where the leading as well as dependent clauses being inserted, will direct to the proper rendering of this mood in each sentence.

PRESENT TENSE (Gr. 171).

30.—1. With some conjunction, adverb, indefinite, or relative, expressed; translated (generally) as the indicative (Gr. 170–3).

Seeing I am in health.	Quum *valēre*.
Have a care (see) what thou doest;—What is done by thee.	Vidēre quis *agĕre*;—Quis *agi* a tu.
There is no (nobody is) covetous man, who does not want.	Nemo avarus esse, qui non *egēre*.
Stay till we return.	Expectare dum *redīre*.
You do not know for whom you get money;—For whom money is gotten by you.	Nescire, quis *parare* pecunia;—Quis pecunia *parari* a tu.

Seeing covetous men always want, though they abound.	Quum avarus semper *egēre*, etiamsi *abundare*.
I wish I may become a scholar (learned).	Utinam *evadĕre* doctus.
— Thou mayest recover.	— Tu *convalescĕre*.
— The king may live long.	— Rex *vivĕre diu*.

Sometimes it is rendered by the participle in *ing*, with *am*, *art*, *is*, *are*, as in the indicative mood; as,

Seeing I am writing letters. Seeing letters are writing.	Quum ego *scribĕre* litera. Quum litera *scribi*.
Seeing he is building a house. Seeing a house is building, &c.	Quum ille *ædificare* domus. Quum domus *ædificari*, &c.

Note.—This tense, after *quasi*, *tanquam*, and the like, is sometimes translated like the imperfect; as, *Quasi intelligant qualis sit*, &c. As if they understood, &c.—Cic. *Tusc.* 1.

31.—2. Without any verb and conjunction expressed (Gr. 145), the signs are, *may*, *can*, *let*, *should*, *would* (Gr. 171–1–3).

By this means (thus) thou mayest get (find) praise. Praise may be gotten (found) by thee.	Ita *invenire* laus. Laus *inveniri* a tu.
Thou canst scarcely find a faithful friend. A faithful friend can scarcely be found by thee.	Vix *reperire* amicus fidelis. Amicus fidelis vix *reperiri* a tu.
Somebody may say.	Aliquis *dicĕre*.
Let us live piously.	*Vivĕre* pie.
I should refuse.	*Recūsare*.
She would pray for help.	*Orare* opis.—Ovid.

Interrogatively.

Should I tell it?	*Narrare?*
What should I think?	Quis *putare?*
Whom should I ask?	Quis *rogare?*
What shouldst thou do here?	Quis tu hìc *agĕre?*
Who can (could, would) believe this?	Quis hic *credĕre?*
Why should she ask this? Why should this be asked by her?	Cur ille *quæritare* hic? Cur hic *quæritari* ab ille?

3. With conjunctions, indefinites, and relatives, the signs are *may*, *can*, &c. (Gr. 171).

That I may speak the truth.	Ut verum *dicĕre*.
I know not what I should do with myself (make myself).	Nescire quis ego *facĕre*.—Ter.
Use thy endeavour that thou mayest be in good health (well).	Dare opera, ut *valēre*.
Love, that thou mayest be loved.	Ut *amari*, amare.
I would have thee (I wish that thou wouldst) write.	Velle* (ut) *scribĕre*.
Beware that thou do not believe it.	Cavēre* (ne) *credĕre*.
He begs that thou wouldst come.	Orare, ut *venire*.
Take care, that he may know.	Curare, ut *scire*.
I am afraid that he may not believe it.	Timēre ut† *credĕre*.—Ter.
If any one should ask.	Si quis *rogare*.
We have nothing, which we can (may) do.	Nihil habēre, quod *agĕre*.
I advise that you would study.	Monēre ut *studēre*.
Though they should deny. Though it should be denied by them.	Etsi ille *negare*. Etsi *negari* ab ille.

IMPERFECT TENSE (Gr. 172).

32.—1. With conjunctions, indefinites, &c., translated as the indicative (Gr. 172–4).

Seeing I did not hear what thou saidst;—What was said by thee.	Quum non *audire*, quis *dicĕre*;—Quis *dici* a tu.
If he knew, what we were now doing;—What was doing now by us.	Si *scire*, quis nunc *agĕre*;—Quis nunc *agi* a ego.

* *Ut* is often understood after *volo*, *nolo*, *facio*, *censeo*, *jubeo*, *opto*, *sino*, *licet*, *oportet*, &c., and *ne* after *cave* (Gr. 632).

† Verbs signifying *to fear*, as *timeo*, *metuo*, *vereor*, *paveo*, are used affirmatively with *ne*, but negatively with *ut*, or *ne non*, and after such verbs, these conjunctions should be rendered *that*, *that not* (An. & Pr. Gr. 962); as, *timeo ne credat*, I am afraid that he may believe it; *timeo ut credat*, I am afraid that he may not believe it (Gr. 633).

When you did not know for whom you got money;—For whom money was gotten by you.	Quum *nescire*, quis *parare* pecunia;—Quis pecunia *parari* a tu.
I staid till they returned.	2 Expectare dum *redire*.
I wish I were in health.	Utinam *valēre*.
— Thou spokest from thy heart.	— Tu *loqui* ex animus.
— We were wise enough.	— *Sapĕre* satis.
— You used diligence;—Diligence was used by you.	— Tu *adhibēre* diligentia;—Diligentia *adhibēri* a tu.

Sometimes it is rendered by the participle in *ing* with *was, wert, were;* as,

While I was writing letters. While letters were writing.	Dum *scribĕre* litera. Dum litera *scribi*.
While he was building a house. While a house was building, &c.	Dum ille *ædificare* domus. Dum domus *ædificari*, &c.

33.—2. With the signs *would, could, should, might,* either with or without *conjunctions, indefinites,* &c. (Gr. 172).

I would take care.	*Curare*.
He begged that I would come.	3 Orare ut *venire*.
Thou wouldst think thyself happy, if thou wert rich.	*Putare* tu felix, si *esse* dives.
He might say. It might be said by him.	*Dicĕre*. *Dici* ab ille.
The day would fail me, if I should reckon every one.	Dies *deficĕre* ego, si *enumerare* omnis.
We should not suffer it.	Non *sinĕre*.
You would learn willingly, if you were wise.	*Discĕre* libenter, si *sapĕre*.
Men would follow virtue, if they were wise.	Homo *sectari* virtus, si *sapĕre*.

Interrogatively.

What should I do?	Quis *facĕre?*
Wouldst thou not think thyself happy?	Nonne *putare* tu felix?
Might not (would not) he say?	Nonne *dicĕre?*
What would he say?	Quis *dicĕre?*
Should we not do it?	Annon *facĕre?*
Would you suffer it?	Num *sinĕre?*
Would they believe?	An *credĕre?*

PERFECT TENSE (Gr. 173).

1. *Indefinite.*

34.—1. With conjunctions, indefinites, &c., translated as the indicative.

Though I sought for thee yesterday. Though thou wert sought for by me yesterday.	Licet *quærĕre* tu heri. Licet *quæsĭtus esse* a ego heri.
I do not know whither you went.	Nescire quò *profectus esse.*
Who can doubt, but God created the world?—But the world was created by God?	Quis dubitare, quin Deus *creare* mundus? Quin mundus *creatus esse* a Deus?
You know, how great praise we got.	Scire, quantus laus *adeptus esse.*
Though many did not believe these things. Though these things were not believed by many.	Quanquam multi non *credĕre* hic. Quanquam hic non *credĭtus esse* a multus.
I wish I satisfied the master.	Utinam *satisfacĕre* præceptor. (Gr. 397. III.)
— Thou spokest truth.	— *Dicĕre* verum.

35.—2. Without a conjunction, the sign is *might.*

Perhaps I might be in an error (might err).	*Errare* fortasse.—PLIN. *Epist.* 1, 23.
Perhaps I might add more kind expressions.	Forsitan *addĕre* blanditia plus.—OVID. *Met.* 7. 816.
Perhaps the Sabine [women] might be unwilling.	Forsitan Sabina *nolle.*—OVID. *Amor.* 1, 8, 39.
Perhaps Ulysses might keep his wife's birth (natal) day.	Ulysses *agĕre* forsan dies natalis conjux.—OVID. *Trist.* 5, 5, 3.

2. *Definite.*

36.—1. With conjunctions, indefinites, &c., translated as the indicative.

Though I have made trial. Though trial has been made by me.	Etiamsi *facĕre* periculum. Etiamsi periculum *factus esse* a ego.

Tell me, what you have got.	Dicĕre mihi quis *nactus esse.*
I know a man, who has promised.	Nôsse homo, qui *promittĕre.*
Seeing we all have sinned.	Quum omnis *peccare.*
I am glad, that you have escaped.	Gaudēre, quòd *evadĕre.*
I desire to know, what they have done;—What has been done by them.	Avēre scire, quis *agĕre;*—Quis *actus esse* ab ille.

Passives with the signs *am, art,* &c., as in the indicative mood.

Though I am (be) reduced to straits.	Licet *redactus esse* ad angustiæ.
Seeing the work is finished.	Quum opus *fīnītus esse.*
Since the city is taken.	Quum urbs *captus esse.*
Since we are conquered.	Quum *victus esse.*
Since her parents (the parents of her) are found.	Quum parens ejus *repertus esse.*

Come, gone, run, set, &c., with the signs *am, art, is, are.*

Since thou art come quickly.	Quum *advenire* citò.
Since he is gone.	Quum *abire.*
Since he is entered into the city.	Quum *ingressus esse* [in] urbs.
Since the sun is risen.	Quum sol *ortus esse.*
Since the time is past.	Quum tempus *præterire.*
Since the labour is lost.	Quum opera *perire.*
Though we are (be) set together on the grass.	Etiamsi *considĕre* in herba. (Gr. 608. R. LI.)
I wish the twenty pounds be not lost.	Utinam viginti minæ non *perire.*

Note.—This tense, after *quasi, tanquam,* and the like, may sometimes be rendered as the pluperfect; as, *Quasi jam satis veneratus miratusque sim,* As if I had, &c. PLIN. Paneg. *Perinde ac si jam vicerint.* CIC. *Perinde eris, ac si gratiam retulerim.* SENEC.

37.—2. With the signs *may have,* or as the indicative.

That (lest) he may not have lost, the gamester does not cease to lose.	Ne non *perdĕre,* non cessare perdĕre lusor.—OVID.

Then I should have saved the Capitol in vain.	Tunc ego nequicquam Capitolium *servare*.—Liv.
Thou fearest that I have not received thy epistle.—That thy epistle has not been received by me.	Verēri, ut (Gr. 633) *accipĕre* tuus epistola;—Ut tuus epistola *acceptus esse* a ego.—Cic. *Att.*
I am afraid that he may have taken it ill.	Verēri, ne (Gr. 633) ille graviùs *ferre*.—Ter. *Eun.* 1, 2.
I fear that I may have taken pains (undertaken labour) in vain.—That thou mayest have exceeded moderation;—That she may have heard these things.	Metuĕre, ne (Gr. 633) frustra *suscipĕre* labor;—Ne *excedĕre* modus;—Ne ille hic *audire*.—Plaut. *Casin.* 3, 3, 12, & 7.

Passives signifying a thing but just now past, have the English BE instead of HAVE BEEN, or they may be rendered by the indicative mood.

EXAMPLES.

Perhaps the work may be (is) finished.	Fortasse opus *n.* *finītus esse*.
Perhaps he may be (is) reduced to poverty.	Fortasse *redactus esse* ad paupertas.
I fear, that the city may be (is) taken.	Verēri, ne urbs *captus esse*.

Also, *come, gone, set,* &c., have the sign BE or IS instead of HAVE.

EXAMPLES.

Perhaps the mother may be (is) come.	Forsitan mater *venire*.—Ovid. *Ep.* 18.
I fear that he may be (is) returned already.	Metuĕre, ne (Gr. 633) *redire* jam.—Ter. *Eun.* 3, 5.
I fear that I may be (am) come too late.	Metuĕre, ne (Gr. 633) *venire* serò.—*Vid.* Cic. *Att.* 14, 19.
I fear that the time is past;—That the labour is lost.	Metuĕre ne (Gr. 633) tempus *prœterire*; Ne opera *perire*.

38.—3. This perfect of the subjunctive sometimes inclines very much to a future signification; and is therefore called, by some grammarians, the proper future of that which is named the potential mood.

The signs are *should, would, could, may, can.*

EXAMPLES.

I should choose rather to be poor.	*Optare* pauper esse potiùs.
I would not do it without your order.	Non *facĕre* injussu tuus.
Thou wouldst choose rather to be in health than to be rich?	*Præferre* valēre, quàm dives esse.—HOR.
Who would say that the covetous man is rich?	Quis *dicĕre* avarus (Gr. 671) esse dives?
You would play more willingly than study.	*Ludĕre* libentiùs quàm *studēre.*
They will be angry, if they should know it.	Irasci, si *resciscĕre.*
If I should now hang myself, I should fool away my pains, and besides my pains, I should spend a halter in vain, and should create pleasure to my enemies.	Si nunc ego 31 suspendĕre, meus opera *ludĕre*, et præter opera, restis frustra *sumptifacĕre*, et inimicus meus voluptas *creare.*—PLAUT. *Casin.* 2, 7, 1.

The passive form here is *amatus sim;* which is scarcely used, except in deponents; as, *Ubivis faciliùs passus sim, quàm in hac re, me deludier.* TER. *And.*

This tense is resolvable by *velim* or *possim* with the infinitive mood, or by the present subjunctive; as, *Optârim*, i. e. *Velim optare,* or *optem.* Sometimes by the present indicative; as, *Deos audisse crediderim;* i. e. *Credo.* It respects either the time present (as in that passage of Plautus above); or indefinitely any time whatever.

This tense may sometimes be rendered by the sign SHALL; as, *Quin etiam corpus libenter obtulerim, si repræsentari morte mea libertas civitatis potest.* CIC. *Phil.* 2. "I shall willingly offer my body, if the liberty of the city may be presently established by my death." Sometimes by the sign CAN; as, *Quis dubitârit, quin ægrotationes animi, ex eo, quòd magni æstimetur ea res, ex qua animus ægrotat, oriantur?* CIC. *Tusc.* 4. "Who can doubt, that," &c.

This tense is also sometimes equivalent to the future-perfect tense; as, *Ac non id metuat, ne, ubi eam acceperim, sese relinquam,* "When I shall have received her." TERENT. *Eun.* 1, 2.

PLUPERFECT TENSE (Gr. 174).

39.—1. With conjunctions, indefinites, &c., translated as the indicative.

Because I had received a kindness. Because a kindness had been received by me.	Quòd *accipĕre* beneficium. Quòd beneficium *acceptus esse* a ego.
If thou hadst restrained thy passion. If passion had been restrained by thee.	Si *cohibēre* iracundia. Si iracundia *cohibĭtus esse* a tu.
He who had offered injury. By whom injury had been offered.	Ille qui *inferre* injuria. A qui injuria *illātus esse.*
If they had kept promise.	Si *servare* promissum.
I did not know whether he had thanked (given thanks to) him or not.	Nescire an *agĕre* gratia ille, *necne.*
I wish I had obeyed.	Utinam *parēre.*
I wish you had made trial.	Utinam *facĕre* periculum.

Come, gone, run, set, &c., with the signs *was, wert, were.*

When he was gone away before.	Quum ille *abire* antea.
When the time was past.	Quum tempus *præterire.*
When the labour was lost.	Quum opera *perire.*
Seeing the summer was come.	Quum æstas *venire.*
After the sun was set.	Postquam sol *occĭdĕre.*
When the morning star was risen.	Quando Lucifer *ortus esse.*
After we were set together on the grass.	Postquam *considĕre* in herba. (Gr. 608. R. LI.)
As soon as we were got to the city.	Simul ac *pervenire* ad urbs.

40.—2. With the signs, *might have, would have, could have, should have, ought to have,* and *had* for *would have* or *should have.*

If he had (should have) commanded it, I would have obeyed.	Si *jubēre*, *parēre.*—*Vid.* Cic. *Am.* c. 11.
Thou shouldst (oughtest to) have called me.	*Vocare.*—Virg. *Æn.* 4, 678.
Cæsar would never have done this, nor suffered it.	Cæsar nunquam hic *facĕre*, neque *passus esse.*—Cic. *Att.* 14, 13.
We could not have escaped this mischief.	Non *effugĕre* hic malum.

You should have (ought to have) imitated him, and should have resisted.

Imitatus esse ille, et *resistĕre.*

The good might have conquered, and the rogues might have been defeated.

Vincĕre bonus, et *victus esse* improbus. — Cic. *pro Sext.*

I feared that we had taken pains (undertaken the labour) in vain:—That pains had been taken (labour undertaken) in vain by us.

3 Verēri, ne (Gr. 633) frustra *suscipĕre* labor:—Ne labor frustra *susceptus esse* a ego.

— That they had heard these things.—That these things had been heard by them.

— Ne ille *audire* hic.—Ne hic *auditus esse* ab ille.

— That they had returned.

— Ne ille *redire.*

Interrogatively.

Wouldst thou have obeyed? — An *parēre?*

Wouldst thou not have obeyed? — Annon (nonne) *parēre?*

Would Cæsar have done or suffered this? Would not Cæsar have suffered this? — An Cæsar hic *facĕre* aut *passus esse?* Nonne Cæsar hic *passus esse?*

Who would have done this? — Quis hic *facĕre?*

Could we have escaped? — An *effugĕre?*

Note.—The verbs *come, gone, set,* and the like, have the sign BE instead of HAD here also.

41.—3. There is a peculiar use of this pluperfect of the subjunctive, when a thing is signified as future at a certain time past referred to. It is rendered by *should,* or as the imperfect of the subjunctive or indicative (Gr. 174); as, *Tuis denunciavi, si rursus tam multa* attulissent, *omnia relaturos?* "I declared to your servants, that if they brought (should bring) so many things again, they should carry them all back again." Plin. *Ep.* 28, 6. *Testabatur Cocles, nequicquam eos fugere, si transitum hostibus pontem a tergo* reliquissent, "If they left, or should leave the bridge," &c. Liv. *l.* 2. *Imperaret quod vellet; quodcunque* imperavisset ["whatever he commanded or should command"], *se esse facturos.* Cæs. *B. Civ.* 3. *Ibi futuros Helvetios, ubi Cæsar* constituisset ["should appoint"], *atque eos esse* voluisset ["should be willing to have them to be"]. *Id. B. Gall.* 1. *Oraculum datum est, Athenas victrices fore, si rex* interfectus esset ["was slain or should be slain"]. Cic. *Tusc.* 5. (Gr. 174.)

EXAMPLES.

[The following examples may be omitted till after the pupil has gone over the future of the infinitive.]

Thou promisedst that thou wouldst write, if I desired (should desire) it.	Promittĕre tu scripturus (esse), si *rogare.*—Plin. *Epist.* 14, 5.
Thou saidst that thou wouldst come, if thou didst (shouldst) obtain leave.	Dicĕre tu venturus esse, si *impetrare* venia.
They decreed a reward if any one should discover.	Decernĕre præmium, si quis *indicare.*—Sal.
He declared that we should be punished (suffer punishment) if we did (should do) that:—If that was (should be) done.	Denunciare ego daturus esse pœna, si is *facĕre*:—Si is *factus esse.*
Unless we came (should come) the next day.	Nisi posterus dies (R. xl.) *venire.*
Marius said he would make an end of the war in a short time, if they made (should make) him consul.	Marius dicĕre sui brevis tempus (Gr. 565. R. xli.) confecturus (esse) bellum, si sui consul *facĕre.*
Xerxes proposed a reward to him who invented (should invent) a new pleasure.	Xerxes præmium proponĕre is qui novus voluptas *invenire.*—Cic. *Tus.* 5.
Xerxes delighted so much (even to this extent) in luxury, that he proposed a reward by proclamation to him, who found (should find) a new kind of pleasure.	Xerxes eò usque luxuria gaudēre, ut edictum præmium is (32) proponĕre, qui novus voluptas genus *reperire.*—Val. Max. 9, 1.
Plato declared that the world (the circle of lands) would then, and not till then (at last), be happy, when either wise men should begin to reign, or kings to be wise.	Plato, tum demum terra orbis beatus futurus (esse), 3 prædicare, quum aut sapiens regnare, aut rex sapĕre *cœpisse.*—*Id.* 7, 2.
Plato thought that states would then, and not till then (at last), be happy, when (if) either learned and wise men should begin to govern them, or those who governed should employ their whole study in learning and wisdom.	Plato 3 putare, tum denique beatus (Gr. 180–8) esse respublica, si aut doctus et sapiens regĕre is *cœpisse*, aut qui 32 regĕre omnis suus studium in doctrina et sapientia *collocare.*—Cic. *ad Q. Fr.* 1. 1.

Examples of this kind are very frequent in Cæsar, and in Cic. de Divinatione, it being the usual style of recitals of laws, speeches, and predictions; the future-perfect tense in the law, speech, or prediction, being, in the recital, expressed by the pluperfect, which bears to the future-perfect the same relation as the imperfect does to the present. Compare the following examples.

Fut.-P. If any one shall make (shall have made) bad verses against any one, there is law.	Si malus *condĕre* in quis quis carmen, jus esse.—Hor. *Sat.* 1. 2.
Pluperf. The twelve tables made it capital, if any one should compose (should have composed) verses, which brought infamy to another.	Duodecim tabula caput sancire, si quis carmen *condĕre* qui infamia (32) afferre alter.—Cic. *in Fragm.*
Fut.-P. They promise that they will do what he may command (shall have commanded).	Qui *imperare*, sui facturus (esse) pollicēri. — Cæs. *B. Civ.* 1.
Pluperf. They promised, that they would do what he commanded (should have commanded).	Qui *imperare*, sui facturus (esse) 3 pollicēri.—Cæs. *B. Gall.* 4.
Fut.-P. Their fortune was told thus: He that (who) shall first kiss (have given kisses to) his mother, shall be conqueror.	Sors esse ita reddĭtus: Mater qui *dare* princeps osculum, victor esse.—Ovid. *Fast.* 2. 713.
Pluperf. Apollo answered, that the highest power of the Roman city should be in him, who should give (have given) a kiss to his mother, before all [the rest].	Apollo, penes is summus urbs Romanus potestas futurus (esse), 3 respondēre, qui, ante omnis, mater osculum *dare.*—Val. Max. 7. 2.
Fut.-P. The law says, let him be punished with death, who shall give (have given) assistance to the enemy.	Dicĕre lex, qui hostis opis *ferre*, caput puniri.—Quinc. *Declam.* 318.
Pluperf. The law was written against him who should give (have given) assistance to the enemy.	Adversus is conscriptus lex esse, qui opis *ferre* hostis.—*Ibid.*
Fut.-P. Then we must have that fortune (that fortune is to be had) which the gods shall give (have given).	Tunc habendus esse is fortuna, qui deus *dare.*—Liv. *l.* 30.
Pluperf. They carry word back that they had discoursed (they report that words had been made) in vain; that they must dispute it with arms, and must have that fortune (that that fortune is to be had) which the gods should give.	Frustra verbum factus (esse) renunciare; arma (Gr. 699 & 671) decernĕre esse, habendusque is fortuna, qui Deus *dare.*—*Ibid.*

Note.—When the former verb in such recitals is of the present tense, because it refers to the time past, and is put for the imperfect or perfect, the latter may be either the perfect or pluperfect; as, Pollicentur *sese facturos, quæ imperârit:* Renunciant *habendam esse eam fortunam quam dii* dedissent.

FUTURE TENSE.

42.—This tense is composed of the participle in *rus* and *sim*, and is used with conjunctions, indefinites, and sometimes with the relative *qui*. The sign is SHALL or WILL. (Gr. 170–1.)

I am uncertain yet what I shall do.	Incertus esse etiam, quis *facturus esse.*—TER.
I am glad that I shall see him.	Gaudēre, quòd *visurus esse* is.
Since I shall see thee, I shall write nothing more.	Quum *visurus esse* tu, nihil amplius scribĕre.
I neither know what I should do, nor what I shall do.	Nec quis (33) agĕre, nec quis *acturus esse*, scire.—CIC. *Att.* 7, 10.
I will let (make that) you know on what day I shall come.	Facĕre ut (32) scire, quis dies (Gr. 565) *venturus esse.*—CIC. *Att.* 16, 8.
Neither where, nor when I shall see thee, can I guess.	Nec ubi, nec quando tu *visurus esse*, posse suspicari.—*Ibid.* 11, 13.
I would have thee write (I should wish that thou wouldst write) what thou shalt do.	(33) Velle [ut] (33) scribĕre, quis *esse acturus.*—*Ib.* 7, 22.
I ask whether or no thou wilt do [it].	Quærĕre, *esse*ne *facturus.*—CIC.
I doubt not that thou wilt stay there.	Non dubitare, quin ibi *mansurus esse.*—CIC. *Att.* 9, 10.
Take care that I may know the day on which thou shalt (wilt) go out from Rome.	Curare, ut scire dies, quis (Gr. 565) Roma *exiturus esse.*—*Ib.* 2, 11.
There is nothing so great which I shall (will) not do for thy sake.	Nihil esse tantus, qui non ego tuus causa (Gr. 542) *facturus esse.*—C. *Fam.* 15, 11.
Should I (am I such a man that I should) promise my daughter to him to whom I shall not marry (give) her?	Egon' ut is (33) despondēre filia, qui *daturus* non *esse?*—TER.

43.—The future in *rus* with *essem* instead of the pluperfect subjunctive. The sign SHOULD OR WOULD.

I desired to know what thou wouldst do, and when thou wouldst return. — Scire velle, quis tu *esse facturus*, et quando *esse rediturus*.—CIC. *Att.* 12, 41.

I was glad that I should see him. — Gaudēre, quod *visurus esse* is.

I neither knew what I did, nor what I should do. — Nec quis (32) agĕre, nec quis *acturus esse*, scire.

Neither where nor when I should see thee, could I guess. — Nec ubi, nec quando tu *visurus esse*, posse suspicari.

I did not doubt, that thou wouldst stay. — Non dubitare, quin *mansurus esse*.

I did not know the day on which thou wouldst go out. — Nescire dies, qui (Gr. 565) *exiturus esse*.

Should I (am I such a man that I should) promise my daughter to one to whom I should not marry (give) her? — Egon' is ut despondēre filia, qui non *daturus esse*?

INFINITIVE MOOD.

44.—The INFINITIVE MOOD expresses the meaning of the verb in a general manner, without any distinction of person or number; as, *scribĕre*, "to write," (Gr. 152.)

The tenses of the infinitive are three, the *present*, the *perfect*, and the *future*—and, in the active voice, the *future-perfect*.

In Latin, the tenses of the infinitive express its action as past, present, or future, not with regard to the present time as in the other moods, but with regard to the time of the leading verb on which it is dependent. (Gr. 176.)

The infinitive is used in two different ways; viz., without a subject, or with it. (Gr. 177.)

The Infinitive without a subject.

45.—The infinitive without a subject follows a verb or adjective, and is always translated in the same way, whether the preceding verb be present, past, or future (Gr. 178).

EXAMPLES.

I cease to write.	Desĭnĕre *scribĕre.*
Dost thou delay to speak to (him)?	Cessare *allŏqui* (eum)?—Ter.
I desire to become a scholar (learned).	Cupĕre *evādĕre* doctus.
We are forbidden to do injury.	Prohibēri *facĕre* injuria.
Thou oughtest to perform promises.	Debēre *præstare* promissum.
Thou seemest to me to desire wisdom.	Vidēri ego *expetĕre* sapientia.
He seems to become a scholar (learned).	Vidēri *evadĕre* doctus.
Desiring to learn.	Cupiens *discĕre.*
Hastening to go home.	Properans *abire* domus.—(Gr. 558.)
Worthy to be loved.	Dignus *amari.*
Skilful in singing.	Peritus *cantare.*
Prepared to command.	Paratus *imperare.*

46.—The sign TO is omitted when the former verb is *may, can, might, would, could,* made by *licet, volo, nolo, possum, debeo,* &c. (Gr. 147 & 668, Note 1.)

I cannot write.	Non posse *scribĕre.*
Money may be taken away.	Pecunia posse *erĭpi.*
It cannot be done.	Non posse *fĭĕri.*
Virtue cannot die.	Virtus non posse *emŏri.*
All would (all wish to) know.	*Scire* velle omnis.
You may (it is allowed to you to) go home.	Licet tu (Gr. 223–6 & 409) *ire* domus. (Gr. 558.)
I could not write.	Non 3 posse *scribĕre.*
It could not be done.	Non posse *fĭĕri.*
Mutius could burn his hand.	Mutius posse *urĕre* manus.
He would not take [it].	3 Nolle *accipĕre.*
That could not be prevented.	Is non posse *cavēri.*
We might not (it was not allowed to us to) come.	Non licēre ego (Gr. 223 6 & 409) *venire.*

To is likewise omitted after the English words *must, bid, dare, let,* and *make* (An. & Pr. Gr. 877).

EXAMPLES.

I must (it behoves me to) write a letter.	Oportet ego (Gr. 423) *scribĕre* epistola.

He bid me come.	Jubēre ego *venire.*
We dare not refuse.	Non audēre *recusare.*
I will not let you go.	Non siněre tu *abire.*
The darkness made us wander.	Tenebræ facěre ego *errare.*

47.—The present infinitive is generally translated as the perfect without *to*, when it comes after the past tenses of *possum*, *volo*, *nolo*, *malo*, translated *could*, *would*, *would not*, *would rather;* and with *to* after the same tenses of *debeo* and *oportet* translated *ought;* as, *melius fieri non potuit*, "It could not have been done better." *Dividi oportuit*, "It ought to have been divided."

EXAMPLES.

Thou never couldst have (hast been able to) come more seasonably than thou comest now.	Nunquam 3 posse magis opportunus *venire*, quàm nunc advěnire.—PLAUT.
There could have been (able to be) no living at all without arts.	Sine ars vita omnino nullus *esse* (40) posse.—CIC.
Cities could not have been (able to be) built without an assembly of men.	Urbs sine cœtus homo non 40 posse *ædificari.*—*Ib.*
There could have been (able to be) neither navigation, nor agriculture, without the assistance of men.	Neque navigatio, neque agricultura, sine opera homo *esse* (40) posse.—*Ibid.*
It is evident, that men could not have lived (been able to live) conveniently without the assistance of men.	Perspicuus esse, home sine homo opera commŏdè *vivěre* non posse, *perf. infin.*
I would have come if I could.	3 Velle *venire*, si (40) posse.
What would you have had (did you wish) me do for you?	Quis 3 velle ego *facěre* tu?—TER. *Phor.* 1, 5.
They themselves were held with the same difficulties with which they would have (had wished to) shut up the Romans.	Qui difficultas Romanus *clauděre* 4 velle, idem ipse tenēri.—CÆS. *B. Gall.* 8.
He had a knife wherewith he would have slain (with which he wished to slay) himself.	Ferrum 3 habēre, qui sui *occīděre* 3 velle.
You ought not to have been a helper to your friend sinning.	Non 3 debēre adjutor *esse* amicus peccans.

48.—*Videor*, "I seem," followed by the dative of its subject, is usually rendered "think." When thus used, the infinitive after it is rendered like the indicative, or like the infinitive with a subject (49 below); as, *Videor mihi esse*, "I think that I am;" lit., "I seem to myself to be."

EXAMPLES.

I think that I (I seem to myself to) get knowledge.	Vidēri ego *adipisci* scientia.
Thou thinkest that thou art become (thou seemest to thyself to have become) an artist.	Vidēri tu factus (*esse**) artifex. (Gr. 326.)
He thinks that he is become (he seems to himself to be) a scholar.	Vidēri sui *evādĕre* doctus. (Gr. 326.)
He thinks that he has (he seems to himself to have) gotten favour.	Vidēri sui adeptus (*esse**) gratia.
You think that you (you seem to yourselves to) have obtained the victory.	Vidēri tu consecutus (*esse**) victoria.
They think that they shall (they seem to themselves to be about to) get riches.	Vidēri sui adepturus (*esse**) divitiæ.

Miscellaneous Examples to be turned into Latin.

For the Latin words, see English Vocabulary at the end of the book.

They began to ask assistance.—They had begun to despair.—They endeavour to carry on the war.—Cæsar determined to cut down the woods.—These are said to have a hundred cantons.—He despises to be taught.—Money cannot (knows not to) change nature.—He endeavours to perform his promise.—I (we) did not begin to philosophize on a sudden.—No art can come up to the skill of nature.—The mind always desires to be employed (to act); nor can it endure perpetual inactivity.—It is always advantageous to be a good man, because it is always honorable.

The Infinitive Mood with a subject.

49.—The infinitive mood with an accusative before it as its subject, is usually rendered as the indicative—the particle *that*

* *Esse* is sometimes understood (Gr. 179-6).

being sometimes placed before it, sometimes not (Gr. 179–11, & 180; also 670 & 673).

The infinitive *with its* subject forms a dependent clause, which is sometimes the subject of the verb on which it depends; as, *te istud non audivisse mirum est*, "that you have not heard that, is surprising" (Gr. 670. 1st.): but most commonly its object; as, *miror te non istud audivisse*, "I wonder that you have not heard that." (Gr. 670. 2d.)

PRESENT TENSE.

50.—1. When the preceding verb is of the present or future tense, the present-infinitive is likewise translated as the present. (Gr. 179–1.)

EXAMPLES.

I say [that] I praise thee;—[That] thou art praised by me.	Dicĕre ego *laudare* tu.—Tu *laudari* a ego.
I see [that] thou desirest knowledge;—[That] knowledge is desired by thee.	Vidēre tu *expetĕre* scientia.—Scientia *expĕti* a tu.
We know [that] God governs the world;—[That] the world is governed by God.	Scire Deus *gubernare* mundus.—Mundus *gubernari* a Deus.
You see [that] we write (are writing) letters;—[That] letters are writing by us.	Vidēre ego *scribĕre* litera.—Litera *scribi* a ego.
I have heard [that] you get riches;—[That] riches are getting by you.	Audire tu *parare* divitiæ.—Divitiæ *parari* a tu.
We know [that] all [men] blame the ungrateful;—[That] the ungrateful are blamed by all.	Scire omnis *culpare* ingratus.—Ingratus *culpari* ab omnis.

51.—2. When the preceding verb is of the imperfect, perfect, or pluperfect tense, the present of the infinitive is translated as the imperfect or perfect-indefinite of the indicative. (Gr. 179–1.)

Thou knewest [that] I was writing letters.—[That] letters were writing by me.	Nôsse ego *scribĕre* litera.—Litera *scribi* a ego.
— [That] he reverenced his parents, and followed virtue.	— Ille *reverēri* parens suus, et *sectari* virtus.

— [That] we gave our minds (endeavour) to learning (letters).	— Ego *dare* opera litera.
— [That] they were talking.	— Ille *fabulari*.

PERFECT TENSE.

52.—1. When the preceding verb is of the present or future tense, the perfect of the infinitive is translated as the perfect of the indicative, indefinite or definite. (Gr. 179–2.)

Note.—In the compound forms of the infinitive, i. e. the perfect infinitive passive, and the future, and the future-perfect infinitive active, the participle must always be of the same gender, number, and case as the accusative before it.

1. *Indefinite.*

I say [that] I sought for thee. —[That] thou wert sought for by me.	Dicĕre ego *quærĕre* tu. —Tu *quæsītus esse* a ego.
I think [that] thou didst well.—[That] this was well done by thee.	Putare tu bene *facĕre*.—Hic bene *factus esse* a tu.
We know [that] God created the world.—[That] the world was created by God.	Scire Deus *creare* mundus. —Mundus *creatus esse* a Deus.

And so in the other examples, 50, 51.

2. *Definite.*

I say [that] I have often sought for thee.—[That] thou hast been often sought for by me.	Dicĕre ego sæpe *quærĕre* tu.—Tu sæpe *quæsītus esse* a ego.
— [That] thou hast spoken well.	— Tu *locūtus esse* bene.
— [That] she has found her parents.	— Ille *reperire* parens.

And so in the other examples, 50, 51.

The following examples are in accordance with the statement above; see No. 13.

Thou believest [that] I am reduced to want.	Credĕre ego *redactus esse* ad egestas.
— [That] the work is finished.	— Opus *n. fīnītus esse*.

— [That] the city is taken.	— Urbs *captus esse.*
— [That] we are conquered.	— Ego *victus esse.*
— [That] her parents (the parents of her) are found.	— Ejus parens *repertus esse.*
He thinks [that] thou art come quickly.	Putare tu *advenire* citò.
— [That] they are gone.	— Ille *abire.*
— [That] they are entered into the city.	— Ille *ingressus esse* (in) urbs.
— [That] the sun is set.	— Sol *occidĕre.*
— [That] the moon is (up) risen.	— Luna *ortus esse.*
— [That] the time is past.	— Tempus *præterire.*
— [That] the labour is lost, &c.	— Opera *perire*, &c.

53.—2. When the preceding verb is of the imperfect, perfect, or pluperfect tense, the perfect of the infinitive is translated as the pluperfect of the indicative. (Gr. 179–2.)

I told thee [that] I had sought for thee before. — [That] thou hadst been sought for by me before.	Dicĕre tibi ego *quærĕre* tu antea.—Tu *quæsĭtus esse* a ego antea.
Thou knewest [that] thou hadst promised the day before.	7 Scire tu *promittĕre* pridie.
Thou knewest [that] the master had often forbidden that.—[That] that had been often forbidden by the master, &c.	7 Scire præceptor sæpe *prohibĕre* is.—Is sæpe *prohibĭtus esse* a præceptor, &c.

For the following, see No. 13 above.

Thou saidst [that] he was gone away before.	Dicĕre ille *abire* antea.
— [That] the time was past.	— Tempus *præterire.*
— [That] the labour was lost.	— Opera *perire.*
— [That] the summer was come.	— *Venire* æstas.
— [That] the sun was set.	— Sol *occidĕre.*
— [That] the moon was risen,	— Luna *ortus esse*, &c.

FUTURE TENSE.

54.—1. When the preceding verb is of the present or future tense, the future of the infinitive with *esse* is translated as the future of the indicative. (Gr. 179–3.)

Note 1.—The verbs *esse* and *fuisse* in the future and future-perfect infinitive are often understood (Gr. 179–4).

Note 2.—Deponent verbs have the future of the infinitive like active verbs (Gr. 179–8). The future-infinitive passive consists of the former supine and *iri;* as, *scriptum iri* (Gr. 179–7).

EXAMPLES.

1. Importing *will* or *purpose.*

Examples with the sign WILL.*

I say [that] I will write letters.	Dicĕre ego *scripturus* (*esse*) litera.
Thou sayest [that] thou wilt write letters.	Tu dicĕre tu *scripturus* (*esse*) litera.
He says [that] he [himself] will write letters.	Dicĕre sui *scripturus* (*esse*) litera.
We promise [that] we will do our endeavour.	Ego promittĕre ego *daturus* (*esse*) opera.
You promise [that] you will send.	Tu promittĕre tu *missurus* (*esse*).
They promise [that] they will give (use) diligence.	Ille promittĕre sui *adhibiturus* (*esse*) diligentia.

Examples with the sign SHALL.

I say [that] letters shall be written by me.	Dicĕre litera *scribi* a ego.
— [That] thou shalt know.	— Tu *sciturus* (*esse*).
— [That] he shall know.	— Ille *sciturus* (*esse*).
— [That] you and they shall know.	— Tu et ille *sciturus* (*esse*).
Thou sayest [that] letters shall be written by thee.	Dicĕre litera *scribi* a tu.
He says [that] letters shall be written by himself.	Dicĕre litera *scribi* a sui.
— [That] I shall know the whole matter.	— Ego *sciturus* (*esse*) res omnis.
— [That] thou shalt hear.	— Tu *auditurus* (*esse*).
— [That] the queen shall hear.	— Regina *auditurus* (*esse*).

* Whether *will* or *shall* is the auxiliary in the English future, it makes no difference in the form of the Latin verb.—No. 19, Note.

2. Signifying *bare event.*

Examples with the sign SHALL.

I believe [that] I shall see.	Credĕre ego *visurus* (*esse*).
Thou believest [that] thou shalt get the victory.	Credĕre tu *potiturus* (*esse*) victoria. (Gr. 484.)
He believes [that] he shall go.	Ille credĕre sui *iturus* (*esse*).
We believe [that] we shall obtain leave.	Ego credĕre ego *impetraturus* (*esse*) venia.
You believe [that] you shall get (make) an estate.	Tu credĕre tu *facturus* (*esse*) res.
They believe [that] they shall get friends.	Ille credĕre sui *inventurus* (*esse*) amicus.

Examples with the sign WILL.

I believe [that] leave will be obtained by us.	Credĕre venia *impetrari* a ego.
— [That] thou wilt get the victory.	— Tu *potiturus* (*esse*) victoria. (Gr. 484. R. XXVI.)
I believe [that] he will go.	Credo ille *iturus* (*esse*).
— [That] you and they will stay.	— Tu et ille *mansurus* (*esse*).
Thou believest [that] I will see.	Tu credĕre ego *visurus* (*esse*).
— [That] he will hear.	— Ille *auditurus* (*esse*).
He hopes [that] I will not go.	Sperare ego non *iturus* (*esse*).
— [That] thou wilt obtain.	— Tu *impetraturus* (*esse*).
— [That] we will do our endeavour. [That] endeavour will be used by us.	— Ego *daturus* (*esse*) opera. Opera *dari* a ego.
We hope [that] they will get friends. [That] friends will be gotten by them.	Sperare ille *inventurus* (*esse*) amicus. Amicus *inveniri* ab ille.

55.—2. When the preceding verb is of the imperfect, perfect, or pluperfect tense, the future of the infinitive with ESSE is rendered by *would* or *should.* (Gr. 179–3.)

I said [that] I would write letters.
Thou saidst [that] thou wouldst write letters.
He said [that] he would write letters.
We promised [that] we would do our endeavour

You promised [that] you would send.
They promised [that] they would give diligence.
I said [that] letters should be written by me.
— [That] thou shouldst know.
— [That] he should know.
— [That] you and they should know.
Thou saidst [that] letters should be written by thee.

And so on through the rest of the examples at Num. 54, turning the former verb into the perfect tense, and the sign *will* into *would*, and *shall* into *should*.

56.—3. The future of the infinitive with FUISSE (i. e., the future-perfect), is always rendered by *would have*, or *should have*, whatever be the tense of the preceding verb.

I shewed [that] I would have satisfied him.	Ostendĕre, ego is (Gr. 397) *satisfacturus fuisse.*—C. *Att.* 1, 1.
He will think, [that] I would (should) not have written.	Existimare, ego *scripturus* non *fuisse.*—*Ib.* 11, 29.
Dost thou think, I would (should) have said these things?	Censēre, ego hic *dicturus fuisse?*—Cic. *Fin.*
Dost thou think, [that] I would (should) have undertaken so great labours?	An censēre, ego tantus labor *suscepturus fuisse?*—Cic. *de Sen.*
We should not have thought, [that] thou wouldst have done that, unless, &c.	Non putare, tu ille *facturus fuisse*, nisi, &c.—Plin. *Paneg.*
I am assured (it is well known to me), [that] Cæsar would neither have done nor suffered that.	Mihi exploratum est, Cæsar hic neque *facturus*, neque *passurus fuisse.*—Cic. *Att.* 14, 14.
I say [that] he would not have sold these things.	Dicĕre, ille hic non *fuisse venditurus.*—Cic. *in Verr.*
What do we think, they would have done?	Quis arbitrari, is *facturus fuisse?*—Cic. *de Am.*
Nobody shall persuade me, [that] Paulus and Africanus would have attempted so great things unless, &c.	Nemo ' mihi persuadēre, Paulus et Africanus tantus *fuisse conaturus*, nisi, &c.—Cic. *de Senec.* 28.

57.—When the former verb speaks of men in general, it may very elegantly be varied by the passive voice.

PRESENT TENSE.

They think thee Thou art thought	to be wise.	Putare tu Tu putari	*sapĕre.*
They thought him He was thought	*to be* wise.	Putare ille Ille putari	*sapĕre.*

PERFECT TENSE.

They say [that] Romulus founded Rome.	Dicĕre Romulus *condĕre* Roma.
Romulus is said to have founded Rome.	Romulus dici *condĕre* Roma.
They say [that] Rome was founded by Romulus.	Dicĕre Roma *condĭtus esse* a Romulus.
Rome is said to have been founded by Romulus.	Roma dici *condĭtus esse* a Romulus. (Gr. 326.)
They said [that] Romulus had founded Rome.	Dicĕre Romulus *condĕre* Roma.

FUTURE TENSE.

They believe that the king will come.	Credĕre rex [*esse*] *venturus.*
The king is believed to be about to come.	Credi rex [*esse*] *venturus.*

Miscellaneous Examples to be turned into Latin.

For the Latin words, see English Vocabulary at the end of the book.

Do you think *that such excellent men did* such things without reason?—Ancient philosophy thought *that a happy life was placed* in virtue alone.—I deem it not improper *that* 11 *I should write* to you.—I desired *that you should understand* this now.—I desired *that you should understand* this afterwards.—We think *that you can* very easily *explain* that—*that you will explain* that—*that you have explained* that.—We thought *that you could* very easily *explain* that—*that you had explained* that—*that you would explain* that—*that you would have explained* that.—You know *that I think* the same thing—*that I thought* the same thing.—You knew *that I thought* the same thing.—I suppose *that you prefer* to experience our silence.—I supposed *that you wished rather*, &c.—It is evident *that man consists* of body and mind.—It is innate to all and as it were engraven on the mind *that there are* gods.

PARTICIPLES.

58.—Participles are parts of the verb which contain no affirmation, but express the meaning of the verb considered as a general quality or condition of an object (Gr. 182). They have the form of adjectives, and, like them, agree with their substantives in gender, number, and case (Gr. 264). The participles in the active voice are the present in *ns*, and the future in *rus;* in the passive voice, the perfect in *tus*, *sus*, or *xus*, and the future in *dus*. For the time, meaning, and use of these, see Gr. 182, § 49. Also participles of the active voice, and all the participles of deponent verbs except the future in *dus*, govern the case of their own verbs. (Gr. 682. See also Gr. 688).

Present Participle.

59.—The participle of the present tense ends in *ns*—is active in signification, and is commonly rendered by the English participle in *ing*.

I praising thee.	Ego *laudare* tu.
Thou desiring wisdom.	Tu *expĕtĕre* sapientia.
God governing the world.	Deus *gubernare* mundus.

And so in the rest of the examples in the indicative mood, present tense.—No. 5, above.

Future Participle Active.

60.—The future participle active ends in *rus*, and is rendered by the circumlocution "about to;" as, *scripturus*, "about to write."

I [being] about to praise thee.	Ego *laudaturus* tu.
Thou [being] about to write.	Tu *scripturus*.
He [being] about to do his endeavour.	Ille *daturus* opera.

We [being] about to give thanks.	Ego *acturus* gratia.
What are you going (about) to do?	Quis *facturus* esse.—Ter.
He was going (was about) to say, O miserable me!	Me miserum! *dicturus* 2 esse.—Ovid.
I was just going (about) to give you it.	*Daturus* jam 3 fuisse.—Ter. *Heaut.* 4, 5.

61.—This participle with *esse* in the present tense, is usually translated as the future of the indicative, and often used instead of it.

I shall give (to) him nothing.	Nihil ego *esse* ille *daturus.* —Plaut. (Gr. 501).
Will not you tell me?	Non *dicturus esse?*—Ter.
My father will stay for my uncle.	Pater *mansurus* patruus *esse.*—Ter. *Phor.*

See above, No. 20.

62.—This participle with *fui*, and sometimes with *eram*, may be translated as the pluperfect subjunctive, and may often be varied by that tense.

Those things are done, which Cæsar would not have done.	Qui Cæsar non *facturus fuisse*, is fĭĕri.—Cic. *Att.* 14, 14.
He would have perished, if he had been left.	*Periturus fuisse*, si relinqui.—Quint. *Decl.* 5.
He would have wept for me being taken away.	Me *fleturus* ademptus illo *fuisse.*—Ov. *Trist.* 4, 10.
He would not have read the letters.	Non *lecturus fuisse* litera.
He would have done it.	*Facturus fuisse.*
Thou wouldst have done me a greater kindness (peformed more), if thou hadst denied quickly.	Plus *præstāturus fuisse*, si citò 10 negare.
Thou wouldst have been the greatest glory of the Muses.	Gloria Pierĭdes summus *futurus esse.*—Ov. *de Pon.* 4, 8, 70.
He would have amended [it], if he might (had been allowed).	*Emendaturus*, si 10 licēre, *esse.*—Ov. *Trist.* 1, 7.

Perfect Participle Passive.

63.—The perfect participle passive ends in *tus*, *sus*, *xus*, and is rendered by the present, past, or perfect participle passive in English; as, *amatus*, "being loved," "loved," or "having been loved."

1. Passives with the sign *being*, or *having been*.

Thou being sought for by me yesterday.	Tu *quæsītus* a ego heri.
Thou having been often sought for by me in vain.	Tu sæpe *quæsītus* a ego *frustra*.
The world, being (having been) created out of nothing, lasts still.	Mundus, *creatus* ex nihilum, durare adhuc.
Men, being brought to poverty, are slighted.	Homo, *redactus* ad paupertas, contemni.
The city, being taken, was burnt by the enemy. The enemy burnt the city, being taken.	Urbs, *captus*, 3 incensus esse ab hostis. Hostis urbs *captus* 3 incendĕre.

Without any Sign.

The conquered army.	Acies *victus*.
Ploughed land.	Terra *aratus*.
Armed enemies domineer in the taken city.	Hostis *armatus captus* dominari in urbs.
Time past.	Tempus *n*. *præteritus*.

2. *Deponent Verbs.*

Deponents, having an active signification under a passive form, are rendered by the sign *having*, or *who have*.

I having (who have) tried to speak.	Ego *expertus* loqui.—SENEC.
Thou having got riches, wilt find friends.	Tu, *nactus* divitiæ, invenire amicus.
He having spoken thus, held his peace.	Sic ille *fatus*, tacēre.
I congratulate thee, who hast (having) got the victory.	Gratulari tibi *potitus* victoria. (Gr. 484.)
They having often attempted in vain, desisted from the attempt.	Ille sæpius *conatus* frustra, conatus 3 desistĕre.—CÆS.
O you who have (having) suffered more grievous things.	O (vos) *passus* gravior.—VIRG.
Believe those who have (having) tried.	Credĕre *expertus*. (Gr. 405, 5th.)

In such deponents as have the passive signs, instead of *have* and *had* (see above, No. 14, &c.), this participle is also translated like those of passive verbs; as, *ortus*, "risen," or "being risen." So *mortuus, profectus, reversus, ingressus, experrectus*, &c.

The sun being risen was covered with clouds.	Sol *ortus* nubes 3 obductus esse.
They being entered into the city.	Ille *ingressus* [in] urbs.
They being returned home.	Ille *reversus* domus. (R. LX.)
We being awaked, slight vain dreams.	*Experrectus*, vanus somnium contemnĕre.

This participle in deponents may be often translated as the participle of the present tense.

Give pardon to me confessing.	Dare venia [ego] *fassus*.—Ov.
Their (of them) fathers going from home took care of that.	Pater [is] *profectus* domus (Gr. 556 & 558) 3 curare is.
He stood leaning on his spear.	*Nixus* hasta stare. (Gr. 484.)

Future Passive Participle in DUS.

64.—The future participle in *dus* has a variety of significations. After a noun it is rendered like the present infinitive passive; as, *homo amandus*, "a man to be loved." Hence,

The English of the infinitive mood passive, coming after a noun, or a substantive verb, must be rendered into Latin by the participle in *dus*.

Injury to be avoided.	Injuria *fugiendus*.
Injury is to be avoided.	Injuria esse *fugiendus*.
God to be worshipped.	Deus *colendus*.
God is to be worshipped.	Deus esse *colendus*.
Our good name (fame) is not to be neglected.	Non *negligendus* esse fama.
An office to be discharged.	Munus *n*. *fungendus*.
Pleasure to be enjoyed.	Voluptas *fruendus*.—Cic.
She is not to be obtained.	Ille non esse *potiundus*.
A thing to be boasted of.	Res *gloriandus*.—Cic.
Wine is to be denied to children.	Vinum *negandus* esse puer.

There is a kind of (some) reverence to be used towards men.

Adhibendus esse reverentia quidam adversus homo.—Cic. *Off.* 1.

Friends are to be admonished and chid: and that is to be taken kindly, which is done out of good will.

Amicus esse *monendus* et *objurgandus:* et is *accipiendus* esse amicè, qui benevolè fiĕri.—Cic. *Am.*

His (of him) safety is to be despaired of who cannot hear truth.

Hic salus *desperandus* esse, qui verum audire nequire.—*Ibid.*

Though strength should (may) be wanting, yet a good will (willingness) is to be commended.

Ut decesse vires, tamen esse *laudandus* voluntas.—Ov.

Whatsoever thou sufferest deservedly (from merit), is to be borne meekly.

Leniter, ex meritum quisquis 7 pati, *ferendus* esse.—Ov.

Virtue is to be preferred to gold, and good health to pleasure.

Virtus *anteponendus* esse aurum, et bonus valetudo voluptas.

Friendship is to be preferred before (to) all worldly things.

Amicitia *anteponendus* esse omnis res humanus.—Cic. *Am.*

Life was given to be used (i. e. was lent).

Vita 3 datus esse *utendus.* —Pedo.

Neighbours borrow vessels (ask vessels to be used).

Vicinus rogare vas *n. utendus.*—Cato.

I borrow this (I receive this to be used).

Hic accipĕre *utendus.*

Life was lent us (we received life to be used).

Vita accipĕre *utendus.*

That which we have borrowed (received to be used) is to be returned.

Is, qui accipĕre *utendus, reddendus* esse.

65.—The participle in *dus* as a predicate, in connection with the verb *esse*, often denotes necessity, propriety, or obligation, and is rendered by *must*, *ought*, &c., and the expression is equivalent to that made by the gerund in *dum* with the verb *est*, *erat*, *fuit*, &c., No. 67. (Gr. 182–6, & 531.)

We must beware of pride. (Pride is to be avoided.)

Cavendus esse superbia.

We must do our endeavour. (Endeavour is to be used.)

Dandus esse opera.

We must apply ourselves to (endeavour is to be used for) virtue, if we would (we wish to) either live happily or die happily.	*Dandus* esse opera virtus, si velle vel beatè vivĕre, vel beatè mori.
We ought to keep a promise. A promise is to be kept.)	*Servandus* esse fides.
We ought to keep a promise (a promise is to be kept) made (given) even to an enemy.	*Servandus* esse fides, etiam hostis datus.
Thou oughtest to restrain thy tongue (thy tongue is to be restrained by thee) most carefully then, when thy mind is moved with passion.	Lingua tu esse *continendus* diligentissimè tum, quum animus iracundia (Gr. 630) movēri.—Cic. *ad Q. Fr.*
In all things diligent preparation ought (is) to be made before thou goest about (undertakest) them.	In omnis res *adhibendus* esse præparatio diligens, priusquam aggrĕdi. (Gr. 627–4.)—Cic. *Off.* 1.

Miscellaneous Examples to be rendered into Latin.

For the Latin words, see English Vocabulary at the end of the book.

No one, when he looks (looking) at the whole earth, will doubt concerning the providence of God.—The Deity ruling within us forbids us to depart.—My mind exalting itself looked forward to the future.—The third line received the enemy as they came (coming) forward.—Following (having pursued) with their swords (those) attempting to pass over, they slew a great part of them. Tarquin surrounded by a band of armed men rushed into the forum, then when all were (being) struck with fear, sitting on the royal seat before the curia, he ordered the fathers to be summoned.—Whilst they were (they being) overwhelmed with grief, Brutus holding before him the knife taken from the wound of Lucretia (and) dripping with gore, says.—Valerius returned in triumph (triumphing) to Rome.—When these things being commonly spoken of and believed, vexed the mind of the consul, having called the people (the people being called) into council, he went down to the assembly with the fasces lowered.—All things 2 had to be done by 3 Cæsar at one time; the standard had to be displayed; the signal, to be given by the trumpet; the soldiers to be recalled from the work; the line of battle to be formed; the soldiers to be harangued; the signal to be given.

THE GERUND.

66.—The gerund is a kind of verbal noun, used only in the singular number. It represents the action or state expressed by the verb as a thing now going on, and at the same time, if in the nominative, or in the accusative before the infinitive, as the subject of discourse; and the oblique cases as the object of some action or relation. They are construed in all respects as nouns, and also govern the case of their verbs. (Gr. 698.)

In meaning and use, the gerund resembles the English present participle used as a noun (An. & Pr. Gr. 462), and the Greek infinitive with the article prefixed. (Gr. 714).

The Gerund in Dum *of the Nominative Case.*

67.—The gerund in *dum* of the nominative case is always joined with the verb *est*, *erat*, *fuit*, &c., and is rendered by *must*, *ought to;* or, *I am*, *thou art*, *he is*, &c., *obliged* or *forced to.*

Note.—The nominative case in English must be the dative in Latin. (Gr. 699.)

EXAMPLE.

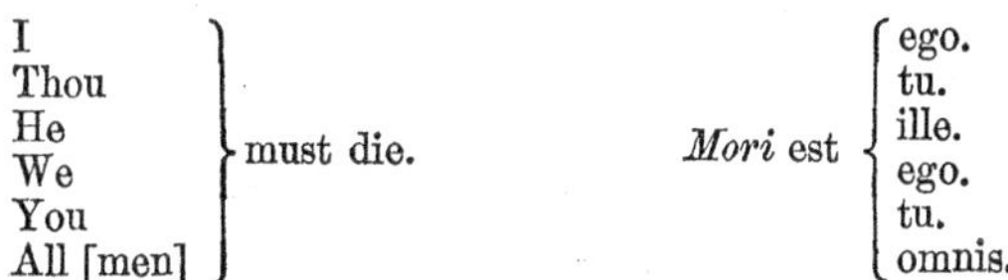

I, Thou, He, We, You, All [men]	must die.	*Mori* est	ego. tu. ille. ego. tu. omnis.

This dative case is often understood.

We must beware.	*Cavēre* esse (ego).
We ought to stand to promises.	*Stare* esse promissum.
We ought always to consult for peace.	Pax semper *consulĕre* esse. —Cic. *Off.* 1.
We must take care that we do not give ourselves to laziness.	*Cavēre* esse, ne ego desidia 7 dedĕre.
We must pray.	*Orare* esse (ego).
We must resist old age, and we must fight against it as against a disease.	*Resistĕre* esse [ego] (Gr. 405–3d) senectus, et *pugnare* esse contra is, tanquam contra morbus.

I must stay here longer, but thou oughtest to go home now. — *Manēre* esse ego hic diutiùs, at tu *ire* domus (Gr. 553 & 558) nunc 1 esse.

Why dost thou loiter? Thou oughtest to make haste. — Quid cessare? *Properare* 2 esse [tu].

We foolish men are catched with pleasure, whose temptations we ought to resist; and we ought to fight against the love of it as against a disease. — [Ego] stultus homo capi voluptas; qui illecebra (Gr. 405–3d) *resistĕre* 1 esse; et *pugnare* 1 esse contra amor is, tanquam contra morbus.

Thou oughtest to have stood to thy promises. — *Stare* [tu] 2 esse promissum.

Cato was obliged to die rather. — Cato *mori* potiùs 2 esse.—Cic. *Off.* 1.

Next we must speak of the gerund in *di*. — Deinceps de gerundium in *di dicĕre* esse [ego].

The Gerund in Di.

68.—The gerund in *di* follows a former substantive, or an adjective which governs a genitive case. (Gr. 332 & 349.)

Gerunds, supines, and participles, govern the same cases as the verbs to which they belong. (Gr. 682.)

The desire of increasing wealth. — Libido *augēre* opes.

The fear of losing money. — Metus *amittĕre* pecunia.

The way of living. — Via *vivĕre.*

The desire of learning. — Cupiditas *discĕre.*

Desirous of learning. — Cupidus *discĕre.*

Wrath is a desire of revenging. — Iracundia esse *ulcisci* libido.—Cic. *Tusc.* 3.

Children cannot judge which way of living is the best. — Puer non posse judicare quis via *vivĕre* optimus(30) esse.—Cic. *Off.*

The best way of living is to be chosen, and custom will make (render) it pleasant. — Optimus *vivĕre* via eligendus esse, isque jucundus consuetudo reddĕre.—*Ad Her.*

Covetous men are tormented, not only with a desire of increasing those things which they have, but also with the fear of losing [them]. — Avarus cruciari, non solùm libido *augēre* is qui habēre, sed etiam *amittĕre* metus.—Cic. *Par.* 1.

The greatness of the advantage ought to drive us to undergo the labour of learning. — Magnitudo utilitas debere ego ad (70) suscipĕre *discĕre* labor impellĕre.—Cic. *Or.* 1.

He who shall finish well and laudably the course of life (living), given by nature, shall go to heaven.	Ille, qui rectè et honestè curriculum *vivĕre* a natura datus conficĕre, ad cœlum ire.—Cic.
Covetousness is very miserable in the desire of getting, and not happy in the enjoyment of having.	Avaritia cupiditas *quærĕre* miserrimus esse, nec *habēre* fructus felix.—Val. Max. 9, 4.
The mind of man is drawn by the delight of seeing and hearing.	Homo mens *vidēre audire*que delectatio duci.—Cic.

Sometimes it may be rendered by the sign *to*, like the infinitive mood.

A desire to revenge.	Libido *ulcisci.*
A desire to increase riches.	Libido *augēre* divitiæ.
A desire to get.	Cupiditas *quærĕre.*
A temptation to sin.	Illecebra *peccare.*
There is a time to act, and a time to rest.	Esse tempus *agĕre*, et tempus *quiescĕre.*
A cause to repent.	Causa *pœnitēre.*

Sometimes by *in.*

Moderation in playing is to be kept.	Modus *ludĕre* esse retinendus.—Cic.

The Gerund in Do *of the Dative Case.*

69.—The gerund in *do* of the dative case follows an adjective denoting usefulness or fitness. (Gr. 382 & 703.)

Seed useful for sowing.	Semen n. utilis *serĕre.*—Plin. 19. 11.
Paper not good (useless) for writing.	Charta inutilis *scribĕre.*—*Id.* 13, 12.
Legs fit for swimming.	Crus *n.* aptus *natare.*—Ov.
He is not able to pay (for paying).	Non esse (habilis, idoneus) *solvĕre.*

The Gerund in Dum *of the Accusative Case.*

70.—The gerund in *dum* of the accusative case follows a preposition governing the accusative case. (Gr. 704).

Ready to write.	Paratus ad *scribĕre.*
Apt to learn.	Aptus ad *discĕre.*

A reward for teaching. — Merces ob *docēre.*

Man is born to labour. — Homo natus esse ad *laborare.*

Virtue allures men to loving. — Virtus allicĕre homo ad *diligĕre.*

Use all diligence to learn. — Adhibēre omnis diligentia ad *discĕre.*

Children are too inclinable to lying. — Puer nimium propensus esse ad *mentiri.*

Things necessary to life (living). — Res necessarius ad *vivĕre.*

He makes haste (hastens) to repent who judges quickly. — Ad *pœnitēre* properare citò qui judicare.—PUBL.

Do not come to punishing, when thou art (being) angry. — Ne (No. 25) accedĕre ad *punire*, iratus.—CIC. *Off.* 1.

We are not only inclined to learn, but also to teach. — Non solùm ad *discĕre* propensus esse, verùm etiam ad *docēre.*

A true friend is more inclinable to do kindness (to deserve well) than to ask returns (ask again). — Verus amicus propensior esse ad bene *merēri*, quàm ad *reposcĕre.*—CIC.

While we are (during) going, we shall have time enough to talk (talking). — Inter *ire*, habēre satis (Gr. 592] tempus ad *fabulari.*

These things are easy to be determined (to determining). — Hic esse facilis ad *judicare.*—CIC.

The Gerund in Do *of the Ablative Case.*

71.—The gerund in *do* of the ablative case follows a preposition expressed or understood, or is placed without a preposition as the ablative of manner or cause. (Gr. 705.)

Pleasure is found in (is derived from) learning. — Voluptas capi ex *discĕre.*—CIC.

To obtain by begging. — *Orare* impetrare.

Anger is to be debarred in punishing. — Ira esse prohibendus in *punire.*—CIC. *Off.* 1.

The mind is nourished by learning. — Mens *discĕre* ali.—CIC. *Off.* 1.

A wife governs by obeying. — Uxor *parēre* imperare.—PUBL.

We learn to do ill, by doing nothing. — Nihil *agĕre*, malè agĕre discĕre.—SEN.

We increase grief by mentioning it. — Augēre dolor *commemorare.*—CIC.

They say that Regulus was killed by (with) waking. Aio, Regulus *vigilare* necatus esse.—Cic. *Off.* 3.

Nothing is so hard, but it may be found out by searching. Nil tam difficilis esse, quin *quærĕre* investigari (Gr. 627–3) 7 posse.—Ter.

A drop makes a stone hollow, not by violence, but by often falling. Gutta cavare lapis, non vis, sed sæpe *cadĕre*.—Ov.

He that advises thee to (that thou) do [that] which thou doest already, praises [thee] in advising. Qui monēre ut facĕre qui jam facĕre, ille *monēre* laudare.—Ov.

Miscellaneous exercises on the Gerunds.

For the Latin words, see English Vocabulary at the end of the book.

Nominative, No. 67.—Young men ought to acquire, old men ought to enjoy.—The disciples of Pythagoras were obliged to be silent five years (Gr. 565).—We ought to praise the good.—I say that we must admit the truth.—We ought to have resisted the enemy.—Each one must exercise his own judgment.

Genitive, No. 68.—Avaricious men are tormented not only with a passion for acquiring, but also with the fear of losing.—Frugality is the science of avoiding superfluous expenses, or the art of using property with moderation.—He dreads the difficulty of speaking.

Dative, No. 69.—Coarse paper is not fit for writing.—This water is good for drinking.—Is that horse fit for running?—This seed is useful for sowing.—Nature has given to frogs legs fitted for swimming.—This is common to studying and writing.

Accusative, No. 70.—We are inclined not only to learn but also to teach.—As the ox was born for ploughing, the dog for tracking, so man was born for understanding and acting.—The Parthians are more disposed to act than to speak.—As we walk we will talk together.

Ablative, No. 71.—A man munificent in giving and not severe in exacting.—Anger should be forbidden in punishing.—Plato did not deter Aristotle from writing.—Virtue is given to man by instructing and persuading.—By doing nothing men learn to do ill.—The laws of Lycurgus train youth by hunting, running, being hungry, being thirsty, being pinched with cold, and by being greatly heated.

GERUNDIVES.

72.—The participle in *dus* of transitive verbs, and also of *medeor*, *utor*, *abutor*, *fruor*, *fungor*, and *potior*, is often used in the oblique cases in the sense of the gerund. Thus used, it is called a *gerundive* participle, and agrees with its substantive in gender and number, and both take the case which the gerund would have in the same place (182–7 & 707); thus,

Gerund . . .—Cupidus augendi opes. Gerundive.—Cupidus augendarum opum.	*Desirous of increasing wealth.*
Gerund . . .—Aptus ferendo onus. Gerundive.—Aptus ferendo oneri.	*Fit to bear the burden.*
Gerund . . .—Ad discendum artes. Gerundive.—Ad discendas artes.	*To learn arts.*
Gerund . . .—Faciendo injuriam. Gerundive.—Faciendâ injuriâ.	*By doing injury.*

1. The gerund in *di.*

The fear of losing money; (of money to be lost.)	Metus { amittĕre pecunia. / *amittendus* pecunia.
The covetous man is tormented with the fear of losing [his] money; (of money to be lost.)	Avarus cruciari metus *amittendus* pecunia.
The way of requiting a kindness; (of a kindness to be requited.)	Ratio { remunerâri beneficium. / *remunerandus* beneficium.
The hope of getting the town; (of the town to be gotten.)	Spes { potiri oppidum. (Gr. 484.) / *potiundus* oppidum.—CÆS.
Moderation in enjoying pleasure; (of pleasure to be enjoyed.)	Modus { frui voluptas. (Gr. 484.) / *fruendus* voluptas.
For the sake of exercising his memory; (of memory to be exercised.)	Gratiâ { exercēre memoria. / *exercendus* memoria.

2. The gerund in *do* of the dative.

Fit to bear a burden. (Fit for a burden to be borne.)	{ Aptus ferre onus. / Aptus *ferendus* onus.
A hand fit to carry a shield (for a shield to be carried).	Manus aptus *ferendus* clypeus.—OVID. *Art.* 1.

That the rich might contribute, who were able to bear the burden (for the burden to be borne).	Ut dives conferre, qui onus *ferendus* [par] 8 esse.—Liv. 2, 9.
Fit to endure the toil (for the toil to be endured).	Idoneus *perpetiendus* labor.—Col. 1, 9.

3. The gerund in *dum* of the accusative.

To love men. (To men to be loved.)	{ Ad amare homo. Ad *amandus* homo.
We are inclined by nature to love men (to men to be loved).	Natura propensus esse ad *diligendus* homo.—Cic. *Leg.*
To contemn pleasures. (To pleasures to be contemned).	{ Ad contemnĕre voluptas. Ad *contemnendus* voluptas.
Human nature is weak to contemn pleasures (for pleasures to be contemned).	Humanus natura imbecillus esse ad *contemnendus* voluptas.
To help men. (To men to be helped.)	{ Ad juvare homo. Ad *juvandus* homo.
Man was made (born) to help and preserve men (for men to be helped and preserved).	Homo natus esse ad *juvandus* et *conservandus* homo.—Cic. *Fin.* 3.
To enjoy pleasures. (For pleasures to be enjoyed.)	{ Ad perfrui voluptas. (Gr. 484.) Ad *perfruendus* voluptas.—Cic.
To discharge his office. (For his office to be discharged.)	{ Ad fungi munus suus. (Gr. 484.) Ad *fungendus* munus suus.
A disturbed eye is not well disposed to discharge its office (for its office to be discharged.)	Conturbatus oculus non esse probè affectus ad suus munus *fungendus*.—Cic.
To consider things. (For things to be considered.)	{ Ad considerare res. Ad *considerandus* res.

4. The gerund in *do* of the ablative.

Men use care in getting horses (in horses to be gotten), and are negligent in choosing friends (in friends to be chosen).	In equus *parandus* cura adhĭbēre homo, in amicus *eligendus* negligens esse.
But the greatest diligence is to be used in getting friends (in friends to be chosen).	Maximus autem diligentia adhibendus esse in amicus *comparandus*.—Cic. *Am.*

In managing affairs. (In affairs to be managed.)	In gerĕre res. In *gerendus* res.
In managing most affairs (in most affairs to be managed), slowness and procrastination is hurtful.	In plerique res *gerendus*, tarditas et procrastinatio noxius esse. (Gr. 268.)
In contemning pleasure. (In pleasure to be contemned.)	In contemnĕre voluptas. In *contemnendus* voluptas.
Honesty consists in contemning pleasure (in pleasure to be contemned).	Honestas in voluptas *contemnendus* consistĕre.—CIC.
By enjoying pleasures. (By pleasures to be enjoyed.)	Frui voluptas. (Gr. 484.) *Fruendus* voluptas.
By enjoying pleasures (by pleasures to be enjoyed) the grief for wanting them increases.	*Fruendus* voluptas crescĕre (68) carēre dolor.—PLIN. *Epist.* 8, 5.
Than requiting a good turn. (Than a favour to be requited.)	Referre gratia. *Referendus* gratia.
There is no duty more necessary than requiting a good turn (a favour to be requited).	Nullus officium *referendus* gratia magis necessarius esse.—CIC. *Off.* 1.
In discharging offices. (In offices to be discharged.)	In fungi munus. (Gr. 484.) In *fungendus* munus.

The participle in *dus* is elegantly put for the infinitive mood active, or the subjunctive with *ut*, after *curo, habeo, mando, conduco, loco,* &c. (Gr. 686).

He took care to do that.	Curare id	facĕre. *faciendus.*
He commanded the boy to be brought up.	Mandare	puer ali. ut puer ali. 4 puer *alendus.*

Miscellaneous Examples to be rendered both by Gerunds and Gerundives, as above.

For the Latin words, see English Vocabulary at the end of the book.

A desire seized Romulus of building a city.—All judicial proceedings have been devised for the sake either of terminating controversies or of punishing crimes.—Either pleasures are foregone for the sake of obtaining greater pleasures, or pains are undergone for the sake of escaping greater pains.—Dry wood is a proper material for eliciting fire.—The rest of the time is adapted for reaping and gathering the fruits.—Some games are useful for sharpening the wits of boys.

Pythagoras went to Babylon to learn the motions of the stars; thence he went to Crete and Lacedæmon to become acquainted with the laws of Minos and Lycurgus.—The eyelids are most skilfully formed both for enclosing the pupils and for opening them.—Similarity of character is the firmest bond for forming friendships.—There was no time not only for fitting the insignia but even for putting on their helmets and removing the covering from their shields.—Virtue is seen in despising and rejecting pleasures.—Many (persons) use care in getting money, (but) are negligent in using it rightly.—Honesty consists in despising pleasure.—No duty is more necessary than requiting a favor.

SUPINES.

73.—Supines are defective verbal nouns, of the fourth declension, having only the accusative and the ablative singular. (Gr. 183–2).

The former Supine.

74.—The supine in *um* has an active signification, governs the case of the verb (Gr. 682), and is used after verbs signifying motion to a place. (Gr. 712).

I will go to see.	Ire *spectare.*
I am come to beg leave.	(14) Venire *orare* venia.
He sent to ask help.	Mittĕre *rogare* auxilium.

The latter Supine.

75.—The supine in *u* has usually a passive signification—sometimes also an active, and follows such adjectives as signify *easy*, *hard*, *good*, *bad*, &c. (Gr. 183–2 & 716.)

Easy to { understand. / be understood.	Facilis *intelligĕre.*
Pleasant to { hear. / be heard.	Jucundus *audire.*

A thing hard to { do. / be done.	Res difficilis *facĕre.*
A thing worthy to be related.	Res dignus *referre.*
These things are unseemly to behold.	Hic esse deformis *vidēre.*—OVID.
It is hard to say, what is best to be done.	Difficilis esse *dicĕre*, quis 7 esse optimus *facĕre.*
A true friend is a thing hard to find (be found).	Difficilis res esse *invenire* verus amicus.
Let nothing filthy to be spoken or to be seen, touch those doors, within which there is a child.	Nil *dicĕre* fœdus *vidēre*ve, hic limen tangĕre, intra qui puer esse.—JUV.

It is used also after these substantives, *fas, nefas, opus ;* as, *Ecce ! nefas visu.*—Ov.

English Examples to be turned into Latin.

For the Latin words, see English Vocabulary at the end of the book.

Supine in um.—The ambassadors assembled about Cæsar to congratulate him. (Gr. 207, Obs. 3.)—The commanders of the King of Persia sent ambassadors to Athens to complain.—The Vejentes send negotiators to Rome to implore peace.—They went to see Italy.—Hannibal was recalled to defend his country.—Mæcenas went to play, I and Virgil went to sleep.

Supine in u.—A narrative easy to be understood.—Virtue is difficult to be found.—Incredible to relate!—Thou wilt do what seems best to be done.—This is proper to be said.

SYNTAX.

PART II.

251.* Rule I.—Substantives denoting the same person or thing, agree in case.

In this rule, the word "substantive" includes nouns, pronouns personal and relative, adjectives used substantively, and all words or phrases used as substantives. The substantive added is said to be in apposition with that which precedes, and must take its case. It is added to express some *attribute*, *description*, or *appellative* belonging to it, and must be in the same member of the sentence with it, i. e. subject or predicate. The substantive in apposition, whatever be its case, is without the case-sign in English. (Gr. 52.) The word "for," or "as," which sometimes precedes the noun in apposition in English, is occasionally made by *ut* or *quasi*, but has usually no corresponding word in Latin.

When the word in apposition has different forms to denote the different genders, it should correspond in gender, and, if the sense permit, in number also, to the word preceding.

Beware of pleasure, the mother of all evils.	Cavere *voluptas*, *mater* omnis malum.—Cic.
Plato the philosopher calls pleasure the bait to (of) evils.	*Plato philosophus* appellare *voluptas esca* malum.—Cic.
Do not thou (be thou unwilling to) reject glory, the fruit of true virtue.	Nolle repudiare *gloria fructus* verus virtus.—Cic.
Let flattery the promoter of vices be far removed from friendship.	*Assentatio* vitium *adjutrix* procul (25) amovēri ab amicitia.—Cic.

* In Part II, the numbers at the beginning of paragraphs refer to the running numbers in the Latin Grammar; also all numbers in parentheses above 75, and those distinguished by Gr. before them, whether in parentheses or not. But numbers, in parentheses, from 1 to 75, not distinguished by Gr. before them, refer to the running numbers in Part I. Numbers made by Roman letters, refer to the Rules of Syntax in the Latin Grammar.—See also "Explanations," p. 4.

How like to us is an ape, the most foul beast?	*Simia* quàm similis turpissimus *bestia* nos?—ENN.
Otho, a brave man, and my intimate friend, restored dignity to the equestrian order.	*Otho*, *vir* fortis, et necessarius meus, equester ordo restituĕre dignitas.
Themistocles, the commander in the Persian war, freed Greece, the home of freedom, from servitude.	*Themistocles*, *imperator* bellum Persicus, *Græcia domus* libertatis 6 servitus liberare.
Brutus and Cassius, the slayers of Cæsar, excited a great war.	*Brutus* et *Cassius*, *interfector* Cæsar, ingens bellum movēre.
Titus, the darling of mankind, was called a most excellent prince.	*Titus*, humanus genus *deliciæ*, bonus princeps vocari.
Grecian soldiers, his chief hope, came unto Darius.	Græcus *miles*, præcipuus *spes*, ad Darius pervenire.

1. An infinitive mood may be put in apposition with a substantive; as,

There is so great a love of sinning in some, that this very thing to sin delights them.	Tantus in quidam peccare libido esse, ut *hoc* ipse is (Gr. 627) delectare, *peccare*.—CIC. *Off.* 2.

256. A possessive pronoun, being equivalent to the genitive of its substantive pronoun, has a noun in apposition with it in the genitive.

Vatinius despises the law of me (his) enemy.	Vatinius contemnĕre *meus* lex, *homo* inimicus.
This pursuit has been approved of by thy judgment, a grave and learned man.	Hic studium, *tuus* judicium 3 probari, *vir* gravis et eruditus.

To this part of Syntax is usually referred the common remark that a noun or pronoun containing the answer to a question must be in the same case with the interrogative word in the question itself; thus, *Quis creavit mundum?* Ans. *Deus.* This, however, is evidently not a case of apposition but of ellipsis, and when the ellipsis is supplied, the answer will be, *Deus creavit mundum;* hence, *Deus* is in the nominative, not because *quis* is the nominative, but because, like *quis*, it is the subject of a verb, and of course comes under the principle mentioned (Gr. 304.). The pupil may illustrate this by supplying the ellipses in the following examples:

Who is poor? *Ans.* The covetous man [is poor].

Quis esse pauper? *Resp.* *Avarus* [esse pauper].

Of what men is there great scarcity? *Ans.* [There is great scarcity] Of the good.

Quis vir esse magnus *penuria?* *Resp.* [Esse magnus penuria] *Bonus.*

To what is pleasure an enemy? *Ans.* [Pleasure is an enemy] To virtue.

Quis inimicus esse voluptas? *Resp.* [Voluptas esse inimicus] *Virtus.*

Whom ought we to worship? *Ans.* [We ought to worship] God.

Quis debēre venerari? *Resp.* [Debēre venerari] *Deus.*

With what are fishes catched? *Ans.* [Fishes are catched] With a hook.

Quis capi piscis? *Resp.* [Piscis capi] *Hamus.*

With what are men catched? *Ans.* [Men are catched] With pleasure.

Quis capi homo? *Resp.* [Homo capi] *Voluptas.*

Than what has God given nothing to man more excellent? *Ans.* [God has given nothing to man more excellent] Than understanding and reason.

Quis (XXIV) Deus homo nihil præstabilior dare? *Resp.* [Deus homo nihil præstabilior dare] *Mens* et *ratio.* —CIC. *de Sen.*

The words understood being thus supplied, the reason of the exceptions from the rule will be evident; as, *Cujum pecus est?* Resp. [*Est pecus*] *Laniorum.* *Cujus est domus?* Resp. *Nostra* [*est domus*]. (Gr. 121. Obs. 1.)

To this question, *Quid est tibi nomen?* What is thy name?—the answer may be either in the nominative or dative case; because it may be indifferently said in Latin, *Est mihi nomen Sulpicius*, or *Est mihi nomen Sulpicio.* So PLAUTUS, *Mihi nomen Sosia est*, Amph. 1, 1. *Nomen Arcturio est mihi.* (Gr. 262.)

For other exceptions, see Gr. 260 & 262.

English Examples to be turned into Latin.

The Romans waged war with Tigranes, king of the Armenians.—The consul, a very brave man, has been sent with an 6 army.—How often hast thou endeavoured to slay me when (consul) elect?—How often, when consul?—Experience, an excellent instructor, has taught this.—I pass by Athens, that inventress of all learning.—To Cæsar, as quæstor, farther Spain fell by lot.—The use of gold and silver, as the material of all crimes, was abolished by 3 Lycurgus.

263.—Rule II. An adjective agrees with its substantive in gender, number, and case.

264.—Expl. This rule applies to all adjectives, adjective pronouns, and participles, and requires them to be put in the same gender, number, and case, with the substantives which they qualify, or of which they are predicated.

Past labours are pleasant. — *Actus labor jucundus* esse.

Wickedness is always fearful. — Semper *timidus scelus* esse. —Stat.

Worldly (human) things are frail and fading. — *Res humanus* esse *fragilis* et *caducus*.

Nobody was on a sudden very debauched. — *Nemo* repentè 3 esse *turpissimus*.—Juv.

Time past never returns. — *Præteritus tempus* nunquam reverti.—Cic.

And a word once let go (uttered) flies not to be recalled. — Et semel *emissus* volare *irrevocabilis verbum*.—Hor.

True honour consists (is placed) in virtue. — *Verus decus* in virtus *positus* esse.—Cic.

The way to the stars from the earth is not easy. — Non esse ad astrum *mollis* e terra *via*.—Sen.

For thy interest is concerned, when the next house is on fire (next wall burns). — Nam *tuus res* agi, *paries* quum *proximus* ardēre.—Hor.

We all haste to one mark. — *Ego omnis meta* properare ad *unus*.—Pedo.

Every one thinks his own condition the most miserable. — *Suus* quisque *conditio miserrimus* putare.—Cic.

Live ye innocent, God is at hand (a deity is present). — *Innocuus* vivĕre, numen adesse (Sup. *vos*).—Ov.

You live as if you were [about] to live always. — *Tu* vivĕre tanquam semper *victurus*.

Pride joined [to them] spoils excellent virtues. — Inquinare *egregius adjunctus superbia mos*.—Cic.

Letters (i. e. learning) adorn prosperity (prosperous things), and afford succour and comfort to adversity (adverse things). — Litera *secundæ res* ornare, *adversæ* (*res*) perfugium et solatium præbēre.—Cic. *pro Arch.*

There is nothing so easy but it is hard, when thou dost it with an ill-will (unwilling). — *Nullus* esse tam *facilis res*, quin *difficilis* 7 esse, quum (*tu*) *invītus* 7 facĕre.—Ter. *He.* 4.

265–268.—When an adjective qualifies, or is predicated of two or more substantives taken together, it becomes plural, and, in gender, prefers the masculine to the feminine, and the feminine to the neuter. (Gr. 265. 266.) But if the substantives denote things without life, the adjective may be neuter. (Gr. 267.) Also, whatever be the gender or number of the substantives, the adjective sometimes agrees with the last, and is understood to the rest. (Gr. 268.)

Many sons, daughters, grandsons, grand-daughters placed Metellus on the funeral pile.	Metellus *multus filius*, *filia*, *nepos*, *neptis* in 4 rogus 3 imponĕre.
Men, beasts, fishes, and birds were created by God.	*Homo*, *bestia*, *piscis*, et *avis*, a Deus 3 creari.
Empire, liberty, and life were taken away.	*Regnum*, *libertas*, et *vita* 3 *adimi*.
The king and the royal fleet set out together.	*Rex* regisque *classis* una 3 *proficisci*.
Benefit and injury are contrary to each other.	Inter sui *contrarius* esse *beneficium* et *injuria*.
The wall and gate were struck by lightning.	*Murus* et *porta* de cœlum *tactus* esse.

269.—When the noun to which an adjective or adjective-pronoun belongs is obvious, and may be easily supplied, it is often omitted; and the adjective, taking its gender, number, and case, is used as a substantive, and may have another adjective agreeing with it. This is particularly the case with neuter adjectives, when the adjective in English qualifies the word *thing* or *things;* or the reference is to something of a general or indefinite nature, without any regard to sex.

The good love the good.	*Bonus* diligĕre *bonus*.
He is only a little better than the worst of all.	Esse tantum paulo melior *pessimus*.
Great rewards await the good.	Prœmium magnus manēre *bonus*.
The wicked shall suffer punishment in hell (with those below).	*Impius* apud *inferi* pœnæ luĕre.—Cic.
Neither Pompey could bear an equal, nor Cæsar a superior.	Nec Pompeius 2 ferre *par*, nec Cæsar *superior*.
The slaves who were in the vestibule, when they saw armed men, thinking it was all over with their mistresses, cried out that men had been sent to kill the female captives.	Servus qui in vestibulum esse, ut *armatus* 2 conspicĕre ratus *actus* esse de domina, vociferāre *missus* esse qui 3 occidĕre *captus*.

We cannot all of us do all things.	Non *omnis* posse *omnis*.
The gods above regard the affairs of mortals (mortal things).	Aspicĕre *superus mortalis.*
Nature is content with few things.	Natura *paucus* contentus esse.—Cic.
I see and approve of better things, I follow worse things.	Vidēre *melior* probareque, *deterior* sequi.—Ovid.
Look always at heavenly things, contemn and neglect earthly (human) things.	Spectare semper *cœlestis*, contemnĕre et negligĕre *humanus.*—Cic.
God sees all things.	Deus cernĕre *omnis.*
Death devours all things.	Mors *omnis* devorare.
There is no desire of a thing unknown.	*Ignotus* nullus cupido esse. —Ovid.
All do not admire and love the same things.	Non omnis *idem* mirari amareque.—Hor.
We always hanker (strive) after what is [a thing] forbidden and desire things denied.	Niti in *vetĭtus* semper, cupĕreque *negatus.*—Ovid.
All excellent things are rare.	*Omnis præclarus* esse *rarus.*—Cic.
Let us contemn these worldly (human) things as small, thinking upon things above and heavenly.	*Hic humanus* ut *exiguus* contemnĕre (25), cogitans *superus* et *cœlestis.*—Cic. *Acad.*
The least of evils are to be chosen.	*Minimus* de malum *eligendus* esse.—Cic. *Off.* 3.
Bad things are near to good.	*Malus* esse *vicinus* bonus. —Ov.
In excellent things those are great, which are next to the best.	In præstans res *magnus* esse is, *qui* esse optimus *proximus.*—Cic. *de Orat.*

270, 271.—Adjectives qualifying, or predicated of, an infinitive mood or part of a sentence, are put in the neuter gender.

To talk of one's self *is* the property of old age.	De sui ipse *dicĕre* esse *senilis.*
To err is human.	*Humanus* esse *errāre.*
How long the life of any one of us will last is uncertain.	*Incertus* esse *quam longus ego quisque vita futurus* 7 esse.
It is a great thing to have the same monuments of ancestors.	*Magnus* esse *idem habēre monumentum majores.*
When will that to-morrow come?	Quando *cras iste* venīre?

To recede from one's right is sometimes not only liberal but advantageous.	*De suus jus decedĕre* nonnunquam esse non modo *liberalis* sed *fructuosus*.

273.—The adjectives *primus*, *medius*, *ultimus*, &c., are placed before their substantives, and often signify the first, the middle, the last, &c., part of a thing.

At the entrance of the province.	In *primus* 6 *provincia*.
The middle of the night.	*Medius* 1 *nox*.
To the farthest part of the province.	In *ultimus* 4 *provincia*.
On the top of the mountain.	In *summus* 6 *mons*.
Behind these, he places the rest of the army.	Post is (*fem.*) *ceter exercitus* locāre.

274.—An adjective agreeing with a substantive, generally the subject of a verb, sometimes modifies the meaning of the verb itself, and is translated like an adverb.

The Greeks drew near early in the morning, and gladly engaged in battle.	*Græcus matutinus* 3 appropinquare, *lætus*que 4 prœlium 3 inīre.
We delivered up ourselves to thee entirely and altogether.	3 Tu penitus *totus*que *ego* 3 tradĕre.
An augury came to Remus first.	*Prior* 3 *Remus* augurium 3 venire.
The Romans assembled in great numbers.	*Romanus frequens* convenire.
Avarice and luxury entered Rome at a late period.	4 Roma *serus avaritia* atque *luxuria* 3 immigrāre.

The following exercises correspond to the remaining observations and exceptions under Rule II, to which reference is made by the numbers prefixed.

275.—They gazed on the statues and ornaments, some in one place and some in another.	Signum et ornamentum *alius alius* in *locus* intuēri.—Cic.
Living one in one way and another in another.	*Alius alius mos* vivens.—Sall.
The soldiers in their joy (joyful) address themselves one to one, and another to another.	Miles *alius* 4 *alius* lætus appellāre.

They at one time think one thing, at another time another, concerning the same things.

Ille *alias alius* idem de res sentīre.

The cavalry slip off, some in this way and some in that.

Eques *alius alia* dilabi.

276.—Those places which were less secure he fortified, some with ditches, others with ramparts, and others with towers.

Qui minus tutus 2 esse alius fossa, *alius* vallum, *alius* turris 2 munīre.

It is one thing to rail at, another to accuse.

Alius esse maledicĕre, *alius* accusare.

Of whom (which two) the one lost an army, the other sold one.

Qui *alter* exercitus 3 perdĕre, *alter* 3 vendĕre.

He loves the one sister, I the other.

Alter ille amāre soror, ego *alter*.

277.—The best men most regard posterity.

Optimus quisque maxime posteritas servīre.

Every learned man despises (or all learned men despise) the Epicureans.

Epicureus *doctissimus quisque* contemnĕre.

It is the custom to sow all the heaviest grains.

Mos esse *gravissimus quisque* granum serĕre.

278.—Three thousand two hundred of the Samnites were slain.

Samnis *cæsus* esse *tres mille* ducenti.

Lofty Ilium was consumed.

Altus (fem.) *crematus* (fem.) esse Ilion (scil. urbs).

Pergamus was destroyed by the sword.

Excisus (fem.) esse *Pergamum* ferrum.

279.—A great part of the men were either wounded or killed.

Magnus *pars* homo *vulneratus* aut *occisus* esse.

The slaves conspired to arm themselves and seize (that being armed they would seize) upon the citadel.

Servitium conjurāre ut arx *armatus* 8 occupare.

281.—They are every one insane.

Uterque insanīre.

On the same day they each of them lead forth the army from the stationary camp.

Idem dies *uterque is* ex castra stativus exercitus *educere.*

Let them have each one what is his own.

3 Sui *quisque* 7 *habere* qui suus esse.

They were selected, every tenth man to punishment.

Decimus *quisque* ad supplicium 3 legi.

282.—I do not want medicine, I console myself.

Non egere 6 medicina *ego ipse* consolari.

He acquired to himself the greatest glory.	*Sui ipse* parĕre laus magnus.
He who knows himself, will feel that he has something in him divine.	Qui *sui ipse* 6 noscĕre aliquis sentīre sui habēre (Gr. 671) divinus.
283.—We sometimes allow our own liberty to be undermined.	*Noster ipse* libertas interdum subrui pati.
By his own power alone Mithridates reduced Cappadocia.	*Suusmet unus* opera Mithridates Cappadocia 3 capĕre.
My prayers when present will not avail him to whom my name when absent has been (for) an honor.	3 Is *meus præsens* preces non profuturus 1 esse 3 qui nomen *meus absens* 3 honor 3 esse.
I will be satisfied with our own friendship.	Contentus esse *noster ipse* amicitia.

Miscellaneous English Examples to be turned into Latin.

I received many letters from you, all written with care. The best laws, without any exception, will be taken away by this one.—Death is shameful in flight, glorious in victory.—No forgetfulness will ever blot out my remembrance of your favours to me (to us).—The city Rome, I foolishly supposed [to be] like this our [city].—A great part of the men were either wounded or killed (Gr. 279).—The slaves conspired to arm themselves and seize upon the citadel.—In a free state the tongue and mind ought to be free.—Menelaus and Paris being armed, fought for Helen and [her] riches.—Gnats seek for acid things, but do not fly to sweet things.—To advance was difficult, to retreat hazardous. It is astonishing how much that availed to the harmony of the state.—No artist can by imitation attain to the skill of nature.—Of all the provinces, Spain was subdued last.—The river Marsyas flows through the midst of the city.—At break of day, the top of the mountain was occupied by Labienus.—To take uncertain things for certain [things] is very foolish.

The Relative and Antecedent.

284.—Rule III. The relative *qui, quæ, quod*, agrees with its antecedent in number and person. See also Gr. 285, 286.

Beware of pleasure, which is a deadly mischief to men.	Cavēre *voluptas, qui* esse capitalis pestis homo.

Follow virtue, in which true honour consists (is placed).

Colĕre *virtus*, *f.* in *qui* verus decus *n.* positus esse.

The covetous man, who always wants, cannot be rich.

Avarus, *qui* semper egēre, non posse esse dives.

He does valiantly, who is able to be miserable.

Fortiter *ille* facĕre, *qui* miser esse posse.—Mart.

Be sparing of time, which [being] once past never returns.

Tempus *n.* (Gr. 405. 2d) parcĕre, *qui* semel præteritus nunquam reverti.

Those things are scarcest which are best.

Rarissimus esse *is*, *qui* esse optimus.

Worldly (human) things are to be despised, which are frail and fading.

Despiciendus esse *res* humanus, *qui* fragilis et caducus esse.

Follow (cultivate) the study of letters (i. e. learning) which adorn prosperity (prosperous things) and afford succour and comfort to adversity (adverse things).

Colĕre studium *literæ*, *qui* secundæ res ornare, adversæ [res] perfugium et solatium præbēre.—Cic. *pro Arch.*

They seem to take the sun out of the world, who take friendship out of the world.

Vidēri tollĕre sol e mundus, *qui tollĕre* amicitia e vita.—Cic. *Am.*

He is not blessed who knows, but he who does good (a good thing).

Non beatus esse *qui scire* bonus, sed *qui facĕre.*—Sen. *Ep.* 75.

There is one who has begun lately to dispute, that the soul dies at the same time with the body.

Esse (quidam) *qui cœpisse* nuper dissĕrĕre, anima interire simul cum corpus.—Cic. *Am.*

He is more valiant that (who) [conquers] himself, than he that (who) conquers the strongest towns.

Fortior esse *qui* sui, quam *qui* fortissimus *vincĕre* oppidum.

Govern thy passion (mind); which, unless it obeys, governs.

Animus regĕre; *qui*, nisi parēre, *imperare.*—Hor.

He is wise to no purpose (in vain), that (who) is not wise for himself.

Nequicquam sapĕre, *qui* sui non *sapĕre.*—Plaut.

He that (who) has much, desires more.

Qui multum *habēre*, plus cupĕre.—Sen.

He confesses the fact, who avoids the trial.

Fatēri facinus *n.* is, *qui* judicium *fugĕre.*

He is happily wise, that (who) is wise by another's danger (or trial).

Feliciter is sapĕre, *qui* alienus periculum *sapĕre.*—Plaut.

He that desires (who shall wish) to avoid error, will give (employ) time and diligence to the considering of things (to things to be considered).

Qui effugĕre error *velle*, adhibēre ad res considerandus (Gr. 707) tempus et diligentia.—Cic. *Off.* 1.

What better nature is there in man than theirs (of those) who think themselves born to help men?

Quis esse melior in homo natura quàm is, *qui* sui natus ad homo juvandus (Gr. 707) *arbitrari* ?—Cic. *Tusc.* 1.

Take example by (make trial from) others, which may be of use to thee.

Periculum ex alius facĕre, tu *qui* ex usu *esse*.—Ter.

Those injuries that (which) happen through some sudden passion (motion) are less than those that (which) are done on purpose and designedly.

Levior is esse injuria, *qui* repentinus aliquis motus *accidĕre*, quàm is, *qui* consultò et cogitatò *fiĕri*.—Cic. *Off.* 1.

The good things of fortune are just as his (of him) mind is that (who) possesses them: to him, who knows [how] to use them, [they are] good [things]; [to him] that does not use them well, [they are] bad [things].

Bonum fortuna perinde esse, ut is animus *qui* is *possidēre* : *qui* uti *scire*, is bonum; *qui* non *uti* rectè, [ei] malum.—Ter.

He that (who) gives the greatest things that he could is abundantly grateful.

Is *qui*, quàm 3 posse *dare* maximus, gratus abundè esse.—Ov.

Many contemn honours, with the desire of which some are inflamed.

Multus honor contemnĕre, *qui cupiditas* quidam inflammari.—*Id.*

Study for knowledge, than which nothing is more pleasant.

Studēre scientia, 6 *qui* (Gr. 467) nihil esse *jucundior*.

A good man does good to whom he can [do good]; hurts nobody.

Vir bonus prodesse, *qui* posse [*prodesse*]; nocēre (Gr. 405–1st) nemo.—Cic. *Off.* 3.

Some think nothing right but what (that which) they do themselves.

Quidam nisi *qui* ipsi *facĕre* nihil rectus putare.—Ter.

We are most lavish in throwing away of time, of which alone covetousness is laudable.

Profusissimus esse in tempus jactura, *qui* unus honestus *avaritia* esse.—Sen.

God affords (furnishes to) us abundance and plenty of all things which nature requires.

Deus omnis res, *qui* natura *desiderare*, abundantia et copia ego suppeditare.—Cic. *Am.* 23.

Death is terrible to those with whose life all things are extinguished, not to those whose praise cannot die.

Mors terribilis esse is, *qui* cum *vita* omnis extingui; non is, *qui laus* emŏri non posse.—Cic. 2 *Par.*

Friendship is the only thing in the world (in human affairs), concerning the usefulness of which all agree with one mouth.

Unus amicitia esse in res humanus, de *qui utilitas* omnis unus os *n.* consentire.—Cic. *Am.*

They are unjust, both who do (who bring) injury, and who do not keep off injury from them to whom it is offered (brought).

Injustus esse, et *qui inferre*, et, *qui* ab hic, *qui inferri*, non *propulsare* injuria.—Cic. *Off.* 1.

There is certainly a God, that (who) both hears and sees [those things] which we do.

Esse profectò Deus, *qui*, *qui* ego *gerĕre*, *audire*que et *vidēre.*—Plaut.

285.—The relative with its clause is sometimes put before the antecedent and its clause.

He is not truly rich, who is not endued with virtue.

Qui non esse præditus (Gr. 462) virtus, [*ille*] non esse verè dives.

Even they hate (have for hatred to themselves) injustice, who do it.

Etiam *qui* facĕre, [*illi*] odium (Gr. 427) habēre injuria.—Syr.

That which is honest is profitable.

Qui honestus, *is* utilis esse.—Cic.

[That] which is excellent, the same is difficult.

Qui præclarus esse, *idem* arduus esse.—Cic. *Tusc.* 3.

They who are blessed (endued) with wealth and plenty, ought to be liberal and charitable.

Qui (Gr. 462) opes et copiæ esse præditus, *is* debēre esse (Gr. 326) liberalis et benefĭcus.

Thou wilt always have those riches alone, which thou shalt have given to the poor.

Egenus *qui* 6 dăre, solus semper habēre *opes.*—Mart.

Every one thinks that which he himself suffers, the most grievous of all.

Qui ipse pati, *is* omnis gravissimus quisque putare.

Let every one exercise himself in this [art], which art he knows.

Qui quisque 9 nosse ars, in *hic* sui exercēre.—Cic.

All things which are produced in the earth, are created for the use of men.

Qui in terra gigni, ad usus homo *omnis* creari.—Cic. *Off.* 1, *c.* 7.

Men judge that to be done well in another, which they cannot do themselves. — Homo, *qui* facĕre ipse non posse, *is* rectè fĭeri in alter judicare.—Cic. *Am.*

Then, and not till then (at last), we all understand our blessings (good things), when we have lost those things which we had in our power. — Tum denique omnis noster intelligĕre bonum, quùm *qui* in potestas 3 habēre, *is* amittĕre.—Plaut.

The English relative *that* is rendered into Latin in the same manner as *who* and *which* (An. & Pr. Gr. 748).

He gives twice that (who) gives quickly. — Bis dăre, *qui* citò dăre.

He that (who) conquers passion, conquers the greatest enemy. — Iracundia *qui* vincĕre, hostis vincĕre maximus.

He that (who) gives himself up to pleasures, is not worthy of the name of a man. — *Qui* tradĕre (Gr. 501) sui voluptas, non esse dignus (Gr. 462) nomen homo.

Knowledge, that (which) is remote from justice, is to be called craft rather than wisdom. — Scientia, *qui* remotus esse a justitia, calliditas potiùs quàm sapientia esse appellandus.—Cic. *Off.* 1.

A burden that (which) is borne well, is made light. — Levis fĭeri, *qui* bene ferri onus.—Ov. *Am.*

Examples under Observations and Exceptions.

The following examples illustrate the observations and exceptions under Rule III, indicated by the numbers prefixed.

287.—*a.* You are not reading my words (= the words of me) who have been banished to the Ister. — Nec *meus* verbum legĕre *qui* submovēri ad Ister.

A few conspired against the republic, concerning which (conspiracy) I will speak as truly as possible. — *Conjurāre* paucus contra respublica, de *qui* quam verissime 5 posse 5 dicĕre.

b. The Lacedæmonians killed their king Agis, which never before happened among them. — *Agis rex Lacedæmonius, qui* nunquam antea apud is accidere, *necāre.*

The slaves, which had never been done before, were set free and made soldiers. — *Servus*, *qui* nunquam ante fieri, *manumitti et miles* 3 *fĭĕri.*—Cæs.

A thanksgiving of fifteen days was decreed, which before that time happened to no one.

Dies quindecim supplicatio 3 *decerni*, *qui* ante is tempus 3 accidĕre 3 nullus.—Cæs.

288.—The Helvetians are bounded on one side by the river Rhine, which separates the Helvetian territory from the Germans.

Helvetius contineri unus ex pars *flumen Rhenus*, *qui* ager Helvetius a Germanus dividĕre.—Cæs.

Cæsar determined to advance to the Scheldt which flows into the Meuse.

Cæsar ad *flumen Scaldis qui* influĕre in Mosa ire constituere.—Cæs.

289.—Pausanias betook himself to Colonæ, which is a place in the territory of Troas.

Pausanias *Colonæ*, *qui locus* in ager Troas esse, sui conferre.

Mago enticed the Suffetes, which is the chief magistracy among the Carthaginians, to a conference.

Mago ad colloquium *Suffetes*, *qui* summus 3 Pœnis *magistratus* esse, elicĕre.

Men have fenced with walls their united dwelling-places, which we call cities.

Homo *domicilium* suus conjunctus, *qui urbs* dicĕre, mœnia 3 sepīre.

290.—Themistocles sent to Xerxes the most faithful (one) of his slaves that he had.

Themistocles de servus suus *qui* habēre *fidelissimus* ad Xerxes mittĕre.

The Volscians being conquered in battle, lost Volscæ, the best city which they had.

Volsci, acies victus, Volscæ *urbs qui* habēre *optimus* perdĕre.

291.—The ships and captives which had been taken in the naval battle at Chios were restored.

Navis captivusque, *qui* ad Chius navalis prœlium capi, restitui.

293.—Whomsoever (=all whom) I have heard complaining of you, I have satisfied in every possible way (in every way that I could).

Quicunque de tu queri (Gr. 668, Note 3) audīre, *quicunque* posse *ratio* 3 placāre.

He joined himself to whatever standard (i. e. to any standard which) he had met with.

Quicunque signum occurrĕre sui aggregare.—Cæs.

Whatever things are needful for the attack of next day, are got ready during the night.

Quicumque ad proximus dies oppugnatio opus esse, noctu comparari.—*Ib.*

0 *The Relative in Latin used as the Demonstrative in English.*

295–296.—In English, the relative and its antecedent must always be in the same sentence, and as the relative follows the antecedent it cannot begin a sentence. In Latin, however, the relative often begins a sentence, and refers to some word or idea as its antecedent, in a sentence going before. When thus used, the relative, *without* a noun following it, is usually rendered by the personal pronoun preceded by a connective; and *with* a noun following it, by the demonstratives *this*, *that*, *these*, *those*.

By this battle the war of the Veneti was ended.	*Qui prœlium* bellum Veneti 3 confici.—CÆS.
And he sets forth the consternation of the Romans.	*Qui* timor Romanus 1 ponĕre.—CÆS.
And when he was heard.	*Qui* ubi 3 audiri.—CÆS.
And he too could not deny the young man. And Dion so admired and loved him that he gave himself wholly up to him.	*Qui* quidem adolescens negare non posse. *Quem* Dion adeo admirari atque adamare ut sui totus is tradĕre.
This occurrence indeed was very opportune for putting an end to the business.	*Qui* quidem *res* ad negotium conficĕre (Gr. 707) maxime 2 esse opportunus.—CÆS.
When this (viz. the fleet) arrived.	*Qui* (classis) ubi 3 convenīre.
And when Ariovistus saw these [men] near him in the camp, he cried out.	*Qui* cùm apud sui in castrum Ariovistus 10 conspicere, 3 conclamāre.—CÆS.
In this thing Cæsar revenged not only public but also private injuries.	*Qui* in *res* Cæsar non solum publicus sed etiam privatus injuriæ 3 ulcisci.—*Ib.*
For this reason also the Helvetii excel the rest of the Gauls in bravery.	*Qui* de *causa* Helvetius quoque reliquus Gallus virtus præcedĕre.—*Ib.*
And this place they had fortified with a very high double wall.	*Qui locus* duplex altissimus murus 4 munīre.—*Ib.*
This state of things has generally ruined great states.	*Qui res* plerumque magnus civitas 3 pessumdăre.—SALL.

To this belongs the construction of *quod* mentioned (Gr. 296).

In regard to what you write, that you wish to know what is the state of the republic; there is very great discord.	*Qui* scribĕre, 4 tu 11 velle (Gr. 671) scire qui 7 esse respublica status; summus dissensio esse.
298.—At this age which we have mentioned, Hannibal went with his father into Spain.	*Hic qui* dicĕre *ætas*, Hannibal cum pater in Hispania proficisci.

299.—The people whom you know being judges.

Judex (sing.) *qui* noscĕre populus (Gr. 695).

300.—No one was ever so shameless, as silently to dare (lit., who would silently dare) to wish from the immortal gods, so many and so great things as the immortal gods have bestowed on Cn. Pompey.

Nemo unquam tam impudens esse qui a deus immortalis *tot* et *tantus* res tacitus 8 audēre (Gr. 643. 2d) optare *quot* et *quantus* deus immortalis ad Cn. Pompeius deferre.

No ball is, in every thing, such as another ball is.

Nullus esse pila omnis 6 res *talis qualis* 7 esse pila alius.

Our men slew as great a number of them as the length of the day permitted (was).

Tantus is multitudo noster interficĕre *quantus* esse dies spatium.—Cæs.

English Examples to be turned into Latin.

How can *he* praise temperance *who* 7 places his chief good in pleasure?—*Who* has been found *that* 8 blamed my consulship except Clodius?—What is so much according to nature as for old men *to die*, *which* happens to young ones also (287, *b*).—Consider this *animal which* we call *man* (289).—They infer *many* (*things*) *which* will be said in these books.—All (persons) by nature follow *those* (things) *which* seem good.—*He who* does not fear death procures for himself a great security to a happy life.—The *desires which* arise from nature are easily satisfied.—*Many* (things) harass and trouble me *which* I can bring out in conversation.

The consuls came to that army which I had in Apulia.—Friendship which has ceased, was never true friendship.—Virtue and learning are riches which no thief can take away.—Posterity will discover many arts which we have not yet discovered.—No animal which has blood can be without a heart.—He who easily believes, is easily deceived.—The things which are right, are deservedly commended.—They who seem to be doing nothing, are often doing greater things than others.—It is ridiculous to ask what we cannot attain.

I have received two letters from you, dated at Corcyra, in one of which, you congratulated me because you had heard that I preserve my ancient dignity; in the other, you said, that you wished what I had done would turn out well and happily. But if it is dignity to think well of the state, and to commend to honest men what you think, I do preserve my dignity: but if dignity consists in this, if that either you are able in fact to accomplish what you think, or, in short, to defend it with a freedom of speech, there is not indeed any vestige of dignity remaining with me; and I am well off, if I can master myself, so that I bear patiently those events which partly are at hand, and partly impend; which is difficult in a war of this sort, the event of which exhibits slaughter on the one side, and slavery on the other.

The Verb and its Nominative.

303.—Rule IV. A verb agrees with its nominative in number and person.

I love truth; I would have (I wish) the truth (to be) told to me; I hate a liar.	*Ego* verum *amare;* verum *velle* ego dici; mendax *odisse.* —Plaut.
Thou hast done thy duty.	*Tu facĕre* officium tuus.
The covetous man always wants.	Semper *avarus egēre.*—Hor.
Wickedness reigns.	*Nequitia regnare.*
Nobody is born without faults.	*Nemo nasci* sine vitium.—Hor.
Passion soon dies with a good man.	Bonus apud vir citò *mori iracundia.*—Publ.
We old men dote sometimes.	*Delirare* interdum (*nos*) senex.—Plaut.
Honour nourishes arts; and we are all encouraged to our studies by glory.	*Honos alĕre* ars; omnisque (*nos*) *incendi* ad studium gloria.—Cic.
Years slip away.	*Labi annus.*—Cic.

304.—The subject of a verb is sometimes an infinitive mood or part of a sentence. (Gr. 304 & 309.)

To die is necessary.	Necesse esse *mori.*—Cic.
It is like a man (is human) to mistake.	Humanus esse *errare.*
It is a kind of (some) pleasure to weep.	Esse quidam *flĕre* voluptas. —Ov.
To talk of one's self is the property of old age (is senile).	*De sui ipse dicĕre* senilis esse.—Cic. *Sen.*
To subdue the mind, to restrain passion, is an excellent thing.	Animus *vincĕre,* iracundia *cohibēre* præclarus esse.—Cic.
To excel in knowledge is thought noble; but to be ignorant is accounted disgraceful.	*In scientia excellĕre,* pulcher putari; *nescire* autem, turpis duci.

To be serviceable to (deserve well of) the republic is glorious.	*De respublica bene merēri*, præclarus esse.—Cic.
It is contrary to duty not to keep promises.	*Promissum non servare* contra officium esse.—Cic.
To take uncertain things for certain (things) is very foolish.	*Incertus pro certus habēre*, stultissimus esse.—*Ib.*
It is a great fault to speak things [that ought] to be kept silent.	Gravis esse culpa, *tacendus loqui.*—Ov.
In great things it is enough to have been willing.	In magnum *velle* sat esse. —*Prop.*
How hard is it [for one] not to discover his crime by his looks (countenance)?	Quam difficilis esse *crimen non prodĕre vultus?*—Ov.
Not to know what happened before thou wert born, is to be always a child.	Nescire quid accĭdĕre (34) antequam nasci (34), *esse semper puerum esse.*—Cic. *Or.* 34

SPECIAL RULES.

312.—Rule I. Two or more substantives singular taken together have a verb in the plural; taken separately the verb is usually singular.

Note.—In the compound tenses of the passive voice, the participle must be made to agree with the subject of the verb, as in Gr. 265–267.

(Taken together.)

Justice and bounty procure friends.	*Justitia et benignitas conciliare* amicus.
Rage and anger hurry on the mind.	*Furor iraque* mens *præcipitare.*—Virg.
Rashness, lust, and idleness, always torment the mind, and are always turbulent.	*Temeritas, libido, et ignavia* semper animus *excruciare*, et semper *turbulentæ esse.*—Cic.
Eagerness, and covetousness, and boldness, make men blind.	Cæcus *reddĕre cupiditas, et avaritia et audacia.*—*Ib.*
Gold and purple exercise the life of men with cares.	*Aurum et purpura* cura *exercēre* homo vita.—Lucr.
The wicked and the covetous (man) are to be esteemed poor.	*Improbus et avarus inops existimandus esse.*
Castor and Pollux were seen to fight on horseback in the Roman line.	In acies Romanus *Castor* et *Pollux* ex equus pugnāre *vidēri.*

Fineness, closeness, whiteness, (and) smoothness are regarded in paper. — *Spectari* in charta (*pl.*) *tenuitas*, *densitas*, *candor*, *lævor*.

313.—Exc. But after several nominatives, the verb sometimes agrees with the one nearest it, and is understood to the rest. This occurs most frequently when the nouns denote things without life, or abstract ideas; or when each of the nominatives is preceded by *et*, or *cum* (*quum*), or *tum*. But if what is asserted is true of them only jointly, the verb must be plural: or if one of the nominatives is plural, the verb is commonly, though not always, plural.

Every virtue draws us to itself, but justice and liberality effect that most of all. — Omnis virtus ego ad sui allicere, sed *justitia* et *liberalitas* is maxime *efficĕre*.—Cic.

The bond of human society is reason and speech. — Societas humanus vinculum *esse ratio* et *oratio*.—*Id.*

The consciousness of a life well spent, and the remembrance of good deeds, is very pleasant. — *Conscientia* bene actus vita, et benefactum *recordatio jucundissimus esse*.—*Id.*

Understanding, reason, and prudence, is in old men. — *Mens*, *ratio*, et *consilium*, in senex *esse*.—*Id.*

Praise, honour, and dignity, accrues to those who have got wisdom. — Ad is, qui sapientia adipisci *laus*, *honos*, *dignitas*, *confluĕre*.—*Id.*

Let us consider what excellency and dignity there is in the nature of man. — Considerare, quis (Gr. 627–5) *esse* in natura homo *excellentia* et *dignitas*.—Cic. *Off.* 1.

Our application and carefulness is to be stirred up, that we may do nothing rashly and inconsiderately. — *Excitandus esse animadversio* et *diligentia*, ut nequid temere ac inconsideratè (627–1, 2d) agĕre.—*Id.*

About the same time both Marcellus came to Rome, and the consul Q. Fulvius. — Sub idem tempus et *Marcellus* et *Q. Fulvius consul* Roma (553) *venīre*.

There was in Miltiades both the greatest kindness and wonderful affability, great authority with all the states, an illustrious name, and the highest renown in military affairs. — In 6 Miltiades *esse* quum summus *humanitas*, tum mirus *comitas*; magnus *auctoritas* apud omnis civitas, nobilis *nomen*, *laus* 2 res militaris maximus.

The forehead, the eyes, the countenance, often deceive. — *Frons*, *oculus*, *vultus* sæpe *mentiri*, *pl.*

314.—Bocchus, with his foot soldiers, attacks the rear of the Roman army. — *Bocchus*, *cum pedes*, postremus Romanus acies (273) *invadĕre*.—Sall.

The leader himself, with some chief men are taken. — Ipse *dux*, *cum* aliquot *princeps capi*.—Liv.

Romulus, with his brother Remus, will give laws. — *Quirinus* cum frater *Remus* jus *dăre*.

315.—Both thou and all my friends have fallen into one common ruin. — Et *tu* et omnis meus *amicus corruĕre*.

Thou and I to-day speak to each other (between us) with the greatest frankness. — *Ego* ac *tu* simpliciter (*superl.*) inter ego hodie *loqui*.

You (*sing.*) and I were together all that time. — *Ego* atque *tu* omnis ille 4 tempus unà *esse*.

Both thou and I are in fault. — Et *ego* et *tu esse* in culpa.

(Taken separately.)

Either the temple of Jupiter or the town occupies a part of the plain. — Pars planitia aut Jupiter *templum* aut *oppidum tenēre*. —Liv.

Whether a slave or a freeman shall do it, let it be done well. — Sive *servus* sive *liber* 9 *facĕre*, probe factum esto.—*Id.*

From the Cimmerii, some god, or nature, or the situation of that place which they inhabited, had taken away the sight of the sun. — Cimmerius aspectus sol, *deus* aliquis, sive *natura*, *adimĕre*, sive is locus qui incolĕre *situs*.—Cic.

If a thrush or any other peculiar [delicacy] shall be given thee, let it fly thither. — *Turdus* sive alius *privus dari* tu, 7 *devolare* illuc.—Hor.

Exc.—When the nominatives are disjunctively connected by *aut*, *neque*, &c., the verb is sometimes plural; and it is always so when the substantives are of different persons. (Gr. 313 *in fin.*).

According as inclination or friendship took possession of them. — Ut *studium* aut *gratia* quique 3 *occupăre* (pl.)

If neither thou nor I have done these (things), poverty has not permitted us to do [them]. — Hic si neque *ego* neque *tu facĕre*, non sinĕre egestas ego facĕre.

316.—Rule II. 1. A collective noun expressing many as one whole, has a verb in the singular number.

At the same time both the army showed itself (was shown) and the fleet was entering the harbour.	Idem tempus et *exercitus ostendi* et *classis intrāre* portus.—Liv.
So great a multitude threw stones and darts.	Tantus *multitudo* lapis et telum *conjicĕre.*—Cæs.
The greatest part of men labour under (are tossed to and fro by) the same malady.	Maximus *pars* homo morbus *jactāri* idem.—Hor.
The fickle crowd are divided into opposite courses.	*Scindi* incertus studium in contrarius *vulgus.*—Virg.

Rule II. 2.—When a collective noun expresses many as individuals, the verb must be plural.

Part load the tables with food, and replace the full goblets.	*Pars* epulæ *onerāre* mensa et plenus *reponĕre* poculum. —Virg.
Part cut the flesh into pieces and fix it, while yet quivering on the spit.	*Pars* viscera in frustum *secāre* veruque tremens *figĕre.*—*Id.*
317.—When the army of the enemy had been put to flight on the left wing, they pressed our army severely on the right wing.	Cum hostis *acies* a sinister cornu in fuga 10 *converti*, a dexter cornu vehementer noster acies 2 *premĕre.*
Gaul takes great delight in beasts of burden, and procures them at a great price.	*Gallia* maxime *delectari* 6 jumentum, isque impensus *parare* 6 pretium.
318.—Each of them leads forth his army from the stationary camp, on the same day.	Idem dies *uterque* is ex castra stativus *educĕre.*—Cæs.
Both hasten on the work, and move their pliant arms.	*Uterque* (fem.) *festināre*, brachiumque doctus movēre. —Ov.
The rest of the multitude, every tenth man, were selected by lot for punishment.	Ceter multitudo sors, decimus *quisque* ad supplicium *lectus* (esse).
As one brought aid to another, they began to resist more boldly.	Quum *alius alius* subsidium *ferre*, audacius resistĕre cœpisse.

English Examples to be turned into Latin.

The liberty of the Roman people is at stake.—The inclinations of the citizens have been different.—Fear 2 made you a good man.

—Our reasoning agrees; (our) language differs.—The remembrance of slavery will make liberty more pleasant.—No one interrupts me; all respect me.—We wish to determine truly.—We, we the consuls are deficient (in our duty).—To do wrong is never useful (Gr. 270, 271).—To betray (our) country is a sin.

Seleucus and Antiochus waged war on account of Asia.—Ninus and Semiramis acquired great glory.—To separate the mind from the body is nothing else than to learn to die.—To salute kindly, and to address each one courteously, is never unpleasing.—In the meantime, all Greece being divided into two parties, turned their arms from foreign wars as it were upon their own bowels; wherefore, two bodies are made out of one people, and the soldiers are divided into two hostile armies.—After the battle, no woman lamented her lost husband; all lamented their own hap, because they had not fallen for their country.

319.—RULE V. The predicate substantive or adjective after a verb, is put in the same case as the subject before it.

Anger is a short madness.	*Ira furor* brevis *esse.*
Anger is the beginning of madness.	*Ira esse initium* insania.
Frugality is a great income.	Magnus *vectigal parsimonia esse.*
Drunkenness is a voluntary madness.	*Ebrietas esse* voluntarius *insania.*—SEN.
Virtue is the perfection of reason.	*Virtus esse perfectio* ratio.
Virtue is the sole and only nobility.	*Nobilitas* solus *esse* atque unicus *virtus.*—JUV.
A good life is the way to heaven.	Probus *vita esse via* in cœlum.—CIC. *Somn.*
Honour is the reward of virtue.	*Honor esse præmium* virtus.
Envy is its own punishment.	*Invidia supplicium esse* suus.
Deferring is the greatest remedy of passion.	Maximus ira *remedium dilatio esse.*—SEN.
Justice is the mistress and queen of virtues.	*Justitia esse domina* et *regina* virtus.
Revenge is the pleasure of a weak and little mind.	Infirmus *esse* animus exiguusque *voluptas ultio.*—JUV.

A magistrate is a speaking law, and the law is a dumb magistrate. — *Magistratus esse lex* loquens, et *lex esse* mutus *magistratus.*—Cic. *Leg.* 3.

A magistrate may (is able to) be called a speaking law. — *Magistratus dici* posse *lex* loquens.

Patience too often offended becomes fury. — *Furor fĭĕri* læsus sæpius *patientia.*—Publ.

Socrates was judged the wisest man by the oracle. — *Socrates* oraculum *sapientissimus* 3 *judicari.*

In every thing the agreement of all nations is to be thought the law of nature. — Omnis in res omnis gens *consensio lex* natura *putandus* esse.—Cic.

Why am I called (saluted) a poet? — Cur *ego poeta salutari?*—Hor.

Note.—An infinitive mood may be put instead of a nominative after substantive verbs, &c., in the predicate.

To live well is to live twice. — Bene vivĕre *esse* bis *vivĕre.*

To suppose is to assent to a thing unknown. — Opinari *esse assentiri* res incognitus.—Cic.

To give wine to children is to increase fire with fire. — Vinum puer dăre *esse* ignis ignis *incitare.*

To receive a benefit is to sell [one's] liberty. — Beneficium accipĕre, libertas *vendĕre esse.*—Pub.

This is cheating (to deceive). — Hoc *esse decipĕre.*—Cic.

321.—Not to believe rashly is the sinews of wisdom. — *Non temĕre credĕre nervus esse* sapientia.—*Id.*

To be content with what one has (with one's own things) is the greatest and most certain riches. — (4 Hominem) *contentus esse res suus*, maximus *esse* certissimusque *divitiæ.*—Cic. *Par.* 6.

It is great riches to a man to live sparingly with a contented mind. — *Divitiæ* grandis homo *esse*, *vivĕre parcè æquus animus.*—Luc.

321, *a.*—Every mistake is not to be called folly. — Non omnis *error stultitia* esse *dicendus.*—Cic.

Inconstancy, which is a fault. — *Inconstantia*, *qui* esse *vitium.*—Cic. *Leg.* 1.

Hate thou calumny, which is a great fault. — 6 Odisse *calumnia*, *qui* esse *vitium* magnus.

Just glory, which is the fruit of true virtue, is not to be rejected. — Justus *gloria*, *qui* esse *fructus* verus virtus, non esse repudiandus.—Cic.

That animal endued with reason which we call man. — Ille *animal* præditus ratio, *qui* vocare *homo*.—Cic.

Charity, which is a thing most conducive to the living happily. — *Caritas*, *qui aptissimus* esse ad quiete vivĕre.—Cic.

325.—The accusative (Gr. 671) or dative before the infinitive of a copulative verb, requires the same case after it in the predicate.

Accusative before the Infinitive.

The poet says, that anger is a short madness. — Poeta dicĕre, *ira esse* brevis *insania*.

Cicero says, that anger is the beginning of madness. — Cicero dicĕre, *ira esse initium* insania.

It may (is able to) be truly said, that the magistrate is a speaking law, and that the law is a dumb magistrate. — Verè dici posse, *magistratus esse lex* loquens, et *lex esse* mutus *magistratus*.

We have heard that Socrates was judged the wisest man by the oracle. — Accipĕre *Socrates* oraculum *sapientissimus esse judicatus*.—Cic.

I reckon frugality to be the best income. — Optimus *vectigal* ducĕre *esse parsimonia*.—*Id.*

And so in the other examples under R. V.

Dative before the Infinitive.

It is not given to all to be noble and wealthy. — Non dări *omnis esse nobilis* et *opulentus*.

It is permitted to all to be good if they wish. — Licēre *omnis esse bonus* si velle.

In an easy cause, any one may be (it is permitted to any one to be) eloquent. — In causa facilis, 3 *quivis* licēre *esse disertus*.

Give the following examples according to both the forms mentioned (Gr. 326 & 327).

326.—We all desire and hope to become old men. — *Omnis* velle et sperare *fiĕri senex*.—Cic. *Sen.*

Not so many desire to be endued with virtue as to seem so. — Non tam *multus* virtus *esse præditus*, quàm vidēri velle.

I would choose to live poor honestly, rather than to get riches dishonestly.
Optare (38) honestè *pauper vivĕre* potiùs, quàm inhonestè parare divitiæ.

I had (I wish) rather (to) be in health than (to) be rich.
Malle valēre, quàm *dives esse.*

If thou desirest, in good faith, to be a good man, suffer a man to (that some one) contemn thee.
Si velle, bonus fides, *esse vir* bonus, sinĕre (ut) 7 contemnĕre tu aliquis.—SEN. *Ep.*

327.—It is allowed to no one to be negligent.
3 *Nemo* licēre *esse negligens.*

It is given to the good only, to be truly happy.
Bonus (Gr. 272) solus dări *esse* verè *beatus.*

It is not given to all to be noble and wealthy; but all may (it is permitted to all to) be good if they wish.
Non dări *omnis esse nobilis* et *opulentus;* sed licēre (Gr. 409) *omnis esse bonus* si velle.

English Examples to be turned into Latin.

He was afterwards made prætor and consul.—He openly desires to be made a tribune of the people.—The countenance is a certain silent expression of the mind.—Experience is the best master.—To the consul, he 2 appeared a good quæstor; and to you all, a most excellent citizen.—Nothing is generous which is not just.—He seems to me most dignified, who arrives by his virtue at a higher station.—The opinion of Bibulus 3 was first given.—You will come, beloved and respected by all.—I love your little daughter, and know for certain her to be lovely.—A worthy man, with great difficulty, suspects others to be wicked.

CONSTRUCTION OF THE GENITIVE.

GENITIVE GOVERNED BY NOUNS.

332.—RULE VI. One substantive governs another in the genitive, when the latter substantive limits the signification of the former.

The souls of men are immortal.
Animus homo esse immortalis.—CIC. *Sen.*

There is a great scarcity of good men.
Esse magnus *penuria bonus.*—CIC. *Am.*

The unskilfulness of youth (of beginning age) is to be governed by the wisdom of old men.	*Inscitia* iniens *ætas senex prudentia* regendus esse.—Cic. *Off.* 1.
The remembrance of past evils is pleasant.	*Memoria* præteritus *malum* jucundus esse.
Many had (wish) rather (to) suffer the loss of life, than of a good name (of fame).	Multus malle facĕre *jactura vita*, quàm *fama*.
Pain is often the cure of pain.	Dolor sæpe esse *medicina dolor*.
The manner of our life and of human nature is so ordered, that one (another) age arises out of another.	Ita *ratio* comparatus esse *vita* noster et *natura* humanus, ut alius ætas (LIV.) oriri ex alius.—Cic. *Am.*
The anger of God is slow.	*Ira Deus* lentus esse.
The power of custom is great.	*Consuetudo* magnus *vis* esse.—Cic.
The consent of all is the voice of nature.	*Omnis consensus natura vox* esse.—*Id.*
The body is as it were (as if) the vessel or receptacle of the soul.	Corpus quasi vas esse aut *receptaculum animus.*—Cic. *Tusc.* 1.
Forgetting is the remedy of injuries.	*Injuria remedium* esse oblivio.
In my judgment piety (dutifulness) towards parents is the foundation of all virtues.	Meus judicium pietas erga parens esse *fundamentum virtus* omnis.—Cic. *Pl.*
Forgetfulness is the companion of drunkenness.	*Comes ebrietas* esse oblivio.—Mac.
The desires of riches, glory, pleasures (the desire of riches, the desire of glory, the desire of pleasures), are diseases of the mind.	*Cupiditas divitiæ, gloria, voluptas,* esse *morbus animus.* Cic. *Fin.*
It is the saying of Demetrius, Nothing seems to me more unhappy than he to whom nothing of adversity ever has happened.	*Demetrius vox* esse, Nihil ego vidēri infelicior (XXIV.) is, qui *nihil* unquam evenire *adversum.*—Seneс.
The inventor of the brazen bull being first shut into [it], deservedly handselled the dismal work of his own art; to whom Phalaris said, O admirable inventor of punishment, do thou thyself first handsel thy own work.	Æneus *taurus repertor* teterrimus *ars* suus *opus*, primus inclusus, meritò 3 auspicari; Qui Phalaris, *Pœna* mirandus *repertor*, ipse tuus princeps imbuĕre, 3 dicĕre, opus.—Val. Max. 9, 2. & Ov. *Trist.* 3, 11.

Thou, O money, art the cause of a solicitous life; and thou, O money, affordest nourishment to the vices of men.

Solicitus tu *causa*, pecunia, *vita* esse; Tuque *homo vitium* alimentum (*pl.*), pecunia, præbēre.—PROP.

1. Sometimes, instead of *of*, or the sign of the possessive, the latter substantive has the preposition *to*, *at*, *for*, *in*, *on*, *between*, &c., before it in English; as,

The descent to hell is easy.

Descensus Avernus esse facilis.

Virtue is the only way to praise and honour.

Virtus esse unus *via laus* et *honor*.

God has regard to the pious and the impious.

Deus habēre *ratio pius* et *impius*.—CIC. *Leg.* 2.

The pleasures of the body are the baits and allurements to evils.

Voluptas corpus esse *esca* atque *illecebra malum*.

Riches are enticements to evils.

Opes esse *irritamentum malum*.—OV.

Certainly the only way to a happy life is [lies open] by virtue.

Semita certè tranquillus per virtus patēre unicus *vita*. JUV.

2. Sometimes the sign *for*; as,

Ambition and contention for honour is very miserable.

Ambitio et *honor contentio* miserrimus esse.—CIC. *Off.* 1.

Let alone light hopes and strivings for riches.

Mittĕre levis spes et *certamen divitiæ*.—HOR.

Through anger for the virgin taken away.

Ereptus *virgo ira* (XXXV.) —VIR.

3. Sometimes the sign *in*; as,

I am wont to admire thy wisdom in other things.

Cætera *res sapientia* tuus admirari solēre.—CIC.

Skill in the civil law.

Prudentia jus civilis.—*Id.*

Faithfulness is steadfastness and truth in promises (words) and agreements.

Fides esse *dictum conventum*que *constantia* et *veritas*. —*Id.*

Justice consists (is employed) in giving to every one his own, and in faithfulness in contracts (things contracted).

Justitia versari in tribuendum suum quisque, et in *res* contractus *fides*.—CIC. *Off.* 1.

Temperance keeps a moderation in all things.

Temperantia servare *res* omnis *modus*.

Order, and constancy, and moderation, in all words and actions, gain (excite) the approbation of those with whom a man lives (it is lived).

Ordo, et constantia, et *moderatio*, *dictum* omnis atque *factum*, movēre (Gr. 313) approbatio is, qui cum (Gr. 223–3) vivi.—Cic. *Off.* 1.

Friendship is nothing else, but a very great agreement [of opinion] in all divine and human things.

Amicitia nihil aliud esse, nisi omnis *res* divinus atque humanus summus *consensio*.—Cic. *Am.*

The consciousness of a right intention (will) is the greatest comfort in adverse affairs.

Conscientia rectus voluntas maximus *consolatio* esse *res* incommŏdus.—Cic.

Boldness in bad things is called valour by some.

Malus *res audacia* fortitudo vocari a quidam.—Sal.

So great carelessness in a thing very necessary is to be blamed.

Res maximè necessarius tantus *incuria* vituperandus esse.—Cic.

4. Sometimes the sign *between;* as,

Distinctions are to be made between kindnesses received.

Acceptus *beneficium delectus* esse habendus.

335.—One substantive may govern two genitives; as,

Marius's insatiable greediness of honour (the insatiable greediness of honour of Marius).

Inexplebilis *honor Marius fames*.—Flor.

God's love of [to] men.

Deus amor homo.

The infamy of the vices of the father often redounds on the son.

Infamia vitium pater sæpe redundare ad filius.—Cic. *Am.*

Men sought the securities of cities, with the hope of preserving (of the preservation of) their effects.

Homo *spes custodia res* suus urbs præsidium quærĕre.—Cic. *Off.* 1.

The backwardness of Sabinus in preceding days encouraged the Gauls.

Gallus hortari superus *dies Sabinus* cunctatio.

On account of the ancient injuries of the Helvetians to the Roman people, Cæsar sought satisfaction from them in war.

Cæsar, pro vetus *Helvetii injuria populus* Romanus ab is pœna bellum repetĕre.—Cæs.

336.—Who is there who can compare the life of Trebonius with (that of) Dolabella

Quis esse, qui 7 posse conferre vita Trebonius cum *Dolabella?*

Agesilaus, after he had entered into the port, which is called [the port] of Menelaus, being attacked with disease, died.

Agesilaus quum 10 venīre in 4 portus, qui *Menelaus* vocāri, in 6 morbus implicitus 3 decedĕre.

337.—Ariovistus refused neither his (Cæsar's) friendship nor (that) of the Roman people.

Ariovistus neque *suus*, neque populus Romanus gratia 3 repudiāre.

All *mine* is nevertheless *thine.*

Omnis *meus* esse, autem *tuus.*

Then the Salii celebrate in song the deeds of Hercules.

Tum Salii 6 carmen *Herculeus* factum ferre.

Tages seemed to have had (to have been of) the appearance of a boy, but the prudence of an old man.

Tages *puerilis* 6 species 3 vidēri sed *senilis* esse 6 prudentia. (Gr. 339.)

English Examples to be turned into Latin.

Great is the power of conscience.—The proof of eloquence is the approbation of the hearers (of those hearing).—The privation of every pain has been rightly called pleasure.—The whole life of philosophers is a meditation on (of) death.—The body is indeed as it were the receptacle of the soul.—A sudden storm at (of the) sea frightens sailors (those sailing).—The weakness of the body 3 hindered not the vigour of the mind.—Frugality is the virtue *of a private* man, not *of a king.*—I assume to myself a father's authority.

A love of pleasure and an attachment to (the desire of) virtue cannot easily exist (be) in the same person.—The meditating on future evils softens their approach.—The foundation of eloquence, as of other things, is wisdom.—The love of the people is greatly excited by the very report and opinion of liberality, beneficence, justice, fidelity, and all those virtues which belong to gentleness of manners, and to good nature.

The knowledge and the practice of virtue is the fittest defence of old age, not only because these never forsake us, even at the extremity of life; but also because the consciousness of a well spent life, and the recollections of many kind actions are most pleasant.—Your remembrance of your father's friendship and of his affection, has given me (brought to me) incredible joy.—The gods of the people are many; of nature, one.—This is mine and my brother's native country.

339.—Rule VII. A substantive added to another, to express a property or quality belonging to it, is put in the genitive or ablative.

1. *Genitive.*

Live mindful of how short a life thou art.

Vivĕre memor quàm (Gr. 627–5) esse *brevis ævum.*

Pythagoras was a man of no mirth.

Pythagoras esse vir *nullus hilaritas.*—Cic.

The little ant [a creature] of great labour, draws with its mouth, and adds to its heap, whatever it can.

Parvulus *magnus* formica *labor* os trahĕre quicunque posse, atque addĕre acervus. —Hor.

It is evident, that there is some deity of a most surpassing wisdom (mind), by whom all things are governed.

Perspicuus esse, esse numen aliquis *præstantissimus mens,* qui omnis (Gr. 635) regi.—Cic. *N. D.* 2.

It is so evident that there is a God, that I can scarcely think him [to be] in his wits (of a sound mind) who denies it.

Esse Deus ita perspicuus esse, ut, qui id (Gr. 635) negare, vix is [esse] *sanus mens* existimare.—Cic.

2. *Ablative.*

Simonides was a man of a great memory.

Simonides esse vir *magnus memoria.*

The mob is of an inconstant humour.

Vulgus esse *ingenium mobilis.*—Sall.

God cannot be ignorant of what mind every one is.

Deus ignorare non posse *quis mens* quisque (Gr. 627–5) esse.—Cic. *Div.* 2.

I know of what manners this age is.

Nôsse seculum hic *quis mos* (Gr. 627–5) esse.—Plaut.

Themistocles was [a man] of so great a memory, that he knew the names of all the citizens; but Cato, of a much better memory.

Themistocles esse *tantus memoria,* ut omnis civis nomen percipĕre (34): Cato verò multò *melior memoria.* —Cic. *Sen.*

They that (who) prefer themselves before (to) all, are [persons] of intolerable arrogance.

Qui sui omnis (Gr. 399) anteponĕre, *intolerabilis arrogantia* esse.—Cic. *Ad. Her*

Young men are commonly of a careless humour, and account [those things] the best (first) which are delightful at present, nor do they look a great way before them (provide for a long time).

Adolescens ferè *animus* esse *omissus*, et, suavis in præsentiâ qui (Gr. 635) esse, primus habēre, neque consulĕre in longitudinem.—Ter. *Heaut.* 5, 2.

We may (it is allowed us to) see this, that they who were before good-humoured (of affable manners) are changed by prosperity (prosperous things).

Hic vidēre licet, is, qui antea *commŏdus mores* 3 esse, prosperæ res immutari.—Cic. *Am.*

Scipio Africanus was [a man] of most courteous behaviour (manners), of very great dutifulness to his mother, liberality to his sisters, goodness to his [servants], justice to all.

Scipio Africanus esse *mores facillimus*, *summus pietas* in mater (L.), *liberalitas* in soror, *bonitas* in suus, *justitia* in omnis.—*Id.*

Of how great innocence ought generals to be? Of how great moderation? Of how great fidelity? Of how great skill? Of how great wit? Of how great courtesy?

Quantus innocentia debēre esse imperator? *Quantus temperantia? Quantus fides? Quantus facultas? Quantus ingenium? Quantus humanitas?*—Cic.

English Examples to be turned into Latin.

The consul himself [a man] of little and mean mind.—They are endowed with (are men of) the best disposition, the greatest wisdom, the most perfect harmony.—Men of the lowest stations are delighted with history.—Oppianicus himself 2 was of a cruel and severe disposition.—Furranius, a man of the highest integrity and innocence, was of the same opinion.—He is of a certain incredible strength of mind.

343.—Rule VIII. An adjective in the neuter gender without a substantive, governs the genitive.

There is much good in friendship, much mischief in discord.

Multum bonum esse in amicitia, *multum malum* in discordia.—Cic.

We have not [too] little time, but we lose a great deal.

Non *exiguum tempus* habēre, sed *multum* perdĕre.—Sen.

Take so much meat and drink, that your strength may be repaired, not oppressed.

Adhibēre *tantum cibus* et *potio*, ut refĭci vires, non ut opprĭmi.—Cic.

How much good there is in friendship, may (is able to) be perceived from quarrels and discords.

Quantum bonum (Gr. 627-5) esse in amicitia, ex dissensio et discordia percĭpi posse.—Cic. *Am.*

One example of luxury or covetousness does a great deal of (much) mischief.

Unus exemplar luxuria aut avaritia *multum malum* facĕre.—Sen. *Ep.* 7.

How much of blind night have mortal minds?

Quantum mortalis pectus *n.* cæcus *nox* habēre?—Ov.

What means (wishes to itself) the covetousness of old age (senile covetousness)? for can any thing be more absurd than to seek so much the more provision by how much the less of the journey remains?

Avaritia senilis quid sibi velle? Posse enim quidquam esse absurdior, quàm quò *minus via* restare, eò *plus viaticum* quærĕre?—Cic. *Sen.* 18.

We must resist passions with all our strength, if we would (we wish to) pass over that (this) life which is given [us] quietly and peaceably.

Omnis vires (LXI.) repugnare esse (Gr. 403) perturbatio, si velle *hoc*, qui 3 dari *vita*, tranquillè placidèque traducĕre.—Cic. *Tusc.*

In what darkness, and in how great dangers, is this life passed over?

Qualis in tenebræ, quantusque periculum degi *hoc ævum?*—Lucr.

The belly gives a very great deal of (very much) trouble to mankind (the human race), for the sake of which the greater part of mortals live.

Plurimum negotium humanus genus alvus exhibēre, qui (XXXV.) causa major pars mortalis vivĕre.—Plin. 26, 8.

If the crow could eat silently (being silent), he would have more meat, and much less of quarrelling and envy.

Si corvus 8 posse pasci taciturnus, habēre *plus dapis*, et *rixa* multò *minus invidia*que.—Hor.

It is a miserable thing to see so many [people] living badly, nay rather perishing badly.

Miserabilis esse vidēre *tantum* malè *vivens*, imò malè *periens*.

English Examples to be turned into Latin.

After the battle much gold and other riches were found in the camp of the Persians.—As much money as any one has in his chest, so much credit has he; and he that has little money has likewise little credit.—Cicero had less courage than Julius Cæsar, but he had more honesty.—What news is there in the city about Nero? a little before his death he leaned down upon a bed and drank some warm water.

349.—Rule IX. Verbal adjectives, or such as imply an operation of mind, govern the genitive.

Live mindful of death.

Vivĕre *memor mors*.—Aus.

All men hate [those that are] unmindful of a good turn (kindness).

Omnis odisse *immĕmor beneficium*.—Cic. *Off.* 2.

Most men are desirous of new things.

Plerique homo esse *cupidus res* novus.

Be not more desirous of contention than of truth.

Ne 7 esse *cupidior contentio*, quàm *veritas*.—Cic.

If thou art conscious to thyself of no fault, do not fear.

Si nullus *culpa* tu *conscius* esse, ne (25) *timēre*.

What nation does not love a mind grateful and mindful of a good turn (kindness)?

Quis natio non gratus animus et *beneficium memor* diligĕre?—Cic. *L.* 1.

Be ye even now mindful of old age about to come, so no time will pass away idle to you.

Venturus *memor* jam nunc esse *senecta*, sic nullus vobis tempus abire iners.—Ov.

A mind solicitous about [that which is] future is miserable.

Animus *futurum anxius* calamitosus esse.—Sen.

A good conscience (a mind conscious of what is right) laughs at the lies of fame.

Conscius mens *rectum* fama mendacium ridēre.—Ov.

The mind of men is ignorant of fate and future fortune.

Nescius mens homo *fatum sors*que futurus esse.—Virg.

Our native soil draws us all with I do not know what sweetness, and does not suffer us to be forgetful of itself.

Nescio quis natalis solum dulcedo cunctus ducĕre, et *immĕmor* non sinĕre esse *sui*.—Ov.

Time that eats up all (devouring of) things.

Tempus *edax res*.—*Id.*

The heat of his countrymen bidding [him do] ill things, does not shake a just man, and [one that is] tenacious of his purpose, from his fixed mind (steady resolution).

Justus et *tenax propositum* vir, non civis ardor pravum jubens, mens quatĕre solidus. —Hor.

Virtue is a lover of itself.

Virtus esse *amans sui*.—Cic.

Every nature is a lover of itself; neither is any thing more desirous of things like itself than nature.	Omnis natura esse *diligens sui;* neque quicquam esse *appetentior similis* (Gr. 385) sui, quàm natura.—Cic.
Virtue is a reward to itself, not (nothing) wanting praise, not (nothing) desiring outward help.	Ipse sui virtus pretium esse, nil indigus (xi.) laus, nil *opis* f. externus *cupiens.* —Claud.

English Examples to be turned into Latin.

Posterity of all ages will never be unmindful of this affair.—The Greeks are more desirous of disputation than of truth.—Ye have always been desirous of glory, and greedy after praise beyond other nations.—Do I seem to you so forgetful of my own firmness, so unmindful of my own actions?—They were not so mindful of your merit as (they were) enemies of your glory.—All men hate him who is unmindful of a favor.

355.—Rule X. Partitives and words placed partitively, comparatives, superlatives, interrogatives, and some numerals govern the genitive plural.

No beast (none of beasts) is wiser than the elephant.	*Nullus bellua* prudentior esse elephantus.—Cic.
Peace is the best of things.	Pax *optimus res* esse.—Sil.
There is none (nobody) of us without fault.	*Nemo ego* esse sine culpa. —Sen.
Nothing can be said so absurd, which is not said by some one of the philosophers.	Nihil tam absurdus dici posse, quod non (Gr. 635. lv.) dici ab *aliquis philosophus.*—Cic.
There is no man (nobody of men is) so savage, whose mind a belief (opinion) of a God has not possessed.	*Nemo homo* tam immanis esse, qui mens non (Gr. 635) imbuĕre Deus opinio.—Cic. *Tusc.*
Set before your eyes every one of these kings.	Ponĕre ante oculus *unusquisque* hic *rex.*—Cic. *Par.* 1.
The king did not know (was ignorant) whether of them was Orestes.	Rex ignorare *uter is* (Gr. 627–5) esse Orestes.—Cic. *Am.*
The least of evils are to be chosen.	*Minimus malum* eligendus esse.—Cic.

Nature covers man alone of all living creatures (animals) with the riches of others (another's riches).

Natura homo *unus animans* omnis alienus velare opes.—PLIN. 7. 1.

Note.—The partitive does not always take its gender from the genitive case, but sometimes agrees with the former substantive; as, *Albunea, nemorum quæ maxima*, VIRG. *Æn.* 7. 83. *Dulcissime rerum*, HOR. *Maxime rerum*, OV.

Oxen only of [all] animals feed walking backwards.

Bos *animal solus* retro ambulans pasci.—PL. 8, 45.

The chameleon only of [all] animals neither uses meat nor drink always, nor any other nourishment than [that] of air.

Chamæleon *m. solus animal* nec cibus (XXVI.) nec potus semper uti, nec alius quàm aër alimentum.—*Id.* 33.

All things are not alike fit for all.

Omnia non pariter *res* esse omnis aptus.—PROP.

358.—The most excellent of the Persian kings were Cyrus and Darius, the son of Hystaspes: the former of these fell in battle among the Massagetæ.

Excellens rex Persæ esse Cyrus et Darius, Hystaspes filius; *prior hic* apud Massagĕtæ in prœlium cadĕre.

359.—Give [me some] proof if you are [one] of these priestesses of Bacchus.

Cedĕre signum, si hic Baccha esse.

360.—Thales was the wisest among the seven.

Thales *sapiens in septem* esse.

I made myself one of those who had come to the waters.

Ego *unus ex is* facĕre, qui ad aqua 10 venire.

He was made tribune of the people first among noblemen.

Tribunus plebs fiĕri *primus inter homo* nobilis.

That was the second of the three things.

Is esse *de tres secundus.*

Themistocles sent to the king by night, [one] of his servants whom he accounted the most faithful.

Themistocles noctu *de servus* suus, qui habēre fidelis, ad rex mittĕre.

English Examples to be turned into Latin.

Who of the Greek rhetoricians ever drew any thing from Thucydides?—*None of the beasts* is wiser than the elephant.—Set before your eyes *every one of these kings.*—The *least of evils* are to be chosen.—*No one* (nemo) *of mortals* is wise at all times.

—The last of all the Roman kings was Tarquin the Proud.—Thales the Milesian, first of all among the Greeks, ascertained the reason of the eclipse of the sun.—Of these opinions, which is true?—Nothing can be said so absurd which 7 is not said by some of the philosophers.

361.—Rule XI. Adjectives of plenty or want govern the genitive or ablative.

1. *Genitive.*

The fables of the poets are full of vanity.	Fabula poëta *plenus* esse *futilitas.*—Cic. *N. D.*
All [places] are full of fraud and perfidiousness and snares.	*Fraus*, et *perfidia*, et *insidiæ*, *plenus* esse omnis.—Cic.
All [that are] endued with virtue are happy.	Omnis *virtus compos* esse beatus.—Cic. *Tusc.* 5.
Man, who is partaker of reason and speech, is more excellent than beasts, which are void of reason and speech.	Homo, qui esse *particeps ratio* et *oratio*, præstantior esse fera, qui esse *expers ratio* et *oratio.*
But the mind of man is endued with reason in vain, unless it become also endued with virtue.	Sed animus homo frustra esse *compos ratio*, nisi 30 evādĕre quoque *compos virtus.*
Virtue is made long-lived by verse, and free from the grave.	Carmen fĭĕri vivax virtus, *expers*que *sepulcrum.*—Ov.
We are not wanting, but prodigal, of time.	Non *inops tempus*, sed *prodigus* esse.—Sen.
All things are full of God.	*Deus plenus* esse omnis.—Cic.
Solitude, and a life without friends, is full of snares and fear.	Solitudo, et vita sine amicus, *insidiæ*, et *metus plenus* esse.—*Id.*

2. *Ablative.*

Human life is never free from troubles.	Vita humanus nunquam *molestia* esse *vacuus.*
Rich men have many nights full of fears.	Nox multus *timor plenus* habēre dives.
When one is loaded with wine, he is not master of himself.	Quum quis *vinum gravis* esse, esse *impos sui* (gen.).—Sen. *Ep.* 83.

English Examples to be turned into Latin.

What word is there in the letter which is not *full of humanity, duty, benevolence?*—Truly we shall be happy when we shall be, 6 our bodies being left, *free from* both *passions* and *contentions.*—A mind *free from disorders* makes men perfectly and absolutely happy.—His countenance 2 was *full of fury;* his eyes, *of wickedness;* his discourse, *of insolence.*—The mind during sleep is *without* (*free from*) *sensations* and *cares.*

GENITIVE GOVERNED BY VERBS.

364.—RULE XII. *Sum* governs the genitive of a person or thing to which its subject belongs as a possession, property, or duty.

It is not [the part] of a wise man to say, I will live well to-morrow.	Non *esse sapiens* dicĕre, cras bene vivĕre.—MART.
Doting is [the infirmity] of old men, but not of all old men.	Deliratio *esse senex*, sed non omnis *senex.*—CIC.
Rashness is [the property] of youth (blooming age), prudence of old age.	Temeritas *esse florens ætas*, prudentia *senectus.*—CIC. *Sen.*
It is [the part] of a vain person to commend, of a fool to disparage himself.	Laudare sui *vanus*, vitupe-rare *stultus esse.*—SEN.
It is [the property] of a great mind to slight injuries.	Magnus *animus esse* injuria despicĕre.—*Id.*
It is [the part] of a generous and magnificent mind to help and to do good.	Generosus et magnificus *animus esse* juvare et prodesse.—*Id.*
It is [the part] of an arrogant person to neglect what every one thinks of him.	*Arrogans esse*, negligĕre quid de sui quisque (Gr. 627–5) sentire.—CIC. *Off.* 1.
It is [the property] of a great wit to apprehend beforehand (foresee by reflection) things future, and not to suffer (cause) that he may be forced to say (that it may be to be said) at length, I had not thought it.	*Ingenium* magnus *esse*, præcipĕre cogitatio futurus, nec committĕre, ut aliquando dicendus (LIV.) esse, non putare.—*Id.* 1, 23.

There are two sorts of injustice; one [is] theirs that do (who bring) injury, the other theirs who do not keep off injury from those to whom it is offered (done).

Injustitia duo genus *n.* esse; unus [*esse*] *is*, qui inferre, alter *is*, qui ab hic, qui inferri, non propulsare injuria. —Cic. *Off.* 1.

It may happen to (it is the property of) any man to err; [but] it is [the property] of none but a fool to persist in error.

Quivis *homo esse* errare; *nullus* nisi *insipiens* in error perseverare.—Cic.

367.—If [my] memory perhaps shall fail me, it is your [part] to (that you may) put me in mind.

Si memoria fortè deficĕre, *tuus esse* ut suggerĕre.—Cic. *Fin.*

It belongs to us (it is ours) to understand.

Noster esse intelligĕre.—*Id.*

It is your business, Cato, to look to it.

Esse tuus, Cato, vidēre.—Cic.

English Examples to be turned into Latin.

It is the mark of a brave man not to be disturbed in adversity.—It is a wise man's business to determine who 7 is a wise man.—It is not becoming your gravity and wisdom to bear your misfortune too immoderately.—366. The Pythagoreans relate that the Orphean poem was the work of one Cecrops.

369.—Rule XIII. *Misereor*, *miseresco*, and *satăgo*, govern the genitive.

Pity thy poor companions.

Miserēri inops *socius.*—Juv.

Take [ye] pity, I pray you, upon the Arcadian king.

Arcadius, quæso, *miserescĕre rex.*—Virg.

Clinia is employed enough in (is busy with) his own affairs.

Clinia *satagĕre res* suus.—Ter.

Those who ought to take compassion on me cease not to envy me.

Qui debēre *miserēri ego* non desinĕre invidēre.—Cic.

At length take compassion on the allies.

Aliquando *miserēri socius.* —Cic.

371.—How he is deceived in his mind.

Ut 3*falli animus.*—Ter.

He is disgusted at me.

Fastidire ego.—Plaut.

I did not hear sufficiently, and yet I am not mistaken as to their conversation. — Nec satis exaudīre nec *sermo falli* tamen.

372.—Refrain from anger and fierce contention. — *Abstinēre ira*, calidusque *rixa*.

Cease at length from tender complaints. — *Desinĕre* mollis tandem *querela*.

It is time to give over the battle. — Tempus *desistĕre pugna*.

373.—Rule XIV. *Recordor*, *memini*, *reminiscor*, and *obliviscor*, govern the genitive or accusative.

1. *Genitive.*

He will remember (reflect upon) his own villanies with sorrow. — Iste cum dolor *flagitium* suus *recordari*.—Cic.

A good man easily forgets injuries. — Vir bonus facilè *oblivisci injuria*.

It is a pleasant thing to remember labours past. — Dulcis esse *meminisse labor* actus.

God himself commands thee to remember death. — Ipse jubēre *mors* tu *meminisse* Deus.—Mart.

A man that (who) is pitiful towards a calamitous person, remembers himself. — Homo qui in 6 homo calamitosus esse misericors, *meminisse sui*.—Publ.

That which any one loves very much, he cannot forget. — Qui quisque vehementer amare, *is* non posse *oblivisci*.

Let young men, when they shall have a mind (shall wish) to give themselves to diversion, beware of immoderateness, and remember modesty. — Adolescens, quum dăre sui jucunditas velle, (25) cavēre intemperantia, et *meminisse verecundia*.—Cic. *Off.* 1.

2. *Accusative.*

I remember all the stages of thy life (age). — Omnis *gradus* ætas *recordari* tuus.—Cic.

Thou art [one] of a happy memory, who usest to forget nothing but injuries. — Tu esse (vii.) memoria felicissimus, qui *oblivisci nihil* solēre, nisi *injuria*.—Cic.

Good men remember benefits. — Bonus *beneficium meminisse*.

He ought to remember kindnesses upon whom they are bestowed, not he to mention, who bestowed them.	*Officium meminisse* debēre is, in qui collātus esse, non commemorare is, qui 3 conferre.—Cic. *Am.*
Remember those things, which are worthy of your character.	*Reminisci is*, qui dignus (xxiii.) tuus persona esse.—Cic.
376.—I wish to know whether you remember yourself.	Velle scire ecquid *de tu* 7 *recordari.*
Remember the palla.	*De palla* 9 *memini.*
Never mention God but with caution, fear, and reverence.	Ne unquam 6 *meminisse Deus* (*de Deus*) nisi cautè, timidè et reverenter.

English Examples to be turned into Latin.

No one, Dolabella, *can* now *pity* either *you* or your *children*, whom you have left miserable in want and solitude.—It is peculiar to folly (Gr. 385) to discern the faults of others and *to forget her own.*—*Have* you *forgotten* your own (*tuus*) *accusation?*—He himself shall certainly recognize and *remember* his own *crimes* with some pain.—The old man told us not only of all his actions, but even of his sayings.—It is a pleasant thing *to remember labours* past.—The leader of the Helvetii exhorted Cæsar to (that he should) *remember* both the former disaster of the Roman people, and the ancient valour of the Helvetii.

CONSTRUCTION OF THE DATIVE.

DATIVE GOVERNED BY NOUNS.

378.—Rule XV. Substantives frequently govern the dative of their object. See also Nos. 379–381.

The cause of the poverty of Abdolonymus was (his) honesty.	Causa *Abdolonymus*[b] *paupertas*[a] esse probitas.
Are you my servant (a servant to me), or I yours (to you)?	Tu *ego*,[b] aut *tu*[b] ego *servus*[a] esse?
They cast themselves weeping at the feet of Cæsar.	Sui flens ad *pedes*[a] *Cæsar*[b] 3 projicĕre.

The knees of the boldest soldier have trembled a little when the signal of battle was given, and the heart of the greatest commander has palpitated.

6 Signum pugna datus (Gr. 690) ferox *miles*[b] paululum genu[a] 3 tremĕre, et magnus *imperator*[b] *cor*[a] exsilire.

The same love is destruction to the herd and to the herdsman (the master of the herd).

Idem amor *exitium*[a] *pecus*[b] esse; pecusque *magister*.[b]

I know not what eye bewitches my tender lambs.

Nescire quis tener oculus *ego*[b] fascinare *agnus*.[a]

THE DATIVE GOVERNED BY ADJECTIVES.

382.—RULE XVI. Adjectives signifying profit or disprofit, likeness or unlikeness, govern the dative. Also 383.

Nothing is so like death as sleep.

Nihil esse tam *similis mors*, quàm somnus.—CIC.

Is there any thing more like madness than anger?

An esse quidquam *similior insania*, quàm ira?—CIC. *Tusc.*

In the grave, the poor needy man will be equal to [those that are] rich.

In sepulchrum *par dives* pauper egenus esse.—CORN. GALL.

It is a hard thing to find words equal to great grief.

Difficilis esse magnus *dolor par* verbum reperire.—SEN.

Passionateness is an enemy (unfriendly) to prudence.

Iracundia esse *inimicus consilium*.—CIC.

Pleasure is an enemy (unfriendly) to reason and to virtue.

Voluptas esse *inimicus ratio* et *virtus*.

Nothing is so much an enemy (so unfriendly) to the mind (understanding) as pleasure.

Nihil esse tam *inimicus mens*, quàm voluptas.—CIC. *Sen.*

Cruelty is a very great enemy (very unfriendly) to the nature of men.

Homo *natura* maximè esse *inimicus* crudelitas. — CIC. *Off.* 3.

Nothing is more agreeable to the nature of man, than beneficence and liberality.

Nihil esse *natura* homo *accommodatior* (XXIV.) beneficentia et liberalitas.—*Id.* 1.

Fortune is sometimes kind to me, sometimes to another.

Fortuna nunc *ego*, nunc *alius benignus* esse.—HOR.

I am nearest to myself.

Proximus esse egomet *ego*.—TER. *An.* 4. 1. 12.

Let not your ears be easy to accusers.

Ne esse auris *criminans facilis.*—SEN.

That is becoming, which is agreeable to the excellency of man.

Decorus is esse, qui esse *consentaneus excellentia* homo.—CIC. *Off.* 1.

The good things of fortune are common to the righteous and wicked.

Bonum fortuna *communis* esse *probus* et *improbus.*—CIC.

Some things are common to man with beasts.

Quidam esse *homo* cum bestia *communis.*—*Id.*

Death is common to every age.

Omnis *ætas* mors *communis* esse.—*Id.*

We are all easy to be taught (docile) to imitate base and naughty things.

Docilis (LXII.) *imitandus turpis* ac *pravus* omnis esse. —JUV.

Archytas, when he had been made [a little] too angry with his bailiff, says, How (in what manner) would I have dealt with (treated) thee, if I had not been angry?

Archytas, quum *villicus* (39) factus esse *iratior*, Quis tu modus, inquit, accipĕre, nisi iratus (32) esse?—CIC. *Tusc.* 4, 36.

I would have punished (taken satisfaction from) thee, says Archytas to his bailiff, if I had not been angry with thee.

Sumĕre a tu supplicium, inquit Archytas villicus, nisi *tu iratus* (32) esse.—VAL. MAX. 4, 1.

A good conscience (a mind conscious to itself of right).

Mens *sui conscius* (IX.) rectum.

A plain diet (simple food) is best for man: a heaping together of tastes (of savoury dishes) is hurtful, and sauces are more pernicious.

Homo utilissimus esse cibus simplex: coacervatio sapor pestifer, et condimentum perniciosior.—PLIN.

Think yourself born for praise and glory, not for the belly, not for sleep and delight.

Arbitrari tu *natus laus* et *gloria*, non *abdomen*, non *somnus* et *delectatio.*—CIC.

We are born in this condition, creatures liable to no fewer diseases of the mind than of the body.

Hic conditio natus esse, animal *obnoxius* non paucior animus, quàm corpus *morbus.* —SEN. *de Ir.* 2.

If thou canst not (shalt have been unable to) be the best, at least (use thy) endeavour that thou mayest be next to the best.

Si 6 nequire esse optimus saltem dare opera ut *optimus* (LIV.) esse *proximus.*—PLAUT.

This is indeed common to all philosophers.

Hic quidem *communis* esse omnis *philosophus.*

EXCEPTIONS.

385.—A good man seeks [one] like himself.

Vir bonus *sui similis* quæ-rĕre.—Cic. *de Am.*

The bad would have (the bad wish) the good be bad, that they may be like themselves.

Malus bonus malus esse velle, ut (Liv.) esse *sui similis.*—Plaut.

There is something like understanding (reason) in a brute.

Esse quiddam *similis mens* in bellua.—Cic.

Death is very like sleep.

Somnus simillimus mors esse.

It is to be wished, that they that are over the commonwealth may be like the laws, which are moved (drawn) to punish (punishing), not by passion, but by equity.

Optandus esse, ut is, qui præesse (Gr. 393) respublica, *lex similis* esse, qui ad (Gr. 704) punire non iracundia, sed æquitas duci.—Cic. *Off.* 1.

Temperance is the enemy of (unfriendly to) lusts; and lusts are the enemies of (unfriendly to) the understanding and soul.

Temperantia esse *inimicus libido;* libido autem esse *inimicus mens* et *animus.*—Cic. *Off.* 3, 33.

Plain and open persons, who think that nothing ought (is) to be done underhand (secretly) or by stratagem, lovers of truth, enemies (unfriendly) to tricking, are beloved.

Homo simplex et apertus, qui nihil ex occulto, aut ex insidiæ agendus [esse] putare, veritas cultor, *fraus inimicus,* dilĭgi.—Cic. *Off.* 1.

It is the common fault of all, that we are too intent upon wealth in old age.

Vitium *communis omnis* esse, quŏd nimium ad res in senecta attentus esse.—Ter.

A certain care of those [creatures] which are procreated [by them] is the common [property] of all animals.

Communis animans omnis esse cura quidam is [animans *n.*], qui procreatus esse.—Cic. *Off.* 1, 4.

Cato the elder was almost of the same time (contemporary) with Scipio Africanus.

Cato major *Scipio Africanus* ferè *æqualis* esse.—Cic. *Off.* 3, 1.

The search of truth is proper to man.

Homo proprius esse verum inquisitio.—Cic. *Off.* 1.

It is the property of the guilty to tremble.

Proprius esse *nocens* trepidare.—Sen.

386.—Almost all men are prone to pleasures.

Plerique omnis homo *ad voluptas propensus* esse.—Cic. *Off.* 1.

The nature of almost all boys is inclined to idleness and play.	Ingenium omnis ferè puer esse *proclivis ad otium et lusus.*
Let a prince be slow to punishment, swift to [give] rewards; and let it grieve him as often as he is forced to be severe.	Esse *piger ad pœnæ* princeps, *ad præmium velox ;* et dolēre quoties cogi esse ferox. —Ov.
Some are more liable to some diseases, and others to others (others are more liable to other diseases).	Alius *ad* alius *morbus* (Gr. 275) *proclivior* esse.—Cic.
We are by nature inclined to liberality.	Natura *propensus* esse *ad liberalitas.*—Cic.

Examples of the Accusative with ad.

387.—All [people] are not fit for friendship.	Omnis *ad amicitia idoneus* non esse.—Cic. *Am.*
The necks of oxen are naturally fitted for the yoke.	Bos cervix *natus* esse *ad jugum.*—Cic.
Mankind (the race of men) is born for justice and honesty (honour).	Genus homo *ad justitia* et *honestas natus* esse.—*Id.*
A man good for nothing.	Homo *ad* nullus *res utilis.* —*Id.*
Old age brings this vice to men; we are more intent upon wealth than is sufficient.	Hic vitium senectus afferre homo; *attentior* esse *ad res* quàm sat esse.—Ter.
A disturbed mind is not fit to discharge its duty.	Conturbatus animus non esse *aptus ad* (LXII.) *exsequendus munus* n. suus.—Cic. *Tusc.* 3.
We all are too apt to learn to imitate naughty things.	Ego *ad pravus* (LXII.) *imitandus* nimis *docilis* esse omnis.
388.—Jugurtha stations his foot soldiers nearer the mountain.	Jugurtha *propior mons* pedes collocāre.
The Ubii live nearest to the Rhine.	Ubii *proximus Rhenus* incolěre.
389.—This was agreeable to (in accordance with) the letters which I had received at Rome.	Is esse *consentaneus cum* is *literæ* qui ego Roma 4 recipěre.
Often you appeared somewhat impudent, which is very unlike you (foreign from you).	Sæpe, qui *a tu alienus* esse subimpudens vidēri.

390.—Homer has sunk to the same repose as others.	Homerus *idem alius* sopīri 6 quies.

English Examples to be turned into Latin.

Your discourse against Epicurus was pleasing to our (friend) Balbus.—Antony is equal to Catiline in wickedness.—Nothing is so congenial to our intellectual faculties as metres (numbers) and tones (voices).—Good health is more pleasing to those who have recovered from a dangerous illness, than to those who have never been sick.—Men can be very useful to men.—The same labours are not equally painful to the commander and the soldier, because honour itself 7 renders the commander's labour lighter.—385. Why dost thou always defend men unlike thyself?—Nor indeed do I understand why Epicurus 9 rather chose to pronounce the *gods like men*, than *men like the gods.*

The Dative governed by Verbs.

GENERAL RULE.

391.—Rule XVII. All verbs govern the dative of the object or end, to which the action or state expressed by them, is directed. Also No. 392.

Praise is due to virtue.	Laus *deběri virtus.*
The greatest reverence is due to a child.	Maximus *deběri puer* reverentia.—Juv.
We owe dutifulness to our parents.	*Parens* noster *debēre* pietas.—Sen.
We must beware lest we open our ears to flatterers.	Cavēre esse (Gr. 701) ne (liv.) *patefacěre* auris *assentator.*—Cic. *Off.* 1.
That which thou dost well, thou dost for thyself, not for another.	Qui bene facěre, *facěre tu,* non *alius.*—Plaut.
Punishments are prepared for the wicked in hell (with the infernal gods).	*Impius* apud inferi pœna *præparatus* esse.—Cic. *de Inv.*
Nature engages us to our parents and country.	*Parens* et *patria* natura ego *conciliare.*—Cic.
The wise man makes a fortune himself for himself.	Sapiens ipse *fingěre* fortuna *sui.*—Plaut.

Has not nature set a bound (measure) to desires?	Nonne *cupido statuĕre* natura modus?—Hor.
The sun shines even to the wicked.	Etiam *sceleratus* sol *lucēre.* —Sen.
[That] which may happen to one body, may happen to any body.	*Quivis* posse *accidĕre*, qui *quisquam* [*accidĕre*] posse.—Publ.
Let him wish for no (nothing) more, to whom that has happened, which is enough.	Qui satis esse, *qui contingere*, hic nihil amplius optare. —Hor.
Many good things have happened to many beyond expectation.	Multus præter spes *multus evenire* bonum.—Plaut.
A return to heaven is open to every very good soul, when it is gone out of the body.	Optimus quisque *animus*, quum e corpus 6 excedĕre reditus ad cœlum *patēre.*—Cic. *Am.* 4.
We were not born for ourselves only.	Non *ego* solùm *nasci.*—Cic.
The covetous man gets riches for others, not for himself.	Avarus *alius* non *sui* divitiæ parare.
So you oxen carry plows not for yourselves.	Sic tu non *tu ferre* aratrum bos.
And you sheep bear fleeces not for yourselves.	Et tu non *tu* vellus *ferre* ovis.
And you birds make nests not for yourselves.	Et tu non *tu nidificare* avis.
And you bees make honey not for yourselves.	Et tu non *tu mellificare* apis.—Donat. *vit. Virg.*

English Examples to be turned into Latin.

It is the part of a wise man to please God, to do good to men, to take care of himself, to provide for his own safety, to be concerned for his friends and study their interest, to do harm to no one, to displease nobody, neither to hurt the miserable nor lay snares for the innocent.—A good man favours the good and rejoiceth with them upon any happy event; he is always disposed to spare the vanquished and forgive what is past; he neither entertains resentment nor flatters any one; he envies nobody but imitates the worthy.—You must be the servant of (It behoves you to serve) philosophy, that true liberty may be your portion (may happen to you).—Why do you yield and give way to fortune?—No man can serve pleasure and virtue at the same time.

SPECIAL RULES.

393.—I. *Sum* and its compounds govern the dative (except *possum*).

A word is enough to the wise.	Dictum *sapiens* sat *esse.*
It can be well with no wicked man (to nobody wicked).	Bene *esse* posse *nemo* improbus.—Cic.
That which is enough for nature, is not [enough] for man.	Qui *natura* satis *esse*, *homo* non *esse.—Id.*
A great fortune is a great slavery to its master.	Fortuna magnus magnus *dominus esse* servitus.
The covetous man is rich to his heir, but poor to himself.	Avarus *hæres* dives, pauper at ipse *sui esse.*
There is in youth the greatest weakness of judgment.	*Adolescentia inesse* maximus imbecillitas judicium.—Cic. *Off.* 1.
There is by nature in our minds an (a certain) insatiable desire of seeing truth.	Natura *inesse mens* noster insatiabilis quidam cupiditas verum visendus (Gr. 707).—Cic.
Scornfulness is in the fair.	Fastus *inesse pulcher.*—Ov.
Nature commands us to do good to men.	*Homo prodesse* natura jubēre.—Sen.
We ought to do good one to another.	Debēre *prodesse* alius *alius.*
There are [some] that (who) neither do good to themselves nor to others.	Esse [quidam] qui neque *sui* nec *alius prodesse.*—Cic. *Off.* 2.
Men may do very much good or harm to men (are able to do good or to do harm very much to men).	Homo plurimum *prodesse* aut *obesse* posse *homo.—Id.*
It is a greater thing to do good to many, than to have great wealth.	Major esse *prodesse multus*, quàm magnus opes *f.* habēre.—Cic.
A little is enough to nature, nothing is enough to covetousness.	*Natura* satis *esse* parum; *cupiditas* nihil satis *esse.*—Sen.
As magistrates are above the people, so the laws are above magistrates.	Ut magistratus *præesse populus*, ita lex *præesse magistratus.*
Pollio was not only concerned in all [your] affairs, but took the lead in them.	Pollio, omnis *negotium* non *interesse* solùm, sed *præesse*—Cic.

Let us do that strenuously which is equally profitable (equally does good) to poor and (equally to) rich.	Agĕre gnaviter is, qui æquè *pauper prodesse*, *locuples* æquè.—Hor. *Ep.* 1, 1.
The study of honest virtue equally profits (does good to) the poor and rich.	Virtus honestus *pauper prodesse* studium et *locuples* æquè.

394.—II. The verb *est*, signifying *to be*, or *to belong to*, governs the dative of the possessor. Also No. 395.

Note.—In translating from English into Latin under this rule, the objective case in English becomes the nominative in Latin, and the nominative in English becomes the dative in Latin. See examples, Gr. 394.

Kings have long hands (long hands are to kings).	Manus longus *esse rex.*
Art thou ignorant that kings have long hands (that long hands are to kings)?	An nescire longus *rex esse* manus? (Gr. 671.)—Ov.
So long as the sick man has life (as life is to the sick man) there is hope.	Dum *ægrotus* anima *esse*, spes esse.
Many animals have quicker senses (quicker senses are to many animals) than man.	Sensus agilior *esse* multus *animal* quàm *homo.*—Sen.
Man has some resemblance (some resemblance is to man) with God.	*Esse homo* similitudo quidam cum Deus.—Cic.
The soul has a struggle (a struggle is to the soul) with this heavy flesh, lest it should be drawn away or depressed: it tends thither from whence it was sent down.	*Animus* cum hic caro *f.* gravis certamen *esse*, ne (31) abstrăhi aut sidĕre: niti illò unde 3 demitti.—Sen.
The (Gr. 579) less wealth (by how much the less of things, by so much) the less covetousness the Romans had (was to the Romans). Riches brought in avarice.	Quantum minus (Gr. 343) res, tantum minus (Gr. 343) cupiditas 2 *esse Romanus.* Divitiæ avaritia 3 invehĕre. —Liv.
396.—Even if I have not wanted, as you think, talent for this undertaking, I have certainly wanted learning and leisure.	Etiamsi *ego* ut tu putare ad hic opus ingenium non *deesse* doctrina certe, et otium deesse.
I have not this (lit. this is wanting to me).	Hic *ego deesse.*

Nothing was less wanting to Darius than multitude of soldiers.	Non quisquam parum *Darius* quam multitudo miles *deesse.*
Poverty wants many things, covetousness all things (many things are wanting to poverty, all things to covetousness).	*Deesse inopia* multus, *avaritia* omnis.—PUB. SYR.
A covetous man wants as well that which he has, as that which he has not (as well, &c. is wanting to a covetous man).	Tam *deesse avarus* qui habēre, quàm qui non habēre. —*Id.*

397.—III. Verbs compounded with *satis*, *bene*, and *male*, govern the dative.

He does a kindness to himself, that (who) does a kindness to a poor man.	*Sui benefacĕre* ipse, qui *egenus benefacĕre.*
If thou dost a kindness to the good, that kindness is not lost.	Si *benefacĕre bonus*, is beneficium haud perire.
If thou dost any kindness to a bad man, that kindness is lost.	*Malus* si quid (30) *benefacĕre*, is beneficium interire.—PLAUT.
That kindness which is done to the good, is not lost.	Qui *benefiĕri bonus*, haud perire.—*Id.*
We are said to satisfy him whose desire we fulfil.	*Satisfacĕre* dici *is* qui desiderium implēre.—CAI. DIG.

English Examples to be turned into Latin.

The safety of his country *was* dearer *to him* than the sight of it.—[My] books now profit me nothing.—Men both profit and hurt men very much.—I have now no business with him.—I had not the oppŏrtūnity of consulting with you when we were together.—396. If any one possesses these things (if these things are supplied to any one) they assist him a little in (as to) others. —III. He satisfied both nature and the laws.—If any one reviles me, he seems to me petulant or absolutely mad.—Of what good man did Gellius ever speak well?

399.—IV. Many verbs compounded with these ten prepositions, *ad*, *ante*, *con*,—*in*, *inter*, *ob*,—*post*, *præ*, *sub*, and *super*, govern the dative.

Ad.

Stick to justice and honesty.	*Adhærescĕre justitia* et *honestas.*
The good take to themselves the good [for] companions.	Bonus bonus *sui* (I.) socius *adsciscĕre.*
Take care that thou dost not (lest thou) rashly assent to things unknown.	Cavēre ne temere (30) *assentiri incognitus.*—Cic. *Off.* 1.
Fame delights to add false things to true.	Fama gaudēre falsus *addĕre verus.*—Ov.
Do not lay hands on other men's goods.	Ne (25) *afferre* manus alienus *bonum.*—Cic.
Give not thy mind to pleasure.	Ne (25) *addicĕre* animus *voluptas.*—Sen.

Ante.

Prefer virtue before (to) riches, and those things which are honest to those things which seem profitable.	*Anteponĕre* virtus *divitiæ,* et is qui esse honestus *is* qui vidēri utilis.
Where can you find him that (who) prefers the advantage of a friend before (to) his own [advantage]?	Ubi iste invenire qui commodum amicus (LIV.) *anteponĕre suus?*—Cic. *Am.*
Virtue excels all things.	Virtus *anteire* omnis *res.*—Plaut.
The least excellence of the mind excels all the good things of the body.	Minimus animus præstantia omnis corpus *bonum anteire.*—Cic.
Many have preferred private quiet before (to) public employments.	Multus privatus otium *negotium* publicus *anteferre.*
The unlearned and savage sort of men always prefer profit before (to) honour; but the civilized and polished sort prefer dignity before (to) all things.	Indoctus et agrestis genus *n.* homo *anteferre* semper utilitas *honestas*; sed urbanus et politus genus *res* omnis dignitas *anteponĕre.*—Cic.
Always remember (have in readiness) how much the nature of man excels beasts.	Semper in promptu habēre, quantum natura homo *bestia* (Gr. 627–5) *antecedĕre.*—Cic. *Off.* 1.
One day spent well, and according to the precepts of virtue and religion, is to be preferred to a sinning immortality.	Unus dies bene, et ex præceptum virtus et religio actus, peccans *immortalitas anteponendus* esse.

Con.

Themistocles killed himself (procured death for himself). — Themistŏcles *sui* mors *consciscĕre.*

A sword is ill trusted with (to) an angry man. — Malè *iratus* ferrum *committi.*—Sen. *de Ir.*

Socrates durst not trust himself with anger: I would beat thee, says he to his servant, if I were not angry. — Socrates non 3 audēre sui *ira committĕre:* (33) Cædĕre tu, servus ait, nisi 8 esse iratus.—*Id. ibid.* 1. 15.

In.

Many dangers hang over us continually. — Multus *ego impendĕre* periculum perpetuò.

Death hangs over men always, as the stone over Tantalus. — Mors *homo*, quasi saxum *Tantalus*, semper *impendĕre.*—Cic. *Fin.*

A good man envies nobody. — Probus *invidēre nemo.*—Cic.

Nothing is happy to him, over whom some terror always hangs. — Nihil esse is beatus, *qui* semper aliquis terror (Gr. 636) *impendĕre.*—*Id.*

To indulge pleasure is the beginning of all mischiefs. — *Voluptas indulgēre* initium esse malum omnis.—Sen.

So does the sick man hanker after waters being forbidden him. — Sic interdictus *imminēre* æger *aqua.*—Ov.

It is a wretched thing to depend (lean) upon another man's reputation. — Miser esse *alienus incumbĕre fama.*—Juv.

Indulge your body so much as is sufficient to good health. — *Corpus* tantum *indulgēre,* quantum bonus valetūdo satis esse.—Sen.

Bitter enemies deserve better of us than those friends that (who) indulge sins, and drive us into mischief (fraud) by obsequiousness. — Meliùs de ego merēri acerbus inimicus, quàm is amicus qui *peccatum indulgēre,* et obsequium ego in fraus impellĕre.—Cic. *Am.*

Fern [that is] to be burned grows in neglected fields. — Neglectus urendus filix *innasci ager.*—Hor.

He must (it behoves him to) denounce war against his lusts and pleasure, who would (who may wish to) be good. — (Gr. 423) Oportēre is qui (Gr. 636) velle esse bonus, bellum *indicĕre cupiditas* et *voluptas.*

Inter.

God is amongst us.

Interesse ego Deus.—Sen.

God is present to our minds, and intervenes in the midst of our thoughts (to our middle thoughts).

Deus *interesse animus* noster, et *cogitatio* medius *intervenire.*—Sen.

God, the beholder of all things, is present in darkness; is present also in our thoughts, [which are] as it were (as if) another darkness.

Deus speculator omnis *tenebræ interesse; interesse* et *animus* noster, quasi alter *tenebræ.*—Min. Felix.

Ob.

Youth creeps upon childhood, old age upon youth.

Adolescentia *pueritia, adolescentia* senectus *obrepĕre.*—Cic. *Sen.* 2.

Many uneasinesses (displeasing things) are met with by him that lives (occur to him living) long.

Multus pœnitendus *occurrĕre vivens* diu.—Publ. Syr.

It is not [the part] of a courageous man to expose himself to dangers without cause, than which nothing can be more foolish.

Non esse (Gr. 364) magnanimus vir, *offerre* sui *periculum* sine causa, (Gr. 467) qui nihil posse esse stultior. — Cic. *Off.* 1.

Post.

Children commonly value all things less than (postpone all things to) play.

Puer ferè omnis *lusus postponĕre.*

Dost thou wonder, seeing thou valuest all things less than (postponest all things to) money, that nobody loves thee?

Mirari, quum tu 7 *postponĕre* omnis (*pl.*) *nummus,* quod tu nullus (30) amare?—Hor.

Præ.

Friendship is better than (excels) relationship.

Amicitia *præstare propinquitas.*—Cic. *Am.* 5.

A good name is better than (excels) riches.

Existimatio bonus *præstare divitiæ.*

The soul is much better than (much excels) the body.

Animus *corpus* multùm *præstare.*—Cic. *Leg.*

Man far excels other living creatures (other animals), and [one] man [another] man, an understanding man a fool.

Homo longè *præstare* cæter *animans,* et vir *vir,* intelligens *stultus.*

Prefer virtue to riches, friendship to money, and profitable things to pleasant.

Præferre virtus *divitiæ*, amicitia *pecunia*, et utilis *jucundus*.

Prefer not thyself to others, because of abundance of fortune.

Ne (25) *præferre* tu *alius*, propter abundantia fortuna. —Cic.

Mars presides over arms.

Mars *præsidēre arma.*—Ov.

Sub.

Nothing flourishes always: age succeeds age.

Nihil semper florēre; ætas *succedĕre* ætas.—Cic.

One world does not suffice the Pellean young man.

Unus Pellæus *juvenis* non *sufficĕre* orbis.—Juv.

It is a king-like thing, believe me, to help [those that are] fallen.

Regius, credĕre (Gr. 403) ego, res esse *succurrĕre lapsus.*—Ov.

Super.

Mourning often comes in the midst of mirth.

Luctus sæpe *lætitia supervenire.*

402.—Some verbs compounded with these prepositions, sometimes, instead of the dative, govern the case of the preposition; such as *ante-eo*, *-cedo*, *-cello*, *-venio*, *-verto; præ-cedo*, *-curro*, *-verto*, *-sto*, *-gredior; sub-eo*, &c.

EXAMPLES.

The nature of man exceeds all living creatures (all animals).

Natura homo omnis *animans anteire.*—Cic.

They affect us with a kind of (with a certain) admiration, who are thought to go before others in virtue.

Admiratio quidam afficĕre, qui *anteire cæter* virtus putari.—Cic. *Off.* 2.

Many have gone before us to death, all the rest will follow us.

Multus *ego antecedĕre* ad mors, omnis reliquus sequi.—Sen.

We are angry at God, because some one goes beyond us, forgetting how many men are behind us. Consider how many (by how much) more thou goest before than thou followest.

Deus (Gr. 403) irasci, quòd aliquis *ego* (30) *antecĕdere*, oblītus quantum (viii.) homo retro (Gr. 627–5) esse. Considerare quanto *plures* (Gr. 627–5) *antecedĕre* quam (Gr. 627–5) sequi.—*Id.*

English Examples to be turned into Latin.

We are all partakers of that reason and superiority by which we *excel the brutes.*—These adjoining gardens *bring* his memory *to my mind.*—These things are reputable to those whose *rank they suit.*—Who can *prefer* impious [persons] *to religious?*—The spear of Cæsar *brings* both hope and confidence *to many* wicked men.—Antony desired *to place* a diadem *on Cæsar.*—Many and various kinds of death *hang over mankind.*—This I cannot commend, that he did not *relieve such men.*—The poets make a rock *hang over Tantalus* in the shades below.—Who first gave names to all things?—He prefers the pleasures of the belly to the gratification of the eyes and ears.

403.—V. Verbs govern the dative which signify to profit or hurt;—to favor or assist, and the contrary;—to command and obey, to serve and resist;—to threaten and to be angry;—to trust. Also Nos. 404, 405.

1. Verbs signifying *to profit* or *hurt.*

Whosover shall spare the bad, does harm to the good.	*Bonus nocēre*, quisquis 6 *parcĕre malus.*—*Id.*
Flattery can harm nobody, but him who delights in it (is delighted with it).	Assentatio *nocēre* posse *nemo*, nisi *is* qui is delectari.—Cic. *de Am.*
Many of our good things hurt us.	Multus bonum noster *ego nocēre.*—Sen.
If you do good to any one for your own sake, it is not to be reckoned a favour, but usury.	Si tuus ob causa *quisquam* (30) *commodare*, beneficium ille habendus non esse, sed fœneratio.—Cic.
Other men's things please us more, our things others.	Alienus *ego*, noster plus *alius placēre.*—Pub.
[That] is kept with great danger, which pleases many.	Magnus periculum custodiri, qui *multus placēre.*—*Id.*
It is a commendation to displease the bad.	*Malus displicēre* laus esse.
Let whatever has pleased God please man.	*Placēre homo*, quicquid *Deus placēre.*—Sen.

Phrases.—*Consŭlo tibi*, I consult for thee [thy good], or, I take care of thee. *Tibi consultum volo* I wish thy good.

We ought to consult for peace.	*Pax consulĕre* debēre.
Human affairs are taken care of (it is consulted for human affairs) by the providence of God.	Deus providentia *consŭli res* humanus.—Cic.
We ought to consult [for the good] of men, and to be serviceable to human society.	*Consulĕre homo*, et *servire societas* humanus, debēre.
Nature teaches this, that [one] man should wish the good of (wish to consult for) [another] man.	Natura hoc præscribĕre, ut homo *homo consultum* (31) velle.—Cic. *Off.* 3.
It is not so well [acted] with human affairs, that the best (better) things should please the major part; a multitude is an argument of the worst.	Non tam bene cum res humanus agi, ut melior *plures* (LIV.) (31) *placēre;* turba esse argumentum pessimus.—Sen.

2. Verbs signifying *to favour* or *assist*, and their contraries.

Pardon thou another often, never thyself.	*Ignoscĕre* sæpe *alter*, nunquam *tu.*—Pub. Syr.
Pardon others many things, thyself nothing.	*Ignoscĕre alius* multus, nihil *tu.*—Aus.
All men love (study for) liberty by nature.	Omnis *libertas* natura *studēre.*
Every one favours (studies) his own advantage.	Quisque suus *studēre commŏdum.*
We are soon satisfied in (please) ourselves; we easily assent to those that affirm (affirming) that we are very good or very wise: We are so fond of (so indulge) ourselves, that we are willing to be praised.	Citò *ego placēre;* optimus ego esse aut sapientissimus *affirmans* facilè *assentiri:* Adeò *indulgēre ego*, ut laudari (LIV.) velle.—Sen.
He that (who) hath taken this upon (to) himself, to correct the manners of others, and reprove sins, who would pardon him, if he himself should deviate from his duty in any thing?	Qui sui (XVII.) hoc sumĕre, ut mos (LIV.) (30) corrigĕre alius, ac peccatum reprehendĕre, quis *hic* (31) *ignoscĕre*, si quis in res ipse ab officium (38) declinare?—Cic. *Ver.* 3.
They are easily pardoned (it is easily pardoned to them) who do not endeavour to persist in, but to recall themselves from their error.	*Ille* facilè (impers.) *ignosci*, qui non perseverare, sed ab erratum sui revocare moliri. —Cic.

Many great men have lamented that favour did not answer their merits.

Plorare suus non *respondēre* favor multus homo summus *meritum.*—Hor.

3. Verbs signifying *to command*, *obey*, *serve*, or *resist.*

To govern thy passion and thy tongue, when thou art angry, is [a piece of] great wisdom.

Moderari animus et *oratio* quum (Gr. 630) esse iratus, magnus sapientia (xii.) esse. —Cic.

He is not happy, who does not think himself to be so, though he commands the world.

Non esse beatus, esse sui [beatum] qui non putare, licet (liv.) *imperare mundus.*—S.

Wise men command their lusts, which others serve.

Sapiens *imperare cupiditas* suus, *qui* cæter *servire.*—Cic.

Temperance commands pleasures.

Temperantia *voluptas imperare.*—Sen.

Rule thy tongue.

Lingua temperare.—Pl.

How shall he command others, who cannot command his own lusts?

Quomodo *alius imperare*, qui non posse *imperare cupiditas* suus?—Cic. *Par.* 5.

To obey God, is liberty.

Deus parēre, libertas esse. —Sen.

Every thing obeys riches.

Omnis res *divitiæ parēre.* —Hor.

Let the appetite obey reason.

Appetitus *obtemperare ratio.*

Honesty at the present offends those whom it opposes; afterwards it is commended by those very persons.

Fides in præsentiâ is *qui resistĕre*, offendĕre; deinde ab ille ipse laudari.—Plin. *Ep.* 3. 9.

No power can withstand the hatred of many.

Odium multus nullus opes posse *obsistĕre.*—Cic.

The mind ought to obey reason, and to follow whither that leads.

Parēre debēre animus *ratio*, et quò illa (liv.) ducĕre sequi.—Cic. *Tusc.* 2.

Let arms give place (yield) to the gown.

Cedĕre arma *toga.*—Cic.

Dissembling is repugnant to opposes) friendship.

Simulatio *repugnare amicitia.*

Be not a slave to passion, which you ought to resist.

Ne *servire iracundia*, *qui* debēre *resistĕre.*

He is to be accounted free who is a slave to no baseness.

Liber is existimandus esse, qui nullus *turpitudo servire.* —*Ad Her.*

He is not to be accounted a free [man] who obeys his lusts.

Non esse liber habendus, qui *cupiditas obedire*.—Cic. *Par.*

We do not easily withstand the allurements of pleasure.

Non facilè *obsistĕre blanditiæ* voluptas.—Cic. *Sen.*

Do not (be unwilling to) comply [with] a friend requiring any thing of thee which is not right.

Nolle *obsĕqui amicus* postulans a tu aliquis qui non (lv.) esse rectus.—Cic. *de Am.*

All is in this, that thou shouldst command thyself.

Totum in is esse, ut *tu* (liv.) *imperare*.—Cic.

When it is advised, that we should command ourselves, this is advised, that reason should restrain rashness, and should command the inferior part of the soul.

Quùm præcĭpi, ut *egomet ipse* (31) *imperare*, hoc præcĭpi, ut ratio (31) coërcēre temeritas, *imperare*que inferior *pars* animus.—Cic. *Tusc.* 2.

He that (who) shall not moderate his passion (anger), will wish that to be undone which resentment shall put him upon (shall have advised).

Qui non *moderari ira*, infectus velle esse, dolor qui 6 suadēre.—Hor.

He that does not withstand injury, if he can, is in fault as well as if he should do injury.

Qui non *obsistĕre injuria*, si posse, tam esse in vitium quàm si injuria (31) inferre. —Cic. *Off.* 1.

Withstand beginnings: a cure is prepared too late, when mischiefs are grown strong through long delays.

Principium obstare: serò medicina parari, quùm malum per longus (14) invalescĕre mora.—Ov.

The body must (is to) be exercised, and so disposed, that it may (be able to) obey reason.

Exercendus esse corpus, et ita afficiendus, ut *obedire ratio* posse.—Cic. *Off.* 1.

4. Verbs signifying *to threaten*, or *to be angry with.*

He threatens many who does injury to one.

Multus minari, qui unus facĕre injuria.—Pub.

There is a great part of men which is not angry with the faults, but with the offenders.

Magnus pars homo esse, qui non *peccatum*, sed *peccans irasci*.—Sen.

It is [the part] of a madman to be angry with those things which are without (want) life, or with dumb animals.

Demens (xii.) esse *hic irasci*, qui (xxv.) anima carēre, aut mutus *animal.*—*Id.*

How foolish a thing is it to be angry with those things which neither have deserved, nor are sensible of our anger?

Quàm stultus esse *hic irasci*, qui ira noster nec merēre, nec sentire?—SEN.

It signifies (it is for) nothing to be angry with him who does not value thee a rush.

De nihilo esse *ille irasci*, qui tu non flocci (Gr. 498) facĕre.—PL.

Anger is nothing better, often worse, than those faults at which it is angry.

Ira nihilo melior (XXIV.) sæpe pejor esse, hic delictum *qui irasci*.—SEN.

Thou oughtest not to have been very angry at so small a fault.

Non (36) debēre graviter (Gr. 668. n. 2) *irasci* tantulus *peccatum*.

It is recorded (it is transmitted to memory), that Pisistratus, when a certain drunken guest had said many things against his cruelty, said, that he was no more angry at him, than if one had run against him being blindfolded (with his eyes tied up).

Memoria prodi (XXXII.) Pisistratus, quum multus in crudelitas is, ebrius quidam conviva (39) dicĕre, dicĕre, non magis sui *ille succensēre*, quàm si quis obligatus oculus in sui (39) incurrĕre.—SEN.

A partial esteem of ourselves makes us passionate, and we are not willing to suffer those things which we would (wish to) do. But let us set ourselves in that place in which he is with whom we are angry.

Iniquus ego æstimatio iracundus ego facĕre, et qui facĕre (33) (LV.) velle, pati nolle. Quin is locus ego constituĕre, qui ille esse *qui irasci*.—*Id.*

5. Verbs signifying *to trust*.

Beware, lest thou trust thyself too much.

Cavēre, ne nimium *tu* (LIV.) *confidĕre*.—CIC.

Let nobody trust too much to prosperity (prosperous things).

Nemo *confidĕre* nimium secundæ *res*.—SEN.

Believe not any one more than yourself of yourself.

Ne *quis* de tu plus quàm *tu* (25) *credĕre*.—HOR.

We are wont not to believe a lying person even when he speaks (speaking) truth.

Mendax *homo* ne verum quidem dicens *credĕre* solēre. —CIC. *Div.* 2.

Men believe their eyes more than their ears.

Homo amplius *oculus* quàm *auris credĕre*.—SEN.

No fortune is more dangerously trusted (it is trusted to no fortune less well) than [to] very good.

Nullus *fortuna* minus bene (imp.) *credi*, quàm optimus. —SEN.

Guardianship is to be managed to the advantage of those who are committed to trust, not [to the advantage] of them to whom it is committed.	Tutēla ad is utilitas qui commissus esse (alicui), non ad is, *qui commissus esse*, gerendus esse.—Cic. *Off.* 1.
It is not safe to believe (it is not well trusted to) fame; she is often a liar, and feigns many things.	Non bene *fama* (imp.) *credi;* esse mendax is sæpe, et plurimus fingĕre.
We ought not quickly to believe those things, which are told us concerning any one's backbitings.	Non debēre citò *credĕre hic*, qui narrari de quisquam obtrectatio.—Sen. *de Ir.*
406.—So great calamities threaten you.	Tantus *in tu impendēre* ruina.
Though on every side all terrors threaten me.	Licet undique omnis *in ego* terror 7 *impendēre.*
They wish their days and months to agree with the course of the sun and moon.	Suus dies mensisque *congruĕre* velle *cum* sol lunaque *ratio.*

408.—The English word *to*, after a verb of motion, is commonly made by the preposition *ad* or *in* followed by an accusative; thus,

A part of Gaul inclines to the north.	Pars Gallia *vergĕre ad Septentrio.*
The desire of dominion incites two kindred and neighbouring nations to arms.	Cupīdo imperium duo cognatus vicinusque populus *ad arma stimulāre.*
It belongs to parents and teachers to exhort children to patience, peace, and concord, though they be provoked to fightings.	*Attinēre ad* parens et præceptor *hortari* puer *ad* patientia, pax, et concordia etiamsi (30) *lacessi ad* pugna.
Apply thyself to the study of learning and virtue, which tends to thy praise and happiness.	*Applĭcare* tu *ad* studium doctrina et virtus, qui *spectare ad* laus et felicitas tuus.
The loadstone draws iron to itself.	Magnes ferrum *ad* sui *allicĕre.*—Cic.
Later or sooner we [all] haste to one place.	Serius aut citiùs sedes *properare ad* unus.—Ov.
We are all drawn to the desire of knowledge.	Omnis *trahi ad* cognitio cupiditas.—Cic.
It is very laudable to apply riches to beneficence and liberality.	Honestissimus esse divitiæ *ad* beneficentia et liberalitas *conferre.*—Cic. *Off.* 1.

We were born for society and the community of mankind (of the human race), and therefore we ought always to contribute something to the common advantage.	*Ad* societas et communitas genus humanus 8 *nasci*, itaque semper aliquid *ad* communis utilitas debēre *afferre*. —Cic.
There are two things that most of all put men upon (which chiefly impel men to) mischief, luxury and covetousness.	Duo res esse qui homo maximè *impellĕre ad* maleficium, luxuries et avaritia. —*Ad Heren.*
Thou oughtest to apply thy prudence and understanding to the good of men.	*Ad* homo utilitas prudentia et intelligentia tuus *conferre* debēre.

English Examples to be turned into Latin.

I desire *to assist that company* in whatever things 7 I can.—It is not allowable for the sake of one's own advantage to *hurt another*.—I favoured the commonwealth which I have always favoured, and your dignity and glory.—I will overcome my disposition and *command myself*.—He *commands those desires which* others *obey*.—*He opposed the designs* of the daring with authority.—That softer part of his soul submits to reason as a modest soldier [submits] to a severe commander.—He obeys himself and follows his own rules.—*He threatens* the same punishment to *the best citizens*.—Marcellinus was angry with you.—I am by no means accustomed to be rashly angry with my friends.—You say indeed many things, but no one *believes you*.—I recommend myself entirely to your love and affection.

409.—Rule XVIII. An impersonal verb governs the dative. Also 410.

Thou mayest (it is lawful for thee to) be good and happy.	*Licēre tu* esse (Gr. 327) *bonus et beatus*.
Thou mayest not (it is not lawful for thee to) hurt another for the sake of thy own advantage.	Non *licēre tu* commodum tuus (xxxv.) causa nocēre (Gr. 403) alter.—Cic.
A good man is not at liberty (it is not lawful for a good man) not to return a kindness if only he can do it.	*Vir* bonus non *licēre* non reddĕre beneficium, si modo is facĕre (31) posse.—*Id.*
A man may (it is lawful for a man to) keep a holiday without luxury.	*Licēre homo* sine luxuria agĕre festus dies.—Sen.

He that (to whom it) agrees well with poverty, is rich. — *Qui* cum paupertas bene *convenire*, dives esse.—SEN.

That only which is honest is good, as the Stoics are of opinion (honesty only is good as it pleases the Stoics). — Honestum solus bonus esse, ut *Stoicus placēre*.—CIC. *Off.* 3.

410.—An intransitive verb may be changed into the impersonal in *tur* (Gr. 223–3), when the subject of the verb is a word signifying a multitude (as, *multi*, *omnes*, &c.); or any one whoever (as, *quivis*, *ullus*, *aliquis*, *quisquam*, &c.); as, *fletur*, i. e. *ab omnibus*, for *flent omnes*, they all weep. *Vivitur exiguo meliùs*, for *Homo vivit exiguo meliùs*, a man (i. e. any one) lives better with a little. (Gr. 410. *Expl.*)

Through virtue men go to heaven (it is gone to the stars). — Per virtus *iri* ad astrum; *for* homines eunt.

A man does not live (it is not lived) safely, and without fear, without friendship. — Non tutò et sine metus *vivi* sine amicitia; *i. e.* Non ullus vivit.

A man does not live (it is not lived) pleasantly, unless he live (unless it be lived) wisely, honestly, and justly. — Non jucundè *vivi*, nisi sapienter, honestè, justèque (30) *vivi*.

War is to be undertaken, that we may live (that it may be lived) in peace without injury. — Suscipiendus esse bellum, ut in pax sine injuria (LIV.) *vivi*.—CIC.

The advantages of others are envied (it is envied to, &c.). — *Invidēri* commŏdum (Gr 403) alius.—*Id.*

Men sin (it is sinned) every where. — *Peccari* ubique.

They sin (it is sinned) within the Trojan walls and without. — Iliacus intra murus *peccari* et extra.—HOR.

No prudent man (nobody prudent) punishes, because an offence has been committed (it has been sinned), but that offences may not be committed (lest it may be sinned). — Nemo prudens punire, quia 3 *peccari*, sed ne (LIV.) *peccari*.—SEN. *de Ir.*

Men offend (it is sinned) against justice two ways, both by doing injury and by omitting of defending. — *Peccari* in justitia duo (XXXV.) modus, et inferendus (LXII.) injuria, et prætermittendus (LXII.) defensio.—CIC.

The foundations of justice are, first, that nobody be hurt (that it be hurt to no one), then that the — Fundamentum esse justitia, primùm (Gr. 403) nequis (31) *nocēri*, deinde ut com-

common good be consulted (that service be done to the common good). — munis (Gr. 403) utilitas (31) *serviri.*—Cic.

The discourse shows a fault to be in the manners, when people are forward to speak (it is spoken forwardly) of the absent for the sake of detraction (of detracting). — Sermo vitium inesse mos indicare, quum studiosè de absens detrahĕre (xxxv.) causa *dici.*—*Id.*

Through the vices of men they come (it is come) to battles. — Homo (xxxv.) vitium ad prælium 3 *veniri.*—*Prop.* 2.

The pupil may be accustomed to vary these passive impersonals by the active voice.

411.—These verbs *potest*, *cœpit*, *incipit*, *desinit*, *debet*, and *solet* before the infinitive of impersonals, become impersonal also; as, non *potest credi tibi*, "you cannot be believed."

Through virtue men may go to heaven (it may be gone to the stars). — Per virtus *posse iri* ad astrum.

A man cannot live (it cannot be lived) safely without friendship. — Non *posse vivi* tutò sine amicitia.—Cic. *Fin.* 2.

A man cannot live (it cannot be lived) pleasantly, unless he live (unless it be lived) wisely, honestly, and justly. — Non *posse* jucundè *vivi*, nisi sapienter, honestè, justèque (30) *vivi.*—Cic. *Fin.* 1.

Men are wont to sin (it is wont to be sinned) every where. — *Solēre peccari* ubique.

It uses to concern the public. — *Solēre interesse* respublica.

I begin to be ashamed (it begins to ashame me) of my fault. — *Incipĕre pudēre* ego peccatum meus.

I ought to be sorry (it ought to grieve me) for my fault. — *Debēre pœnitēre* ego peccatum meus.

Cease to be dissatisfied with (let it cease to repent thee of) thy condition. — *Desinĕre pœnitēre* tu sors tuus.

Do nothing which thou mayest repent of (it may repent thee of). — Nihil (25) facĕre, qui tu *pœnitēre* (LV.) *posse.*—Cic.

They ought to be sorry for (it ought to repent them of) their fooleries. — Ineptiæ suus is *pœnitēre debēre.*

The praise and glory of others uses to be envied (it uses to be envied to the praise, &c.). — Alius laus et gloria (Gr. 403) *invidēri solēre.*—Cic.

Thou oughtest to pity (it ought to pity thee of) the needy.

Debēre miserēre tu egenus.

It often uses to happen ill to good men, and very well to the bad.

Sæpe *solēre* malè *evenire* bonus, et optimè improbus. (Gr. 398.)

Fame cannot well be believed (it cannot be well trusted to fame).

Non *posse* bene *credi* (Gr. 403) fama.

It is very great folly to be afflicted with grief, when thou art sensible (understandest) that no good can be done (by it).

Summus esse stultitia mœror conficĭ, quum (30) intelligĕre nihil *posse profĭci*.—Cic. *Tusc.* 3.

One cannot come (it cannot be come) to wisdom without the liberal studies.

Sine liberalis studium ad sapientia *veniri* non *posse*.—Sen.

Long time demolishes every thing: But wisdom cannot be harmed (it cannot be hurt to wisdom).

Nihil non longus demoliri ætas: At sapientia (Gr. 403) *nocēri* non *posse*.

Men cannot dispute (it cannot be disputed) well with passionateness or obstinacy.

Cum ira aut pertinacia rectè *disputari* non *posse*.—Cic. 1. *Fin.*

I could never be persuaded (it could never be persuaded to me) that souls died when they were gone out of these mortal bodies.

Ego nunquam *persuadēri posse*, animus, quum ex hic corpus mortalis (39) exire, emŏri.—Cic. *de Sen.*

God uses to consult and provide not only for all mankind, but also for each particular man (it uses to be consulted and provided by God not only for the whole race of men, but also for particular persons).

Non universus solum genus homo, sed etiam singuli, a Deus *consŭli* et *providēri solēre*.—Cic. *Nat. D.*

412.—Impersonal verbs have sometimes a nominative case before them.

Candid peace becomes men, cruel anger wild beasts.

Candidus *pax* homo, trux *decēre ira* fera.—Ov.

If any thing is unbecoming in others, let us avoid it ourselves.

Si quid dedecēre in alius, vitare ipse.—Cic. *Off.* 2.

We see more in others than in ourselves, if any fault is committed.

Magis in alius cernĕre, quàm in egomet ipse, *si quid delinqui*.—*Id.*

Beware the day before, lest thou shouldst (mayest) do that which may trouble thee the day after.

Pridie (25) cavēre, ne facĕre *qui* tu *pigēre* postridie. —PLAUT.

That which is allowed is unpleasing.

Qui licēre, ingratus esse.—Ov.

Half of our time is slept away.

Dimidium ætas noster *edormiri*.

In the longest life there is very little time that is lived.

In longissimus vita minimum esse *qui vivi*.—SEN. *Ep.* 99.

Whatever sin is committed by many is unpunished.

Quicquid multus *peccari*, inultus esse.—LUC.

In injuring the life of a father, many sins are committed.

In pater vita (72) violandus *multa peccari*.—CIC. *Par.* 3.

N. B. Most impersonal verbs have a nominative case expressed or understood, or something in place of it. *Refert*, *interest*, *decet*, *delectat*, *juvat*, *oportet*, *libet*, *licet*, &c., have an infinitive mood or clause answering to the question *who* or *what*, that supplies the place of a nominative case to them; as, What is the concern of subjects? *Ans.* To obey the laws. And so in the other examples at Rule XVIII, Ex. I, II, III. There are, however, some impersonal verbs that have no nominative or subject understood, such as *pluit*, *gelat*, and the like; but especially passive impersonals; as *curritur*, *statur*, &c., the design of these verbs being nothing else but to express the bare thing or action itself, without the least regard to any person or suppositum. (Gr. 413. Obs. 3.)

EXCEPTIONS.

415.—EXC. I. *Refert* and *interest* govern the genitive.

It is the concern of (it concerns) subjects to obey the laws.

Civis referre lex (Gr. 399) obtemperare.

It is the concern of (it concerns) all men to endeavour (to use endeavour) for virtue.

Interesse omnis dare opera virtus.

It very much concerns the public, that all should consult for peace and concord.

Vehementer *interesse respublica*, ut omnis (31) consulĕre pax et concordia.

It much concerns the common good, that youth be well educated.

Multum *interesse utilitas* communis, juventus probè institui.

It is of very great importance in composing (it very much concerns composition), which [words] you put before others (which).

Plurimum *referre compositio* quis (Gr. 399) quis (Gr. 627–5) anteponĕre.—QUINCT.

When king Lysimachus threatened the cross to Theodorus, It is all one to (it nothing concerns) Theodorus, says he, whether he rots on the ground or on high.

Quum rex Lysimachus (XXIX.) Theodorus crux (32) minari, *Theodorus*, inquit, nihil *interesse* (Gr. 559) humusne, an sublimè (Gr. 627–5) putrescĕre.—C. *Tusc.* 1.

416.—But instead of the genitives *mei*, *tui*, *sui*, &c., the possessives *mea*, *tua*, *sua*, *nostra*, *vestra*, are used.

It concerns thee not to believe rashly.

Tuus referre non temere credĕre.

That which thou dost well, thou dost for thyself; it concerns thee most.

Bene qui facĕre, tu facĕre; *tuus* is *referre* maximè.—PLAUT.

Who is there that does not love modesty in youth, though it does nothing concern him?

Quis esse, qui pudor in adolescentia, etiamsi *suus* nihil (30) *interesse*, non (LV.) diligĕre?—CIC. *Fin.*

Cease to ask that which nothing concerns thee.

Tuus qui nihil *interesse*, percontari desinĕre.—TER.

419.—EXC. II. These five, *miseret*, *pœnitet*, *pudet*, *tædet*, and *piget*, govern the accusative of the immediate, with the genitive of the remote object. Also No. 420.

I am ashamed (it ashames me) of my fault.

Pudēre ego peccatum meus.

He that is sorry for (he whom it repents of) a fault is almost innocent.

Qui pœnitēre peccatum, pæne esse innocens.—SEN.

I judge him worthy of punishment, who is not ashamed (whom it does not ashame) of his fault.

Qui non *pudēre peccatum*, hic pœna dignus judicare.—CIC. *de Or.*

He doubles the sin, that is not ashamed (whom it does not ashame) of his fault.

Geminare peccatum, *qui delictum* non *pudēre*.—CIC.

I am sorry for and ashamed (it grieves and ashames me) of my folly.	*Ego stultitia* meus *pigēre* et *pudēre*.—Cic.
Is he concerned for (does it ashame him of) the fact?	Num *factum* (*eum*) *pudēre?*—Ter.
There are some men that are neither weary nor ashamed (whom it neither wearies nor ashames) of their lust and infamy.	Esse homo, *qui libido infamia*que suus neque (lv.) *tædēre*, neque (lv.) *pudēre*.—Cic.
Pity thou (let it pity thee of) the needy.	*Miserēre tu egenus.*
They that have lived otherwise than became them, are most sorry for (it most repents those who have lived, &c. of) their sins when death approaches (death approaching).	*Is*, qui, secus quàm 8 decēre, vivĕre, *peccatum* suus, (lx.) mors appropinquans, maximè *pœnitēre*.—Cic. *Div.* 1.
I am not very much dissatisfied with (it does not repent me very much of) my fortune.	*Ego* meus *fortuna* non nimis *pœnitēre*.—Cic.
Every one is dissatisfied with (it repents every one of) his own lot.	Suus *quisque sors pœnitēre.* —Cic.
If thou art sorry for (if it repents thee of) thy fault, thou wilt take care not to (lest thou) commit any such thing hereafter.	Si *tu peccatum* tuus *pœnitēre*, cavēre ne quid talis posthac (31) *committĕre.* — Cic. *Off.* 1.

Note.—An infinitive mood sometimes supplies the place of the genitive. (Gr. 421, Obs. 7.)

He is almost innocent, who repents (whom it repents) that he has sinned.	*Qui pœnitēre peccare*, pæne esse innocens.—Sen.
Art thou not ashamed (does it not ashame thee) to allot the relicts (leavings) of life to virtue and a good mind?	Non *pudēre tu* reliquiæ vita virtus et bonus mens *destinare?—Id.*
I am not ashamed (it does not ashame me) to confess that I do not know that which I do not know.	Non *ego pudēre fatēri* [me] nescire [id] qui (Gr. 656) nescire.—Cic.
There is no fear lest thou shouldst repent (lest it should repent thee) that thou hast striven in kindness first.	Non metus, officium ne *tu certare* prior (liv.) *pœnitēre.* —Virg.

423.—Exc. III. *Decet*, *delectat*, *juvat*, and *oportet*, govern the accusative of a person with the infinitive.

It becomes a young man to be modest. — *Decēre adolescens esse* verecundus.—Plaut.

There are [some] that delight (whom it delights) to lead an idle life. — Esse *qui* (Gr. 638) *delectare* segnis *traducĕre* vita.

And there are [some] that delight (whom it delights) to ply their studies. — Et esse *qui* (Gr. 399) studium *invigilare* (Gr. 638) *juvare*.

We must (it behoves us to) choose the least of evils. — Ex malum minimus *oportēre* (*nos*) *eligĕre*.—Cic.

He ought (it behoves him) to obtain, who asks a reasonable thing. — *Impetrare oportet is*, qui æquus postulare.—Plaut.

Integrity and innocence ought (it behoves integrity, &c.) to be in him that (who) accuses another. — *Integritas* atque *innocentia esse oportēre* in is, qui alter accusare.—Cic.

He that accuses another of dishonesty ought (it behoves him who, &c.) to look upon himself. — Qui alter incusare probrum, *is* ipse sui *intuēri oportēre*.—Plaut.

Men ought (it behoves men) to reckon that God sees all things, that all things are full of God. — *Homo existimare oportēre*, Deus omnis cernĕre, omnis Deus plenus esse.

Thales said that men ought (that it behoved men) to reckon that God sees all things, &c. — Thales 3 dicĕre, *homo existimare oportēre*, Deus omnis cernĕre, &c.—Cic. 2 *Leg.*

All people ought (it behoves all people) then most of all to meditate with themselves how to (by what means they may) bear adverse calamity when things are most prosperous. — *Omnis*, quum secundus res esse maximè, tum maximè sui cum *meditari oportēre*, quis pactum (xxxv.) adversus ærumna (Gr. 627–5) ferre.—Ter.

Thou oughtest (it behoves thee) to eat, that thou mayest live; not to live, that thou mayest eat. — *Esse oportēre* (*te*), ut vivĕre; non *vivĕre* ut esse.—*Ad Heren.*

Oportet elegantly has the subjunctive (*ut* being understood) with a nominative. (Gr. 425.)

Thy mind must (it behoves that thy mind) judge itself rich, not the speech of men, not thy possessions. — *Animus* tuus *oportēre* sui (30) *judicare* dives, non homo sermo, non possessio tuus.—Cic. *Par.*

Thou must (it behoves that thou) love me myself, not my things, if we are (about) to be true friends.

Ego ipse [ut *tu*] (30) *amare oportēre*, non meus, si verus amicus futurus sum.—CIC. *Fin.* 1.

Every one must take care (it behoves that every one consult) for himself.

Sui *quisque* (30) *consulĕre oportēre*.—CIC.

Place not the hope of thy affairs in the rewards of men (in human rewards); virtue itself ought to (it behoves that virtue itself) draw thee to true honour by its own charms.

Nec spes ponĕre res tuus in præmium humanus; suus tu illecebræ *oportēre* ipse *virtus* (30) *trahĕre* ad verus decus.—CIC. *Som. Scip.*

Things to be observed concerning Impersonal Verbs.

Note 1.—The word that seems to be the nominative case in English is frequently such case in Latin as the impersonal verb has after it; as, I may, *licet mihi;* I am at leisure, *vacat mihi;* I repent, *pœnitet me;* I am ashamed, *pudet me;* I am weary, *tædet me;* If you please, *si placet tibi.*

Note 2.—But if *must* or *ought* be rendered by *oportet*, the nominative case to *must* or *ought* in English must in Latin be put to the verb following, and made such case as that requires before it; as, I must go, *oportet me ire*, or *ut ego eam.*

See examples above in Exc. III.

Note 3.—If the verb following be impersonal, the nominative case to *must* or *ought* must be such case in Latin as the impersonal requires after it; as, *Oportet credi mihi*, I ought to be believed.

A witness being an enemy must not be believed. (It ought not to be trusted to a witness being an enemy.)

Inimicus *testis credi* non *oportēre*.—CIC.

When one shall have once forsworn himself, he ought not to be believed afterwards (it ought not to be trusted to him afterwards).

Ubi semel quis 6 pejerare, *is credi* postea non *oportēre.* —CIC.

English Examples to be turned into Latin.

It by no means *becomes an orator* to be in a passion.—Honesty is the only excellency as *the Stoics are of opinion* (as it pleases the Stoics).—*It is lawful for no man* to sin.—If *you are tired of such citizens*, show it.—*I am quite tired of my life*, all things are so very full of the utmost distress.—*Neither myself nor others shall repent of my industry.*—Indeed *I am not ashamed of you*, whose memory I have always admired, but (I am ashamed) *of Chrysippus.*—*I am grieved for the very walls and buildings.*—*It is of great consequence to Cicero* that I should be present (Gr. 671) at his studies.—*It is of great consequence to your private affairs* that you come (Gr. 671) as soon as possible.—*It pleases me* very much that you are of a cheerful mind.—2. *You ought* long since, Catiline, 11 to have been dragged to death at the command of the consul.—*You ought* to be well furnished with the precepts of philosophy.

427.—Rule XIX. The verbs *sum*, *do*, *habeo*, and some others, with the dative of the object, govern also the dative of the *end* or *design*. Also No. 428.

Note.—Some other verbs, as, *forem*, *do*, *duco*, *verto*, *tribuo*, *habeo*, *relinquo*, &c., also govern two datives.

Letters are a remedy for forgetfulness.	Literæ [bb]*subsidium* [b]*oblivio* [a]*esse.*
Covetousness is a great mischief to men.	Magnus [bb]*malum* [b]*homo* [a]*esse* avaritia.
Every one minds his own pleasure (his own pleasure is for a care to every one).	[bb]*Cura* [a]*esse* suus [b]*quisque* voluptas.—Ov.
Cruelty is hated by (is for hatred to) all, and piety and clemency beloved by (for love to) all.	[b]*Omnis* [a]*esse* [bb]*odium* crudelitas, et [bb]*amor* pietas et clementia.
There is nothing that (which) can be a greater advantage, and a greater glory to thee, than to do kindnesses to (to deserve well of) as many as may be.	Nihil esse, qui *tu* major [bb]*fructus*, et major [bb]*gloria* [a]*esse* (Gr. 639) posse, quàm bene merēri de quàm plurimus.—Cic. *Ep. Fam.* 10, 5.
Go on, young men, as you do, and pursue (apply to) the study of learning; that you may (be able to) be an honour to yourselves, and a benefit to your friends, and an advantage to the public.	Pergĕre, ut facĕre, adolescens, atque incumbĕre in studium doctrina; ut [b]*tu* [bb]*honor*, et [b]*amicus* [bb]*utilitas*, et [b]*respublica* [bb]*emolumentum esse* (LIV.) posse.—Cic. *de Or.*

It is not only to be reckoned (given) not a commendation, but even a fault, to them that (who) injure one, that they may do good to another. — Qui nocēre alius (Gr. 403) ut prodesse alius, [b] *hic* non modò non [bb] *laus*, verùm etiam [bb] *vitium* [a] *dandus* esse. —Cic. *Off.* 1.

The dative of the person is sometimes understood. (Gr. 432.)

EXAMPLES.

That which thou spendest in religion [divine things] is gain. — Qui in res divinus (Gr. 644) sumĕre, [bb] *lucrum* [a] *esse* [[b] *tibi*]. —Plaut.

All men hate injustice (have injustice for hatred to themselves). — Omnis [bb] *odium* [a] *habēre* injuria [[b] *sibi*].

English Examples to be turned into Latin.

I wish that thing 7 *may be a satisfaction to him.*—7 *Let him have* myself *for his example.*—Apply then for (seek) that office in which 7 you can *be of great service to me.*—*He was of great use both to me* and *my brother Quintus.*—A large house often *becomes* a disgrace to the owner.—To go upon the stage and *to be a spectacle to the people, was a disgrace to nobody* in these nations.

CONSTRUCTION OF THE ACCUSATIVE.

ACCUSATIVE GOVERNED BY VERBS.

436.—Rule XX. A transitive verb in the active voice governs the accusative.

SPECIAL RULES.

437.—I. A transitive deponent verb governs the accusative.

Beware of intemperance. — *Cavēre intemperantia.*
Wealth finds friends. — Res *amicus invenire.*
Complaisance begets friends, [plain] truth hatred. — Obsequium *amicus*, veritas *odium parĕre.*—Ter.

A life well spent makes old age pleasant. — Vita bene actus jucundus *efficĕre senectus.*

Benefits get friends, and [one] good turn begets [another] good turn. — Beneficium *parĕre amicus,* et gratia *gratia parĕre.*

Use makes artists. — Usus *facĕre artifex.*—Ov.

Anger begets hatred. — Ira *odium generare.*

Love overcomes all difficulties. — *Vincĕre* amor omnis *difficultas.*—Cic.

Time consumes iron and stone. — *Consumĕre ferrum lapis*que vetustas.—Ov.

Care follows increasing money. — Crescens *sequi* cura *pecunia.*—Hor.

One night awaits all men. — Nox *manēre* unus *omnis.*—*Id.*

Can riches make a man wise? — Divitiæne *homo* prudens *reddĕre* posse?—*Id.*

Riches change [men's] minds, breed pride and arrogance, procure envy. — Divitiæ *mutare animus, superbia* et *arrogantia parĕre, invidia contrahĕre.*

Men see the advantages of base things with fallacious judgments, they do not see the punishment. — *Emolumentum* res turpis fallax judicium *vidēre* homo, *pœna* non *vidēre.*—Cic. *Off.* 3.

Virtue both gives quiet of life, and takes away the terror of death. — Virtus et vita *tranquillitas largiri,* et *terror* mors *tollĕre.*—Cic.

Do not thou lay down thy eyes for sweet sleep, before (sooner than) thou hast recounted all the actions of the long day. — Ne priùs in dulcis (25) *declinare lumen* somnus, omnis quàm longus 6 *reputare actum* dies.—Aus.

Keep thy mind, eyes, hands, from other men's things. — Ab alienus *mens, oculus, manus, abstinēre.*—Cic.

A stomach, seldom fasting, disdains ordinary things. — Jejunus rarò stomachus *vulgaris temnĕre.*—Hor.

We ought to beware lest those vices deceive us which seem to imitate virtue. For knavery imitates prudence, pride greatness of mind, prodigality liberalness, fool-hardiness valour, and superstition religiousness. — Cavēre (Gr. 699) esse, ne (LIV.) *fallĕre ego* is vitium, qui *virtus* vidēri *imitari.* Nam *prudentia* malitia, *magnitudo* animus superbia, *liberalitas* effusio, *fortitudo* audacia, et *religio* superstitio *imitari.*—Cic. *Or. Partit.*

I will leave your dreams; I will proceed to your crimes. — *Relinquĕre somnium* tuus; venire ad scelus.—Cic.

438.—II. An intransitive verb may govern a noun of kindred signification in the accusative. Also No. 439.

He that will live a happy life, must (it behoves him who shall wish to live a happy life, that he) be endued with virtue.	Qui beatus *vita vivĕre* 5 volle, is virtus præditus (31) esse oportēre.—Sen.
It is but a small part of life which we live.	Exiguus pars esse vita *qui* ego *vivĕre.*—Sen.
[That time] which we live is but a moment, and less than a moment.	Punctum esse, *qui vivĕre,* et punctum minus.—Sen.
He serves a very miserable slavery who serves his lusts.	Miserrimus *servire servitus,* qui servire (Gr. 403) cupiditas suus.

English Examples to be turned into Latin.

The voluntary virtues *surpass the virtues* not voluntary.—No one *avoids pleasure* itself, because it 7 is pleasure.—All men 3 *admired his diligence* and *acknowledged his genius.*—When he says "*Know thyself,*" he says "*Know* thy own *mind.*"—*Drive that rascal* from those places.—*Observe the sorrow* and *grief* of all these persons.—They *lost* not only *their goods* but *their honour* also.—Your ancestors first *conquered all Italy.*—Time *does* not only not *lessen this grief,* but even increases it.—There is no one so old who 7 does not think he may *live a year.*—They will live a safer life under my protection.—Why have they not *run the same course* at this time *which they ran before?*

440.—Obs. 1. Verbs signifying to *name, choose, appoint, constitute,* and the like, besides the accusative of the object, take also the accusative of the *name, office, character,* &c., ascribed to it. All such verbs, in the passive, have the same case after, as before them. (Gr. 320.)

Antony called his flight victory, because he had escaped alive.	Antonius *fuga* suus quia vivus exire *victoria vocāre.*
The Julian clan calls Iulus the founder of their name.	*Iulus* gens Julius *autor* nomen suus *nuncupāre.*
The people made Ancus Marcius king.	*Ancus Marcius rex* populus *creāre.*

The recollection of pleasures enjoyed renders life happy.	Voluptas perceptus recordatio *vita beatus facĕre.*
Wisdom offers herself to us as the surest guide to pleasure.	Sapientia certus *sui* ego *dux præbēre* ad voluptas.
Ancus Marcius was made king by the people.	*Ancus Marcius rex* a populo *creari.*
Thunder on the left is reckoned a very good omen on all occasions except at elections.	*Fulmen* sinister *auspicium* optimus *haberi* ad omnis res præterquam ad comitia.
Homer, Virgil, and Horace, are justly esteemed most excellent poets.	*Homerus*, *Virgilius*, et *Horatius*, bonus *poeta* merito *existimari.*
441.—Obs. 2. A certain Elysius was bitterly lamenting the death of his son.	Elysius quidam graviter filius *mors mœrēre.*
Permit me first to give vent to this fury.	Hic sinĕre ego *furĕre* antè *furorem.*
What fish would taste like the sea itself.	Quis piscis *sapĕre* ipse *mare.*
The sweet muses have usually smelt of wine in the morning.	*Vinum* (*pl.*) fere dulces *olēre* mane Camēnæ.
442.—History ought not to go beyond the truth.	Historia non debēre *egredi* supra *veritas.*
We will go hence, some to the parched Africans, part to Scythia, and we will come to the rapid Oaxis of Crete, and to the Britons far separated from the whole world.	Ego hinc, alius sitiens ire Afri; pars Scythia, et rapidus Cretæ Oaxes venire, et penitus totus divisus orbis Britannus.—VIRG. *Sup. ad.*

443.—The accusative after many verbs depends on a preposition with which they are compounded.

1st. The planet Venus is called Lucifer when it goes before the sun.	Stella Venus Lucifer dici quum *antegredi sol.*
The Venetians dwell around a gulf of the sea.	Veneti *sinus circumcolĕre* mare.
Apollonius laughed at philosophy.	Apollonius *irridēre philosophia.*
The Samnites descend into the plain which lies between Capua and Tifata.	Samnis descendĕre in planities qui *Capua Tifataque interjacēre.*
The Euphrates flows through the midst of Babylon.	Euphrates *Babylonia* medius *permeare.*

2d. Cæsar leads his army across the Loire, and reaches the territories of the Bituriges. — Cæsar *exercitus Liger transducĕre* atque in Bituriges finis pervenire.

Hannibal led ninety thousand infantry [and] twelve thousand cavalry across the Ebro. — Nonaginta *mille* pedes, duodecim *mille* eques Hannibal *Iberus traducĕre.*

Cæsar conveyed a great part of the cavalry across the river. — Equitum magnus *pars flumen* Cæsar *trajicĕre.*

445.—Rule. The infinitive mood or part of a sentence is often used as the object of a transitive verb instead of the accusative.

Tarquin resolved to send to Delphi. — Tarquinius Delphi *mittĕre statuĕre.*

Cæsar gave orders to advance the standards, and extend the maniples. — Signum *inferre* et manipulus *laxare* Cæsar 3 *jubēre.*

I wish to leave the city before it dawns. — *Exire* ex urbs priusquam lucescĕre *velle.*

Dicæarchus wishes to make out that souls are mortal. — Dicæarchus *velle efficĕre animus esse mortalis.*

The philosopher will show that the sun is great. — *Magnus esse sol* philosophus *probare.*

I desire to know what you think of these things. — *Quis de is* 7 *cogitare scire* velle.

I wish to be a judge, not a teacher. — *Judex* 4 ego *esse*, non *doctor velle.*

I wish you would answer me. — *Velle ut* 3 *ego* 7 *respondēre.*

CONSTRUCTION OF THE VOCATIVE.

The vocative is used to designate the person or thing addressed, but forms no part of the proposition with which it stands, and it is used either with or without an interjection. (Gr. 448.)

449.—Rule XXI. The interjections, *O*, *heu*, and *proh* (*pro*), are construed with the vocative.

Then thou, O Jupiter, wilt drive him and his associates from thy altars. — Tum tu, *Jupiter*, hic et hic socius, a tuus ara arcēre.

You, Hannibal, know how to conquer. — Vincĕre scire *Hannibal.*

What is there, Catiline, which now can delight you in this city. — Quis esse, *Catilina*, qui tu jam in hic urbs delectare 7 posse.

Wherefore, Romans, celebrate those days with your wives and your children. — Quamobrem, *Quirites*, celebrare ille dies cum conjunx ac liberi vester.

Good gods! what is there long in the life of man? — O *deus* bonus, quis esse in homo vita diu?

Some fraud is concealed; trust not the horse, O Trojans. — Aliquis latēre error; equus ne credĕre, *Teucri.*

What more important affair, O holy Jupiter! ever occurred not in this city only, but in any country? — Qui res unquam, pro sanctus *Jupiter*, non modo in hic urbs, sed in omnis terra geri major?

451.—O fortunate republic, if indeed it shall have thrust forth this refuse of this city. — O fortunatus *respublica*, si quidem hic sentina hic urbs 6 ejicĕre.—Cic.

CONSTRUCTION OF THE ABLATIVE.

THE ABLATIVE AFTER NOUNS.

456.—Rule XXII. *Opus* and *usus*, signifying need, require the ablative. Also 457.

Let him give pardon easily, who has (to whom there is) need of pardon. — Dare ille venia facilè, qui (Gr. 394) *venia* esse *opus.*—Sen.

There is no need of passionateness to punishing. — *Iracundia* non *opus* esse ad (Gr. 704) punire.—*Id.*

There is no need of an angry chastiser for the restrainment of those that err (of the erring), and of the bad. — Ad correctio errans sceleratusque iratus *castigator* non esse *opus.*—*Id.*

459.—First, there is need of consultation; and when thou hast consulted, [there is] need of timely execution. — Priùs *consultum;* et ubi (21) consulĕre, maturè *factum* esse *opus.*—Sal.

What need is there of more? — Quid *opus* esse *plura?*

He that (who) always desires more, confesses that he has (there is to him) need of getting. Now *who can ever truly call him rich* that has (to whom there is) need of getting?

Qui semper appetĕre amplius, confitēri (Gr. 394) sui *quæsītum opus* esse. Qui autem *quæsītum opus* esse, quis hic unquam verè (38) dicĕre dives?—Cic. *Par.* 6.

Ablative governed by Adjectives.

462.—Rule XXIII. The adjectives *dignus, indignus, contentus, præditus, captus,* and *fretus;* also the participles *natus, satus, ortus, editus,* and the like, denoting origin, govern the ablative. Also 463.

They are men in name only, not in reality, who do [things] unbecoming a man.

Esse homo nomen tantum, non res, qui *homo indignus* facĕre.

Bear a mind worthy of praise.

Gerĕre animus *laus dignus.* —Cic.

Nobody is fit for (is worthy of) friendship, who is not endued with virtue.

Nemo esse *dignus amicitia,* qui non esse *præditus virtus.*

Nothing is more becoming a great and brave man, than clemency and being soon pacified (placability).

Nihil magnus et præclarus *vir dignior* esse, clementia et placabilitas.—Cic. *Off.* 1.

Who would call him a gentleman, who is unworthy of his family?

Quis generosus (38) dicĕre hic, qui *indignus genus* esse? —Juv.

How comes it to pass, that nobody lives contented with his condition (lot)?

Qui fieri, ut nemo *sors* suus *contentus* (liv.) vivĕre?—Hor.

Nature is content with a little.

Natura *parvum contentus* esse.—Cic. *Fin.*

I can live contented with a little.

Possum *contentus* vivĕre *parvum.*—Tib.

Wisdom is always contented with that which is present.

Sapientia semper *is contentus* esse qui adesse.—Cic *Tusc.*

Let him be both blind and deaf (seized both in his eyes and ears).

Esse et *oculus* et *auris captus.*—Cic.

He is descended of illustrious ancestors.

Illustris *majores natus* esse.

I rely (am relying) upon his conduct (the conduct of him).

Hic *consilium fretus* esse. —Ter.

He that shall know himself, will be sensible that he has something divine, and will always do something worthy of so great a gift of God.

Qui sui ipse 6 nôsse, sentire aliquid sui habēre divinus, tantusque *munus* Deus semper *dignus* aliquid facĕre. —Cic. *Leg.* I. 22.

Nothing is more unworthy of a man than the pleasure of the body: nature has begotten and formed us for some (certain) greater things.

Nihil *homo indignior* esse, quàm corpus voluptas: ad major quidam natura ego gignĕre et conformare.—Cic.

Only they who are endued with virtue are rich; for they only possess things both advantageous and everlasting; and they only are content with what they have (with their own things), which is the property of riches.

Qui *virtus præditus* esse, solus esse dives; solus enim possidēre res et fructuosus et sempiternus; solusque *contentus* esse *res* suus, qui esse proprium divitiæ.—Cic. *Parad.* 6.

Xerxes would not have been contented with a new pleasure being found out; for lust shall never (not ever) find a bound.

Xerxes novus *voluptas* inventus non esse *contentus;* neque enim unquam finis invenire libido.—Cic. *Tusc.* 5.

English Examples to be turned into Latin.

Philosophy is *content with few judges.*—Philippus, a man *most worthy of his father*, *grandfather*, and *ancestors*, did the same thing.—Those by whom you were declared consul did not think you *worthy of the light.*—These things are *worthy of thee.*—I see nothing in this Sulla *deserving hatred*, many things *worthy of compassion.*—I think these things shameful and unworthy of me.—He was a wise man and *endued with a certain lofty mind*, and affected with compassion.—Relying on your discernment, I say less than the cause requires.—465. Undertake the care and attention most worthy of your virtue.

The Ablative after the Comparative Degree.

467.—Rule XXIV. The comparative degree without a conjunction, governs the ablative. Also 468.

Nothing is more lovely than virtue.

Nihil esse *amabilior virtus.*—Cic.

What is more desirable than wisdom? what more excellent?	Quid esse *optabilior sapientia?* Quid præstantior?
There is nothing more pleasant to a man than the sweetness of knowledge.	Nihil esse homo *jucundior suavitas* scientia.
What is better than kindness (goodness) and doing good (beneficence)?	Quid esse *præstantior bonitas* et *beneficentia?*
Nothing is greater than use (custom).	Nihil *assuetudo major.*—Ov.
Nothing can be more intolerable than a fortunate fool.	Nihil *intolerabilior* fiĕri posse *insipiens* fortunatus.
Nothing is pleasanter to the mind than the light of truth.	Mens veritas *lux* nihil *dulcior* esse.—Cic.
Wisdom is often better than a sharp right hand.	Sæpe acer *potior* prudentia *dextra* esse.—Val. Flac.
Nothing is sweeter than liberty.	*Libertas* nihil esse *dulcior.* —Cic.
Deeds are more difficult than words.	Factum *verbum difficilior* esse.—Cic.
Nothing is swifter than years.	Nihil esse *velocior annus* —Ov.
Peace alone is better than innumerable triumphs.	Pax unus *triumphus* innumerus *potior.*—Sil.
Nothing is more foolish than foolish laughter.	*Risus* ineptus res *ineptior* nullus esse.—Cat.
The anger of God is more powerful (avails more) than human strength.	*Plus* valēre humanus *vires* ira Deus.—Ov.
The wise man thinks all things less than virtue alone.	Cunctus putare sapiens unus *virtus minor.*—Hor.
The poor man lives a securer life than the lords of the world.	Pauper agĕre mundus *dominus securior* ævum.—Luc. 8.
Old age is more to be feared than death.	*Mors magis* metuendus senectus esse.
One (another) man is more passionate than another.	Alius *alius magis* iracundus esse.—Cic. *Tusc.* 4.
Nothing dries up sooner than a tear.	*Lacryma* nihil *citiùs* arescĕre.—Cic.
Base manners defile fine clothes (clothing) worse than dirt.	Pulcher ornatus turpis mos *cœnum pejùs* collinĕre.—Plaut.
469.—There is no vice worse than covetousness.	Nullus *vitium* tetrior esse quam *avaritia.*

Certainly the ignorance of future evils is better than the knowledge.	Certe *ignoratio* futurus malum utilior quam *scientia*.
It is fit that our country should be dearer to us than ourselves.	Decet carior esse *patria* ego quam *egomet ipse*.
470.—The Roman people saw nothing with more pleasure than the elephants with their towers.	*Nihil* libentius populus Romanus adspicĕre *quam elephantus* cum turris suus.
Xerxes was defeated by the counsel of Themistocles more than by the arms of Greece.	Vinci Xerxes Themistocles magis *consilium quam arma* Græcia.
The multitude, when they have been seized with a groundless superstition, are more obedient to (obey better) their prophets than their leaders.	Multitudo, ubi vanus religio capi, melius *vates quam dux* suus parēre.
471.—I am more than thirty years old.	*Plus triginta annus* (Gr. 565) nasci.
The camp extended more than eight miles in breadth.	Castra *amplius mille* (Gr. 373) passus octo in 4 latitudo patēre.
The soldiers fought very bravely more than four hours.	Miles *amplius hora* (Gr. 565) quatuor fortissime pugnāre.
473.—Many feel their own wrongs more deeply than they ought (right).	Multus injuria suus *gravius æquus* habēre.
The consuls had turned the thoughts of the citizens more than usual to themselves.	Consul *plus solitus* convertĕre in sui civitas animus.
Cæsar is said to be about to come sooner than was expected.	Cæsar *opinio celerius* venīre dici.
Old age is naturally rather loquacious.	Senectus esse natura *loquacior*.
Most of the exploits of Datames are too little known.	*Obscurior* esse Datames gestum plerusque.
474.—The besieged engaged in battle more fiercely than steadily.	Obsessus acriter (magis) quam constanter prœlium inire.
The design of Maraces was not more sagacious in its plan, than fortunate in its issue.	Consilium Maraces non ratio *prudens quam* eventus *felix* esse.
475.—One arose braver than the rest.	Unus *præ cæter* fortior 3 exsurgĕre.

Galba ordered a much higher cross (a cross higher by much) than the rest to be erected.	Galba multus *præter cæterus* altior statui crux jubēre.
The Suevi labour to obtain corn and other productions more patiently than would be expected, according to the usual inactivity of the Germans.	Suevi frumentum cæterusque fructus *patientius quam pro* solitus Germanus inertia laborāre.
477.—The Po is inferior to no river in clearness.	Padus esse *nullus* amnis (gen. pl. 355) claritas *inferior*.
Wisdom accounts all human [things] inferior to virtue.	Sapientia humanus omnis *inferior virtus* ducēre.
478.—We have sought nothing else than the common liberty.	Nec quisquam *alius libertas* communis quærĕre.
479.—[His] opinion was understood [as] more severe than he had intended.	Sententia *gravius atque* ipse sentīre excipi.

English Examples to be turned into Latin.

Who hath ever been *more knowing than this man?*—What is *more shameful than rashness?*—Those things are *clearer than the sun itself.*—What is more desirable than wisdom?—Nothing is *more commendable*, nothing *more worthy* of a great and illustrious 6 man (Gr. 462), *than mildness and clemency.*—My country is much *dearer* to me *than my life.*—What is *more pleasing than literary ease?*—Nothing is *more inconstant than the common people*, nothing *more uncertain than the inclination* of mankind. —There is nothing *more pleasing* to man *than the light of truth.* —What is better in man than a sagacious and good mind?—Of all things by which any profit (any thing) is acquired, nothing is better than agriculture, nothing more advantageous, nothing more pleasing, nothing more worthy of a free man.

Ablative governed by Verbs.

480.—Rule XXV. Verbs of plenty and scarceness for the most part govern the ablative. Also 481.

Nature wants few and small things.	Natura paucus *res* et parvus *egēre.*
Souls are free from (want) death; and verses are free from (want) death.	*Mors carēre* anima; et carmen *mors carēre.*—Ov. *Am.*

He ought to be without (to want) fault, that (who) is prepared to speak against another.

Carēre debēre *vitium*, qui paratus esse in alter dicĕre.—Cic.

Eminent things are never free from (never want) envy.

Nunquam eminens *invidia carēre.*—Vell. Pat.

Dost thou think thou canst find any woman that is without (who wants) fault?

Censērene tu posse reperire ullus mulier, qui (Gr. 638) *carēre culpa?*—Ter.

The belly has no (wants) ears.

Venter *carēre auris.*

To be innocent (to be free from fault) is a great comfort.

Vacare culpa magnus esse solatium.—Cic.

All punishment and chastisement ought to be without contumely (reproach).

Omnis animadversio et castigatio *contumelia vacare* (Gr. 315) debēre.—Cic. *Off.* 1.

Nothing can be honourable that is without (which wants) justice.

Nihil honestus esse posse, qui *justitia vacare.* (Gr. 639.)—Cic.

Fortune frees many bad men from punishment, none from fear.

Multus malus fortuna *liberare pœna*, *metus* nemo.—Sen. *Ep.* 98.

Men abounding in wealth are often puffed up with disdainfulness.

Homo *divitiæ affluens*, sæpe efferri fastidium.—Cic. *Am.*

We see some men flowing with money and wealth, yet to desire those things most with which they abound.

Vidēre quidam homo *circumfluens pecunia opes*que, tamen is desiderare maximè *qui abundare.*—Cic. *Par.* 1.

Tantalus, they say, always wants, always abounds with clear waters.

Tantălus, aio, semper *egēre*, liquidus semper *abundare aqua.*—Ov.

Themistocles was more willing to have (rather wished) a man that (who) wanted money, than money that [wanted] a man.

Themistŏcles 3 malle vir, qui *pecunia* (32) (Gr. 644) *egēre*, quàm pecunia, qui *vir.*—Cic.

He enjoys riches most, that (who) wants riches least.

Is maximè divitiæ (xxvi.) frui, qui minimè *divitiæ indigēre.*—Sen.

483.—A madman needs a keeper.

Insanus *custos egēre.*

Nature decreed (wished) that one man should stand in need of (should need) another.

Natura velle alter *alter indigēre.*—Cic. *Œcon.* 1.

We ought to help those rather than others, who most want relief.

Is (Gr. 403) potissimùm opitulari debēre, qui *opis* maximè *indigēre.*—Cic. *Off.* 1.

It is most certain poverty when you want something.

Certissimus paupertas esse, quùm *aliquid* (30) *indigĕre.* —Cic. *Œcon.*

We have drawn understanding sent down from the heavenly tower, which [creatures] inclining downwards and looking upon the earth want.

Sensus a cœlestis demissus trahĕre arx, *qui egēre* pronus, et terra spectans.—Juv. 15.

English Examples to be turned into Latin.

While they *are free from one kind* of injustice, they fall into another.—You will show that death *is free from every evil.*—While we 7 *are free from guilt* 7 let us bear all human [events] with patience and moderation.—How long then *shall he* who has exceeded all enemies in wickedness *be without the name* of an enemy?—The one, as Isocrates said, *wants a bridle*, the other, *spurs.*—His oration *abounded with every grace.*—We have pursued this quiet and easy life which, as it is *without honour*, 7 may also be without trouble.—Nature herself daily admonishes us how few, how little, how common *things she* 7 *wants.*—483. He expects you, and *wants you.*—I *want your advice.*

484.—Rule XXVI. *Utor*, *abutor*, *fruor*, *fungor*, *potior*, *vescor*, govern the ablative. Also 485.

Note.—To the verbs contained in the Rule may be added, *nitor, gaudeo, assuesco, muto, verto, dono, numero, communico, victito, beo, confido, impertior, dignor, nascor, creor, afficio, consto, prosequor,* which are also followed by the ablative.

Most [people] use too much indulgence towards their children.

Plerique nimius *indulgentia* in liberi suus *uti.*

They that (who) practise liberality, procure good-will to themselves.

Qui *liberalitas uti*, benevolentia sui conciliare.—Cic.

We cannot make use of (use) our understanding well, being filled with much meat and drink.

Mens rectè *uti* non posse, multus cibus et potio (xxv.) complētus.—*Id. Tusc.* 5.

The conveniences which we use, the light which we enjoy, the breath which we draw, are given and bestowed upon us by God.

Commodum *qui uti*, lux *qui frui*, spiritus qui ducĕre, a Deus ego (Gr. 315) dari atque impertiri.—Cic.

The good enjoy eternal life in heaven.	Bonus in cœlum *ævum* sempiternus *frui*.—Cic. *Somn.*
Do not think (beware lest thou believe) that thou wert born for this thing only, that thou mightest enjoy pleasures.	(24) Cavēre (31) credĕre ad hic unus res tu natus esse, ut *frui voluptas*.—Cic. *Fin.* 2.
Use thy ears oftener than thy tongue.	*Auris* frequentiùs quàm *lingua uti*.—Sen.
Men may make use of (may use) beasts for their profit without injustice.	*Bestia* homo ad utilitas suus *uti* posse sine injuria.—Cic.
The young man delights in horses and dogs.	Juvenis *gaudēre equus canis*que.—Hor.
Delight not in vain things.	Ne (25) *gaudēre vanus*.—Sen.
It is a savage cruelty to delight in blood and wounds.	Ferinus rabies esse *sanguis gaudēre* et *vulnus*.—*Id.*
Good men delight in equity and justice.	*Æquitas* et *justitia gaudēre* (*delectari*) vir bonus.
He that delights in punishing is savage.	Qui *pœna frui* (*gaudēre*), ferus esse.—Claud.
Certainly nothing can be better for man than to be free from all pain and trouble, and to enjoy the greatest pleasures both of mind and body.	Certè nihil homo posse melior esse, quàm vacare omnis dolor et molestia, *perfrui*que maximus et animus et corpus *voluptas*.—Cic. *Fin.* 1.
There would be no exportation of those things wherein (with which) we abounded, and no importation of those things that (which) we wanted, unless men performed these offices.	Is res, (xxv.) qui (32) abundare, exportatio, et is, (xxv.) qui (32) egēre, invectio, nullus esse, nisi hic *munus* homo (32) *fungi*.—Cic. *Off.* 2.
What is more glorious than to change anger [into] friendship?	Quid esse gloriosior quàm ira *amicitia mutare?*—Sen.
It becomes thee to rely on virtue rather than on blood.	Tu (Gr. 423) *virtus* decēre potiùs quam *sanguis niti*.—Claud.
Jason got the golden fleece.	Jason aureus *vellus* n. 3 *potiri*.
486.—Cleanthes thought the sun was chief ruler and (ruled and was) lord of all things.	Cleanthes sol dominari et *res potiri* putare.—Cic. *Acad.*
The Helvetii hoped that they could obtain the command of all Gaul.	Helvetii totus *Gallia* 4 sui *potiri* posse sperare.—Cæs.

Men, who could not be a match for other animals, if they were separated, being strengthened by society, are lords of all.	Homo, qui cæter animal par esse non (Gr. 638) (33) posse, si (32) sedūci, societas munitus, *res potiri*.—SEN. *de Benef.* 4.
The Roman people got [the government] of all lands by defending their allies.	Populus Romanus socius (72) defendendus *terra* omnis 3 *potiri*.—CIC. *de Rep.*
487.—Datames performed the part of a soldier.	Datames militaris munus fungi.
I will feed upon sacred laurels.	Sacer laurus vesci.

English Examples to be turned into Latin.

7 Let him *discharge the proper duty* of philosophy.—Your uncle has done his duty.—Why *do I make use of these witnesses*, as if the affair 7 were doubtful or obscure?—That is every one's own (the property of every one) *which every one enjoys and uses.*—That which *makes use of reason* is nobler than that which *does not make use of reason.*—God has not permitted (willed) us to know these things, but only to enjoy them.—7 Use the good while it 7 is present; 7 seek not for it when it 7 is absent.—No one has lived too short a time (little long) who has discharged the entire duty of perfect virtue.

VERBS GOVERNING THE ACCUSATIVE AND GENITIVE.

489.—RULE XXVII. Verbs of *accusing*, *condemning*, *acquitting*, and *admonishing*, govern the accusative of a person with the genitive of a thing. Also 490.

I condemn myself of laziness, i. e. upon the account of, &c.	*Condemnare ego ipse inertia.*—CIC.
Afflictions (adverse things) put men in mind (remind men) of religion (religions).	Res adversus *admonēre homo religio.*—LIV. 5. 51.
Our time slides away silently, it makes no noise, it does not put us in mind (remind us) of its swiftness.	Tacitus labi ætas, nihil tumultuari, nihil *admonēre* [*nos*] *velocitas* suus.—SEN.

Our infirmity often reminds us of mortality.	Imbecillitas noster sæpe *ego admonēre mortalitas.*—*Id.*
Fannius accused Verres of covetousness.	*Fannius Verres* 2 insimulare *avaritia.*—Cic.
494.—You cannot accuse me of negligence in writing (of my letters).	Ego *accusāre* de epistola *negligentia* non posse.
I excuse myself to you in that very thing in which I accuse you.	Ego tu excusare in is ipse, *in qui tu accusare.*
Persons condemned to die (condemned of a capital crime) are punished with death.	Homo *caput damnatus mors multari.*—Cic. *Tusc.*
All mankind (the human race) is condemned to die (death).	Omnis humanus genus *mors damnatus* esse.—Sen.
Nobody has condemned wisdom to poverty.	Nemo sapientia *paupertas damnare.*—*Id.*
Nature, by a fixed law, has condemned degenerate souls to infernal darkness; but to the pious the gate of heaven is open.	Natura fœdus certus degener anima *tenebræ damnare Avernus;* at pius cœlum porta patēre.—Sil. 15.
All the works of mortals are condemned to mortality.	Omnis mortalis opus *n. mortalitas damnatus* esse.—Sen. *Ep.* 91.
He accused him of assassination.	Is *inter sicarius accusāre.*
He accuses the idleness of the young men.	*Inertia* adolescens *accusāre.*

English Examples to be turned into Latin.

Thrasybulus proposed a law, that no one should accuse nor fine another for things previously done.—The judges were so provoked with the answer of Socrates, that they capitally condemned a most innocent man.—Cœlius, the judge, acquitted of injury him who had libelled the poet Lucilius by name upon the stage.—The soldiers were in a rage, and began to charge the tribunes with treason and treachery, and to accuse the centurions of avarice.—He that accuses another of a crime, ought to look well to himself.

495.—Rule XXVIII. Verbs of *valuing*, with their own case, and sometimes without a case, govern such genitives as *magni*, *parvi*, *nihili*. Also Nos. 496–498.

A wise man values pleasure at a very low rate.	Sapiens *voluptas minimum facĕre.*
Epicurus valued pleasure at a very high rate.	Epicurus voluptas quàm *magnum æstimare.*—Cic.
If cunning valuers of things esteem meadows and closes at a great rate, because that sort of possessions can least be damaged (because least injury can be done to that sort of possessions); at how great a rate is virtue to be esteemed, which can neither be taken away by force, nor be stolen?	Si callidus res æstimator pratum et area *magnum æstimare*, quòd is genus possessio minime (*imp.*) nocēri posse; *quantum* esse *æstimandus* virtus, qui nec erĭpi nec surrĭpi posse?—Cic. *Parad.* 6.

499.—So *consulo boni*, *Æqui bonique facio*, I take in good part.

Whatever happens to good men, they take it in good part, they turn it to good.	Quicquid bonus accidĕre, *bonus consulĕre*, in bonum vertĕre.—Sen.
My mind is very calm, which takes all that in good part.	Tranquillissimus esse animus meus, qui totus iste *æquus bonus*que *facĕre.*—Cic.
500.—He set a high value on his meadows.	*Prata multus æstimāre.*
These things he reckons as false.	Is *pro falsus ducĕre.*

English Examples to be turned into Latin.

Corn was in no place *of so much value as* that fellow (Gr. 118. 3. 3d) reckoned.—I can willingly die for Pompey; of all men, I esteem no one more.—I am not ignorant *of what consequence* you 7 esteem (Gr. 627–5) his name.—He greatly values money. —He rates his own authority very highly.—The mind ought now to grow callous and esteem every thing (all things) *as of little value.*—I do not regard *in the least*, the Marsian Augur, nor the Soothsayers.—If you esteem me as much as you certainly do.

Verbs governing the Accusative and Dative.

501.—Rule XXIX. Verbs of *comparing*, *giving*, *declaring*, and *taking away*, govern the accusative and dative. Also No. 502.

1. Verbs of *comparing.*

He compares his old age with that (to the old age) of a strong and victorious horse. — Equus fortis et victor *senectus comparare suus* [sup. *senectutem*].—Cic. *Sen.*

If I may (if it is lawful to) compare great things with small. — *Grandis* si *parvus assimilare* licet.—Ov. *Trist.*

Thus I used to compare great things to small. — Sic *parvus componĕre magnus* solēre.—Virg.

I should compare nothing with a pleasant friend, being in my senses (sane). — *Nil* ego (38) *conferre* jucundus sanus *amicus.*—Hor.

503.—But these verbs more usually have after them an ablative with *cum.*

Compare the longest age of men with eternity, and it will be found very short. — *Conferre* longissimus *ætas* homo *cum æternitas*, et brevissimus reperiri.—Cic. *Tusc.* 1.

When I compare my action with yours, I am much more delighted with mine than yours. — Quum meus *factum cum tuus comparare*, multò magis meus delectari quàm tuus. —Cic.

When Jugurtha had compared the words of Metellus with his actions. — Jugurtha ubi Metellus *dictum cum factum* 3 *componĕre.* —Sal.

2.—Verbs of *giving*, to which may be referred verbs of *restoring*, *promising*, *paying*, *sending*, and *bringing.*

We all easily give right counsels to the sick, when we are well. — Facilè omnis, quum valēre, rectus *consilium ægrotus dăre.* —Ter.

Give not thyself to pleasures nor to sloth. — Ne *tu* (25) *dedĕre voluptas*, neque *desidia.*

Intemperate youth transmits a wasted body to old age. — Intemperans adolescentia effœtus *corpus tradĕre senectus.*—C. *Sen.*

He gives a benefit twice to a poor man, who gives soon. — *Inops beneficium* bis *dare*, qui dare citò.—Publ.

Life has given nothing to mortals without great labour. — *Nil* sine magnus vita laboi *dăre mortalis.*—Hor.

We must impart [something] of our family estate to indigent [persons]. — *Homo* indigens de res familiaris esse (LXI.) *impertire* —Cic. *Off.*

Justice is employed in giving (to) every one his own.

In *tribuĕre suum quisque* justitia versari.—Cic.

Nobody can promise (to) himself to-morrow.

Nemo posse *sui crastinus* [*dies*] *pollicēri*.—Sen.

If thou hast promised any thing to an enemy, thou oughtest (it behoves thee) not to break the promise made to him.

Si *quid hostis promittĕre*, fides *is datus* fallĕre non oportēre.—Cic. *Off.* 1.

Those promises are not to be kept which are hurtful (useless) to those to whom you have promised them.

Promissum non servandus esse is, qui (Gr. 644) esse is, *qui* (Gr. 644) *promittĕre*, inutilis.—Cic. *Off.* 1.

Thou sinnest twice when thou affordest compliance to [one] sinning.

Bis peccare quum *peccans obsequium accomodare*.—Syr.

What? do you, then, when you are angry, yield up the government of your mind to that passion?

Quid? tunc quum esse iratus, *permittĕre* ille *iracundia dominatus* animus tuus?—Cic. *de Rep.*

Give not the reins to thy mind [when it is] warm (i. e. in a passion); allow a space, and a short delay.

Ne *frænum animus* (25) *permittĕre* calens; dare spatium, tenuisque mora.—Stat.

When thou hast (shalt have) given thyself up to carelessness and idleness, do not thou call upon the gods.

Ubi *socordia tute* atque *ignavia* 6 *tradĕre*, neutiquam Deus (25) implōrare.—Sall.

When thou givest a benefit to a deserving [person], thou obligest all.

Beneficium dignus ubi *dare*, omnis obligare.—Pub.

Antipater says that it is not (denies that it is) the part of a good man to pay any one counterfeit money for good: and Cicero agrees with him [in it].

Esse bonus vir (xii.) *solvĕre quisquam* adulterinus *nummus* (*plur.*) pro bonus, negare Antipater; isque (Gr. 399) assentiri Cicero. —Cic. *Off.* 3.

Gratiam referre alicui, to requite any one. *Gratificari aliquid alicui*, to gratify one in any thing. *Dăre operam rei*, to mind or study a thing.

Parents often gratify their children in (with) that which does harm to them.

Parens sæpe *gratificari id liberi*, qui ille (Gr. 399) obesse.

They say [that] Tarquinius said, that he had understood then when he was in banishment (was an exile) what faithful friends he had had, and what unfaithful ones, when he could now requite (return a favour to) neither.

Tarquinius dicĕre ferre, tum quum exul (33) esse sui intelligĕre, quis fidus amicus (39) habēre, quisque infidus, quum jam *neuter referre gratia* (33) posse.—Cic. *Am.*

3.—Verbs of *declaring*, to which belong verbs of *explaining*, *showing*, *denying*, &c.

I declared my thoughts to you in my former letter.

Meus *cogitatio* 3 *explicare tu* superior literæ.—Cic. *Att.*

The boy discovered the whole matter to his mistress.

Puer *res* omnis *domina indicare.*—*Id.*

If cross Nature hath denied (to) me beauty, I make up (repay) the defects of my beauty by [my] wit.

Si *ego* difficilis *forma* Natura *negare*, ingenium forma damnum rependĕre meus.—Ovid.

4.—Verbs of *taking away.*

Time takes away grief from people.

Dies *adimĕre ægritudo homo.*—Ter.

Take not away from another [what is] his own.

Ne *suus* (25) *adimĕre alter.* —Plaut.

Pain takes away from a man the enjoyment of all good things.

Auferre homo fructus bonum omnis dolor.

From whom would not solitude take away the enjoyment of all pleasures?

Quis non (31) *auferre fructus* voluptas omnis solitudo? —Cic. *Am.*

Should not a wise man, if he be ready to die with (should be exhausted by) hunger, take away meat from another man [who is] good for nothing? No, by no means.

Nonne sapiens, si fames (30) conficior, (38) *auferre cibus* alter *homo* ad nullus res utilis? Minimè verò.—*Id. Off.* 3.

The Nile falling down (precipitating itself) takes away hearing from those that dwell near it (from the dwellers near) with its noise.

Nilus præcipitans sui, fragor *auditus accola auferre.*—Plin.

To take away from another, is both against (foreign from) justice and against nature.

Detrahĕre alter, et alienus a justitia et contra natura esse.—Cic.

If every one of us should take away what he could from every one, for the sake of his own advantage, the society of men must needs (it is necessary that the society of men) be overturned.

Si unusquisque ego (31) *detrahĕre qui quisque* (31) posse emolumentum suus (xxxv.) gratia, societas homo [ut] (liv.) everti necesse esse.—*Id. Off.* 3. 6.

Every one (not nobody) can take away life from a man, but nobody virtue.

Eripĕre vita nemo non *homo* posse, at nemo *virtus*. Sen.

The labour of poets delivers all things from fate, and gives eternity to mortal nations (peoples).

Vates labor *omnis fatum eripĕre*, et populus donare mortalis ævum.—Luc. 9.

Naughty folly is thought to depart from him to whom God gives an estate.

Qui res dăre Deus, *hic decedĕre* pravus putari stultitia.—Hor. *Ep.* 2, 2.

503.—Verbs of *taking away* have frequently the ablative with *a*, *ab*, *e*, *ex*, *de*; as,

Death takes us away from evils.

Mors *a malum ego abducĕre.*—Cic. *Tusc.* 1.

Clodius took away the consular money from the senate.

Clodius *pecunia* consularis *auferre a Senatus.*—*Id.*

Use your endeavour to (that you may) bring them off from their lewd temper (depravity of mind.

Dare opera ut *ille de pravitas* animus *deducĕre.*—*Id.*

Philosophy has dispelled darkness from the mind as from the eyes.

Philosophia *ab animus*, tanquam *ab oculus*, *caligo dispellĕre.*—Cic.

English Examples to be turned into Latin.

He *compares himself to me.*—He *compares* his *old age to the old age* of a strong horse.—503. I do not *compare him with the* greatest *men.*—What shall I say of Democritus?—Whom *can we compare with him?*—Your Nicanor gives [to] me excellent assistance.—I impart a share of my trouble to no one; of my glory, to all good [men].—I will most religiously observe and carefully do *what I promise to you.*—I have sent to thee a copy of Cæsar's letter.—I have sent to thee the eulogy of Porcia, in a corrected state.—He has told the whole affair to his master.—It is the part of a fool to declare his sentiments to every body.—What is Sicily if thou take from it (Gr. 502) the culture of the soil?—He took away credit from the merit of those.

VERBS GOVERNING TWO ACCUSATIVES.

508.—RULE XXX. Verbs of *asking* and *teaching*, govern two accusatives, the one of a person, and the other of a thing. Also Nos. 509, 510.

I ask pardon of thee, confessing my crimes.

[b] *Tu* [bb] *venia*, confessus (63–2 in fin.) crimen, *poscĕre*.—CLAUD.

We all beg peace of thee.

[bb] *Pax* [b] *tu poscĕre* omnis.—VIRG.

Ask God for life and safety.

[b] *Deus* [bb] *vita rogare* et *salus*.—SEN.

Want teaches some persons temperance.

Egestas [b] *aliquis* [bb] *temperantia docēre.*

Friends advertise us of many things.

Amicus [b] *ego* [bb] *multus admonēre.*

I request this of you, so as (so that) I cannot request it with greater earnestness.

Hoc tu ita *rogare*, ut (XXXV.) major studium rogare non posse.—CIC. *ad Q. fr.*

See that you also conceal this very thing from my wife.

Uxor quoque ipse hic *res* ut (30) *celare*, facĕre.—TER.

511.—We flee to thee, we desire help of thee, we give up ourselves wholly to thee.

Ad tu confugĕre, *a tu opis petĕre*, tu ego totus tradĕre.—CIC. *Tusc.* 5.

Ask nothing of a friend but [what is] honest and right.

Nihil nisi honestus et rectus *ab amicus postulare.*—CIC. *Am.*

Staberius began to demand hostages from the inhabitants of Apollonia.

Staberius *obses ab Apolloniātes exigĕre* cœpisse.

You will see what your past life, what your studies demand of you.

Quis actus tuus vita, quis studium *a tu* 7*flagitāre*, tu vidēre.

The whole province demanded of me this service.

Hic *a ego munus* universus provincia *poscĕre.*

I inquired of Massinissa concerning his kingdom; he inquired of me concerning our republic.

Ego Masinissa *de* suus *regnum;* illa ego, *de* noster *respublica percontari.*

512.—Cæsar detains Liscus; he inquires of [him] alone [respecting] those [things] which he had spoken in the assembly. He asks the same things privately of others.

Cæsar Liscus retinēre: *quærĕre ex solus*, is qui in conventu dicĕre. *Idem* secreto *ab alius quærĕre.*

English Examples to be turned into Latin.

I ask this favour of you by my right.—He first asks you your opinion.—If 6 I shall ask you any thing, will you not answer?—Though we may (7 posse) conceal the thing (Gr. 687) from all gods and men; yet we ought to do nothing (nothing is to be done) unjustly.—He admonished me of that thing.—511. I beg this of you in such a manner that I cannot (7 posse) beg more earnestly.—This I beg and insist on from you.—512. The Athenians entreated aid from the Lacedæmonians.—He entreats this of (from) the king in many words.

Verbs governing the Accusative and Ablative.

514.—Rule XXXI. Verbs of *loading*, *binding*, *clothing*, *depriving*, and their contraries, govern the accusative and ablative. Also Nos. 515, 516.

The poet fills the mind (breast) with imaginary terrors.

Poeta *pectus* falsus *terror implēre.*

God has filled the world with all good things.

Deus *bonum* omnis *explēre mundus.*

The inhabitants of Crotona desired to enrich the temple of Juno with choice paintings.

Crotoniatæ *templum* Juno egregius *pictura locupletare* velle.

Nature has adorned Germany with armies of very tall men.

Natura *Germania decorare* altissimus homo *exercitus.*

He loads the ships with provisions.

Commeatus navis onerāre.

Æolus had resolved, when night should cover the earth with darkness, to bury them under the waves.

Æolus statuĕre, cum nox 8 *obruĕre terra tenebræ, is fluctus opprimĕre.*

But when indisposition deprived me of sleep, I determined to write this I know not what.

Sed cum *ego* ægritudo *somnum* 8 *privare*, hic nescire quis scribĕre instituĕre.

Thou hast stripped and plundered Apollonius of all his money (silver).

Apollonius omnis *argentum spoliare* ac *depeculari.*

Nature has clothed and protected the eyes with the most delicate membranes.

Natura *oculus membrana* tenuissimus *vestire* et sepire.

Here the air is more extended, and clothes the fields with resplendent light.

Largior hic *campus* æther et *lumen vestire* purpureus.

518.—The earth abounds with wild beasts. *Terra fera scatēre.*

They had now filled the prison with merchants. *Complēre* jam *mercator carcer.*

Construction with Passive Verbs.

519.—Rule XXXII. Verbs that govern two cases in the active voice, govern the latter of these in the passive. Also Nos. 520–523.

RULE SUBDIVIDED.

I. Verbs of *accusing*, *condemning*, *acquitting*, and *admonishing*, in the passive, govern the genitive (Gr. 520).

He was accused of a fault, of which he was innocent. *Culpa argui*, qui esse insons.

He was condemned for [keeping up] the public money. 3 *Condemnari pecunia* publicus.—Cic.

Do not (be unwilling to) take it ill that you are put in mind of your duty. Nolle ægrê ferre tu *officium* tuus *commonēri.*

He that is accused of a [wicked] action, or he that is called in question about any thing, is called *reus* (an accused person). But he that is accused of a fault, is not consequently in fault. Qui *accusari facinus*, aut qui postulari de res aliquis, vocari reus. Sed qui reus esse culpa, non continuò in culpa esse.

For many very innocent persons have been brought to trial for life (have been accused of a capital crime), and condemned to death (of a capital crime). Multus enim homo innocentissimus *caput accusatus*, et *caput damnatus* fuisse.

II. Verbs of *valuing*, in the passive, govern such genitives as *magni*, *parvi*, *nihili* (Gr. 521, and 498).

No possession is to be valued at a higher rate than virtue. Nullus possessio *plus æstimandus* esse quam virtus.

Money is esteemed of great value by the miser. Pecunia avarus *magnus æstimari.*

The favour of a worthless man is lightly esteemed. Nequam homo *parvus pendi.*

Pleasure is estimated at a very low rate by a wise man. | 3 Sapiens voluptas *minimum æstimari.*

III.—Verbs of *comparing*, *giving*, *declaring*, and *taking away*, in the passive, govern the dative. (Gr. 522.)

Death is rightly compared to sleep. | Mors rectè *comparari somnus.*

What virtue is to be compared to charity and liberality? | Quis virtus *comparandus* esse *beneficentia* et *liberalitas?*

Epicurus was too much given to pleasure. | Epicurus nimis *voluptas* 3 *dedi.*—Cic.

The way to true happiness is showed to us from the word of God only. | Via ad verus felicitas ex solus Deus verbum *ego ostendi.*

Virtue can neither be taken away nor stolen from any one. | Virtus nec *erĭpi* nec *surrĭpi quisquam* posse.—Cic.

IV.—Verbs of *asking* and *teaching*, in the passive, govern the accusative. (Gr. 623.)

Let God be asked for life and safety. | Deus *rogari vita* et *salus.*

We are advertised of many things by friends. | *Admonēri multus* ab amicus.—Plin.

The virgin takes pleasure (delights) to be taught Ionian dances. | Virgo *motus docēri* gaudēre Ionicus.—Hor.

Cato being asked his opinion, made a speech to this effect. | Cato *rogatus sententia* hujuscemodi oratio habēre.

V.—Verbs of *loading*, *binding*, *clothing*, *depriving*, and their contraries, in the passive, govern the ablative. (Gr. 524.)

All the cities are filled with grief and slaughter. | *Luctus* atque *cædes* omnis oppidum *complēri.*

The neck of the bull is loaded with the plough. | Taurus cervix *onerari aratrum.*

The ships are loaded with provisions. | *Commeatus* navis *onerari.*

The tree is clothed with vines. | *Amiciri vitis* arbor.

526.—The old man is girded with his useless sword, i. e. girds himself (Gr. 136–3). | Senior inutile *ferrum cingi.*—Virg.

Thus having spoken, he is then arrayed in the long-haired helmet of Androgeos, and in the beautiful ornament of his shield.

Sic fatus, deinde comans Androgeos *galea*, clypeusque *insigne* decorus *indui*.—VIRG.

527.—In Greece, to go upon the stage is considered a disgrace to nobody.

Ire in scena in Græcia, *nemo*[bb] *turpitudo*[b] *duci*.

English Examples to be turned into Latin.

I was not first asked [my] opinion.—All things must (are to) be intrusted to fortune, we struggle without [any] hope.—That province was given to him.—Pardon and impunity were granted to the others.—Cluentius was asked his opinion concerning the decisions.—The duties of justice are to be preferred to the pursuit of knowledge.—The glory of virtue is transmitted by fathers to their children as their best inheritance.—A proper (its own) season has been assigned to every part of life.—The prisoner is accused of a crime so great, that that (viz., the trial) being postponed (Gr. 690), the State could not exist.—Good reputation was preferred by Agesilaus to the most wealthy kingdom.—His cloak of gold was taken off from Olympian Jupiter, and a woollen robe was put upon him.

528.—RULE XXXIII. Passive verbs frequently govern the dative of the doer. See also 529, 530.

I had rather (I am more willing to) be approved by one good man than by many bad men.

Malle *probari* unus *bonus*, quàm multus *malus*.—AUS.

(I had rather (I am more willing) that one good man should like me, than many bad.)

(Malle unus *bonus* ego *probare*, quàm multus *malus*.)

By whom has not the wealthiness of rich Crœsus been heard of?

Dives *audiri quis* non opulentia Crœsus?—OV.

Who has not heard of the wealthiness of Crœsus?

Quis non *audire* opulentia Crœsus?

Glory has been gotten by many (many have gotten glory), by ingenuous arts.

Ars ingenuus *quæri* gloria *multus* (*multus quærĕre* gloria).—OV.

To [people that are] sailing, those things that (which) stand seem to move (to be moved).

Navigans movēri *vidēri* is, qui stare.—CIC.

[People that are] sailing think those things to move (to be moved) that (which) stand.

Navigans putare is movēri, qui stare.

It is not perceived by [one] that always lives (always living) in laudable exercises, (one that always lives (always living) in laudable exercises does not perceive), when old age creeps upon him.

Semper in studium honestus *vivens* non *intelligi* (semper in studium honestus *vivens* non *intelligĕre*), quando (LIV.) obrepĕre senectus.—CIC. *Sen.*

531.—The passive participle in *dus* has the agent or doer almost always in the dative (Gr. 182–6); sometimes also, the perfect participle.

The path of death must once be trod (is to be trod) by all.

Semel *omnis calcandus* esse via letum.—HOR.

Consider, that nothing is to be desired by thee in the world (in life), but that which is laudable and excellent.

Cogitare, nihil in vita *tu expetendus* esse, nisi qui laudabilis et præclarus (LIV.) esse.—CIC.

Let us always live so, as to think that an account must be given by us.

Semper ita vivĕre, ut ratio *ego reddendus* [esse] 31 arbitrari.—CIC.

Wars detested by mothers.

Bellum *mater detestatus.*—HOR.

Glory has been gotten by many by ingenuous arts.

Ars ingenuus *quæsitus* esse gloria *multus.*—OV.

I must read Cato Major more frequently.

Legendus ego sæpe esse Cato Major.

And now the weather is to be feared by the ripe grapes.

Et jam matūrus *metuendus* (esse) Jupiter *uva.*

English Examples to be turned into Latin.

I am here a barbarian, because I am not understood by any one.—By whom has not the nocturnal studies (wakefulness) of Demosthenes been heard of?—The desire of glory is the last to be laid aside (is last put off) even by wise [men].—None of thy sisters have been heard of, or seen by me.—In governing a republic (Gr. 707), a continual remaining in one opinion has never been commended (praised) by eminent men.—On account of the same prodigy, a nine-day festival was undertaken by the Romans, at the public cost.—Often has it been fought successfully by a few active [men] against a multitude.—Virtue must (is to) be reverenced by all.—The labours of the body should (are to) be diminished by old men.—This orator, if any [other], ought to be read by a young man (by youth).

After passive verbs, the *principal* agent or actor, if voluntary, is usually expressed in the ablative with the preposition *a* or *ab* (Gr. 530).

Poverty shows by whom thou art loved.	Paupertas ostendĕre *a quis* (Gr. 627–5) *amari.*—Sen.
Poverty shows who loves thee.	Paupertas ostendĕre *quis* (Gr. 627–5) *amare* tu.
He is miserable, who neither loves any one, nor is himself beloved of any one.	Miser esse, qui neque diligĕre quisquam, nec ipse *ab ullus dilĭgi.*—Cic. *Am.*
He is miserable, who loves not any one, and whom nobody loves.	Miser esse, qui non diligĕre quisquam, quique *nemo diligĕre.*
Nothing can be well done by an angry person.	Nihil rectè *fiĕri* posse *ab iratus.*—Cic.
An angry person can do nothing rightly.	*Iratus* nihil rectè facĕre *posse.*
Not only the mind, but also the body, is discomposed by passion.	Non modò animus *ab ira perturbari*, sed etiam corpus. —Cic.
Passion not only discomposes the mind, but also the body.	*Ira* non modò animus *perturbare*, sed etiam corpus.
The affairs of a good man are never neglected by God.	Bonus vir res nunquam *a Deus neglĭgi.*—Cic.
God never neglects the affairs of a good man.	*Deus* nunquam *negligĕre* res vir bonus.
Care is taken (it is consulted) both for states, and for particular persons by God.	*A Deus* et civitas et singulus homo *consŭli.*—Cic.
God consults both for states and for particular persons.	*Deus consulĕre* et civitas et singulus homo.
It was excellently written by Plato (Plato wrote excellently), that we were not born for ourselves only.	Præclarè 3 *scribi a Plato* (præclarè 3 *scribĕre Plato*), ego non ego solùm natus esse. —Cic. *Off.* 1.
The vulgar [sort] think that honest which is commended by most (which most commend).	Vulgus is honestus putare, qui *a plerique laudari*, (qui *plerique laudare*). — Cic. *Tusc.* 2.
Perdiccas is slain at the river Nile by Seleucus and Antigonus.	Perdiccas apud flumen Nilus interfĭci *a Seleucus* et *Antigonus.*

We are so formed by nature (nature hath so formed us), that we do not seem to be made for sport and jest.

Ita 3 *generari a natura*, (*natura* ita ego *generare*), ut non ad ludus jocusque factus esse (30) vidēri.—Cic. *Off.* 1.

The pleasures of the body were truly called by Plato the allurements and baits to evils.

Voluptas corpus verè *a Plato* 3 *dici* illecebræ et esca (vi.) malum.—Cic. *de Phil.*

Plato truly called the pleasures of the body, &c.

Plato verè 3 *dicĕre* voluptas corpus, &c.

Snares are laid for souls by pleasure, (pleasure lays snares for souls.)

Animus (Gr. 403) *tendi* insidiæ *a voluptas*, [*voluptas tendĕre* insidiæ animus.]—C.

The covetous man does not possess riches, but is possessed by riches, (riches possess him.)

Avarus non possidēre divitiæ, sed *a divitiæ possidēri*, [*divitiæ possidēre* ille.]—Val. Max.

Note.—The preposition before the ablative case is sometimes omitted, especially when the ablative expresses the cause, manner, or instrument, as well as the agent, and that agent is not a living being.

EXAMPLES.

We are forbidden by the law of nature to do injury.

Lex natura *prohibēri* facĕre injuria.—Cic. *Off.* 1.

The law of nature (*or*, nature by its law) forbids us to do injury.

Lex natura (*vel*, natura lex suus) *prohibēre* ego facĕre injuria.

All things are governed by the divine mind and providence.

Omnis *regi* divinus *mens* et *providentia*.—Cic.

The divine mind and providence govern all things; or, God governs all things by his providence.

Divinus *mens* et *providentia regĕre* omnis; vel, *Deus regĕre* omnis *providentia* suus.

Excellent tempers (wits) are excited by glory.

Præclarus ingenium *gloria incitari*.—Cic.

Glory excites excellent tempers.

Gloria incitare præclarus ingenium.

Nobody was ever made immortal by idleness.

Nemo unquam *ignavia* immortalis 3 *fiĕri*.—Sall.

Idleness never made any one (ever made nobody) immortal.

Ignavia nemo unquam immortalis 3 *facĕre*.

Prosperity is (prosperous things are) adorned, and adversity is (adverse things are) helped by learning.

Literæ res secundæ *ornari*, adversæ *adjuvari*.—Cic.

Learning adorns prosperity (prosperous things), helps adversity (adverse things).	*Literæ ornare* res secundæ, *adjuvare* adversæ.
Griefs are mitigated by time.	Dolor *mitigari vetustas.*
Time mitigates griefs.	*Vetustas mitigare* dolor.
Men are deceived by the appearance of good.	Homo *decĭpi species* bonum.
An appearance of good deceives men.	*Species* bonum *decipĕre* homo.
We are all drawn by the desire of praise.	*Trahi* omnis laus *studium.* —Cic.
The desire of praise draws us all.	Laus *studium trahĕre* ego omnis.
Good-will is got by benefits.	Benevolentia *beneficium capi.*—Cic.
Benefits get good-will.	*Beneficium capĕre* benevolentia.
Men are catched with pleasure, as fishes with a hook.	*Voluptas capi* homo, ut *hamus* piscis.—Cic.
Pleasure catches men as a hook does fishes.	*Voluptas capĕre* homo, ut *hamus* piscis.
Profit is outweighed by honesty.	Commodum *præponderari honestas.*—Cic.
Honesty outweighs profit.	*Honestas præponderare* commodum.
Fortune is formed to every man by his own manners.	Fortuna *suus* quisque *fingi mos.*—Cic.
His own manners form fortune to every man.	*Suus* quisque *mos fingĕre* fortuna.—Cor. Nep.
Every man forms fortune to himself by his own manners.	Quisque sui fortuna *fingĕre suus mos.*
The manners of men are changed by adversity (adverse things), as well as by prosperity (prosperous things).	*Mutari* mos homo *adversæ res*, perinde atque *prosperæ.* —Cic. *Am.*
Adversity (adverse things) changes the manners of men, as well as prosperity (prosperous things).	*Adversæ res mutare* mos homo, perinde atque *prosperæ.*
The good delight in (are delighted with) the conversation of the good.	Bonus bonus *familiaritas delectari.*—Cic. *Am.*
The conversation of the good delights the good.	Bonus *familiaritas delectare* bonus.

Every one is most drawn by his own delight.	Suus quisque *studium* maximè *duci.*
His own delight draws every one most.	Suus *studium* quisque *ducĕre* maximè.
Stones are made hollow by water: A ring is worn away by use.	Saxum *cavari aqua: consūmi* annulus *usus.*—Ov.
Water makes hollow stones: Use wears away a ring.	*Aqua cavare* saxum: *usus consumĕre* annulus.
The wicked are always tormented by their conscience (the consciousness of their mind).	Improbus animus *conscientia* semper *cruciari.*—Cic.
Conscience (consciousness of mind) always torments the wicked.	Animus *conscientia* semper *cruciare* improbus.
God gave reason to man, by which the appetites of the mind might be governed, (which might govern the appetites of the mind.)	Deus ratio homo 3 dare, *qui* (Gr. 641, 642) *regi* animus appetitus, (*qui* (Gr. 641, 642) *regĕre* animus appetitus).—Cic. *N. D.* 2.

English Examples to be turned into Latin.

I have indeed been provoked by thee to write (to writing, *gerund*).—Philosophers wish all things to be their own, and to be possessed by themselves.—Deiotarus, the son, was called king by the Senate.—The traveller is not always killed by the robber; but sometimes the robber [is killed] by the traveller.—Friendship was given by nature [to be] the assistant of virtues, not the companion of vices.—A public slave was sent with a sword to kill Marius (Gr. 707), who had been taken by that commander in the Cimbrian war.—(*Note.*) Alexander was carried off by disease at Babylon.—No tree can be planted, of such long duration, by the culture of a husbandman, as by the verse of a poet.—The King of the Parthians, terrified by the fame of Nero, sent his children as hostages to Cæsar.

CONSTRUCTION OF CIRCUMSTANCES.

CIRCUMSTANCES OF LIMITATION.

534.—Rule XXXIV. Respect wherein and the part affected, are expressed in the ablative. Also Nos. 535–537.

On the other part, C. Antonius, being diseased in his feet, commits the army to his lieutenant.	Ex alter pars C. Antonius, *pes æger*, legatus exercitus permittĕre.
Ennius was very eminent in respect of genius, but unskilled in art.	Ennius *ingenium maximus*, *ars rudis* esse.
The thing seems to me to be in practice excellent; in theory, ordinary.	Res ego vidēri esse, *facultas præclarus*, *ars*, *mediocris*.
I am indeed grieved in mind.	Equidem angi *animus*.
I tremble in my whole mind and in every joint (lit. all joints).	Contremiscĕre *totus mens*, et omnis artus.
[He] who is prior in respect of time is preferable in point of right.	Qui *tempus* prior, *jus* potior esse.
He is to me in age, a son; in kindnesses, a father; in affection, a brother.	Hic ego esse, *ætas*, filius; *beneficium*, pater; *amor*, frater.
538.—Æneas remained, in countenance and shoulders, like a god.	Restare Æneas, *os humerus*que Deus similis.
I am covered over as to my broad shoulders and stooping neck with the skin of a tawny lion.	*Latus humerus* subjectusque *collum* fulvus insterni pellis leo.
In all things like Mercury, both in voice, and complexion, and golden locks, and the graceful limbs of youth.	Omnis Mercurius similis, voxque, colorque, et crinis flavus, et membrum decorus juventa.
539.—As to Naucrates, whom I wished to meet, he was not in the ship.	*Naucratis*, qui convenire velle, in navis non esse.
But as to that person whom you seek, I am he.	Sed *iste* qui quærĕre, ego esse.
Except the name, Bocchus, as to other things, was ignorant of the Roman people.	Bocchus, præter nomen, *ceterus* ignarus populus Romanus.—SALL.
As to other things, keep quiet.	*Ceterus* 7 quiescĕre.
As to that, I fear that you suspect that he is somewhat angry with you.	*Iste*, vereor ne tu ille succensēre *aliquis* 7 suspicari.
540.—The man of upright life (upright in respect of life), and free from wickedness, needs not Moorish javelins.	Integer *vita scelus*que purus, non egēre Maurus jaculum.—HOR.
I am distracted in mind (as to my mind).	Discruciari *animus*.

541.—A shield of hollow brass I fix on the opposite door-posts.

Æs cavus clypeus postis adversus figĕre.—VIRG.

A statue of marble.

Statua de marmor.

English Examples to be turned into Latin.

In eloquence, Caius Gracchus has nobody his equal; he is grand in diction, wise in sentiment, and dignified in his whole style.—The wild bees are rough in their appearance, much more passionate, but excellent in labour.—Pamphilus was a Macedonian by nation.—Tullia, the wife of Tarquin, was not dissimilar in her character.—How long shall he who excels all enemies in wickedness, be without the name of an enemy?—The Lacedæmonian Agesilaus was king in name, not in power.—C. Marius, born of equestrian rank, was pure in his life, excellent in war, [but] most pernicious in peace.

THE ABLATIVE OF CAUSE, MANNER, &C.

542.—RULE XXXV. The cause, manner, means, and instrument, are put in the ablative. Also 543.

An incurable limb must be (is to be) cut off with iron.

Immedicabilis membrum *ferrum* exscindendus esse.

All things may be done with money.

Omnis *pecunia* effĭci posse.—CIC.

Men are catched by pleasure, no less than fishes with a hook.

Voluptas capi homo, non minùs quàm *hamus* piscis.

Years go on after the manner of running water.

Ire annus *mos* fluens aqua.—OV.

The year runs on full gallop (with horses put on).

Admissus labi annus *equus*.—*Id.*

You will imitate any thing with wet clay.

Argilla quidvis imitari udus.—HOR.

All agree with one mouth concerning the usefulness of friendship.

De amicitia utilitas omnis unus *os* n. consentire.—CIC. *Am.*

Injury is done two ways, either by force or fraud.

Duo *modus* fĭĕri injuria aut *vis* aut *fraus*.—CIC. *Off.* 1.

Bear patiently (with a patient mind) that which thou canst not help (alter).

Æquus *animus* (25) ferre, qui mutare (Gr. 644) nequire.

Let us always worship God with a pure, sincere, and honest mind.	Deus semper purus, integer et incorruptus *mens* venerari. Cic. *de N.* 2.
He that sincerely (in good faith) worships God, loves priests also.	Qui bonus *fides* Deus colĕre, amare et sacerdos.—Stat.
What madness is it to bring on death by wars? It is at hand, and comes privately with a silent foot.	Quis furor esse *bellum* arcessĕre mors? Imminēre, et tacitus clam venire ille *pes*. m.—Tib.
Many (much) more men have been destroyed by violence of men, than by all other calamities.	Multo plus homo homo *impĕtus* delēri quàm omnis reliquus *calamitas*. — Cic. *Off.* 2.
Covetousness of money affects many men with great inconveniences.	Multus magnus *incommodum* afficĕre pecunia cupiditas.—Cic.
By what steps, I pray, did Romulus ascend to heaven? Was it not by his actions (by things done) and virtues?	Quis tandem *gradus* Romulus 3 ascendĕre in cœlum? Nonne *res* gestus atque *virtus*?—Cic. *Par.* 1, 3.
Who would not extol the friendship of Pylades and Orestes with the greatest praises?	Quis amicitia Pylades et Orestes non maximus *laus* (31) *efferre*?—Cic. *Am.*
They live like (after the manner of) brutes, who refer all things to pleasure.	Vivĕre pecudis *ritus*, qui omnis ad voluptas referre.—Cic. *Am.*
Money lost is lamented with true tears.	Plorari *lacryma* amissus pecunia verus.—Juv.
Our religion teaches that we should love (be affected towards) our neighbours as (in the same manner in which towards) ourselves.	Religio noster præcipĕre, ut idem *modus* erga proximus affectus (31) esse, *qui* erga egomet ipse.—Cic. *Am.* 16.
Among the causes of our evils one is, that we live according to examples, and are carried away by custom.	Inter causa malum noster (una) esse, quòd vivĕre ad exemplum, et *consuetudo* abdūci.—Sen.
That which is done by precedent, men think is also done rightly.	Qui *exemplum* fiĕri, is etiam *jure* fiĕri putare homo.—Cic.
Drunkenness often pays for the jolly madness of one hour with the wearisomeness of a long time.	Ebrietas unus hora hilaris insania (xx.) longus tempus *n.* *tædium* sæpe pensare.—Sen.

The divine anger proceeds to vengeance with a slow pace, and compensates the slowness of the punishment with the greatness (heaviness) of it.

Lentus *gradus* ad vindicta divinus procedĕre ira, tardi-tasque supplicium *gravitas* compensare.—VAL. MAX. 1, 1.

Injuries are overcome by good turns much more genteelly than they are repaid with the obstinacy of mutual hatred.

Speciosiùs multo *beneficium* vinci injuria, quàm mutuus odium *pertinacia* pensari.—*Id.* 4, 2.

We are all worse by liberty.

Deterior omnis esse *licentia.*—TER.

There are some [who are] men not in reality, but in name.

Esse quidam homo, non *res*, sed *nomen.*—CIC.

The cause.

Men were born for the sake of men.

Homo homo *causa* 3 generari.—CIC. *Off.* 1.

Wrong nobody for thy own interest's sake.

Nemo violare tuus commodum *gratia.*—CIC.

Malice (ill-will) is glad at another's misfortune, and envy is troubled at another's good.

Malevolentia lætari (gaudēre) alienus *malum*, et æmulatio angi alienus *bonum.*—CIC.

The greater part of men is destroyed (perishes) by pleasures.

Voluptas homo pars major perire.—SEN.

A whole herd falls in the fields through the scab and mange of one hog.

Grex *m.* totus in ager unus *scabies* cadĕre et *porrigo* porcus.—JUV.

Do thy endeavour that nobody may (do this lest any one should) hate thee through thy own desert.

Id (25) agĕre, ne quis tuus tu *meritum* (36) odisse. —PUB.

What is more foolish, than that one should value (be pleased with) himself for that, which he himself did not do?

Quid stultior esse quàm (LVIII.) aliquis *is* sui (Gr. 405) placēre, qui ipse non 3 facĕre. —SEN.

It is inquired, through what thing Ægisthus became an adulterer: The cause is evident (is in readiness); he was idle.

Quæri, Ægisthus quis *res* (Gr. 627–5) esse factus adulter: In promptu causa esse; desidiosus 2 esse.—OV.

The manners of men are changed by adversity (adverse things), as well as prosperity (prosperous things).

Mutari mos homo adversæ *res* perinde atque prosperæ. —CIC.

It is folly to die for fear of death.

Stultitia esse *timor* mors mori.—SEN. *Ep.* 70.

It is no excuse of sin, if you should sin for the sake of a friend.

Nullus esse excusatio peccatum, si amicus *causa* (38) *peccare.*—CIC.

Some young men, either by a certain felicity, or through goodness of nature, or the management of their parents, follow a right course of life.

Nonnullus adolescens sive *felicitas* quidam, sive *bonitas* natura, sive parens *disciplina*, rectus vita via sequi.—CIC. *Off.* 1.

All men love themselves naturally (by nature).

Omnis *natura* sui ipse diligĕre.—CIC.

Virtue is neither lost by shipwreck nor by fire, nor is it changed by the alteration of seasons and times.

Virtus neque *naufragium* neque *incendium* amitti, nec tempestas, nec tempus *permutatio* mutari.—CIC. *Par.* 6.

Pythagoras thought it to be a wickedness, that body should be fattened with body, and [one] animal live by the death of another animal.

3 Credĕre esse scelus *n.* (LVIII.) pinguescĕre *corpus* corpus, alterque animans *m.* animans vivĕre *letum*, Pythagŏras.—OV.

Minds grow wanton most commonly by prosperity (prosperous things); nor is it easy to bear good fortune (advantages) with an even mind.

Luxuriare animus *res* plerumque secundæ; nec facilis esse æquus commodum *mens* pati.—OV. *Art Am. lib.* 2.

544.—He suffers either from avarice or miserable ambition.

Aut ob avaritia, aut miser ambitio laborăre.—HOR.

The grains were not ripe in the fields on account of the colds.

Propter frigus, frumentum in ager maturus non esse.—CÆS.

Care should be taken lest some should be punished, others not so much as called in question for the offences (causes).

Cavēre 701 esse, ne *idem de causa* alius plecti (Gr. 627), alius ne appellari (Gr. 627) quidem.—CIC.

545.—I did not hesitate to ask that from thee by letter.

Non dubitare is a tu per literæ petĕre.—CIC.

Is it not better to die bravely, than to lose a miserable life in a disgraceful manner?

Nonne emori per virtus præstare, quam vita miser per dedecus amittĕre.—SALL.

Those things that (which) are done with passion, can neither be done well, nor approved by those that are by (who are present).

Qui *cum perturbatio* fiĕri, is neque rectè fiĕri posse, nec ab hic, qui adesse, approbari. —CIC. *Off.* 1.

Nothing can be well done with anger.

Cum ira nihil rectè fĕri posse.—Cic. *Off.* 1.

Who would say, that it is better to do any thing basely with pleasure, than honestly with pain?

Quis (38) dicĕre, melius esse turpiter aliquid facĕre *cum voluptas*, quàm honestè *cum dolor?*—Cic. *de Fin.* 5.

English Examples to be turned into Latin.

Some are moved by grief, others by passion (cupidity).—It cannot be told how much 9 I was delighted with your yesterday's discourse.—I am not so much pleased with news as with your letters.—Our morals have been corrupted and vitiated by the admiration of wealth.—Every one is attracted most by his own pursuit.—8 I should think envy, procured by virtue, not envy, but glory.—All these things are regulated by nature.—He who fears that which cannot be avoided, can, on no account, live *with a quiet mind.*—Some amusement is allowed to youth by the consent of all.—All Italy has been inflamed with the love of liberty.—He offended no one *in word, deed,* or *look.*—The Roman people expressed [their] pleasure by a very great shouting.—We are inclined by nature to (Gr. 707) love (loving) mankind (men).—(Obs.) I cannot write the rest, by reason of my tears.—The ædiles, with the greatest fidelity and acceptableness, divided a large quantity of corn to the people.

CIRCUMSTANCES OF PLACE.

The place WHERE, *or* IN WHICH.

548.—RULE XXXVI. The name of a town denoting the place *where*, or *in which*, is put in the genitive.

549.—EXC. But if the name of the town *where*, or *in which*, is of the third declension, or plural number, it is expressed in the ablative. Gr. 548–550.

Genitive.

It is said that Milo walked (Milo is said to have walked) through the course at Olympia, carrying (while he carried) an ox on his shoulders.

Olympia per stadium ingressus esse Milo (57) dici, quum humerus (32) sustinēre bos.—Cic. *Sen.*

In that taxation which the Vespasians [being] censors made, three persons at Parma gave in 120 years; at Brixellum one 125; two 130 at Parma; one 131 at Placentia; one woman 132 at Faventia; at Bononia one, but at Ariminum three 137.

Is census qui Vespasianus censor 3 agĕre, centeni viceni annus *Parma* tres 3 edĕre; *Brixellum* unus centum viginti quinque; *Parma* duo centeni triceni; *Placentia* unus centum triginta et unus; *Faventia* unus mulier centum triginta duo; *Bononia* unus, *Ariminum* verò tres centeni triceni septeni.—PLIN. 7, 50.

Hear, O young men, the speech of Archytas the Tarentine, which was delivered to Cato when he was at Tarentum, [being] a young man: He said, that there was no mischief more pernicious given to men by nature, than the pleasure of the body.

Audire, adolescens, oratio Archytas Tarentinus, qui 3 tradi Cato, quum (32) esse adolescens *Tarentum*: Nullus capitalior pestis, quàm corpus voluptas, homo 2 dicĕre esse a natura datus.—CIC. *Sen.*

Ablative.

There was one Arganthonius at Gades, that (who) reigned eighty years.

3 Esse Arganthonius quidam *Gades*, qui octoginta annus regnare.—CIC. *Sen.*

Such an one as the learned are wont to call a wise man, we have heard of none (nobody) in [all] the rest of Greece; at Athens, but one.

Qualis eruditus solēre appellare sapiens, in reliquus Græcia nemo; *Athenæ*, unus accipĕre.—CIC. *de Am.*

So much [respect] was nowhere given to age as at Lacedæmon; old age was nowhere more honoured.

Nusquam tantum 2 tribui ætas quantum *Lacedæmon;* nusquam 2 esse senectus honoratior.—CIC. *de Senec.*

At Athens an action was allowed by law (was appointed) against ungrateful persons.

Athenæ adversus ingratus actio 3 constitui.—VAL. MAX.

The place WHITHER, *or* TO WHICH.

553.—RULE XXXVII. The name of a town denoting the place *whither*, or *to which*, is put in the accusative.

Let him sail to Anticyra. — Navigare *Anticy̆ra.*—Hor.

He went (he betook himself) to Syracuse. — *Syracusæ* se 3 conferre.

I think we must remove to Rhodes. If better fortune shall happen, we will return to Rome. — (LXI.) Migrare (esse) *Rhodus* arbitrari. Si melior casus (21) esse, reverti *Roma.*—*Id.*

Anystis the Lacedæmonian, and Philonides, the footman of Alexander the Great, ran from Sicyon to Elis, 1200 furlongs, in one day. — Anystis Lacedæmonius, et Philonides Alexander Magnus cursor, a Sicyon *Elis*, unus dies MCC stadium (XLII.) 3 currĕre.—Plin. 7, 20, 20.

555.—The Albans carry these tidings home. — Hic nunciare *domus* Albanus.

The place WHENCE, *or* FROM WHICH.

556.—Rule XXXVIII. The name of a town *whence*, or *from which*, or *by* or *through which*, is put in the ablative.

I received a packet of letters from Rome. — 3 Accipĕre *Roma* fasciculus literæ.—Cic.

I made my journey by Laodicea. — Iter *Laodicea* 3 facĕre.

An old and constant opinion had spread in all the East, that it was in the decrees of fate (in the fates), that some coming from Judea should obtain the government of the world at that time. — Percrebrescĕre totus Oriens *m.* vetus et constans opinio, esse in fatis, ut is tempus *Judæa* profectus (aliqui) res potiri. (XXVI.)—Suet. *in Vesp.* 4.

DOMUS *and* RUS.

558.—Rule XXXIX. *Domus* and *rus* are construed in the same way as names of towns.

There is always enough for one to be uneasy at (that it may be uneasy), at home and abroad. — *Domus* et foris ægrè quod sit, satis semper esse.—Plaut.

I call [the man] living in the country, thou callest [the man living] in the city, happy. — *Rus* ego vivens, tu dicĕre in urbs beatus.—Hor.

I return home sad. — *Domus* reverti mœstus.—Ter.

I will go to the country. — *Rus* ire.—Ter.

They did not stir (move themselves) from home. — *Domus* sui non 3 commovēre.—Cic.

I see the old man returning from the country. — Video *rus* rediens senex.—Ter.

559.—Tullus Hostilius thought that the bodies of the youths would be more healthy in service than at home. — Credĕre Tullus Hostilius saluber *militia* quam *domus* juvenis corpus fore.

The saying of Plato is too sublime for us, lying on the earth, to look up to it. — Plato vox altus esse quam ut is ego, *humus* stratus, suspicio posse.

562.—We came (it was approached by us) to Britain with all our ships about noon (meridian time). — Accessum (Gr. 530) esse (a nobis) *ad Britannia* omnis navis meridianus ferè (xl.) tempus.—Cæs.

While Cinna tyrannized (Cinna tyrannizing) in Italy, the greater part of the nobility fled to Sylla into Achaia, and then afterwards into Asia. — Dominans (lx. and 694) *in Italia* Cinna, major pars nobilitas ad Sylla *in Achaia*, ac deinde post *in Asia* perfugĕre.—Vell. Pat.

From Europe thou goest to Asia, from Asia thou passest into Europe. — *Ab Europa* petĕre Asia, *ex Asia* transire *in Europa*.—Q. Curt.

I wait for you [at my country-house] in Tusculum. — Ego *in Tusculanum* tu expectare.—Cic.

564.—The Lacedæmonians sent Pausanias with a fleet to Cyprus and the Hellespont. — Lacedæmonius Pausanias cum classis *Cyprus* atque *Hellespontus* mittĕre.

Memmius relates the crimes of Jugurtha at Rome, and in Numidia. — Memmius Roma *Numidia*que facinus Jugurtha memorare.

Rules XXXVI—XXXIX.

English Examples to be turned into Latin.

The expectation of letters detains me *at Thessalonica.*—It had not been doubtful to me, that I should see you *at Tarentum* or *Brundusium.*—Dionysius taught children *at Corinth.*—When you were at Athens, you were often in the schools of the philosophers.—There is a strong (great) report *at Puteoli* [that] Ptolemy is in his kingdom.—Alexander died *at Babylon.*—Æsop was sent by Crœsus to Delphi.—The consul Lævinus led his legions to

Agrigentum.—Dion besought Dionysius to send for Plato to Syracuse.—Timoleon sent for colonists from Corinth.—Cimon set out from Athens for Lacedæmon.—Manlius spent his youth in the country.—Marius died an old man in his own house (at home).—When Tullus shall have returned from the country, I will send him to thee.—He who comes from home, knows not whether he is to (may) return home.—Whose excellence had been known at home and in war.—There is neither (nothing of) gold nor silver in Britain.—What is doing in hither Gaul?—They did not go into Britain.

Circumstances of Time.

565.—Rule XL. Time *when* is put in the ablative. Also Nos. 566, 567.

Death hangs over us every hour.	Mors (Gr. 399) ego *omnis hora* impendēre.—Cic. *Sen.*
Plato died writing in his one and eightieth year.	Plato *unus* et *octogesimus annus* scribens 3 mori.—*Id.*
Let the ground rest on a holiday, let the ploughman rest.	*Lux sacer* requiescĕre humus, requiescĕre arator.—Tib.
Wicked men carry their witness in [their] breast night and day.	Homo sceleratus *nox dies*que suus gestare in pectus testis.—Juv. 13.
God pours out gifts day and night [days and nights] without intermission.	Deus munus sine intermissio *dies* et *nox* fundĕre.—Sen.
If thou shalt lavish away any thing on a holiday, thou mayest (it may be allowed to you to) want on a working day.	*Festus dies* m. si quid (21) prodigĕre, *profestus* egēre (31) licēre.—Plaut. *Aul.* 2, 7.
As swallows in summer time, so false friends are at hand in the serene time of life; as soon as they see (shall have seen) the winter of fortune, they all fly away.	Ut hirundo *æstivus tempus*, sic falsus amicus *serenus* vita *tempus* præstò esse; simul atque fortuna hyems (36) vidēre, devolare omnis.—*Ad Heren.* 4.

565.—Rule XLI. Time *how long* is put in the accusative or ablative. Also 566, 567.

1. *Accusative.*

The covetous man is tormented night and day (days and nights).

Avarus *dies nox*que cruciari.—Cic.

We ought to consider day and night (days and nights) that we must die.

Dies et *nox* cogitare (LXI.) esse, mori (LXI.) esse.—Cic. *Tusc.* 1.

Fatal accidents (fates) surround us on all sides day and night (days and nights).

Dies et *nox* fatum ego undique circumstare.—*Id.*

Demosthenes was almost 300 years before Cicero.

Demosthenes *annus* prope *trecenti* ante Cicero esse.—C.

There is nobody so old, who does not think that he may live a year.

Nemo esse tam senex, qui sui *annus* non (Gr. 641) putare posse vivĕre.—Cic. *Sen.*

No man is certain (nobody has it ascertained) that his riches shall remain to him one day.

Nemo exploratum habēre, divitiæ suus sui permansurus [esse] *unus dies.*—Cic. *Par.*

Arganthonius came to the government 40 years old (aged), reigned 80 years, and lived 120.

Arganthonius ad imperium *quadraginta annus* natus accedĕre, *octoginta* 3 regnare *annus*, et *centum* et *viginti* 3 vivĕre.

They that (they who) prayed and sacrificed whole days, that their children might outlive them, were called superstitious persons.

Qui *totus dies* 2 precari et 2 immolare, ut suus liberi (XVI.) sui superstes esse, superstitiosus 3 appellari.—Cic. *Nat. D.* 2.

2. *Ablative.*

With Pythagoras, scholars were obliged to be silent five years.

Apud Pythagoras, discipulus *quinque annus* (XLI.) tacēre esse.—Sen.

All our life we must learn to live; and all our life we must learn to die.

Totus vita vivĕre (67) discĕre esse; et *totus vita* (67) discĕre esse mori.—Sen.

It is in a manner (it is almost) certain, that Arganthonius reigned 80 years.

Arganthonius *octoginta annus* (52) regnare prope certus esse.—Plin.

569.—T. Larcius was appointed dictator, about ten years after the first consuls.

Dictator institui, decem fere *annus post* primus consul, T. Larcius.

Pythagoras first reached Italy, one hundred and forty years after the death of Numa.	*Annus* fere centesimus et quadragesimus *post* mors Numa, primus Italia Pythagoras attingĕre.
570.—The first Olympiad was established 108 years after Lycurgus undertook to enact his laws.	Centum et octo *annus postquam* Lycurgus lex scribere instituĕre primus ponĕre Olympias.
In a few days after he arrived at Caprea.	In *paucus dies quam* Capreæ attingĕre.
571.—The death of Roscius, four days after he was killed, is announced to Chrysogonus.	Mors Roscius, *quatriduum qui* is occidi, Chrysogŏnus nuntiari.
Four days after these things were done.	*Quatriduum qui* hic geri. —Cic.
572.—It was done sixteen years ago.	*Abhinc annus* fieri sedĕcim.
Carthage was destroyed 177 years ago, when it had stood 667 years.	Carthago dirui, quum stare annus sexcenti sexaginta septem, *abhinc annus* centum septuaginta septem.

Rules XL, XLI.

English Examples to be turned into Latin.

The origin of all this wickedness shall be explained *in its proper time.*—The senate was, *at the same time*, in the temple of Concord.—There are three things which, at this time, 7 may stand in the way of Roscius.—I have now been at war (I now carry on war) for *twenty years* with wicked citizens.—Panætius lived *thirty years* after he had published those books.—The covetous are tormented *night and day.*—You wrote me a letter on your birth-day.—Philotimus brought it to me the day after he had received it from you.—I call to mind, *in the evening*, whatever 9 I have said, heard, or done, every day.—*During all that time*, I was employed *night* and *day* in the study of all the sciences.—They who have been many years bound with chains, step the slower.—Who would choose to exist in that species of pleasure one whole day?

Circumstances of Measure.

573.—Rule XLII. *Measure* or *distance* is put in the accusative, and sometimes in the ablative. Also Nos. 574, 575.

1. *Accusative.*

We ought (it behoves us) not to depart a nail's breadth from a good conscience.

A rectus conscientia non oportēre *transversus unguis* m. discedēre.—Cic.

Italy is 120 miles from Sardinia (Italy is distant from Sardinia 120,000 paces); Sardinia is 200 miles from Africa (Sardinia is distant from Africa 200,000 paces).

Abesse Italia ab Sardinia *centum viginti millia* passus; Sardinia abesse ab Africa *ducenti millia* passus.—Plin.

The city of Saguntum was situated nearly a mile from the sea.

Urbs Saguntum situs esse passus *mille* ferme a mare.

Zama is distant five days' journey from Carthage.

Zama *quinque dies iter* ab Carthago abesse.

2. *Ablative.*

The island Pharus being once a day's sail distant from Egypt, is now joined to it by a bridge.

Pharus insula, quondam dies *navigatio* distans ab Ægyptus, nunc is pons junctus esse.—Plin. 5. 31.

The nation of the Menismini is distant twenty days' journey from the ocean.

Gens Menismini abesse ab oceanus, dies iter viginti.

576.—The Arabs have slender swords, each four cubits long.

Arabs gladius habēre tenuis, longus quaterni cubitum.

The men were each six feet high.

Viri altus esse seni pes.

577.—On the same day he moved forward his camp, and sat down six miles from the camp of Cæsar.

Idem dies, castra promovēre, et *mille* passus *sex* a Cæsar castra *considēre.*

578.—They pitched their camp two miles off.

A mille passus *duo* castra ponĕre.

579.—Rule XLIII. The measure of *excess* or *deficiency* is put in the ablative.

The towers on the walls of Babylon are higher by ten feet than the walls.

Turris in murus Babylon deni *pes* quam murus altus esse.

The sun is many times (parts) larger than the earth.

Sol esse *multus pars* major quam terra.

It is a custom of the Sicilians sometimes to make the month longer by a single day, or by two days.

Esse consuetudo Siculus ut nonnunquam unus *dies* longus mensis 7 facĕre aut *biduum.*

580.—Augustus bore the deaths of his family a good deal more patiently than their disgrace.

Aliquantus patienter mors quam dedecus suus ferre Augustus.

How much more widely the rule of duty extends than that of law.

Quantus latè officium patēre quam jus regula.

By so much the happier every period is, by so much the briefer is it.

1 *Tantus* brevior omnis tempus, *quantus* felicior esse.

The more difficult any thing is, the more honourable [is it].

Qui quis esse præclarior, *hic* difficilior.

Rules XLII, XLIII.

English Examples to be turned into Latin.

He ordered that he should be two hundred miles from the city.—He did not dare to tell a second time how many miles his farm was distant from the city.—It is incumbent on every one not to swerve, in his whole life, a nail's breadth (a nail across) from a good conscience.—Persia extends in length, one thousand six hundred stadia.—The plain of Marathon is ten miles distant from Athens.—Babylon has a citadel including twenty stadia in its circuit; the foundations of the towers are sunk thirty feet into the earth; walls, twenty feet wide, support the hanging gardens.—The temple of the Ephesian Diana is said to have been four hundred feet long, and two hundred broad.—The more men have, the more they desire.—Ireland is less than Britain by half.—The higher the sun, the less is the rainbow.—Thou art in no greater danger than any one of us.

Circumstances of Price.

581.—Rule XLIV. The *price* of a thing is put in the ablative.

I will not buy hope with a price.

Spes *pretium* non emĕre —Ter.

Virtue is valued at a great price every where.

Magnus ubique *pretium* virtus *æstimari.*—V. Max.

Anger and madness are [occasioned] to men by this (from hence) because they value little things at a great [rate].

Inde homo ira et insania esse, quod exiguus *magnum æstimare.*—SEN.

Nothing costs dearer than that which is bought with prayers.

Nullus res cariùs constare quàm qui *preces emi.*—SEN.

Despise pleasures: pleasure does harm (hurts) being bought with pain.

Spernĕre voluptas: nocēre *emptus dolor* voluptas.—HOR.

Bad pleasures cost a man dear (a great price).

Homo (Gr. 399) *magnum* malus gaudium *constare.*

Plato says excellently, that [those things] are too much, which men buy with life.

Egregiè Plato dicĕre, nimius esse qui homo (Gr. 656) *emĕre vita.*—SEN.

Many a place of honour is (very many an honour is) sold for gold.

Plurimus *aurum venire* honos.—Ov.

582.—Exc. But *tanti*, *quanti*, *pluris*, *minoris*, are used in the genitive.

Those things please more which are bought at a dearer rate.

Magis illud juvare, qui *plus emi.*—Juv.

To act considerately is of more [value] than to think wisely.

Consideratè agĕre *plus esse*, quàm cogitare prudenter.—Cic. *Off.* 1.

That which is necessary, is well bought, at how much soever.

Quantum quantum bene *emi*, qui necesse est.—Cic. *Att.* 12, 23.

He taught no man for less than a talent.

Docēre nemo *minus* talentum.—PLIN. 35.

Nothing shall cost a father less than his son.

Res nullus *minus constare* (Gr. 399) pater, quàm filius. —Juv.

They never (they do not ever) consider how dear their pleasures cost them.

Non unquam reputare, *quantum* (Gr. 399) sui gaudium (Gr. 627, 5) *constare.*—Juv. 6.

583.—Chrysogonus bought a vessel of Corinthian brass for so great a price, that those who heard the price reckoned, thought a farm was selling.

Chrysogŏnus vas aliquis Corinthius *tantus pretium* mercari, ut qui pretium enumeratus audire, fundus venire arbitrari.

584.—It is for the interest of the seller that the thing should sell for as much as possible.

Venditor expedire, res *venire quam plurimus.*

English Examples to be turned into Latin.

He purchased the rank of a senator *with money*.—He sold it to some one *for a large sum of money*.—I would most willingly have averted the misfortune from the state, at *my own private loss*.—They valued the Tusculan villa at *five hundred thousand sesterces*, the Formian [estate] *at two hundred and fifty thousand*.—As any one possesses what is *of most value*, so he is to be reckoned richest.—The land is now *of much more value* than it then was.—*Of what consequence* do you think this is to the character of men?—I sell my goods for *no more* than other persons, probably *for less*.

CONSTRUCTION OF ADVERBS.

585.—Rule XLV. Adverbs are joined to verbs, adjectives, and other adverbs, to modify and limit their signification. Also Nos. 586, 587.

He immediately both adopted Jugurtha, and, by his will, made him his heir equally with his sons.	*Statim*que Jugurtha *adoptāre* et testamento pariter cum filius hæres *instituĕre*.—Sall.
But why do we speak so long about one enemy?	Sed cur *tamdiu* de unus hostis *loqui*?—Cic.
I have spoken with brevity and simplicity.	*Breviter simpliciter*que *dicĕre*.—Cic.
That was done justly, moderately, wisely.	Is *juste*, *moderate*, *sapienter*, *fieri*.
Therefore wise men *never* unwillingly, brave men often even willingly, have sought for death.	Itaque mors sapiens *nunquam* invitus, fortis *sæpe etiam libenter*, *appetĕre*.
At no previous time did such consternation take possession of the senate.	*Non unquam aliàs antè* tantus terror senatus invadĕre.
586. — Julius Cæsar married Cornelia, the daughter of Cinna (who was) a fourth time consul.	Julius Cæsar, Cornelia, Cinna *quater consul* filia ducĕre uxor.
588.—Vibius is an absurd poet, but still he is not wholly ignorant nor useless.	Vibius esse poeta ineptus; *nec* tamen scire *nihil*, et esse *non inutilis*.

This thing also occasions some deformity.	Hic res etiam *non nullus* afferre deformitas.
The people are wont sometimes to neglect worthy men.	Populus solēre *non nunquam* dignus prætерīre.
Every one perceives an open flatterer.	Aperte adulans *nemo non* vidēre.
589.—Epicrates owed no money to any one.	Epicrates debēre *nullus* nummus *nemo*.
I never offended Scipio, not even in the smallest particular.	*Nunquam* Scipio, *ne* parvus *quidem* res offendĕre.
590.—In the consulship of Piso, not only was it not permitted to the senate to aid the state, but not even to mourn for it.	Piso consul (Gr. 690) senatus *non solum* juvāre res publicus sed *ne* lugēre *quidem* licet.

CASES GOVERNED BY ADVERBS.

592.—RULE XLVI. Some adverbs of *time*, *place*, and *quantity*, govern the genitive. Also Nos. 593–597.

He that does well, has abettors enough (enough of favourers).	*Sat fautor* habēre, qui recte facĕre.—PLAUT.
Never any man had friends enough (enough of friends have never been to any one of men).	Nunquam quisquam (x.) homo *satis amicus* 3 esse (xxv.)—SALL.
Every one has strength enough to do harm (enough of strength for hurting is to every one).	Nullus non ad nocēre *satis vires* esse (Gr. 394).—SEN.
I must remove to some part of the world (to somewhere of lands).	(67) Migrare esse *aliquo terra*.—CIC.
Nothing is more amiable than virtue; which he who shall have gotten, will be beloved by good men in what nation soever (wheresoever of nations) he shall be.	Nihil esse amabilior virtus; qui qui (21) adipisci, *ubicunque gens* esse, a bonus vir diligi.—CIC. *de Nat. D.*

600.—RULE XLVII. Some derivative adverbs govern the case of their primitives. Also 601.

I hear that Cæsar speaks Latin the most elegantly almost of all orators.	Audire Cæsar omnis fer *orator* Latinè loqui (x.) *elegantissimè*.—CIC. *Cl. O.*

I do not ask what he says, but what he can say agreeably to reason and his own opinion.

Non quærĕre quid (Gr 627–5) dicĕre, sed quid *convenienter* (XVI.) *ratio* (Gr. 627–5) posse et *sententia* suus dicĕre.—Cic. *Fin.*

Nothing dries sooner than a tear.

Lacryma nihil (XXIV.) *citiùs* arescĕre.—*Id. Inv.*

Rules XLVI, XLVII.

English Examples to be turned into Latin.

XLVI.—*In what part* (*Where*) *of the world* are we?—O ye immortal gods! *Of what nation are we?*—In what city do we live?—What government have we?—Good men have no one to take the lead (no leader); our avengers of liberty are *far off*.—Ægypta came to me *the day before the ides of* April.—Philotimus came the day before that day.—I have less strength than either of you.—You have not as yet sufficient strength.—There is protection sufficient in virtue to live (living) well.—XLVII. We sent to Athens *to meet him*.—Though they went (were) out of the way they went down *to meet him*.—Cæsar fortified a camp *as near as possible to the camp* of the enemy.—The quæstors of the province were *in attendance upon me*.—It can be *well with no wicked man*.—Which of us two offends *in a manner more worthy of torture?*—Little gowns were ready for the lictors at the gate.

Cases governed by Prepositions.

602.—Rule XLVIII. Twenty-eight prepositions, *ad*, *apud*, *ante*, &c. (235–1), govern the accusative.

603.—Rule XLIX. Fifteen prepositions, *a*, *ab*, *abs*, &c., govern the ablative.

607.—Rule L. The prepositions *in*, *sub*, *super*, and *subter*, denoting *motion to*, or *tendency towards*, govern the accusative.

608.—Rule LI. The prepositions *in* and *sub*, denoting *situation*, govern the ablative; *super* and *subter*, either the accusative or ablative.

N. B.—Examples of these four rules are to be found in very many of the preceding exercises. The pupil of course must be so familiar with them already, as to render special examples un necessary.

The following are examples in which the preposition is understood. Gr. 611.

A master is in the place of a parent.	Præceptor esse parens *locus.*
One thing is produced in one place, and another in another (another thing is produced in another place).	Alius *alius locus* nasci.—VITRUV.
Nobody tries to descend into himself; but the wallet on the back that goes before them is looked on.	In sui sui tentare descendĕre nemo: at *præcedens* spectari mantica *tergum.*—PERS. 4.
Look back upon those things that hang (things hanging) on thy own back.	*Tuus* pendens respicĕre *tergum.*—*Vide* HOR. *Sat.* 2, 3, 299.
	Sub.
Vice deceives us in the shape of virtue.	Fallĕre ego vitium *species* virtus.—JUV.
	Ex.
Man consists of soul and body.	Homo constare *corpus* et *anima.*—CIC. *Tusc.*
Time consists of three parts, the past, present, and future.	Tempus tres *pars* constare, *præteritum*, *præsens*, et *futurum.*—SEN.
	Ab.
God does not account it [a thing] inconsistent with his majesty to take care of the world and the affairs of men.	Deus non alienus ducĕre *majestas suus*, mundus et res homo curare.—CIC. *de Divin.*
Leave off to debar philosophers from money.	Desinĕre (Gr. 399) philosophus *pecunia* interdicĕre.
Fathers that manage their estate badly use to be debarred from meddling with their goods. (It uses to be debarred from their goods to fathers managing their estate badly.)	Pater malè res gerens (Gr. 399) *bonum* interdīci (Gr. 411) solēre.—CIC. *Sen.*
Fool, dost thou think any other happy besides the wise and good man?	Stultus, putare alius *sapiens bonus*que beatus?—*Vide* HOR. *Ep.* 1, 16.

In is frequently understood before words signifying *place;* as, *terrâ*, *mari*, *domo*, *cœlo*, *campis*, *libro*, &c.

613.—Rule LII. A preposition in composition often governs its own case. Also 614.

Abstain from things forbidden. — *Prohibĭtus* ABS*tinēre.* Sen.

Pythagoras is said to have abstained from all animals. — Pythagoras cunctus *animal* ABS*tinēre* dici.—Juv.

An honest man refrains from injustice, even when impunity is (impunity being) proposed. — Vir probus, etiam impunitas, (LX.) propositus, ABS*tinēre injuria.*

Friendship is excluded out of no place. — Amicitia nullus *locus* EX*cludi.*—Cic. *Am.*

Thou canst exclude death (the fates) out of no place. — Nullus fatum *locus* (31) posse EX*cludĕre.*—Mart.

Let him go out of the court, who shall desire to be pious. — *EXire aula* qui velle esse pius.—Lucan.

Others' disgraces often deter tender minds from vices. — Tener animus alienus opprobrium sæpe ABS*terrēre vitium.*—Hor.

Hercules chose to enter into the way of virtue, rather than that of pleasure. — Præoptare Hercules *via* virtus, quàm voluptas IN*grĕdi.*

Many inconveniences surround the old man; the wretch often gets, and abstains from the things [he has] gotten, and is afraid to use them. — Multus *senex circumvenire* incommŏdum: sæpe quærēre et *inventus* miser *abstinēre*, et timēre uti.—Hor.

An heir comes upon the heir of another, as wave upon wave. — Hæres *hæres* alter, velut unda *supervenire* unda.—*Id.*

A house and land, a heap of brass (money), and gold, will not take off fevers from the sick body, nor cares from the mind of the owner. — Non domus et fundus, non æs acervus et aurum, ægrotus dominus *deducĕre corpus* febris, non *animus* cura.—*Id.*

615.—The soul exists after it has quitted the body. — Animus manēre *e corpus* cum *excedĕre.*

He will never keep his sacrilegious hands from me. — Nunquam *a ego* sacrilegus manus *abstinēre.*

The Lacedæmonians desisted from their long contention. — Lacedæmonius *de* diutinus *contentio desistĕre.*

The law orders us to approach the gods devoutly. — Lex jubēre *adire ad deus* castè.

English Examples to be turned into Latin.

The wisest philosophers have properly looked for the origin of the chief good *in* (from) *nature.*—*From* particular *virtues* certain kinds of duty arise.—Where then is virtue, if nothing is implanted *in ourselves?*—We are ready to refute *without obstinacy*, and to be refuted *without anger.*—He threw the rest of the body *into the sea.*—She married *into* a very distinguished *family.* —7 Let us quit *the theatre*, 7 let us go (come) *into the forum.*— The Porcian law *has removed* the rods *from the body* of all Roman citizens.—Men can scarcely *keep their hands from you.*

SYNTAX OF THE VERB.

CONNECTION OF TENSES. 618.

619.—Rule LIII. Any tense of the subjunctive mood, may follow a tense of the *same class* in the indicative. Also 620.

I. *Primary tenses with their sequents of the same class.* (Gr.618.)

1. *Present.*—In the epistles of Cicero to Atticus, every thing relating to the changes of the republic is so described, that there is nothing which does not appear in them.

In Cicero ad Atticus epistola sic omnis de mutatio respublica *perscribi*, ut nihil in is non *apparēre.*

There is not a province, I think, which Augustus did not visit.

Non *esse* provincia ut opinor qui Augustus non *adire.*

So great is the corruption of bad habit, that the sparks of virtue are extinguished by it.

Tantus *esse* corruptela malus consuetudo, ut ab is tanquam igniculus virtus *extingui.*

2. *Perfect Definite.*—Nature has lavished so great an abundance of things, that those which are produced appear to have been bestowed upon us intentionally, not to have originated accidentally.

Tantus res ubertas natura *largiri* ut is qui gigni donāri consulto ego, non fortuito nasci *vidēri.*

I have attained this by my exploits, that I am thought a safe debtor.

Ego res meus gestus hic *assequi* ut bonus nomen *existimari.*

Few have been found who have exposed their lives to the weapons of the enemy with no reward in view.

Paucus *repĕri* qui nullus præmium propositus (Gr. 690) vita suus hostis telum *objicĕre.*

3. *Future.*—I shall find many whom I can easily persuade of whatever I wish.

Reperire multus qui quisquis velle, facile *persuadēre.*

They could not destroy all witnesses (even) if they wished, for as long as the human race shall exist there will not be wanting some one to accuse them.

Testis omnis si cupĕre interficĕre non posse; nam dum homo genus *esse* qui *accusare* is, non deesse.

I will try to escape hence.

Experiri ut hinc *avolāre.*

If the conversation of Curio shall produce any thing of such a kind that it requires to be written to you, I will subjoin it to my letter.

Si quis Curio sermo ejusmŏdi *afferre*, qui ad tu (Gr. 687) *scribi* is literæ meus adjungĕre.

II.—*Secondary tenses, with their sequents of the same class.* (Gr. 618.)

1. *Imperfect.*—On the other side of the Rhine, Tiberius observed such a mode of life, that he took his food sitting on the bare turf, and often passed the night without a tent.

Trans Rhenus, Tiberius ita vita *instituĕre*, ut sedēre in cespes nudus cibus *sumĕre*, et sæpe sine tentorium *pernoctare.*

I did not suppose that when a consul elect was defended by the son of a Roman knight, his accusers would speak of the newness of his family.

Non *arbitrare*, quum consul designatus ab eques Romanus filius *defendi*, de genus novitas accusator dicĕre.

Other dissensions were of such a kind, that they tended, not to the destruction, but to the change of the state.

Alius dissensio *esse* ejusmŏdi, qui non ad delēre (Gr. 707) sed ad commutare respublica *pertinēre.*

2. *Perfect Indefinite.*—Some fathers of families provided by their will, that victims should be led to the Capitol, and vows discharged for them, because they had left Augustus alive.

Nonnullus pater-familias testamentum cavēre, ut victima in Capitolium *duci*, votumque pro sui *solvi*, quod superstes Augustus *relinquĕre.*

Hannibal promised the Gauls that he would not draw his sword till he came into Italy.

Promittĕre Hannibal Gallus, sui non stringĕre (Gr. 671) ante gladius quam in Italia *venire*.

The State was so arranged by the skill of Servius Tullius, that all the distinctions of patrimony, dignity, age, trades, and offices, were registered.

Servius Tullius sollertia ita *ordinăre* respublica ut omnis patrimonium, dignitas, ætas, ars, officiumque, discrimen in tabula *referri*.

3. *Pluperfect.*—I had heard from himself how generously he had been treated by you.

Ego ex ipse *audire* quam a tu liberaliter *tractări*.

Neither by letter, nor by decree of the senate, had the consuls commanded me what I should do.

Consul neque senatus consultum neque literæ *præcipĕre* ego quis *facĕre*.

The soldiers of Alexander had cut down a great deal of wood, that they might make a passage through the rocks.

Multus materies *cædĕre* Alexander miles, ut aditus per saxum *facĕre*.

621.—They celebrate the spectacle with as much splendour as they could, that they might make the affair brilliant and expected.

Spectaculum 1 *concelebrăre* quantus adparatus, 2 posse ut res clarus exspectatusque *facĕre*.

622.—No one ought to doubt that Cæsar, if it could be done, would call up many from the dead.

Nemo dubitare 1 *debēre* quin multus, si fieri *posse*, Cæsar ab inferi *excitare*.

The shouts were so great, that I think they were heard to that place.

Clamor tantus 3 *esse* ut is usque exaudītus 7 *putăre*.

623.—*Infinitive.* Socrates was accustomed to say that all men were sufficiently eloquent in that which they understood.

Socrates *dicĕre solēre* omnis in is qui *scire* satis esse eloquens.

Tiberius replied to the people of Ilium, that he also grieved for their misfortune, in having lost (because they had lost) their illustrious citizen Hector.

Iliensis populus respondēre Tiberius, sui (Gr. 671) quoque vicis is *dolēre* quod egregius civis Hector *amittĕre*.

They say that Pyrrhus, the greatest master of gymnastic exercises, used to give as a precept to those whom he was training, that they should not be angry.

Pyrrhus, magnus præceptor certamen gymnicus, *solēre* aio hic qui exercēre *præcipĕre*, ne *irasci*.

In the meantime I shall delight myself with the muses; and it will never occur to me (come into my mind) to envy Crassus or to regret that I have not departed from my own course of conduct.

Interea cum musa ego (pl.) delectāre; nec ego (Gr. 380) unquam *venire* in mens Crassus invidēre, neque pœnitēre quòd a ego ipse non *descīscĕre.*

Participles.—Parmenio reached Damascus on the fourth day, the prefect already fearing that no trust had been reposed in him.

Parmenio Damascus quartus dies *pervenire* jam *metuens* præfectus ne sui fides non *habēre.*

When I doubt what is right for me to do, my affection for Pompey has great weight.

Dubitans ego quis ego facĕre par *esse*, magnus pondus afferre benevolentia erga Pompeius.

English Examples to be turned into Latin.

There are some who *have related*, that Marius fell engaging with Telesinus.—Silius *has done* well *in having come* to terms.—Sisygambis said, "O king, you *deserve* that we *should pray* for those things for you which we prayed for formerly for our Darius; and, as I perceive, you *are* worthy of *having surpassed* (Gr. 645) so great a king, not in good fortune only, but in equity." —I think that Cæsar will *take care to withdraw* his troops; for he will gain a victory if he is made consul.—This affair made it very difficult for Cæsar to determine what plan to adopt (brought great difficulty to Cæsar for (*ad*) taking a plan) lest *if he led* his troops rather early (Gr. 473, 2d par.) from their winter quarters, he *should be in straits* (he should labour) for provisions.—Augustus *brought up* his daughter and grand-daughters in such a way, that he even *accustomed* [them] to spinning, and *forbade* [them] to say or do any thing, but what *might be inserted* in the daily register.—*I see* you *are collecting* every thing respecting the republic, which you *think* can give me any hope of a change of affairs (changing affairs).—I *wrote back* immediately to Pompey, that I *was* not *seeking* where I *might be* most safely.

INDICATIVE MOOD.

The indicative mood is used in Latin, to express what is actual and certain, in an absolute and independent manner (Gr. 624).

1. Thebes was now standing.—Romulus founded Rome.

Jam stare Thebæ.—Romulus Roma condĕre.

The liberty of the Roman people is at stake.
Libertas agi populus Romanus.

Our reasoning agrees; our language differs.
Ratio noster consentire oratio pugnare.

What are you doing?
Quis agĕre?

Did you dare to speak against me before the conscript fathers?
Tu apud pater conscriptus contra ego dicĕre *audēre?*

Ancus reigned twenty-four years.
3 Regnare Ancus annus quatuor et viginti.

Cæsar levied two legions; he led forth three from winter quarters; he divided his army into two parts.
Cæsar duo legio conscribĕre; tres ex hiberna educĕre; exercitus in duo pars dividĕre.

We will write letters to-morrow.
Cras literæ scribĕre.

2. In requiting a favour we ought, if we believe Hesiod, to imitate fertile fields which give much more than they have received.
In referre gratia (Gr. 707) si modo Hesiodus *credĕre* debēre imitari ager fertilis qui plus multus affĕrre quam accipĕre.

If you are poor, Æmilianus, you will always continue poor.
Semper esse pauper, si pauper *esse*, Æmilianus.

If these things are not given up, he thus declares war.
Si non *dedi* hic, bellum ita indicĕre.

If thou art a god, said the Scythian ambassadors to Alexander, thou oughtest to bestow benefits on mortals, not to take away theirs.
Si deus *esse*, legatus Scythicus Alexander dicĕre, tribuĕre mortālis beneficium debēre, non suus eripĕre.

3. I will satisfy you if I can.
Ego, si *posse*, facĕre tu satis.

Volumnia ought to have been more attentive to you, and even that which she did she might have done more carefully.
Volumnia *debēre* in tu officiosus esse, et is ipse qui facĕre, *posse* diligens facĕre.

You ought long since to have been led to execution by the command of the consul.
Ad mors tu duci, jussus consul, jampridem *oportēre.*

The army might have been destroyed if any one had dared to conquer.
Delēri *posse* exercitus si quis audēre vincĕre.

4. If men apply reason to fraud and malice, it would have been better that it had not been given than given to the human race.
Si homo ratio in fraus malitiaque convertĕre, non dari ille quam dari humanus genus *bonus esse.*

When it would have become them to stand in the line of battle and fight, then they took refuge in the camp.

Quum in acies stare ac pugnare *decĕre*, tum in castra refugĕre.

5. The Sublician bridge had almost afforded a path to the enemy, if there had not been one man, Horatius Cocles, of distinguished valour.

Pons Sublicius iter pene hostis *dare*, ni unus vir *esse* Horatius Cocles eximius virtus.

The populace would have torn down the effigies of Piso, had they not been protected by the order of the prince.

Populus effigies Piso 2 *devellĕre*, ni jussus princeps protegi.

SUBJUNCTIVE MOOD.

The subjunctive mood is used sometimes in independent, but for the most part in dependent propositions.

THE SUBJUNCTIVE IN INDEPENDENT PROPOSITIONS.

The subjunctive mood is used, apparently at least, in independent propositions (Gr. 625).

1st. I can relate, I think, on sufficient evidence, that Augustus was surnamed Thursinus.

Thursinus cognominatus esse Augustus satis certus probatio *tradĕre.*

Brother, with thy good leave I would say it, this is a sentiment most pernicious to the republic.

Frater, bonus tuus venia *dicĕre* (*perf.*) iste sententia maxime obesse respublica.

I am inclined to accede readily to those who relate that Romulus founded Rome.

Libenter hic qui ita prodĕre *accedĕre* (*perf.*) Romulus Roma condĕre.

Thou canst scarcely [I think] find a man of any nation, age, or rank, whose felicity thou mayest compare to the fortune of Metellus.

Vix ullus gens, ætas, ordo, homo *invenīre* (*perf.*) qui felicitas fortuna Metellus comparāre.

I would not deny that my language appeared to you harsh and atrocious.

Non *negare* (*perf.*) tristis atroxque tu visus oratio meus esse.

Thou knowest not, [I think,] whether anger be a more detestable or unsightly vice.

Nescīre (*pres.*) utrum magis detestabilis vitium esse ira, an deformis.

I would wish thee to be persuaded (that I may persuade thee) that I ask nothing from thee with more earnestness.

Velle 3 tu persuadēre nihil ego magnus studium a tu petĕre.

I wish [for my part] that you would consider with Pomponius whether you can honourably remain at Rome at present.

Velle tu cum Pomponius considerare utrum honestè tu Roma esse posse.

Assuredly I should not a little prefer the mind of Socrates to the fortunes of all those who sat in judgment upon him.

Næ ego haud paulum Socrates animus *malle* quam is omnis fortuna qui de is judicare.

2d. (Gr. 145) So live with an inferior, as thou wouldst wish a superior to live with thee.

Sic cum inferior *vivĕre*, quemadmodum tucum superior velle vivĕre.

Do not allow it to happen, that thou shouldst seem to have been wanting to thyself.

Ne 7 *committĕre* ut tu deesse vidēri.

Let every one become acquainted with his own disposition, and show himself a severe judge both of his own good qualities and faults.

Suus quisque *noscĕre* ingenium, acerque sui et bonum et vitium suus judex *præbēre*.

If I have defended my own safety against your brother's most cruel attack upon me, be satisfied that I do not complain to you too of his injustice.

Si meus salus contra frater tuus impetus in ego crudēlis defendĕre, satis *habēre* nihil ego etiam tucum de is injuria conquĕri.

Let the Stoics look to it whether it be an evil to be in pain.

Esse ne malum dolēre necne, Stoici *vidēre*.

You will say, write nothing at all.

"Nihil," inquam "omnino *scribĕre*."

3d. What wise man will trust to a fragile good?

Quis sapiens bonum *confidĕre* fragilis?

Who will deny that all wicked men are slaves?

Quis *negare* omnis improbus esse servus?

Who can doubt that there are riches in virtue?

Quis *dubitare*, quin in virtus divitiæ esse?

Who hereafter will adore the divinity of Juno?

Quis posthac numen Juno *adorāre*?

What can seem great to him in human affairs, to whom an eternity, and the magnitude of the universe, is known?

Quis *vidēri* is magnus in res humanus, qui æternitas totusque mundus notus esse magnitudo?

Why should I enumerate the multitude of arts, without which life could not have at all existed?	Quid *enumerare* ars multitudo, sine qui vita omnino nullus esse posse?
4th. They report that Alexander said, "If I were not Alexander, I would willingly be Diogenes."	Alexander dicĕre ferre, "Nisi Alexander *esse*, *esse* libenter Diogenes."
These things I could not endure, if I had not my friend Atticus as a partner of my pursuits.	Hic quidem non *ferre* nisi *habēre* socius studium meus Atticus noster.
These things seem ridiculous to you, because you were not present, which, if you were to see, you could not help weeping.	Hic tu ridiculus vidēri, quia non adesse, qui si *vidēre* lacryma non *tenēre*.
If any one were to dig around these plane trees and water them, their branches would not be knotty, and their trunks unsightly.	Si quis hic platănus circumfodĕre, si *irrigare*, non nodosus *esse* ramus et squalidus truncus.
If the gods were to make philosophy a vulgar good, if we were born wise, wisdom would lose what is the best part of it; it would be among accidental things.	Si deus philosophia bonum vulgaris *facĕre*, si prudens *nasci*, sapientia, qui in sui bonus habēre *perdĕre;* inter fortuitus *esse*.

English Examples to be turned into Latin.

Grant indeed that these *are* (Let those be) good things which are so esteemed.—Let these things be so.—I rather think that wild beasts which have (to which are) their food from prey (things taken), are better the more furious they are; but (I confess) I admire the patience of oxen and horses.—The third mode of mining outdoes, in my opinion, the works of the giants.—Who will not with reason wonder that the plane tree has been brought from another hemisphere, only for the sake of its shade?—Buy what is necessary.—Let us remember that justice is to be observed even towards the lowest.—Even in causes in which we have to do (all things are to us) only with the judges, and not with the people, yet, if I were deserted by the audience, I should not be able to speak.—If wisdom were given me with this limitation, that I should keep it shut up, and not give it utterance, I would reject it.—Finally, I *will* so *conduct* myself in the state, as to *remember* always what I have done, and *to provide* that they shall appear to have been accomplished by virtue, and not by accident.

Subjunctive Mood in Dependent Propositions.

The subjunctive mood is used for the most part in dependent clauses, and is preceded by another verb in the indicative, imperative, or infinitive mood, expressed or understood, with which it is connected by a conjunction, a relative, or an indefinite term, and may generally be rendered by the potential in English (142–2d, and 143).

Subjunctive after Conjunctions.

627.—Rule LIV. The conjunctions *ut*, *quo*, *licet*, *ne*, *utinam*, and *dummŏdo*, &c., and words used indefinitely in dependent clauses, for the most part require the subjunctive mood.

1. *Ut*, *quo*, "that," *ne*, *quomĭnus*, "that not," referring to the *result*, *end*, or *design*, take the subjunctive.

It happens to a wise man alone that he does nothing against his own will.	Solus contingĕre sapiens *ut* nihil *facĕre* invitus.
We eat that we may live, not live in order that we may eat.	Edĕre *ut vivĕre*, non vivĕre *ut edĕre*.
Your generals triumphed in such a way that he, though driven back and conquered, still reigned.	Vester imperator ita triumphare, *ut* ille pulsus superatusque *regnare*.
Hannibal so united his troops by a sort of bond, that no mutiny [ever] existed either among themselves or against their general.	Hannibal vinculum quidam ita copia copulāre, *ut* nullus nec inter ipse, nec adversus dux, seditio *extāre*.
The harangues of Thucydides contain so many obscure and involved sentences, that they can scarcely be understood.	Thucydides concio ita multus habēre obscurus abditusque sententia, vix *ut intelligi*.
It behoves a law to be brief, in order that it may be the more easily retained by the ignorant.	Lex brevis esse oportēre *quo* facilius ab imperītus *tenēri*.
The throng (numerous attendance) of men and women at funerals was abolished, that lamentation might be diminished.	Tolli celebritas vir ac mulier in funus, *quo* lamentatio *minui*.
It may happen that a man may think justly, and not be able to express tersely what he thinks.	Fieri posse *ut* recte quis *sentire*, et is qui sentire (30) polite eloqui non *posse*.

It happens to most men, that through the assistance of the art of writing (letters), they relax their diligence in committing to memory. — Plerique accidĕre, *ut* præsidium literæ, diligentia in perdiscendum *remittĕre.*

Take care that thou fall not *anew into sickness.* — Curare *ne* denuo in morbus *incidĕre.*

Death will not deter a wise man from (Gr. 172–3) considering the interests of the republic and his own. — Non deterrēre sapiens mors *quominus* commodum respublica, suusque *consulĕre.*

Parmenio wished to deter the king from drinking (that he might not drink) the potion which the physician had determined to give. — Parmenio deterrēre rex velle, *quominus* medicamentum *bibĕre*, qui medicus dăre constituĕre.

So great is the force of probity that we love it even in an enemy. — Tantus vis probitas esse, *ut* is in hostis etiam *diligĕre.*

English Examples to be turned into Latin.

We read *that* we *may learn.*—It is a custom of mankind *that* they *are unwilling* that the same person should excel in many things.—Oratory moves the minds of judges, and impels them, *so that* they either *hate*, or *love*, or *envy*, or *wish* (the culprit) safe, or *pity*, or *wish* to punish.—It happens, somehow or other, *that* if any fault is committed, we *perceive* it more readily in others than in ourselves.—It very often happens, *that* utility *is at variance* (contends) with virtue.—Trees are covered with a rind or bark, in order *that* they *may be* safer from the cold and from the heat.—It was no obstacle to Isocrates (*from*) *being esteemed* (Gr. 172–3) an excellent orator, that he was prevented from speaking in public by the feebleness of his voice.—It happened *that* in one night all the Mercuries which were in the town of Athens *were thrown down.*

627.—2. *Si*, "if," *ut si*, *quasi*, *ac si*, *æque ac si*, *perinde ut si*, *aliter ac si*, *velut si*, *tanquam*, *ceu*, "as if," expressing a *condition* or *supposition*, commonly take the subjunctive mood.

Live so as if God saw thee. — Sic vivĕre, *tanquam* Deus *vidēre.*—SEN. *Ep.* 10.

As if there was but a little difference (as if it differed but a little). — *Quasi* verò paulum *interesse.*—TER. *Eun.* 4. 4.

We ought to live so, as if we lived in view; to think so, as if somebody could see into the bottom of our breast (our inmost breast). And there is one that can (some one can).

Sic vivĕre (XLVI.) esse, *tanquam* in conspectus *vivĕre;* sic cogĭtare, (LXI.) *tanquam* aliquis in pectus intimus inspicĕre *posse.* Et posse aliquis.—SEN. *Ep.* 83.

As though I had discovered whatever I knew.

Tanquam prodĕre quicquid scire.—JUV. *Sat.* 9.

As if I did not know.

Ceu vero *nescire.*—PLIN.

If thy neighbour have a garment of more value than thou hast, wouldst thou rather have thine own, or his?

Si vicinus tuus vestis pretium major *habēre* quam tu, habēre tuusne an ille malle?

The Stoics give us trifling arguments why pain is not an evil; as if the difficulty were about the word, and not the thing.

Concludĕre ratiuncula Stoici cur dolor non esse malum; *quasi* de verbum, non de res *laborare.*

As if their own affair or honour were at issue.

Quasi suus res aut honos *agi.*

Fabius mentions the capture of M. Atilius in Africa, as if Atilius miscarried at his first landing in Africa.

Fabius M. Atilius captus (Gr. 684) in Africa commemorare, *tanquam* M. Atelius primus accessus ad Africa *offendĕre.*

As if I did not know, that even a woman wrote against Theophrastus.

Ceu vero *nescire*, adversus Theophrastus scribĕre etiam femina.

Some think that God does not exist, because he does not appear nor is perceived; just as if we could see our own mind itself.

Quidam idcirco Deus esse non putare, quia non apparēre nec cerni: proinde *quasi* noster ipse mens vidēre *posse.*

The Pythagoreans abstained from the bean, as if, forsooth, the mind were puffed up by that food.

Faba Pythagoreus abstinēre, *quasi* vero is cibus mens *inflare.*

3. *Ut*, *licet*, *etiamsi*, *quamvis*, "although;" *quin* for *qui non*, or *ut non* or *quominus*, take the subjunctive.

Though truth should obtain no patron or defender, yet she is defended by herself.

Veritas *licet* nullus patronus aut defensor *obtinēre*, tamen per sui ipse defendi.

A dwarf is not great, though he stand on a mountain.

Non esse magnus pumilio, *licet* in mons *consistĕre.*

Although ambition be itself a vice, yet it is frequently the cause of virtues.

Licet ipse vitium *esse* ambitio, frequenter tamen causa virtus esse.

I deny that there was any jewel or pearl which Verres did not search for, examine, [and] carry off.

Negare ullus gemma aut margarīta esse, *quin* Verres *conquirĕre*, *inspicere*, *auferre*.

There is no doubt that he who is called liberal and kind, aims at the discharge of duty, not at profit.

Non esse dubius *quin* is qui liberalis benignusve dici, officium non fructus *sequi*.

There is no one who does not wish to be any where, rather than where he is.

Nemo esse *quin* ubivis, quam ubi esse *malle*.

Caligula was very near (not far from) removing the writings and statues of Livy and Virgil from all the libraries.

Livius ac Virgilius imago et scriptum paulum abesse *quin* Caligula ex omnis bibliotheca *amovēre*.

Hortensius did not hesitate to defend P. Sulla.

Hortensius non dubitare *quin* P. Sulla *defendĕre*.

There is scarcely a day that this Satrius does not resort to my house.

Dies fere nullus esse *quin* hic Satrius domus meus *ventitāre*.

English Examples, under Nos. 2, 3, *to be turned into Latin.*

The Roman prodigies, Horatius, Mucius, Clœlia, *if* they *were* not in the annals, would seem at this day fables.—He who sees these things from a distance, *even though* he *do* not *know* what is going on, knows however that Roscius is upon the stage.—If thou wert here thou wouldst think otherwise.—The day would fail if I should enumerate to what good [men] it has happened ill; to what bad [men] it has happened very well.—Here indeed we behold a great battle, as if other battles were nowhere, as if none were dying in all the city [besides].—Life is short, even if it should extend beyond a thousand years.—I would wish you to undertake this business, just as if it were an affair of mine.—The Sequani stood in awe of the cruelty of Ariovistus [when] absent as much (just) as if he were present before them.

4. *Antequam*, *priusquam*, "before;" *dum*, *donec*, *quoad*, "until;" *modo*, *dum*, *dummŏdo*, "provided;" and the particles of wishing, *utinam*, *O si*, *ut* or *uti*, for *utinam*, commonly take the subjunctive.

In all kinds of business, diligent preparation must be made before you set about it.

In omnis negotium *priusquam aggrĕdi* adhibēre præparatio diligens.

Come hither as soon as possible, before all the troops of the enemy collect.

Huc quam primum venire antequam omnis copia adversarius convenire.

I will return before the moon has twice filled her orb.

Ante reverti *quam* luna bis *implēre* orbis.

Fabius sends the cavalry before, so prepared, that they might engage and delay the whole army till he himself should come up.

Fabius eques præmittĕre sic paratus ut configĕre atque omnis agmen morari, *dum consĕqui* ipse.

If they have not yet gone, there is no reason why they should move till we see how affairs stand.

Si nondum proficisci, nihil esse quod sui movēre, *quoad perspicĕre* qui locus 7 esse res.

The Rhine retains its name and the force of its current where it flows by Germany, until it mingles with the ocean.

Rhenus servare nomen et violentia cursus, qua Germania prævĕhi, *donec* oceanus *miscēre.*

Thou wilt deliver me from great fear, provided there be a wall between me and thee.

Magnus ego metus liberare, *dummodo* inter ego atque tu murus *interesse.*

Nor did Catiline have any concern, provided he could obtain for himself supreme power, by what means he obtained it.

Neque Catilina qui modus assĕqui, *dum* sui regnum *parare*, quisquam pensum habēre.

I wish he could in some way, however false, repel this accusation.

Utinam posse aliquis ratio hic crimen defendĕre, quamvis falsus.

The language of Varro gives me hope of Cæsar, and I wish Varro himself would apply to the cause.

Varro sermo facĕre expectatio Cæsar, atque *utinam* ipse Varro *incumbĕre* in causa.

O that some portion of ancient valour would appear.

O, si solitus quisquam virtus *adesse.*

Would that all the gods and goddesses would destroy thee.

Ut tu omnis deus deaque *perdĕre.*

English Examples to be turned into Latin.

He was unwilling to leave the place till he (Milo) came up.—He was even desirous to be put to torture himself, provided only an investigation took place about his father's death.—I desire while beautiful to become the food of tigers, before unsightly leanness takes possession of my comely cheeks, and the moisture of the tender prey escapes.—Calpurnius Flamma with a chosen band of three hundred [men] occupied the hill on which the enemy were posted (lit. kept possession of (*insessum*) by the enemy) and thus delayed them till the whole army escaped.—O that Paris had then been overwhelmed in the raging waters, when with his fleet he was directing his course (steering) to Lacedæmon.

5. Interrogative words used indefinitely in dependent clauses, or containing an indirect question, take the subjunctive. (Gr. 627–5.)

The Athenians sent to Delphi to inquire what they should do.	Atheniensis mittĕre Delphi consulĕre *quisnam facĕre.*
Pyrrhus asked his ambassadors what they thought concerning the abode of their enemies.	Pyrrhus legatus interrogare, *quis* de hostis sedes *sentire.*
The brothers Lydus and Tyrrhenus being compelled by famine, are said to have cast lots which of the two should quit the country with a part of the population.	Lydus et Tyrrhēnus frater, fames compulsus, sortiri dici, *uter*, cum pars multitudo, patria *discedĕre.*
It is uncertain whether it would have been more beneficial to the State, that Cæsar should be born, or not be born.	In incertum esse *utrum* Cæsar magis nasci respublica *prodesse* annon nasci.
It is asked why the most learned men disagree on the most important subjects.	Quæri, *cur* doctus homo de magnus res *dissentire.*
Who I am you will find out from him whom I have sent to you.	*Quis esse* ex is qui ad tu mittĕre cognoscĕre.—SALL.
See that you think in how great a calamity you are. Consider what your circumstances demand.	Facĕre 7 cogitare (Gr. 657–3) in *quantus* calamitas *esse.* 7 Considerare *quis* tuus ratio *postulare.*
Learn what it is to live.	Discĕre *quis esse* vivĕre.
The mind itself knows not what the mind is.	*Qualis esse* animus, ipse animus nescire.
Learn, good [people], what a virtue and how great it is to live with a little.	*Quis* virtus et *quantus*, bonus, *esse* vivĕre parvus, discĕre.—HOR. *Sat.* 2, 2.
Hear thou now what advantages a slender diet brings with it.	Accipĕre nunc tenuis victus *quis* commodum sui cum *afferre.—Ib.*

Behold what cities, once flourishing, luxury has destroyed.	Aspicĕre florens quondam *quis vertĕre* urbs luxus.—Sɪʟ. 15.
Consider thou, what the laws warn thee of, what the senate (court) commands, how great rewards await the good.	Respicĕre, *quid monēre* lex, *quid* curia *mandare*, præmium *quantus* bonus *manēre*.—Jᴜᴠᴇɴ. *Sat.* 8.
Let us look about us and consider what we are, and what we differ from the other animals, and let us pursue those things for (to) which we were born.	Dispicĕre et cogitare *quid esse*, et *quid* ab animans cæter *differre*, et is sequi ad qui 3 nasci.—Cɪᴄ. *Fin.* 5.
If we consider what excellence and dignity there is in human nature (the nature of man), we shall be sensible that the pleasure of the body ought to be contemned.	Si (30) considerare *quis esse* in natura homo excellentia et dignitas, intelligĕre corpus voluptas contemni oportēre. —*Id. Off.* 1.
Avoid inquiring (to inquire) what shall be to-morrow.	*Quid esse* futurus cras, fugĕre quærĕre.—Hᴏʀ.
It is not allowed to (it is unlawful for) man to know what the morrow (to-morrow's age) brings.	Scire nefas homo esse, ætas *quid* crastinus *volvĕre*.—Sᴛᴀᴛ. *Theb.*
They say that Hercules, as soon as he grew up towards manhood, went out into a solitary place; and there sitting, deliberated with himself a long while, seeing (as he saw) two ways, the one [that] of pleasure, the other [that] of virtue, whether of them it were best (better) to enter upon.	Hercules dicĕre, quum primùm (32) pubescĕre, (52) exire in solitudo; atque ibi sedens, diu sui cum (52) deliberare, quum duo (32) cernĕre via, unus voluptas, alter virtus, *uter* (ʟɪɪ.) ingrĕdi melior *esse*.—Cɪᴄ. *Off.* 1.
Youth (beginning age) is the time given by nature for the choosing what way of life (of living) every one will (is about to) enter into.	Iniens ætas tempus esse a natura datus ad deligĕre, *quis* quisque via vivĕre ingressurus *esse*.
Consider how short life is.	Vita *quàm* brevis *esse* cogitare.—Pʟᴀᴜᴛ.
It is uncertain how long the life of every one of us will be.	Incertus esse *quàm* longus ego quisque vita (42) futurus *esse*.—Cɪᴄ.
Learn ye with how little a man may (it is possible to) prolong life, and how much nature requires.	Discĕre *quàm* parvum *licēre* producĕre vita, et *quantum* natura *petĕre*.—Lᴜᴄ. 4.

Dost thou not see how God has raised the lofty countenances of men towards the stars? — Nonne vidēre homo *ut* celsus ad sidus vultus *tollĕre* Deus?—Sil. 15.

Nature teaches us not to neglect how we carry ourselves towards men. — Ego natura docēre non negligĕre *quemadmodum* ego adversus homo *gerĕre.*—Cic.

It is hard to say how much courtesy and affability of speech engage the minds of men. — Difficilis esse (75) dicĕre, *quantopĕre conciliare* animus homo comitas et affabilitas sermo.—Cic. *Off.* 2.

Behold how much wickedness advances daily, how much sin is committed publicly and privately. — Aspicĕre *quantum* quotidie nequitia *proficĕre*, *quantum* publicê privatimque (xxxiii.) *peccari.*—Sen.

Who knows, whether the gods above may add tomorrow's times to this day's sum? — Quis scire, *an adjicĕre* hodiernus crastinus summa tempus Deus superus?—H.

English Examples to be turned into Latin.

It is often not even useful to know what will be on the morrow.—Cæsar calls Dumnorix to him, brings in his brother, shows him *what* [things] he *blames* in him; *what* he himself *knows*, *what* the state *complains of*, he sets before him. He places guards over Dumnorix that he may know *what* he *does*, *with whom* he *speaks*.—It is uncertain *what* each day or night *may bring forth*.—I have told you (lit. you have) what I fear, what I hope, what I design, for the future; write to me in return what you have done, what you are doing, what you mean to do.—It is hard to tell what the reason is why we are soonest alienated with a kind of (certain) disgust and satiety from those things which most stimulate our senses with pleasure.

Exercises under Observations.

INDICATIVE.

628–629.—If a good reputation is better than riches, and money is so eagerly desired, how much more ought glory to be desired? — *Si* bonus existimatio divitiæ *præstare*, et pecunia tantopĕre *expĕti*, quanto magis gloria esse expetendus?

Catiline in a fury said, "Since I am driven headlong by my enemies, I will extinguish my own conflagration in ruin." — Catilina furibundus, "*Quoniam*, inquam, ab inimicus *agi*, incendium meus ruina exstinguĕre."

No one dances when sober, unless perhaps he is out of his *senses.*	Nemo saltare sobrius, *nisi* forte *insanire.*
I was grieved because I lost an associate and partner of my glorious career.	Dolēre *quod* socius et consors gloriosus labor *amittĕre.*
It is a great kindness of nature, that we must die.	Magnus beneficium esse natura, *quod* necesse *esse* mori.
Every one is involved in a certain plan of life (living) before he has been able to judge what is best.	*Ante* implicari quisque aliquis genus vivĕre *quam posse* qui bonus esse judicāre.
As long as the state exists, trials will take place.	*Tamdiu* fieri judicium *quamdiu esse* civitas.
The Tarquins fought till Brutus killed, with his own hand, Aruns the king's son.	Tarquinius *tamdiu dimicāre*, donec Aruns, filius rex, manus suus, Brutus occidĕre.
The enemy, while they think that they are conquering, began to follow more boldly.	Hostis, *dum* sui *putare* vincĕre, fortiter sequi cœpi.
When he heard these things, he was inflamed with anger.	*Ut* hic *audīre*, exardescĕre ira.

QUUM (CUM), *referring to time only.*

630.—He lived when Sicily was flourishing in resources.	Vivĕre *quum* Sicilia *florēre* opes.
When it is enjoined that we should control ourselves, it is enjoined that reason should restrain rashness.	*Quum præcipi* ut egomet ipse 7 imperare, tum hic præcipi ut ratio 7 coercēre temeritas.
When the consul Carbo was defending the cause of Opimius before the people, he did not deny the death of Gracchus.	*Quum* Opimius causa *defendĕre* apud populus, Carbo consul, nihil de Gracchus nex negare.
I will sail when I shall be able to sail in safety.	*Quum* secure navigare *posse*, navigare.

QUUM (CUM), *referring to cause.*

631.—When the scouts returned, a great multitude was seen from afar: then fires began to blaze throughout the whole plain as the disorderly multitude encamped in a scattered way.	*Quum* speculator *reverti* procul ingens multitudo conspici: ignis deinde totus campus conlucēre cœpisse, *quum* inconditus multitudo laxius *tendĕre.*

When Alcibiades was carrying on these projects, Critias and the rest of the tyrants of the Athenians, sent trusty men to Lysander in Asia.

Hic *quum moliri* Alcibiades, Critias ceterique tyrannus Atheniensis, certus homo ad Lysander in Asia mittĕre.

There was a vast number of prisoners made in the Punic war, whom Hannibal had sold, since they were not ransomed by their friends.

Ingens numerus esse bellum Punicum captus, qui Hannibal, *quum* a suus non *redimi*, venundăre.

Since there is in us design, reason, forethought, it is necessary that God himself have these in greater measure.

Quum esse in ego consilium, ratio, prudentia, necesse esse Deus hic ipse habēre magnus.

632.—What do you wish I should do?

Quis *velle* ? *facĕre ?*

I would wish you would love and defend me as you have been accustomed (to do).

Tu *velle*, ut consuescĕre ego *diligĕre* et *defendĕre.*

I would rather thou hadst given me riches.

Malle divitiæ ego *dăre.*

There are letters extant of Cicero to his brother Quintus, in which he exhorts and admonishes him to imitate his neighbour Octavius.

Extare epistola M. Cicero ad Quintus frater, qui is *hortari* et *monēre imitari* vicinus suus Octavius.

See that you do (it).

Facĕre facĕre.

633.—I fear that you have undertaken labour in vain.

Metuĕre ne frustra labor *suscipĕre.*

I am afraid that while I wish to lessen the labour, I may increase [it].

Verēri, *ne*, dum minuĕre ? velle labor, *augēre.*

Flatterers, if they laud any one, say they are afraid that they cannot by their words come up to his exploits.

Adulator, si quis laudare, *vereri* sui dicĕre, *ut* ille factum verbum consequi *posse.*

It is to be feared that, in a short time, there will be a famine in the city.

Verēri ne, brevis tempus, fames in urbs *esse.*

I was fearing that those things would happen which have come to pass.

Timēre ne evenire is qui accidĕre.

I fear that Dolabella himself may not be able to be of any effectual service to us.

Verēri ut Dolabella ipse satis ego prodesse *posse.*

I add this also which I am afraid I shall not justify [even] to yourself. — Addĕre etiam illo, qui *verēri* tu ipse *ut probare.*

I fear that perhaps I may not appear to have consulted other men's benefit, but my own glory. — *Verēri ne* forte *non* alius utilitas, sed proprius laus servire *vidēri.*

I fear that thou mayest not be able to meet thy present fortune. — *Verēri ne* præsens fortuna tuus sufficĕre *non posse.*

English Examples to be turned into Latin.

When Gyges had turned the stone of the ring to his palm, he was not seen by any one, but he himself saw all things; and again, he was seen when he had turned the ring into its place.—When the Helvetii understood that he had done, in one day, what they themselves had accomplished with great difficulty in twenty days, they send ambassadors to him.—When he had observed these things he accused them vehemently.—To me indeed men seem in this respect (thing) especially to surpass the brutes, in that they are able to speak.—However full thy coffer may be, I shall not think thee rich while I see thee unsatisfied. —Thou wilt deliver me from great fear, provided only there be a wall between me and thee.—I fear that thou wilt not be able to endure all the labours which I see that thou dost undertake. —A bad man fears that his wickedness may get abroad (emanate).

635.—Rule LV. The relative *qui*, *quæ*, *quod*, requires the subjunctive, when it refers to an *indefinite*, *negative*, or *interrogative* word,—to words implying *comparison*,—or assigns the *reason*, *cause*, or *end*, of that which precedes, and also in all cases of *oblique narration.*

This general rule is divided into the following

Special Rules.

636.—Rule I. When the relative *qui*, *quæ*, *quod*, refers to an *indefinite*, *negative*, or *interrogative* word, it requires the subjunctive mood. (Gr. 637.)

Do you ask what it is that has given me pleasure? — *Quis* esse, *qui* ego *delectare*, quærĕre?—Sen.

Hear what (it is that) is maintained by these [philosophers].

Quis esse qui ab hic *dici*, audire.—SEN.

Who knows not how few players there are, and have been, upon whom we could look with patience?

Quis ignorare *quam pauci* histrio esse, esseque, *qui* æquus animus spectare *posse?*—CIC.

Whoever finds fault with the study of philosophy, I cannot truly comprehend what (that is which) he thinks worthy of being commended.

Sapientia studium qui vituperare, haud sane intelligĕre *quisnam* esse *qui* laudandus putāre.—CIC.

It is of no consequence what (it is which) is shewed (presented) to the mirror.

Nihil refert *quis* esse *qui* speculum *ostendi.*—SEN.

There are some who blame this.

Esse, *qui* hic *carpĕre.*—V. PAT.

There were some who surrendered immediately.

Esse, *qui* sui statim *dedĕre.*—TAC.

That in my opinion is not enough, though there are people that think differently.

Is meus opinio, quamquam 7 *esse qui dissentire*, non satis esse.—QUINT.

There were persons who believed that the sound of the trumpet was heard on the lofty hills around.

Esse, *qui credĕre* sonitus tuba collis circum editus audiri.—TAC.

Every age will find something to do.

Omnis ætas *qui agĕre invenire.*—SEN.

Nor as yet has any one been found who refused to die.

Neque adhuc *repertus esse quisquam*, *qui* mori *recusare.*—CÆS.

Many more things are found in the writings of the ancients that merit our approbation, than our rejection.

Multo plus *reperiri* apud vetus *qui* ego probandus *esse* quam qui repudiandus.—COL. R. R.

In his case (lit. in whom, viz. Homer) the most singular circumstance is this, that neither before him has any one been found whom he might imitate, nor after him, who could equal him.

In qui hic maximus esse quod neque ante ille *qui* ille *imitari*, neque post ille, *qui* is æquare *posse inventus esse.*—V. PAT.

The watery element has wherewith it may encircle the earth, not wherewith it may overwhelm it.

Habēre humor *qui ambire* terra (pl.), non qui obruĕre.—SEN.

It is useful to have persons whom you wish first to imitate, and afterwards to excel.	Utilis esse *habēre qui* imitari primum, mox vincĕre *velle.*—Quint.
These seem to most people to have nothing better (Lat. no good thing) to do.	Hic plerique vidēri nil bonus negotium *habēre qui agĕre.*—Sen.
Nor are there wanting, to so noble a contest, leaders who may animate you to similar exertions.	Nec *deesse* tam pulcher certamen dux, *qui* ad similis tu *cohortari.*—Sen.
There are none who weep.	*Qui lacrimare deesse.*—Ov.
So long as the race of men shall exist, there will not be wanting some one to accuse them.	Dum homo genus esse, *qui accusare* is non deesse.—Cic.
There are persons present who exhort you to abandon us.	*Adesse qui* tu *hortari* ut a ego desciscĕre.—Cæs.
There are some here who do not approve of these things.	*Adesse, qui* hic non *probare.*—Cic.
There was one Bebius Massa present who knew [him].	*Adesse qui noscĕre* Bebius Massa.—Tac.
A day will come which will demand [of us] the exercise of this one virtue [thing].	Hic unus res usus *qui exigĕre* dies *venire.*—Sen.
A time will come which will reunite and blend us together.	Venire *aliquis* tempus *qui* ego iterum *jungĕre* ac *miscēre.*—Sen.
Who is there that does not hate Tarquinius Superbus?	*Quis* esse *qui* Tarquinius Superbus non *odisse?*—Cic.
Is this, soldiers, the fight that you have demanded? What man, what god is there whom you can blame?	Hic esse, miles, pugna, qui poscĕre? *Quis* homo, *quis* deus esse, *qui* accusare *posse?*
Who is there that does not wish to appear beneficent?	*Quis* esse *qui* non beneficus vidēri *velle?*—Sen.
What kind of war can there be in which the fortune of the republic has not found him employment?	*Quis* genus bellum esse posse, in *qui* ille non *exercēre* fortuna respublica.—Cic.
Does any body listen to our conference?	*Numquis* esse, sermo noster qui *aucupare?*—Plaut.
You ought not to (there is no reason why you should) believe that any one is made happy by another's misfortune.	*Non esse, qui credĕre* 4 quisquam fieri alienus infelicitas felix.—Sen.
I see nothing else that we can do.	*Nihil* alius vidēre *qui* agĕre *posse.*—Cic.

Have you any occasion for my services? (Lat., Is there any thing on account of which there is need to you of my services?)

Numquis esse, *qui* opera meus tu opus *esse?*—TER.

There is nobody among us (Romans) who has attempted the same thing; no one author among the Greeks who has handled all these subjects.

Nemo apud ego, *qui* idem *tentare; nemo* apud Græcus *qui* unus omnis is tractare.—PLIN.

There was not one man of Numantia that was led in chains.

Unus vir Numantinus *non* esse *qui* in catena *duci.*—FLOR.

There is nothing that is not forced to be somewhere.

Nihil esse *qui* non alicubi esse *cogi.*—CIC.

There was scarcely a shield that was not pierced by several arrows at once.

Vix ullus esse scutum *qui* non plures simul spiculum *perforari.*—CURT.

In all the preceding sentences it will be noticed that the conditions mentioned in the Explanation (Gr. 637) occur, i. e. the antecedent is something indefinite, and the relative clause belongs to the *predicate.* The examples which follow, though resembling the preceding, yet differ in this, that the antecedent is something *definite*, and the relative clause belongs to the *subject*, and of course has the verb in the *indicative.* This nice but important distinction should be carefully noted by every student.

I will by and by show what it is which follows (lit. what that which follows is).

Quis ? *esse qui sequi*, paulo post prosequi.—SEN.

They are bad men who speak ill of the good, i. e. they who speak ill of the good are bad men.

Malus esse homo, *qui* (de) bonus *dicĕre* male.—PLAUT.

Nor ought Cynics to be heard who find fault.

Nec *audiendus* esse Cynicus, *qui reprehendĕre.*

The persons who teach vices, and transfer them from one place to another, are these (belong to this class).

Hic esse *qui* vitium *tradĕre*, et alio aliunde transferre.—SEN.

Many who went to join Catiline at first, were not concerned in the conspiracy.

Esse tamen extra conjuratio *complures qui* ad Catilina initium *proficisci.*—SALL.

Those things which for so many years have consumed the state, were then first discovered.

Tum primum *repertus esse*, *qui* per tot annus respublica *exedĕre.*—TAC.

Those who do not bestow but squander are many.	*Multus esse qui* non *donare* sed *projicĕre.*—SEN.
Those [slaves] who took up (wasted) all your attention, are lost (wanting) to you.	*Deesse* ille *qui* opera tuus *conterĕre.*—SEN.
Nobody is free, who is a slave to his body.	*Nemo* liber *esse*, *qui* corpus *servire.*—*Id.*
Nothing can please which is not becoming.	*Nihil* posse placēre *qui* non *decēre.*—QUINT.

English Examples to be turned into Latin.

A Cæsar shall be born who will bound his empire with the ocean, his fame with the stars.—There is no other Cicero living who can, in a manner sufficiently worthy of the subject, deplore Cicero's unhappy fate.—There is no individual of any nation, who, if he take (having taken) nature for his guide, may not attain to virtue.—Is there any one of all mortal [men] of whom you entertain a more favourable opinion (think better)?—Who is there that prefers not a general to an orator?—He was sad, and saw me sorrowful; for we had heard things which caused solicitude.—There often occur many causes which perplex [men's] minds.—There are some who blame this.—There are very many excellent men who, for their health, resort to these places.—Certain philosophers have been found who denied that the deity had care of human things.—These things I had to remark (say) concerning old age.—Nor, on the other hand, were there wanting persons who, from a foolish vanity, bought superb armour, and magnificent horses, as implements of war.

641.—RULE II. The relative is followed by the subjunctive when the relative and antecedent clauses involve a comparison; or when the latter expresses the purpose, object, or design of something expressed by the former.

N. B. In explanation and illustration of this rule, see Nos. 642–644.

1st.—The Fathers, if you shall have chosen a person worthy to be the successor of Romulus, will confirm.	Pater, si *dignus qui* secundus ab Romulus *numerāri* creare, auctor fieri.—LIV.

You deserve not (are not worthy) to possess things that display such exquisite workmanship.

Non esse *dignus* tu *qui habēre*, qui tam bene factus esse (Gr. 644).

However much I may deserve such an affront, yet it was indecorous in you (you were unworthy) to offer it.

Si ego dignus (*fem.*) hic contumelia esse maxime, at tu *indignus qui facĕre* tamen. —TER.

Perhaps you had nobody fit to be imitated (whom you should imitate).

Tu fortasse *idoneus* esse nemo, *qui imitari.*—CIC.

Cæsar had judged Vibullius Rufus a proper person to send to Pompey.

Vibullius Rufus Cæsar judicare *idoneus qui* ad Pompeius *mittĕre.*—CÆS.

2d.—There is no pestilence so execrable as not to be brought upon man by man.

Nullus *tam* detestabilis pestis, *qui* non homo ab homo *nasci.*—CIC.

Nothing is so mean, nothing so common, of which they have left any part.

Nihil *tam* vilis, neque *tam* vulgaris esse, *qui* pars ullus *relinquĕre.*—*Id.*

No acuteness of human understanding is (so great as to be) able to penetrate the sky [or] enter into the earth.

Nullus acies humanus ingenium *tantus* esse, *qui* penetrare in cœlum, terra intrare *posse.*—*Id.*

No force is so great, that it cannot be weakened and broken by the sword and strength.

Nullus esse *tantus* vis, *qui* non ferrum ac vires debilitari frangique *posse.*—*Id.*

Innocence is such a disposition of mind as hurts nobody.

Esse innocentia affectio *talis* animus, *qui nocēre* nemo. —*Id.*

Thou oughtest to (be such as to) separate thyself from the society of impious citizens.

Talis tu esse oportet *qui* tu ab impius civis societas *sejungĕre.*—*Id.*

My zeal was not of such a nature that it could be passed over in silence.

Non esse meus studium *ejusmŏdi qui* silentium *posse* præteriri.—*Id.*

These dissensions were of such a nature as to have for their object not the overthrow, but a change of (Lat., to pertain not to destroying, but to changing) the commonwealth.

Ille dissensio esse *hujusmŏdi*, *qui* non ad delēre sed ad commutare respublica *pertinēre.*—*Id.*

I am not such a one as to say (i. e. one of those who say) that whatever is seen is such as it seems.

Non *is* esse *qui*, quisquis vidēri, talis *dicĕre* esse, qualis vidēri.—*Id.*

You are not such a person as not to know what you are.

Non tu *is* (Gr. 123–2, *b.*) esse *qui* quid esse *nescire.*—Cic.

Your period of life (age) [is] such that it has now made its escape from the passions of youth;—your (past) life [has been such] that in it you have done nothing that needs an apology.

Is ætas tuus *qui* cupiditas adolescentia jam *effugĕre;*—*is* vita in *qui* nihil excusandus *habēre.*—Tac.

3d.—I am too great for fortune to be able to harm me.

Major esse *quam* 3 *qui posse* fortuna nocēre.—Ovid.

I have done more [exploits] than it is easy for me to comprise in words.

Plus facĕre *quam qui* comprendĕre dictum in promptu ego *esse.*—Ovid.

To Philip not accustomed to hear the truth, the speech of Æmilius seemed too arrogant to be addressed to a king.

Insuetus Philippus verum audire, *ferocior* Æmilius oratio visus esse *quam qui* habendus apud rex *esse.*—Liv.

4th.—I remember that [certain persons] came to me to say that too great allowances were decreed to the deputies.

Ad ego *adire* meminisse *qui dicĕre*, nimis magnus sumtus legatus decerni.—Cic.

The Lacedæmonians sent ambassadors to Athens to accuse Themistocles in his absence.

Lacedæmonius legatus Athenæ *mittĕre*, *qui* Themistocles absens *accusare.*—Nep.

Laws have been invented, that they might at all times discourse with all men in one and the same language.

Lex *esse inventus*, *qui* cum omnis semper unus atque idem vox *loqui.*—Cic.

Anchors were cast to secure the steadiness of the bridge.

Esse jactus ancora *qui* firmitas pons *continēre.*—Tac.

At present all have mules to carry their vessels of crystal, &c.

Omnis jam mulus *habēre qui* crystallinus &c. (vasa) *portare.*—Sen.

644.—It belongs not to a good man to love what (such a thing as) is not of itself lovely.

Non esse bonus vir (Gr. 364) diligēre *qui* per sui non *esse* diligendus.—Cic.

I have set apart the reign of Nerva and the imperial rule of Trajan for my old age, when by the rare felicity of the times you are permitted to think what (such things as) you please, and to speak what you think.

Principatus Nerva, et imperium Trajanus senectus seponĕre; ubi, rarus tempus felicitas, sentire *qui velle*, et *qui sentire* dicēre licet.—Tac.

It was a request, but one which (such a one as) could not be refused.	Preces esse, sed *qui* contradici non *posse.*—TAC.

English Examples to be turned into Latin.

At present there is not only nobody so unskilful as to say that the things which were done in my consulship were blunders; but there is nobody so inimical to his country as not to own, that his country was preserved by my counsels.—There is nothing so important which I ought not, on your account, to perform.—The nature of war is such as should (ought to) animate and fire your minds to an earnest purpose of prosecuting it.—Upon the herald's voice being heard (Gr. 690), the joy was too great (greater than) for the people to contain.—There were persons who thought (Gr. 638) that Letilius had come from Verres as an ambassador, to tell him of his favour and friendship.—Are you the man to follow in disputing, not your own judgment, but to yield to the authority of others?—Many miracles happened by which (such that by them) the favour of heaven, and a particular partiality of the gods (divinity) for Vespasian, was manifested.

645.—RULE III. When the relative with its clause assigns the cause or reason of the action or event announced by the antecedent clause, it requires the subjunctive. See also Nos. 646, 647.

646.—You must be a worthless fellow to (inasmuch as you) mock a foreigner and a stranger.	Nequam tu esse oportēre, homo peregrinus atque advena *qui irridēre.*—PLAUT.
Silius has done well to conclude (the business).	Bene facĕre Silius *qui transigĕre.*—CIC.
I pity you for making so great a man as this your enemy.	Miseret ego tu *qui* hic tantus homo *facĕre* inimīcus tu. —TER.
The king, because he had not known that man, gave most willingly without any suspicion.	Rex, *qui* iste non *nosse,* sine ullus suspicio libentissime dăre.—CIC.
Many have been disapproved of because they spent their life at home.	Multus *qui* domi ætas *agĕre* propterea esse improbatus.—CIC.
O miserable man! to think (because he thought) a barbarian more faithful than his wife.	O 4 miser, *qui* fidelior barbarus *putāre* quam conjux! —CIC.

Is a man called an enemy because he has been [armed] with a weapon?—because he has killed a man?—because he has raised a fire?—because he has taken possession of a temple?

Num appellari inimicus, *qui* cum telum *esse?*—*qui* homo *occidĕre?*—*qui* incendium *facĕre?*—*qui* templum *occupare?*—Cic.

647.—We are constrained therefore not to know our master, because we know not whether we are the servants of the Sun or of the Æther.

Itaque cogi dominus noster ignorare; *quippe qui* nescire Sol, an Æther *servīre.*—Cic.

There Cæsar complained bitterly of my motion (opinion); for he had seen Crassus at Ravenna before, and had by him been incensed against me.

Ibi multus de meus sententia queri Cæsar, *quippe qui* Ravenna Crassus ante *vidēre*, ab isque in ego *esse incensus.*

The Britons display more ferocity as (inasmuch as) a long peace has not yet effeminated them.

Plus ferocia Britannus præferre, *ut qui* nondum longus pax *emollīre.*—Tac.

Nor was Antonius far distant, for he was pursuing with a numerous army.

Neque Antonius procul abesse; *utpote qui* magnus exercitus *sequi.*—Sall.

At the first onset the mountaineers were cut to pieces and dispersed—for to them there was neither honour in victory, nor disgrace in flight.

Primus impetus cæsus disjectusque montanus, *ut* 3 *qui* neque in victoria decus, *esse*, neque in fuga flagitium.—Tac.

English Examples to be turned into Latin.

Behold the fellow's cruelty who (inasmuch as he) does not disguise that he wished (his having wished) to injure an exile.—You blame the idleness of the young men because they do not learn that art thoroughly.—I do not in the least wonder if he hates you, because you call him Tyndarus instead of Philocrates.—I maintain (say) that Crassus is miserable, because by death he has lost his great riches,—that Cn. Pompey is miserable, because he has been bereft of so much glory,—that, in a word, all are miserable, because they enjoy not this light.—To him succeeded Pertinax, already far advanced in life, for he was on the verge of seventy (Lat. had now nearly reached the age of seventy).—The Roman knights, as they had the fates and fortunes of the leading men in their power, robbed the state at their pleasure.—I am a dolt in not having (since I have not) begun to fall in love till to-day.

648.—Rule IV. When *qui* possesses a power equal to *quanquam*, or *etsi is*, or to *si*, *modo*, or *dummodo*, "although—if—provided that he, she, it," &c., it requires the subjunctive mood.

A thing may be burned though it is not kindled.	Posse aliquis esse combustus, *qui non esse* accensus.—Sen.
In fact even Tiberius, though he disliked public liberty, was disgusted with the abject servility of his creatures.	Scilicet etiam Tiberius, *qui* libertas publicus *nolle* tam projectus serviens, patientia tædēre.—Tac.
It is certain that nobody is struck who has (i. e. if, provided he has) first seen the flash or heard the thunder.	Certus esse non quisquam tangi, *qui* prior *vidēre* fulmen, aut tonitru *audire.*—Plin.
There is nothing disagreeable provided you do not set your heart upon it.	Nihil molestus, *qui* non *desiderare.*—Cic.
Nothing can be considered as an evil, if the necessity of nature occasion it.	Nihil posse malum vidēri, *qui* natura necessitas *afferre.* —*Id.*
Can any thing be vexatious to me if (provided) it will be agreeable to you.	An ego posse quisquam esse molestus, *qui* tu gratus *futurus esse.*—*Id.*
There is nothing so easy but it becomes difficult if you do it unwillingly.	Nullus esse tam facilis res, quin difficilis esse *qui* invītus *facĕre.*—Ter.

649.—Rule V. The relative *qui* takes the subjunctive after *unus* and *solus*, when they restrict the affirmation to a particular subject.

You will be the only person on whom the safety of the state will depend.	Tu esse *unus* in qui *niti* civitas salus.—Cic.
It is wisdom alone that dispels gloom from our minds, that does not suffer us to be greatly shocked with fear.	Sapientia esse *unus qui* mœstitia *pellĕre* ex animus, *qui* ego exhorrescĕre metus non *sinĕre.*—*Id.*
This is the only doctrine of the Academics of which no one of the other philosophers approves.	Hic Academicus esse *unus* sententia *qui* reliquus philosophus nemo *probare.*—*Id.*

In those ages of which we now speak, it is the memory, almost alone, that can aid the diligence of teachers (those teaching).	In is de qui nunc loqui ætas, memoria prope *solus* esse *qui* juvare cura docens *posse.*—QUINT.
Pleasure is the only thing that by its own nature invites and allures us to itself.	Voluptas esse *solus qui* ego *vocare* ad sui et *allicĕre* suapte natura.—CIC.
Thou, Cæsar, art the only person in whose victory none has fallen but he who bore arms.	*Solus* esse, Cæsar, *qui* in victoria *cadĕre* nemo, nisi armatus.—*Id.*

English Examples under RULES IV, V, *to be turned in Latin.*

To you also, among many extraordinary [events], this ought not to appear among the last of your glories, that Hannibal, though the gods had granted him victory over so many Roman generals, has yielded to you.—For though he so much disregarded the gods, he used on the least thunder and lightning to close his eyes, muffle up his head, and hide [himself] under a bed.—What can be natural if (provided) the same thing is capable of being excessive.—The nation of the Gauls is the only one left which seems both to be able, and not to be unwilling, to make war on the Roman people.—Pompey is the only man who has surpassed by his valour, not only the glory of those men who now exist, but even the memory (i. e. all that is recorded) of antiquity.

650.—RULE VI. In oblique or indirect discourse the relative requires the subjunctive mood.

Note.—Under this rule special attention should be paid to the explanation and observations connected with it in the Grammar, 651–654. Note also that in the following sentences, in the oblique or indirect part, the Latin words are printed in Italics, and the words under the rule in small capitals.

Cingonius Varro had given his opinion that the freedmen also, who had been under the same roof, should be banished from Italy.	Censēre Cingonius Varro, *Ut libertus quoque* QUI *sub idem tectum* ESSE, *Italia deportari.*—TAC.
Plato remarks excellently, that those objects are the least important which men purchase at the expense of life.	Egregie Plato dicĕre, *Minimus esse,* QUI *homo* EMERE *vita.*—SEN.

Many have heard you say that nobody was rich but the man who could maintain an army with his revenues.	Multus ex tu audīre, quum dicĕre, *Nemo esse dives nisi* QUI *exercitus alĕre* POSSE *suus fructus.*—CIC.
Socrates used to say that all men were sufficiently eloquent in subjects which they understood.	Socrates dicĕre solēre, *Omnis in is* QUI SCIRE *satis esse eloquens.*—*Id.*
The Corsicans reflected that it was an island which they inhabited, that those even whom the cohorts and squadrons of cavalry defended, had been plundered and ravaged by [Otho's] fleet.	Corsi reputare *insula esse* QUI INCOLERE; *direptus vastatusque classis etiam* QUI *cohors alaque* PROTEGERE.—TAC.
Zeno used to say that that man was happy who enjoyed present pleasures, no pain interrupting them.	Zeno dicĕre solēre, *Is esse beatus* QUI *præsens voluptas* FRUI, *dolor non interveniens.*—CIC.
He maintains that it is unjust that a man who is not a soldier should fight with the enemy.	Negare, *Jus esse* QUI *miles non* ESSE, *pugnare cum hostis.*—*Id.*
Alexander said that they were worthy of praise, not who visited the [Eleusinian] mysteries of the Samothracians, but they who by the grandeur of their exploits had exceeded belief.	Alexander dicĕre, *Laus dignus esse non* QUI *Samothraces initia* VISERE; *sed is* QUI *magnitudo res fides* ANTECEDERE.—CURT.
Antonius laid the blame on Mucianus by whose accusations [he observed] his perils had been undervalued.	Antonius culpa in Mucianus conferre (Gr. 655, note), QUI *criminatio* EVILESCERE *periculum suus.*—TAC.
Arcesilaus denied that there was any thing whatever that could be known, not even that which Socrates had reserved to himself: That there was nothing whatever that could be discerned or comprehended.	Arcesilaus negare, *esse quisquam,* QUI *sciri* POSSE, *ne ille quidem ipse* QUI *Socrates sui* RELINQUERE: *neque esse quisquam* QUI *cerni aut intelligi* POSSE.—CIC.
His wife alarmed his fears [by reminding him] that many freedmen and slaves had been standing by, who saw the same things—and that the rewards would be conferred on him alone who should be the first to make the discovery.	Uxor metus intentare *Multus adstare libertus ac servus* QUI *idem* VIDERE—*et præmium penes unus fore,* QUI *indicium* PRÆVENIRE (Gr. 654).—TAC.

Thales, who was the wisest of the seven, said, that men ought to think that all the things which were seen were full of the gods, for that all would be more religious, just as if they were in the most sacred temples.

Thales qui sapientissimus in septem esse dicěre, *Homo existimare oportēre, omnis* QUI CERNI *deus esse plenus; fore enim omnis castior veluti* QUI *in fanum* ESSE *maxime religiosus.*—CIC.

655.—The Africans sent ambassadors to Lacedæmon to accuse Lysander of having endeavoured (that he endeavoured) to corrupt the priests of the temple.

Afer legatus Lacedæmon mittēre qui Lysander accusare (Gr. 643, 4th) QUOD *sacerdos fanum corrumpěre* CONARI.—NEP.

A plane tree is shown there from which Marsyas is said to have been suspended [when] conquered by Apollo.

Ibi ostendi platănus ex *qui* 9*pendēre* (*act.*) Marsyas ab Apollo victus.

656.—They say that good men cultivate that justice which is [justice] not that which is thought [to be so].

Dicěre *vir bonus is justitia sequi* QUI ESSE non is QUI PUTARI.

Critias sent confidential persons into Asia to Lysander to inform him that unless he dispatched Alcibiades, none of those things which he himself had established at Athens could remain in force.

Critias certus homo ad Lysander in Asia mittěre qui is certus facěre (Gr. 643, 4th) *nisi Alcibiades sustollěre, nihil is res fore ratus* QUI *ipse Athēnæ* CONSTITUERE.

They (the chiefs) said that they strove and laboured not less for this, that those things which they had said should not be made public than that they might obtain those things which they wished.

Dicěre *sui non minus is contenděre et laborare, ne is,* QUI DICERE, *enunciari, quam uti is* QUI VELLE *impetrare.*—CÆS.

English Examples to be turned into Latin.

Then at length Liscus discloses what before he had concealed.—That there are some whose authority is of very great weight (avails very much) with the common people, [and] who can do more [though] in a private station than the magistrates themselves.—Divitiacus said that he was the only one who could not be induced to (that he should) swear or give his children as hostages.—Aristotle says that certain small animals are produced near the river Hypanis, which live but a single day.—They say that Tarquin remarked that, being in exile, he had ascertained what faithful, and what unfaithful friends he had, since now he could return a favour to neither.—[He said] That it had happened worse to the victorious Sequani (to the Sequani being victors) than to the conquered Ædui, because that Ariovistus had settled down in their territories, and had seized upon a third part of the territory of the Sequani, which is supposed to be the best of all Gaul.—Themistocles informed Xerxes that it was contemplated that the bridge *which he had made* over the Hellespont should be destroyed.

CONSTRUCTION OF THE IMPERATIVE.

657.—The imperative mood is used to command, exhort, entreat, or permit. (Gr. 149, &c.)

Weep not; and that, whatever it is, let me know, conceal it not, fear not, trust me. — Ne *lacrymare;* atque iste, quisquis esse, *facĕre* ego ut scire, ne *reticĕre*, ne *verēri credĕre* ego.—Ter.

But in the mean time lay down those mattocks, do not toil. — At iste raster interea *dc-ponĕre*, ne *laborare*.—Ter.

Hush, hush, I beseech you, we (*fem.*) are safe. — *Tacēre*, *tacēre*, obsecrare salvus esse.—Ter.

Take this fan; fan her gently (*Lat.* Make a little breeze to her) thus. — *Capĕre* hic flabellum, ventŭlus hic sic *facĕre*.—Ter.

Remove far hence ye profane, and retire from the whole grove. — Procul, O, procul *esse* profanus totusque *absistĕre* lucus.—Virg.

Let the first victor have a steed adorned with trappings. — Primus equus phalera insignis victor *habēre*.—Virg.

Begin Damœtas. — *Incipĕre* Damœtas.—Virg.

Let industry be praised. — *Laudari* industria.

Trust not too much to beauty. — Nimium ne *credĕre* color.

See that you care for nothing else except to recover your health as perfectly as possible. — *Facĕre*, ne quis alius curare nisi ut quam commodè convalescĕre.

Take care of your health. — *Curare* ut valēre.

Do not wish for that which cannot be done. — *Nolle* [ut] is 7 velle, qui fieri non posse.

There is great efficacy in the virtues; arouse these, if perchance they slumber. — Magnus vis esse in virtus; is *excitare*, si forte dormīre.

English Examples to be turned into Latin.

O Jupiter, preserve, I beseech thee, these blessings for us.—Conscript fathers, by the majesty of the Roman people, aid an unfortunate [man], oppose injustice.—Let kings be honoured.—Send ye a present to the Pythian Apollo, and keep yourselves from licentious joy (licentious joy from yourselves).—Do no violence to Ceres.—Go, lictor, bind [those] hands which a little ago acquired empire for the Roman people; veil the head of the deliverer of this city; hang him on the accursed tree; scourge him, either within the Pomœrium, provided [it be] amidst those javelins and spoils of the enemy; or without the Pomœrium, provided [it be] among the tombs of the Curiatii.—Liv.

CONSTRUCTION OF THE INFINITIVE.

The Infinitive without a Subject.

659.—The infinitive without a subject may be regarded as a verbal noun in the singular number, neuter gender, and, in form, indeclinable, but differing from all other nouns, inasmuch as it involves the idea of time, and has all the power of governing that belongs to the verb.—Construed with other verbs, the infinitive may be regarded as in the nominative, and the subject of the verb; or in the accusative as its object. After adjectives, the infinitive may be regarded as in the case which the adjective governs. (Gr. 667.)

The Infinitive as the subject of the Verb.

660.—Rule LVI. One verb being the subject of another, is put in the infinitive. See also Nos. 661, 662.

To do wrong is never useful, because it is always disgraceful.	Nunquam *esse* utilis *peccare* quia semper esse turpis.—Cic.
Not to show gratitude for favours is both base, and is so esteemed among all men: not to love one's parents is impiety.	Non *referre* beneficium gratia et *esse* turpis, et apud omnis habēri: parens suus non *amare* impius *esse*.

To be shipwrecked, to be overturned in a carriage, though severe, are uncommon accidents.

Rarus *esse* casus, etiamsi gravis, naufragium *facĕre*, vehiculum *evertĕre*.

It is disgraceful to say one thing and think another; how much more disgraceful to write one thing and think another.

Turpis *esse* alius *loqui* alius *sentire;* quantus turpior alius *scribĕre* alius *sentire*.

To speak beautifully and oratorically is nothing else than to use the best arguments and the choicest words.

Nihil *esse* alius pulchrè et oratoricè *dicĕre*, nisi bonus sententiam verbumque lectus *dicĕre*.

To write a history seems to me indeed (a work) especially difficult.

Ego quidem in primis arduus (esse) *vidēri res gestus scribĕre*.—SALL.

To act well for the state is honourable, even to speak well is not inglorious; to become renowned either in peace or in war is permitted.

Pulchrum *esse bene facĕre* respublica; etiam *bene dicĕre* haud absurdum *esse;* vel pax vel bellum clarus *fiĕri licēre*. —SALL.

To suffer that which thou mayest prevent is foolish.

Qui cavēre 7 posse, stultus *admittĕre esse*.—TER.

659. 8.—The whole of this philosophising displeases.

Totus hic philosophari displicēre.

The very speaking in Latin is to be regarded as a great source of praise.

Ipse Latinè loqui in magnus laus ponendus *esse*.

For other examples, see No. 304, p. 81.

English Examples to be turned into Latin.

To betray our country is a sin.—To separate the mind from the body is nothing else than to learn to die.—To be entirely unacquainted with our own poets is [a mark] of the most indolent sloth (Gr. 365).—To employ reason and language prudently, to perform what you undertake with deliberation, and, in every circumstance, to discern and to defend what is [of the] true, is becoming; on the other hand, to be mistaken, to blunder, to fail, to be deceived, is as disgraceful as to be delirious.—To think this is [a mark] of prudence (Gr. 365); to do it, of fortitude; [but] both to think and to do it, of perfect and complete virtue.

The Infinitive as the object of a Verb.

663.—Rule LVII. One verb governs another as its object, in the infinitive. See also Nos. 664, 665.

All desire to know.	*Scire velle* omnis.
Nobody makes haste enough to live, i. e. to live well.	*Properare vivĕre* nemo satis.—Mart.
Money cannot (knows not to) change nature.	Natura *mutare* pecunia *nescire.*—Hor.
A good man delights to be admonished.	*Admonēri* bonus *gaudēre.* —Sen. *de Ir.*
Friendship cannot be, but amongst the good. For friendship cannot be without virtue.	Amicitia, nisi inter bonus, *esse* non *posse.* Nam sine virtus amicitia *esse* non *posse.*—Cic. *Am.*
He that does not know how to hold his tongue (to be silent), does not know [how] to speak.	Qui non *nôsse tacēre, nescire loqui.*
Physic cannot (knows not to) take away the knotty gout.	*Tollĕre* nodosus *nescire* medicina podagra.—Ov.
A word let go cannot (knows not to) return.	*Nescire* vox missus *reverti.* —Hor.
Nobody can be happy without virtue.	Nemo *posse esse* beatus sine virtus.—Cic.
Love, if thou wouldst (if thou wishest) to be loved.	Si *velle amari,* amare.—Sen.
Cæsar makes haste to depart from the city.	Cæsar *maturare* ab urbs *proficisci.*
Demosthenes is said to have carefully perused Plato.	*Lectitare* Plato studiosè Demosthenes *dici.*
The bridge over the Iberus was reported to have been nearly finished.	Pons in Iberus prope *effici nuntiari.*
667.—The city was afflicted, being unaccustomed to be vanquished.	Mœstus civitas esse, *vinci insuetus.*
Agricola was accustomed to obey, and taught to mingle the useful with the honourable.	Agricola esse *peritus obsequi, eruditus*que utilis honestus *miscēre.*
Each prince possessed the highest excellence; one was worthy to be elected, the other to elect.	Uterque princeps bonus esse; *dignus*que alter *eligi,* alter *eligĕre.*

668. Note 1, 2.—No one can avoid that which is to come.	Nemo *posse effugĕre* is qui futurus esse.—Cic.
Cities could neither have been built nor peopled without the concourse of men.	Urbs non 10*posse* nec *ædificari* nec *frequentari* sine cœtus homo.—Cic.
How can we have an idea of God except as eternal.	Qui ego *posse intelligĕre* Deus nisi sempiternus.—Cic.

See more examples, No. 46, p. 39.

668. Note 3.—He sees the moon rising.	*Surgĕre vidēre* luna.—Cic.
Do you not hear the zephyrs blowing?	Nec zephyrus *audire spirare.*—Virg.
I see the heaven parting asunder in the middle, and the stars wandering in the firmanent.	Medius vidēre discedĕre cœlum palansque polus stella. —Virg.
669. *Historical Infinitive.*—A short time having intervened, the enemy, upon a signal being given, rushed down from all parts and hurled stones and darts within the rampart. Our soldiers at first, with unimpaired vigour, bravely resisted, and from their more elevated station dispatched no weapon in vain.	Brevis spatium interjectus (Gr. 690) hostis, ex omnis pars, signum datum, (Gr. 690) *decurrĕre*, lapis gæsumque in vallum *conjicĕre.* Noster primò integer vis fortiter *repugnare*, neque ullus frustra telum ex locus superior *mittĕre.*—Cæs.
Meanwhile Cæsar was daily demanding corn from the Ædui.	Interim quotidie Cæsar Ædui frumentum *flagitare.* —Cæs.

English Examples to be turned into Latin.

Let not the wicked presume to appease the gods by gifts.—I have now determined to think nothing upon public affairs.—He hesitated not to erect an edifice upon another man's [ground].—I (we) did not begin to philosophize on a sudden.—No art, no hand, no workman, can, by imitating, come up to the skill of nature.—The mind always desires to be employed about (to do) something, nor can it endure perpetual inactivity.—I desire to know what you think of these things.—The full moon used to produce the greatest tides in the ocean.—Pelopidas did not hesitate to engage as soon as he saw the enemy.—The man hesitated, turned to and fro, blushed.—Her mental powers were of no contemptible character; she could compose verses, tell a pleasant story [move a jest].—The king at first feared nothing, suspected nothing.

THE INFINITIVE WITH A SUBJECT.

670.—The infinitive with a subject possesses the character of the verb, and affirms of its subject, as in the indicative or subjunctive mood, but only in subordinate and dependent propositions. These propositions have a substantive character, and may be regarded sometimes as the subject of a verb; as, *Te non istud audivisse mirum est*, "that you have not heard that is wonderful;" but more commonly as the object after a verb, or in some way dependent upon it; as, *Miror te non scribĕre*, "I wonder that you do not write." See also Note, 670.

671.—RULE LVIII. The subject of the infinitive is put in the accusative. See also Nos. 672–674.

Note 1.—*Me, te, se, illum*, are often understood, and *esse* or *fuisse* is frequently omitted after participles. See Gr. 179, 6, and *Note* 1.

Let the pupil state whether the infinitive clause is the subject or the object of the preceding verb.

N. B.—For the various ways of rendering the different tenses of the infinitive mood after different tenses of the indicative or subjunctive, see at length Gr. 180.

Do not take it ill *that* you are advised.	Ne (25) ferre molestè, *tu monēri*.
Remember *that* passion is the vice of a weak mind.	(27) Meminisse *iracundia esse* vitium animus infirmus.
I confess *that* I have sinned, and I know *that* I have deserved blame.	Fatēri *ego peccare*, et *ego commerēri* culpa scire.—PLAUT.
They say, *that* men see more in another man's business than in their own.	Aio, *homo* plus in alienus negotium *cernĕre* quam in suus.—SEN.
The young man hopes *that* he shall live long. But nobody can be sure (it can be ascertained by nobody) *that* he shall live till the evening.	Adolescens *sui* sperare diu *victurus* (*esse*). Sed nemo (XXXIII.) posse exploratum esse *sui* ad vesper *victurus* (*esse*).—CIC. *de Sen.*
Do not think *that* any virtue is without labour.	Ne (25) existimare ullus sine labor *esse virtus*.—SEN.

Believe thou *that* every day is come (has shined forth) the last to thee.

Omnis credĕre *dies* tu *dilucĕre* supremus.—Hor.

Cato wrote *that* Scipio Africanus was wont to say *that* he was never less at leisure (idle), than when he was at leisure (idle); nor less alone, than when alone.

Scipio Africanus dicĕre *solĭtus* (*esse*) 3 scribĕre Cato, *sui* nunquam minùs otiosus *esse*, quàm quum otiosus; nec minus solus, quàm quum solus (32) esse.—Cic. *Off.* 3, 1.

It is requisite that you be well in mind that you may (be able to) be well in body.

Opus esse *tu* animus *valēre* ut corpus valēre posse.—Cic.

Do you think that such excellent men did such things without reason?

Tu censēre tam egregius *homo gerĕre* res tantus sine causa?—Cic.

I desire that you should understand this.

Velle *tu intelligĕre* hic.—Cic.

We think that you can very easily explain that.

Censēre *tu* facillime *posse* explanare is.—Cic.

You know, Piso, that I think the same thing.

Scire, Piso, *ego sentire* iste idem.—Cic.

I suppose that you prefer to experience our silence.

Arbitrari *tu malle* experiri taciturnitas noster.—Cic.

It is evident that man consists of body and soul.

Esse perspicuus *homo constare* e corpus animusque.—Cic.

It is innate to all, and as it were engraven on the mind, that there are gods.

Omnis innatus esse, et in animus quasi insculptus, *deus esse.*—Cic.

We all know that there are gods.

Omnis scire, *deus esse.*

Alexander ordered the tomb of Cyrus to be opened.

Sepulcrum Cyrus *aperiri* Alexander jubēre.

To be (that a man should be) content with his own possessions is the greatest riches.

Contentus suus res *esse*, magnus esse divitiæ.

It is always advantageous to be a good man, because it is always honourable.

Semper *esse* utilis vir bonus, quia semper esse honestus.

It is right that a victor should spare the vanquished.

Victor parcĕre 3 victus æquum esse.

It is agreed that laws were invented for the safety of citizens.

Ad salus civis *inventus esse lex* constat.

675.—I deem it not improper that I should write to you.

Non puto esse alienus (*ego*) ad tu *scribĕre.*—Cic.

We all desire and hope to become old men.

[a]*Omnis* velle et sperare *fĭeri* [b]*senex.*—Cic. *Sen.*

Not so many desire to be endued with virtue as to seem so.

Non tam [a]*multus* virtus *esse* [b]*prœditus*, quàm vidēri velle.

I would choose to live poor honestly, rather than to get riches dishonestly.

(38) Optare honestè [b]*pauper vivĕre* potiùs, quàm inhonestè parare divitiæ.

I had (I wish) rather (to) be in health than (to) be rich.

Malle valēre, quàm [b]*dives esse.*

If thou desirest in good earnest (faith) to be a good man, suffer a man to (that some one) contemn thee.

Si velle bonus fides *esse* [b]*vir* bonus, sinĕre [ut] (30) contemnĕre tu aliquis.—Sen. *Ep.* 71.

Note 2.—When the former verb has a dative case after it, the word following the infinitive is commonly in the dative likewise. (Gr. 327, 328.)

It is not given to all to be noble and wealthy; but all may (it is in the power of all to) be good if they will (if they wish).

Non dari [a]*omnis esse* [b]*nobilis* et [b]*opulentus;* sed licēre (xviii.) [a]*omnis esse* [b]*bonus*, si velle.

In an easy cause, any one may (it is in the power of any one to) be eloquent.

In causa facilis (xviii.) [a]*quivis* licēre *esse* [b]*disertus.*—Ov.

Nevertheless it may be also made the accusative case, to agree with the accusative which is understood before the infinitive; as, *Licet omnibus esse bonos.* Scil. *eos esse bonos. Cuivis licet esse disertum.* Scil. *eum esse disertum.*

676.—Miltiades, having been long engaged in commands and magistracies, appeared unable to be a private (citizen), especially as he seemed to be drawn by habit to the desire of command.

Miltiades, multum in imperium magistratusque versatus, non *vidēri posse* esse privatus, præsertim quum ad imperium cupiditas trahi vidēri.

Silius Italicus was lately reported to have put an end to his life, on his Neapolitan (estate) by abstinence from food.

Modo *nuntiari* Silius Italicus in Neapolitanus suus inedia vita *finire.*

English Examples to be turned into Latin.

I am very glad that you have got (come) safe to Epirus, and that, as you write, you have had a pleasant voyage.—For it is, in my opinion (as it seems to me), highly decorous that the houses of illustrious men be open to illustrious guests.—See how I have persuaded myself that you are another self (me).—I think that these four qualifications (things) ought to exist in an accomplished general: a knowledge of the art of war, courage, authority, and good fortune.—For I not only allow that you know these things better than I, but also readily permit it.—All believe that there is a divine power and nature.—I add this also, that nature without education has oftener tended to glory and virtue than education without nature.—I 8 could swear by Jupiter, both that I burn with a desire of finding out the truth, and that I think what I say.

677.—Instead of the accusative with the infinitive, in a subordinate clause, the subjunctive with *ut* or *quod*, "that," "in order that," preceding it, is used in certain circumstances; viz.,

1st. When the dependent clause expresses *purpose* or *design*. or when "*that*" is equivalent to "*in order that*," (Gr. 627, 1, 2d.)

Scarcely ever can a parent prevail on himself to conquer nature, so as to banish love towards his children from his mind.	Nunquam fere parens posse animus inducĕre *ut* natura ipse *vincĕre*, *ut* amor in liberi *ejicĕre* ex animus.
Before old age, I took pains to live well; in old age to die well.	Ante senectus curare *ut* bene *vivĕre;* in senectus, *ut* bene *mori*.
We must take care to use that liberality which may benefit our friends, may harm no one.	Vidēre esse (Gr. 699) *ut* is liberalitas *uti* qui 7 prodesse (Gr. 643, 2d) amicus, obesse nemo.
Every animal loves its own self, and, as soon as it has arisen, strives to preserve itself.	Omnis animal sui ipse diligĕre, ac simul ac oriri, is agĕre *ut* sui *conservare*.

2d. This is the case especially after verbs signifying *to endeavour*, *to aim at*, *to accomplish*, such as *facĕre*, *efficĕre*, *perficĕre*, &c.

If virtue can produce this effect that one be not miserable, it will more easily cause that he be most happy.	Si posse virtus *efficĕre ne* miser aliquis *esse*, facile *efficĕre ut* beatus *esse*.

The sun causes every thing to flourish, and grow to maturity in its respective kind.

Sol *efficĕre ut* omnis *florēre*, et in suus quisque genus *pubescĕre.*

Every virtue attracts us to itself, and makes us love those in whom it appears to be found.

Omnis virtus ego ad sui allicĕre, *facĕre*que, *ut* is *diligĕre* in qui ipse inesse vidēri.

Unwillingly indeed I cast L. Flaminius out of the senate.

Invitus quidem *facĕre ut* L. Flaminius e senatus *ejicĕre.*

By his eloquence he effected that the Lacedæmonians should be deprived of the aid of their allies.

Eloquentia *perficĕre ut* auxilium socius Lacedæmonius *privari.*

3d. The infinitive, in English, after verbs signifying *to request, demand, admonish, advise, commission, encourage, command*, and the like, is usually rendered into Latin by the subjunctive with *ut;* sometimes without *ut.*

I admonish scholars to love their preceptors not less than their studies.

Discipulus *monēre ut* præceptor suus non minus quam ipse studium *amare.*

I strongly exhort thee to read carefully, not only my orations, but also these treatises on philosophy.

Magnopere tu *hortari ut* non solum oratio meus, sed hic etiam liber de philosophia diligenter *legĕre.*

If we are not induced to be honest men by honourable feeling, but by some benefit and profit, we are not honest but cunning.

Si non ipse honestas *movēri ut* bonus vir *esse*, sed utilitas aliquis ac fructus, callidus esse, non bonus.

We have not ceased to admonish and exhort Pompey to avoid this great infamy.

Pompeius *monēre* et *hortari* non desistĕre *ut* magnus hic infamia *fugĕre.*

I advise them to be quiet.

Monēre ut conquiescĕre.

Cæsar had given a strong charge to Trebonius not to suffer the town to be taken by storm.

Cæsar Trebonius magnopere *mandare, ne* per vis oppidum expugnari *pati.*

Piso dared to make proclamation that the senate should resume their [ordinary] dress.

Edicĕre audēre Piso *ut* senatus ad vestitus *redire.*

Cæsar gives it in charge to Labienus to visit the Remi and other Belgæ, and keep them in their allegiance.

Cæsar Labienus *mandare* Remus reliquusque Belgæ *adire*, atque in officium *continēre.*

He exhorts and admonishes him to imitate his neighbour Octavius.

Hortari et monēre imitari vicinus suus Octavius.

4th. *Ut* with the subjunctive, and not the infinitive with its subject, usually follows verbs signifying *to happen*, *to occur*, &c.; as, *fit*, *incidit*, *occurrit*, *contingit*; *est*, *restat*, *superest*, &c., (Gr. 627, 1, 4th.)

It happens somehow or other, that if any fault is committed we perceive it more readily in others than in ourselves.	*Fit*, nescire quomodo, *ut* magis in alius *cernĕre* quam in egomet ipse si quis delinquĕre.
It happens to most men that through the assistance which letters (i. e. the art of writing) give, they relax their diligence in committing to memory.	Plerique *accidit ut* præsidium literæ diligentia in perdiscendum *remittĕre.*
It happens to (it is the fortune of) the wise man alone, to do nothing against his will.	Solus hic *contingit* sapiens, *ut* nihil *facĕre* invitus.
It often happens, that utility is at variance with virtue.	Persæpe *evenit*, *ut* utilitas cum honestas *certare.*
It is best to speak every day, many hearing us; for it is rare that any man stands in awe sufficiently of himself.	Optimus *est ut* quotidie *dicĕre*, audiens plures (Gr. 690); rarus *est* enim *ut* satis sui quisquam *verēri.*
It is the main thing in an orator to seem to those before whom he pleads, such as he himself would wish.	Caput *esse* 2 orator *ut* ille apud qui agĕre talis qualis sui ipse optare *vidēri.*

5th. Verbs signifying *willingness*, *unwillingness*, *permission*, *necessity*, &c., sometimes take the subjunctive with *ut* or without it; but more commonly they take the accusative with the infinitive. So also, generally, verbs denoting *seeing*, *hearing*, *feeling*, *thinking*, *saying*, &c. The following sentences may be made both ways.

Those who gave to Greece the forms of her republic, wished the bodies of the youths to be strengthened by toil.	Ille qui Græcia forma respublica dăre, *corpus* juvenis *firmari* labor *velle.*
When I shall have praised some one of thy friends to thee, I wish that he should know that I have done it.	Quum aliquis apud tu laudare tuus familiaris, *velle ille scire* ego is facĕre.
Caligula wished that the Roman people had but one neck.	*Optare* Caligula *ut* populus Romanus unus cervix *habēre.*

Nature does not allow that we increase our own means by the spoils of others.	Natura non *pati ut* alius spolium facultas noster *augēre.*
Phæthon wished to be taken into the chariot of his father.	Phæthon *optare ut* in currus pater *tolli.*

6th. When the dependent clause expresses a *fact* simply, *that* is made by *quod* followed by the indicative.

Besides the dread of a Latin war, this also had been added, that it was sufficiently clear that thirty [different] nations had entered into a conspiracy [against them].	Supra bellum Latinus metus, is quoque *accesserat*, *quod* triginta jam conjurasse populus satis *constare.*—Liv.
Of all that was praiseworthy [in the conduct] of Regulus, that is worthy of admiration, that he gave his opinion that the captives (of the Carthaginians) should be retained.	Ex totus laus Regulus, ille *esse* admiratio dignus, *quod* captivus (Pœni) retinendus 3 *censēre.*—Cic.
But (in this) you are mistaken that you think that I rival Agamemnon.	*Quod* autem ego Agamemnon æmulari *putare*, *falli.*—Nep.

7th. After verbs denoting a feeling of pain or pleasure, and the outward expression of those feelings, such as *gaudeo*, *delector*, *angor*, *doleo*, and the like, *that*, in the sense of *because*, is made by *quod* followed by the indicative or subjunctive, according as the proposition expresses a fact, or only a conception of the mind; or the infinitive with its subject is used.

The following sentences may be made both ways.

I am sorry (it grieves me) that you are displeased.	*Dolēre* ego *quod stomachari.*
I rejoice that my conduct is approved by you.	Meus factum probari abs tu *gaudēre.*—Cic.
They are indignant that you breathe, that you speak, that you have the forms of men.	*Quod spirāre*, *quod* vox *emittěre*, *quod* forma homo *habēre*, *indignari.*—Liv.
Cato said he wondered that a soothsayer did not laugh when he saw a soothsayer.	Cato sui *mirari* aio *quod* non *ridēre* haruspex, haruspex quum videre.—Cic.
678.—I hope you will be wise.	Sperare *futurus esse* (*fore*) *ut sapěre.*

I see that you wish to depart into heaven, and I hope that that will be our lot (happen to us).

Vidēre tu velle in cœlum migrare, et sperare *fore ut contingĕre* is ego.—Cic.

I was not ignorant (I knew well) that this undertaking of mine would lead to various censures.

Non esse nescius *fore ut* hic noster labor in varius reprehensio *incurrĕre*.—Cic.

Ptolemy the astrologer had persuaded Otho that he would be called to the government.

Ptolemæus mathematicus Otho persuadēre, *fore ut* in imperium *adscisci*.—Tac.

The king did not know that the town would have been surrendered to him, if he had waited one day longer.

Rex ignorāre *futurus fuisse, ut* oppidum ipse *dedi*, si unus dies expectare.

679.—That you, my Terentia, should now be so harassed, should lie so in tears and mourning, and that this should be through my fault.

Tu nunc, meus Terentia, sic *vexari*, sic *jacēre* in lacrima et sordes! isque *fieri* mea culpa.—Cic.

That there should be any man so unhappy as I am!

Adeone *esse homo* infelix quidam, ut ego esse.—Ter.

That I vanquished should desist from my undertaking, nor be able to turn away the king of the Trojans from Italy.

Egone inceptum *desistĕre* victus (*fem.*) nec *posse* Italia Teucri avertĕre rex.—Virg.

CONSTRUCTION OF PARTICIPLES.

681.—Rule LIX. Participles, like adjectives, agree with their substantives in gender, number, and case. (Gr. 264.) Also 682.

The praise due to virtue.

Laus debĭtus virtus. (Gr. 522.)

Remember the punishments prepared for the wicked.

Meminisse *pœnæ improbus præparatus*.—*Ib.*

Our ears are to be shut to bad speeches.

Claudendus esse *auris* malus *vox*.—*Ib.*

Anger will do me more (is about to hurt me more) harm than an injury.

Plus *ego* (Gr. 403) *nociturus* esse *ira* quàm injuria.—Sen.

We ought to take care that we make our desire obedient to reason.

39 Curare esse, ut *appetitus ratio* (Gr. 403) *obediens* præbēre.—Cic. *Off.* 1.

Temperance is a moderating of the desires governed by (obedient to) reason.	Temperantia esse moderatio *cupiditas ratio* (Gr. 403) *obediens.*—Cic.
A man that follows (following) pleasure does not much benefit his heir.	*Homo voluptas* (Gr. 403) *obsĕquens* haud multum hæres juvare.—Ter.
I reckon those the most wretched of mortals, [that are] addicted to their belly and lust.	Miserrimus *mortalis* judicare, *venter* ac *libido dedĭtus* (xxxii.)—Sen.
The shadow of the earth hindering the sun makes night.	Umbra *terra sol* (Gr. 403) *officiens* nox efficĕre.—Cic.
There are some animals void of reason, others having the use of (using) reason.	*Animal* (x.) alius *ratio* (xi.) expers esse, alius *ratio* (xxvi.) *utens.*—Cic. *Off.* 1.
All good men will respect (will prosecute) with great honour and benevolence a good magistrate, consulting for his countrymen, and seeking (serving) the common good, forgetting his own interests (advantage), observing the laws, favouring virtue, restraining impiety and debauchery.	*Magistratus* bonus *civis* suus (Gr. 403) *consulens*, et *utilitas* communis (Gr. 403) *serviens*, *oblītus* (xiv.) *commodum* suus, *lex* (Gr. 403) *parens*, *virtus* (Gr. 403) *favens*, *impietas* et *nequitia* (xx.) *coercens*, magnus honor et benevolentia omnis bonus *prosecuturus* (xx.) esse.
Law is right reason, commanding what is right, and prohibiting the contrary.	*Lex* esse rectus ratio *imperans honestus*, *prohibens contrarius.*
How wretched is the bondage of virtue in slavery to pleasure.	Quam miser esse *virtus* famulatus *serviens voluptas* (Gr. 403).
I saw Cato sitting in the library surrounded with many books of the Stoics.	*Cato* vidēre in bibliotheca *sedens*, multus *circumfusus* Stoicus liber.
Alexander [when] dying had given his ring to Perdiccas.	*Alexander moriens* anulus suus dăre Perdiccas.
683.—Hold this as certain, that nothing could have come into being without a cause.	*Ille exploratus habere*, nihil fieri posse sine causa.
The Sicilians have recourse to my aid, which they have long proved and known.	Siculus ad meus fides *qui habēre spectatus* jam et diu *cognitus*, confugĕre.
The Romans have large sums of money invested in Asia.	Romanus in Asia *pecunia* magnus *collocatus habēre.*
I wish you to be relieved from domestic care.	Domesticus cura *tu levatus velle.*

I will find [him] out and bring him to you. — *Inventus* tu *curāre* et *adductus*.

The war being ended, it was ordered that the legions should be discharged. — *Legio* bellum confectum (Gr. 690) *missus fieri* placet.

I will do this for you. — *Hic* ego tu *effectus* redděre.

684.—Nothing was so pernicious to the Lacedæmonians as the abolition of the discipline of Lycurgus. — Lacedæmonius nullus res tantus esse 3 damnum (Gr. 427), quam *disciplina* Lycurgus *sublatus*.

Quinctius Flamininus came as ambassador to king Prusias, whom both the reception of Hannibal and the stirring up of a war against Eumenes had rendered suspected by the Roman people. — Ad Prusias rex legatus Quinctius Flamininus venīre, qui suspectus Romanus et *receptus Hannibal* et *bellum* adversus Eumenes *motus* redděre.

Cæsar and Pompey were not free from the supicion of having crushed Cicero. — Non carēre suspicio *oppressus Cicero* Cæsar et Pompeius.

Ptolemy was the second king after the founding of Alexandria. — Ptolemæus rex alter esse post *Alexandria conditus*.

In the six hundredth year from the building of the city. — Annus ab *urbs conditus* sexcentesimus.

685.—The king sent Hephæstion into the region of Bactriana to provide supplies for the winter. — Rex *Hephæstion* in regio Bactrianus mittěre commeatus in hiems *parare*.

He is a fool who, when he is going to buy a horse, does not examine the animal itself, but its housing and bridle. — Stultus esse *qui* equus *eměre* non ipse inspicěre, sed stratum is ac frenum (*pl.*).

He spoils whatever can be of use to the foe, intending to leave the soil barren and naked. — Quisquis hostis usus esse posse corrumpěre, sterilis ac nudus solum *relinquěre*.

686.—I have given my letter to many persons to copy. — *Epistola* meus multus dăre *describendus*.

In the Sabine war, Tarquinius vowed the erection of a temple in the capitol, to Jupiter greatest and best. — *Ædis* in Capitolium Jupiter Bonus Magnus bellum Sabinus *faciendus* vovēre Tarquinius.

Mummius contracted for transporting pictures and statues into Italy. — Mummius tabula ac statua in Italia *portandus* locare.

The king delivered the infant Cyrus to Harpagus to put to death (to be put to death). — Rex Harpagus Cyrus infans *occidendus* traděre.

687.—Every state must be ruled by some counsel, and that counsel must either be allotted to one, or to certain select persons, or must be undertaken by the multitude and by all.

Omnis respublica consilium quidam *regendus;* is autem consilium aut unus *tribuendus* aut delectus quidam aut *suscipiendus* multitudo atque omnis.

Earth must be (is to be) returned to earth.

Reddendus esse terra *terra* (XXXII.)—Cic.

Life is not to be bought at any (every) price.

Non omnis pretium *vita* (XLIV.) *emendus* esse.—Sen.

Children are not to be filled with meat.

Puer cibus (XXV.) *implendus* non esse.—Sen.

Friendship is to be preferred to all worldly things.

Amicitia omnis humanus *res anteponendus* esse (XXVII. 8).—Cic. *Am.*

Death is to be preferred to baseness.

Mors esse *anteponendus* (Gr. 399) *turpitudo.*—Cic. *Off.* 1.

The exercise and delight of learning is to be preferred before both all the actions and pleasures of wicked men.

Usus et *delectatio* doctrina (Gr. 313) esse omnis improbus et *actum* et *voluptas anteponendus.*—Cic. *Fam.* 9, 6.

A sword is not to be trusted with (entrusted to) children.

Ensis m. puer non (Gr. 522) *committendus* esse.

688.—He thrust his right hand into the altar while it was burning.

Dextra 3 *ara accensus* 3 imponĕre.—Liv.

In a battle which had arisen there, they all perished.

In *prœlium* ibi *exortus,* omnis perire.

During a tempest which had arisen, he was suddenly withdrawn from the sight (eyes) of men.

Inter *tempestas ortus,* repente oculus homo *subduci.*

No one, when he looks at the whole earth, will doubt of the providence of God.

Nemo, cunctus *intuens* terra, de divinus providentia dubitare.

The limbs of Alexander, when he had scarcely entered the river, began suddenly to shiver and to be benumbed.

Alexander, vix *ingressus* flumen, subito horrēre artus et rigēre cœpisse.

The king commands Philip to read the epistle of Parmenio, nor did he remove his eyes from his countenance as he read it.

Rex epistola Parmenio Philippus legĕre jubēre, nec a vultus *legens* movēre oculus.

When we were going to say more he ordered us to depart.

Plus *locuturus* abire *ego* jubēre.

690.—RULE LX. A substantive with a participle whose case depends on no other word, is put in the ablative absolute. See also Nos. 691–693.

Nothing is better than friendship, virtue being excepted.

Nihil amicitia præstabilior esse, *exceptus virtus.* — CIC *Am.*

Nothing better than friendship has been given by God to man, excepting wisdom.

Amicitia nihil melior, *exceptus sapientia*, homo a Deus 3 dari.—*Id.*

Shame being lost, all virtue is lost.

Pudor amissus, omnis virtus (14) perire.

What pleasure of life can there be, friendship being taken away?

Quis posse esse jucunditas vita, *sublatus amicitia?*—CIC.

Love and friendship being taken away, all pleasure is taken away out of the world (life).

*Charitas benevolentia*que *sublatus*, omnis esse e vita sublatus jucunditas.—*Id.*

Thou shalt condemn nobody, the matter not having been examined.

Damnare nemo, *causa* non *cognĭtus.*

A fawning friend may easily (is easily able to) be distinguished and discovered from a true [one], diligence being used.

Blandus amicus a verus facile secerni et internosci posse, *diligentia adhibĭtus.*—CIC. *Am.*

Every good man follows that which is honourable and excellent, despising and contemning pleasure (pleasure being despised and contemned).

Qui pulcher et præclarus esse, *spretus* et *contemptus voluptas*, optimus quisque sequi.—CIC. *Sen.*

Nature has given us the use of life, as it were of money, no [pay] day being appointed.

Natura ego (XXIX.) dare usura vita, tanquam pecunia, *nulla præstitūta dies.*—CIC. *Tusc.* 1.

Dost thou grow milder and better, old age coming on?

Lenior et melior fĭĕri, *accedens senecta?*—HOR.

694.—How well did they live, Saturn being king (while Saturn was king?)

Quàm bene vivĕre, *Saturnus rex* (dum Saturnus esse rex)?—TIB.

The old man is a commender of the time that was (the time spent) he being a boy (when he was a boy), a censurer and corrector of younger [people].

Senex esse laudator tempus actus, *sui puer*, (quum ille esse puer), censor castigatorque minor.—HOR.

The gate is shut too late and in vain, when the loss is (the loss being) already sustained.

Serò et nequicquam *acceptus* jam janua *damnum* claudi.—Juv. *Sat.* 13.

Labour is fruitless, Nature striving (if Nature strives) against it.

Natura reluctans, (si Natura reluctari) labor irritus esse.—Sen.

After a few years had intervened, the war was transferred to Africa.

Pauci *annus interjectus*, bellum in Africa transferri.

When the Samnites were conquered, war was declared against the Tarentines.

Devictus Samnites, Tarentinus bellum 3 indici.

695.—The Romans for the first time fought on sea, in the consulship of C. Duillius and Cn. Cornelius Asina.

Primum Romanus *C. Duillius* et *Cn. Cornelius Asina consul*, in mare dimicāre.

When nature and virtue are our guides no error can possibly be committed.

Natura et *virtus dux*, errāre nullus modus posse.

Under the command of Pausanias, Mardonius was driven from Greece.

Pausanias dux, Mardonius Græcia fugari.

No guilty person (nobody guilty) is acquitted, himself being judge.

Sui judex, *nemo nocens absolvi.*—Juv.

Why does any one want, not deserving it (unworthy), thou being rich (while thou art rich)? Why do ancient temples fall down?

Cur egēre indignus quisquam, *tu dives?* Quare templum ruēre antiquus?—Hor. (*i. e.* Dum tu dives es.)

Thou shalt say or do nothing, Minerva being unwilling.

Tu nihil *invitus* dicĕre facĕreve *Minerva.*—Hor.

Nothing is becoming, Minerva being unwilling, as they say, that is, nature opposing and resisting. For it signifies nothing (for it does not signify) to resist nature, nor to pursue any thing which thou canst not attain.

Nihil decēre, *invitus*, ut aio, *Minerva*, id esse, *adversans* et *repugnans natura.* Neque enim attinēre (Gr. 403) natura repugnare, nec quicquam sequi, qui assĕqui (Gr. 636) nequire.—Cic. *Off.* 1.

While he is a child, the golden age shall arise in all the world.

Qui puer (Gr. 295), totus surgĕre gens aureus mundus. —Virg.

696.—Hannibal having found out that snares were laid for him, sought safety by flight.

Hannibal, *cognitus* (Gr. 182–8) *insidiæ sui parari*, fuga salus quærĕre.

Alexander having heard that Darius was approaching with an army, resolved to oppose him. — Alexander, *auditus Darius appropinquare cum exercitus*, obviam ire constituĕre.—CURT.

Happy as to the other things, with this exception, that you were not present. — *Exceptus quod non simul* 8 *esse*, (Gr. 539) cæter lætus. —HOR.

That they belonged to the enemies not being doubtful to any one. — Haud quisquam *dubius quin hostis esse*.—LIV.

697.—The sky being clear the whole day. — *Serenus* per totus dies.—LIV.

English Examples to be turned into Latin.

My father Micipsa when *dying* commanded me.—In the mean time the common people when the conspiracy was *laid open*, their mind *being changed*, execrated the designs of Catiline; extolled Cicero to the skies; [and], as if *rescued* from slavery, gave vent to joy and gladness.—Galba, *having made* some successful encounters, and *taken by assault* many of their forts, ambassadors *having been sent* to him from every side, and hostages *given*, and peace *being made*, determined to place two cohorts among the Nantuates.—Cæsar having removed first his own horse, then the horses of all out of sight, that the danger of all being made equal, he might take away the hope of flight, having exhorted his men, commenced battle.—All things had to be done by Cæsar at one time; the standard had to be displayed, the signal to be given with a trumpet, the soldiers to be called back, the line to be formed, the soldiers to be encouraged. Cæsar having sent on his cavalry before, followed closely with all his forces.

GERUNDS AND GERUNDIVES.

Gerunds.

699.—RULE LXI. The verb *est*, with the gerund for its subject, implies necessity, and governs the dative of the doer. See also Nos. 700, 701.

Note 1.—The nominative case in English must be the dative in Latin.
Note 2.—The dative case is more commonly understood.

I must govern my tongue. — Lingua (Gr. 403) *moderari esse ego*.—PLAUT.

We must spare tender things.

Parcĕre esse (Gr. 403) tener.—Juv.

We must resist passion.

Resistĕre esse (Gr. 403) iracundia.—Cic.

Meditate daily, that we ought to resist passion.

Quotidie meditari, *resistĕre esse* (Gr. 403) iracundia.—Cic.

We ought not to be very angry with enemies.

Non *esse* graviter *irasci* inimicus (Gr. 403).

They are not to be listened to, who think that we ought to be very angry with enemies.

Non audiendus esse, qui graviter *irasci esse* (Gr. 403) inimicus putare.—Cic. *Am.*

How late is it to begin to live then, when we must leave off?

Quàm serus esse, tum vivĕre incipĕre, quum *desinĕre esse?*—Sen.

We must be upon our guard, lest we should be catched with crafty flattery.

Animadvertĕre esse, ne callidus assentatio (liv.) capi.—Cic. *Am.*

We ought to take care, that the appetite obeys reason.

Efficĕre esse, ut appetitus (Gr. 403) ratio (liv.) obedire.—*Id.*

We ought to be free from all perturbation of mind.

Vacare esse omnis animus (xxv.) perturbatio.—*Id.*

We ought even the more carefully to beware of (we ought to abstain even the more carefully from) those faults (sins) which seem to be small [ones].

Qui parvus vidēri esse, delictum ab hic *esse* etiam diligentiùs *declinare.*—Cic. *Off.* 1.

702.—The gerund in *di*, of the genitive case, is governed like the genitive of nouns (Gr. 333) by substantives or adjectives.

Note.—This gerund is frequently translated as the infinitive mood active.

There are a thousand arts to hurt.

Esse *ars* mille *nocēre.*—Ov.

Pleasure often leaves causes to repent.

Voluptas sæpe relinquĕre *causa pœnitēre.*—Cic.

Nature is a very good guide to live well.

Natura esse optimus *dux f.* rectè *vivĕre.*—Cic. *Am.*

We are all inflamed with a desire to live happily.

Beatè *vivĕre cupiditas* omnis incendi.

The hope of impunity is a very great temptation to sin.

Spes impunitas maximus *peccare illecebra* esse.—Cic.

Nature gives to animals one time to act, another to rest.

Natura tribuĕre animans alius *tempus agĕre*, alius *quiescĕre*.—Cic.

Let us remember that we are come into this world (life) as into a lodging, not as into a home. For Nature has given us here an inn to stay in, not a place to dwell in.

(27) Meminisse ego (52–2) venire in hic vita tanquam in hospitium, non tanquam in domus. Natura enim hic *commorari diversorium*, non *habitare locus* ego dare.—Cic. *de Sen.*

703.—The gerund in *do*, of the dative case, like the dative of nouns, is governed by adjectives signifying *usefulness* or *fitness*, and sometimes by verbs, to denote a purpose.

Iron when red is not fit for hammering.

Rubens ferrum non esse *habilis tundendum.*

Coarse papyrus is not fit for writing.

Charta emporeticus *inutilis* esse *scribendum.*

This water is good for drinking.

Hic aqua esse *utilis bibendum.*

Who is so fit for running as I?

Quis esse tam *idoneus currendum* quam ego?

No seed is good for sowing after four years.

Nullus semen ultra quadrimatus *utilis* esse *serendum.*

In the gnat, nature so formed an instrument, that it was at once pointed for boring and hollow for sucking.

In culex natura telum ita formāre, ut *fodiendum acuminatus* pariter, et *sorbendum fistulosus* esse.

Tiberius promised to rebuild the theatre of Pompey, since no one of the family was able (sufficed) to rebuild it.

Pompeius theatrum Tiberius extruĕre pollicēri quod nemo e familia *restaurandum sufficĕre.*

704.—The gerund in *dum*, of the accusative case, when not the subject of the infinitive, is governed by the prepositions *ad* or *inter*, sometimes by *ante*, *circa*, or *ob* (Gr. 602).

Note.—In the following sentences, the verbs are given in the infinitive, not in the gerund.

We are inclined not only to learn, but also to teach.

Non solum *ad discĕre* propensus esse sed etiam *ad docēre.*

To think well and to act rightly, is sufficient for a good and happy life (for living, &c.).

Bene sentire, rectèque facĕre, satis esse *ad* bene beateque *vivĕre.*

As the ox was born to plough, [and] the dog to track, so man was born for two things, to understand and to act.

Ut *ad arare* bos, *ad indagare* canis, sic homo ad duo res, *ad intelligĕre* et *agĕre* nasci.

Praise cannot induce you to act well.

Tu laus allicĕre *ad* recte *facĕre* non posse.

The marsh hindered the Romans in pursuing.

Palus Romanus *ad insequi* tardare.

The character of boys manifests itself more openly while at play.

Mos puer sui *inter ludĕre* simpliciter detegĕre.

705.—The gerund in *do*, of the ablative case, is governed by the prepositions *a*, *ab*, *de*, *e*, *ex*, or *in;* or without a preposition, as the ablative of manner or cause (Gr. 542).

It is right that a man should be both munificent in giving, and not severe in exacting.

Convenire quum *in dăre* munificus esse, tum *in exigĕre* non acerbus.

Anger should especially be forbidden in punishing.

Prohibendus maxime esse ira *in punire.*

In philosophy the high station of Plato did not deter Aristotle from writing.

Nec Aristoteles in philosophia deterrēre *a scribĕre* amplitudo Plato.

I indeed think that virtue is given to men by instructing and persuading them.

Equidem putare virtus homo *instituĕre* et *persuadēre* tradi.

Socrates, by questioning and interrogating, used to draw forth the opinions of those with whom he discoursed.

Socrates *percunctari* atque *interrogāre*, elicĕre solēre is opinio quicum disserĕre.

English Examples to be turned into Latin.

An orator must observe what is becoming, not in sentiment only, but also in words.—Young men ought to acquire, old men to enjoy.—The disciples of Pythagoras were obliged to be silent five years.—It must either be denied that a god exists, or those who admit it must confess that he is engaged in something.—Avaricious men are tormented not only with the passion for acquiring, but also with the fear of losing.—Frugality is the science of avoiding superfluous expenses, or the art of using property with moderation.—Habit and practice both sharpen acuteness in (sagacity of) understanding, and quicken the rapidity of expression (of speaking).—Nor was it my design to spend my life (age) intent on cultivating the ground or on hunting.—Nitrous water is useful for drinking.—Cæsar was blamed because, during the performance (the looking at the spectacle), he occupied himself in (was at leisure for) reading letters and memorials.—The riper the berry of the olive, the fatter is the juice, and the less pleasant; and the best time for gathering is, when the berry begins to grow black.—The laws of Lycurgus train youth [in labour] by hunting, running, being hungry, being thirsty, being pinched with cold, and being violently heated.—By doing nothing men learn to do ill.

Gerundives.

707.—Rule LXII. Gerunds governing the accusative are elegantly turned into gerundives in *dus*, which, with the sense of the gerund, instead of governing, agree with their substantive in gender, number, and case. Also No. 708.

The following examples may be made by the gerunds also.

A desire seized Romulus and Remus of founding a city in that place where they had been exposed and brought up.	Romulus et Remus cupido capĕre in is locus ubi exponi atque educari, *urbs condĕre.*
Hannibal increased his reputation by his bold attempt of crossing the Alps.	Hannibal opinio de sui augĕre conatus tam audax *trajicĕre Alpes.*
All judicial proceedings have been devised for the sake of terminating controversies, or punishing crimes.	Omnis judicium aut *distrahĕre controversia*, aut *punire maleficium* causa reperiri.
I rejoice that thou art desirous of bringing about peace between the citizens.	*Pax* inter civis *conciliare* tu cupidus esse lætari.
Dry wood is a proper material for eliciting fire.	Lignum aridus materia esse idoneus *elicĕre ignis* (*pl.*).
Cleanthes drew water, and hired out his hands for watering a garden.	Cleanthes aqua haurire, et *rigare hortulus* locare manus.

There are some games not without their use for sharpening the wits of boys.	Esse nonnullus *acuĕre* puer *ingenium* non inutilis lusus.
Pythagoras went to Crete and Lacedæmon, to become acquainted with the laws of Minos and Lycurgus.	Pythagoras Creta et Lacedæmon, ad *cognoscĕre* Minos et Lycurgus *lex*, contendĕre.
No one is more unyielding in granting pardon than he who has often deserved to ask for it.	Nemo ad *dăre venia* difficilis esse quam qui ille petĕre sæpius merēre.
Similarity of character is the firmest bond for forming friendships.	Ad *connectĕre amicitia* vel tenax vinculum mos similitudo esse.
Virtue is seen most of all in despising and rejecting pleasure.	In *voluptas spernĕre* ac *repudiare* virtus vel maxime cerni.
The body must be exercised, that it may obey the reason in executing business and enduring labour.	Exercendus corpus esse, ut obedīre ratio posse in *consequi negotium* et in *labor tolerare.*
Many persons use care in getting horses [but] are negligent in choosing friends.	Multus in *equus parare* adhibēre cura, in *amicus eligĕre* negligens esse.
There is no duty more necessary, than requiting a favour.	Nullum officium esse magis necessarius, *referre gratia.*

English Examples to be turned into Latin.

He who knows himself will understand what means he has for acquiring wisdom.—The rest of the time is adapted for reaping and gathering the fruits.—Wood was brought down from mount Lebanon for constructing rafts and towers.—Either pleasures are foregone for the sake of obtaining greater pleasures, or pains are undergone for the sake of escaping greater pains.—Marius perceived that these [things were] merely glorious and did not tend to terminate the war.—Man enjoys great advantages for gaining and acquiring wisdom.—Nature has furnished the mind of man with senses adapted to the perception of things.—It [is] a difficult subject, and much and often inquired into, whether in conferring a magistracy, or trying a culprit, or enacting a law, it were better to vote secretly or openly.—We have borne and suffered many [things], which ought not to have been borne in a free state, some of us through the hope of recovering our liberty, others from too great a desire of living.

Construction of Supines.

712.—Rule LXIII. The supine in *um* is put after a verb of motion.

Certain persons came to salute the gods.	Aliquis *venire* deus *salutare.*
Know that young Curio came to me to salute [me].	Scire Curio adolescens *venire* ad ego *salutare.*
He sends to ask for those vessels which he had seen.	*Mittĕre rogare* vas is qui vidēre.
The ambassadors of almost all Gaul assembled about Cæsar to congratulate him.	Totus fere Gallia legatus ad Cæsar *gratulari convenīre.*
The people of Veii send negotiators to Rome to implore peace.	Veiens pax *petĕre* orator Roma *mittĕre.*
She came a journey of many days to congratulate you.	Venire is tu tot dies via gratulari.

716.—Rule LXIV. The supine in *u* is put after an adjective noun.

It seems difficult to be said what is the reason.	Vidēri *difficilis dicĕre* quis esse causa.
That not only to be heard but to be seen was most dreadful.	Ille vero *teter audire*, non modo *aspicĕre.*
O the many things grievous to be mentioned, painful to be borne, which I have suffered.	O multus *dicĕre gravis*, *perpeti asper*, qui perferre.
O shameful thing, not only to be seen, but even to be heard!	O 4 res non modo *vidēre fœdus*, sed etiam *audire.*

English Examples under both rules to be turned into English.

Philip was slain by Pausanias at Ægæ, near the theatre, as (when) he was going to see the games.—Divitiacus came to the senate at Rome, to implore assistance.—Ambassadors came from Rome into the camp of the Æqui, to complain of injuries, and to demand a restitution of property according to the treaty.—Hannibal unconquered, was recalled to defend his country.

A narrative easy to be understood.—It is difficult to express how much courtesy and affability of conversation win the minds of men.—Virtue is difficult to be found.—What is so pleasant to know and to hear as a discourse adorned with wise sentiments and weighty words?

720.—RULE LXV. The conjunctions *et*, *ac*, *atque*, *nec*, *neque*; *aut*, *vel*, and some others, couple similar cases and moods. See also Nos. 721, 722.

1. Like cases.

Queen Money gives a wife with a portion, and credit, and friends, and birth, and beauty.

Uxor cum dos, fides*que*, *et* amicus, *et* genus, *et* forma regina Pecunia donare.—HOR.

Nothing is so mischievous as pleasure [is].

Nihil esse tam pestifer *quàm* voluptas [*esse*].—CIC.

The pleasure of the mind is greater than the [pleasure] of the body; and the diseases of the mind are more pernicious than [the diseases] of the body.

Animus voluptas major esse *quàm* [*voluptas*] corpus; *et* morbus animus perniciosior esse *quàm* [*morbus*] corpus.

Drunkenness is nothing else but a voluntary madness.

Ebrietas nihil aliud esse *quàm* voluntarius insania.—SEN. *Ep.* 83.

Whithersoever thou goest, death follows, as a shadow [follows] a body.

Quocunque ingrĕdi, sequi mors, corpus *ut* umbra.—CATO.

Glory follows virtue as a shadow.

Gloria virtus, *tanquam* umbra, sequi.—CIC.

The covetous man is commended as a frugal person.

Tanquam frugi laudari avarus.—JUV. 14.

Nothing is so convenient either for prosperity or adversity, (for things either prosperous or adverse) as friendship [is].

Nihil esse tam conveniens ad res vel secundæ *vel* adversæ *quàm* amicitia [esse].—CIC. *de Am.*

Credulity is an error, rather than a fault.

Credulitas error esse, magis *quàm* culpa.—CIC. *F. Ep.*

Young men fall into diseases more easily than old men.

Faciliùs in morbus incidĕre adolescens *quàm* senex.—CIC.

You may overcome by policy better than by passion.

Consilium melius vincĕre *quàm* iracundia.

It behoves me to comply with my father rather than with my love.

Parens ego obsĕqui (Gr. 403) potiùs, *quàm* amor, oportēre.—TER. *Hec.* 3. 4.

There is no vice worse than covetousness.

Nullus vitium tetrior esse *quàm* avaritia.—CIC.

What is sleep but the image of death?

Quid esse somnus *nisi* mors imago?—CIC.

Nobody ought to boast of any thing but that which is his own. — Nemo gloriari debēre (quoquam) *nisi* (xxxv.) suus.

What will that man do in the dark who fears nothing but a witness and a judge? — Quid facĕre is homo in tenebræ, qui nihil timēre *nisi* testis *et* judex?—Cic. *Leg.*

We cannot maintain friendship, except we love friends as well (equally) as ourselves. — Amicitia tuēri non posse, nisi æquè amicus, *ac* ego ipse (30) diligĕre.—Cic. *Fin.*

We rejoice for the joy of friends as much as for our own [joy]. — Lætari amicus lætitia æquè *atque* noster lætitia.—*Id.*

Time slides away with a constant motion, no otherwise than a river. — Assiduus labi tempus motus, non secus *ac* flumen.—Ov. *Met.* 15.

Anger perishes by staying (by delay), as brittle ice [does]. — *Ut* fragilis glacies, interire ira mora.—Ov.

2. Like moods and tenses.

Honesty is praised and starves. — Probitas laudari *et* algēre.

Virtue procures and preserves friendship. — Virtus conciliare *et* conservare amicitia.—Cic.

The thirst of covetousness is never filled nor satisfied. — Nunquam explēri *neque* satiari cupiditas sitis.—*Id.*

Juvenal says, that honesty is praised and starves. — Juvenalis dicĕre, probitas laudari *et* algēre.

I would more willingly receive than [I would] do injury. — (38) Accipĕre libentiùs, *quàm* (38) facĕre, injuria.

It is better to receive than to do injury. — Accipĕre præstare, *quàm* facĕre, injuria.—Cic.

3. An infinitive mood is often coupled with a noun or pronoun substantive.

Learn ye justice, being warned, and not to contemn heaven. — Discĕre justitia monĭtus, *et* non temnĕre cœlum.

Nothing is the property of so narrow a soul as to love riches. — Nihil esse tam (xii.) angustus animus *quàm* amare divitiæ.—Cic. *Off.* 1.

Nothing is so very common as to want wisdom (to be wise in nothing). — Nihil esse tam valde vulgaris, *quàm* nihil sapĕre.—Cic. *Div.* 2.

723.—The games were performed during ten days, nor was any thing omitted. — *Ludus* decem per dies *fieri*, neque *res* ulla *prætermitti.*

PROMISCUOUS EXERCISES.

[FROM CROMBIE'S GYMNASIUM.]

1.

The Athenians were building the walls of their city. This thing the Lacedæmonians took amiss. Themistocles deceived them by this stratagem: he went to Sparta as an ambassador, and denied to the Lacedæmonians that the walls were building. "But," says he, "if you do not believe me, send trusty men to inspect the city (Gr. 643–4th), and, in the meantime, detain me [here]." This they did.

2.

Themistocles, at the same time, secretly sent a messenger to the Athenians, and advised them (Gr. 677–3d) to detain the Lacedæmonian inspectors at Athens, by whatever means [they could], until they had built the walls, and had recovered him. The Athenians followed (obeyed) his counsel. Themistocles accordingly was recovered: the Lacedæmonian inspectors were restored, and Athens fortified, against the will of the Lacedæmonians (*invitus*, Gr. 690).

3.

The father of a family one day came to Aristippus, and asked him to undertake (Gr. 677–3d) the education of his son (his son to be educated). To the philosopher asking five hundred drachmas as a fee, the father, who was a very covetous man, frightened at the price, said, that he could buy a slave for less (money). "Do so," said Aristippus, "and then you will have two."

4.

Hasdrubal passed over into Italy with a great army, and the Roman empire would have been ruined (it would have been over with the Roman empire), if he had been able to join himself to his brother Hannibal. But Claudius Nero, having left a part of his army in the camp (Gr. 692, Rem.), hastened to Hasdrubal with a few chosen troops, and joined (himself to) his colleague Livius, at the river Metaurus, and these two together (lit. both) conquered Hasdrubal.

5.

After him, Julian obtained the government and made war on the Parthians, in which expedition, I myself was present. He took by assault many towns of the Persians, and received others on surrender. Returning victorious, he was slain by an enemy, on the sixth day before the Calends of July, and in the seventh year of his reign. He was a man remarkable for eloquence, and had a very retentive memory (Gr. 394). He was succeeded by Jovian (Jovian succeeded him), who was elected emperor by the army.

6.

Tiberius Sempronius Gracchus, descended from a very noble family, would not suffer Scipio Asiaticus, though an enemy, to be carried to prison. The latter (Gr. 123–1) [when] prætor, subdued Gaul. In his first consulship, he conquered Spain; in his second, Sardinia. When he was accused of a capital crime (*capitis*) by the people, Sempronius swore that he was not deserving of death, and that, if he should be sent into exile, he would go into exile (Lat., would change his soil) along with him. Upon this (wherefore) he was acquitted.

7.

A war having arisen between the Romans and Albans, Hostilius and Fufetius being leaders, before it came (was come) to a battle, it was agreed (it pleased them) to finish the affair by the combat of a few. There happened to be (there were by chance) among the Romans, three brothers born at one birth, by name Horatii, and, in like manner, three born at one birth among the Albans, named Curatii, equal [to them] in age and strength. It was agreed, therefore, that these should fight for the dominion, and the people to whom (to whichever people) the victors belonged, (they) should rule over the other.

8.

They engaged, and after many wounds given and received (Gr. 688) on both sides, two Romans fell, and the three Albans were severely wounded. The one Horatius, as yet untouched, but not a match for all the Albans (together), that he might divide their force and attack them singly, pretended flight. They followed him one after another as their strength and the pain of their wounds permitted, and, as they came up, he slew them one by one. The Roman accordingly conquered, and these two states were united (joined into one) under the same name.

9.

Curius Dentatus, having subdued the Samnites (Gr. 692, Rem.), said in an assembly, "I have taken so much land that there would have been a desert if I had not taken so many men; and moreover, I have taken so many men that they would have perished by famine, if I had not taken so much land." He divided the fields among (to) the soldiers man by man, giving (them) fourteen acres each, and reserved as many for himself, saying that no man ought to be a general, who would not be content with the share (part) of a common soldier.

[N. B. The pupil may vary the preceding exercise, by putting the words of Dentatus, in the first part, in the oblique or indirect form (Gr. 650, &c.), and the report of his words at the end in the direct form. Similar variations may be made in others also.]

10.

No man was ever milder than Scipio Africanus, and yet, supposing that somewhat of severity was necessary for establishing military discipline, he was on a certain time cruel to his countrymen (citizens); for after he had conquered Carthage (Gr. 692, Rem.), and reduced under his power all who had gone over to the Carthaginians, he inflicted punishment more severely on the Roman deserters, than on the Latin. The former he crucified as fugitives from (of) their country, the latter he beheaded as perfidious allies.

11.

When Porsenna, king of the Etrurians, was endeavouring to restore Tarquinius Superbus to the government, and had taken the Janiculum at the first assault, Horatius Cocles, a man of the greatest bravery, posted himself at the extreme part of the Sublician bridge, and alone withstood the whole force of the enemy, till the bridge was broken down behind him (from behind). Then he threw himself into the Tiber, and swam over to his friends unhurt, either by his fall or by the darts of the enemy.

12.

The Greeks, after the victory, determined to sail to the Hellespont, and to destroy the bridge, that the king might not escape. Themistocles dissuaded them from this (Lat., this to them), by saying (Gr. 689-2) that the king being intercepted would renew the battle; and that despair sometimes achieves what valour cannot. At the same time, he sent a eunuch to the king, informing him, that unless he made his escape quickly, the bridge would be destroyed. Xerxes, therefore, betook himself to flight, and Themistocles thus preserved the victory to the Athenians.

13.

A certain youth had for a long time frequented the school of Zeno [the philosopher]. When he returned home, his father asked (from) him what he had learned. The young man modestly replied, that he would show him that by his conduct (manners). The father was grievously offended and beat him. The son remained perfectly composed and said, "I have learned to bear patiently a father's anger."

14.

In the reign of Cæsar Augustus (Gr. 694), a dolphin, as it is said, contracted an attachment for the son of a poor man, who was accustomed to feed him with bits (fragments) of bread. Every day, the dolphin, when called by the boy, swam to the surface of the water, and being fed from his hand, carried the boy on his back from the shore at Baiæ (the Baian shore) to a school at Puteoli, and brought him back in the same manner. The boy having died, the dolphin, coming oftentimes to the accustomed place, and missing him, is said also to have died of grief.

15.

P. Scipio, surnamed Africanus, from the conquest of Africa (Gr. 684), is believed to have been the son of Jupiter. For, before he was conceived, a serpent of huge size appeared in his mother's bed; and the snake having twisted around him [when] an infant, did not hurt him (hurt him nothing). He undertook no expedition, until he had sat some time in the chapel of Jupiter, as if he was receiving divine counsel (mind). When he was eighteen years of age (born 18 years), he saved the life of his father at Ticinum; and when he was twenty-four years old (had 24 years), he was sent as prætor (Gr. 689–1st) into Spain, and took Carthage on the very day on which he arrived.

16.

A maiden of extraordinary beauty, whom he had taken [captive] in war, he forbade to be brought into his sight, and ordered her to be restored to her father, and her betrothed lover. He conquered, (Gr. 689–1st) and drove out of Italy, Hasdrubal and Mago, brothers of Hannibal, and formed an alliance (friendship) with Syphax, king of the Moors. Having returned home victorious (victor), he was made consul, before the [consular] years (i. e. before the legal age), and being sent into Africa, he conquered Hannibal, who had been compelled to return to Carthage to defend his country (Gr. 707). Being falsely accused of extortion, he went into voluntary exile, where he spent the rest of his life (age).

17.

Xerxes, before the naval battle in which he was defeated by Themistocles, had sent four thousand of armed [men] to plunder (Gr. 643–4th) the temple of Apollo, as if he was carrying on war, not only with the Greeks, but also with the immortal gods. This band was entirely destroyed by rain and thunder. Historians say that this was done, that he might understand how insignificant (nothing) was the strength of men against the immortal gods. The wicked do not reflect with themselves, that to war against heaven (the gods), is to court destruction for themselves.

18.

Xenophon, the disciple of Socrates, was offering (making) a solemn sacrifice, when he heard that his elder son was slain at Mantinea. He did not however desist, but only laid down his crown, and asked how he had fallen. When he understood that his son had fallen in battle, fighting bravely for his country, he calmly replaced the crown upon his head, calling (Gr. 63–2 *in fin.*) the gods to witness, that he received (took) greater pleasure from the bravery of his son, than pain from his death.

19.

Marcus Aurelius, the Roman emperor, applied to the study of wisdom, and, for that purpose, attended the lectures of (Lat., heard) Sextus the philosopher. When he was going out of the palace (Gr. 688) one day, Lucius the philosopher, who had lately come to Rome, met him, and asked him whither he was going, and on what business. Marcus replied, "It is becoming even for an old man to learn, and I am going to Sextus to learn (that I may know) those things which I do not yet know." Lucius, raising his hands to heaven (Gr. 692), exclaimed, O Jupiter! a Roman emperor, now in his old age, goes to school like (as) a boy.

20.

When Plato had come to the Olympic games, [an assembly] the most crowded of all the assemblies in Greece, he lodged with persons unknown to him; and he was unknown to them. Whilst he remained at Olympia, he so attached them to him, by the suavity of his manners, and by his conversations free from all affectation of wisdom, that they rejoiced exceedingly in the society of such a man. He made no mention, however, of the academy, or of Socrates; he told them merely that he was called Plato.

21.

The games being over, when they had come to Athens, Plato received them very kindly. Being very desirous (desiring greatly) to see the philosopher, they say [to him], "Show us that namesake of yours, the disciple of Socrates, whose fame is so great every where. Take us to the Academy." He, softly smiling, as he used to do, said to them, "I am he." The visitors were amazed when they found that they had been so long the companions of Plato without knowing him.

22.

Dion, being banished from Syracuse by the tyrant Dionysius, went to Megara. There, when he wished to have an interview with Theodorus the chief man of the city, and had come to his house for that purpose, being detained a long time at the gate, and finally being refused admittance (prohibited to enter) he said to his companion, calmly, "We must bear this patiently; perhaps we also, when we were in authority (the magistracy), sometimes did such things." By this tranquillity of mind, he rendered the condition of his exile much more tolerable.

23.

Aristides among the Athenians, and Epaminondas among the Thebans, are said to have been such lovers (so loving, fond) of truth, that they never told a lie even in jest. Atticus, also, with whom Cicero lived in the greatest intimacy, neither told, nor could bear a lie. "I hate that [man]," said Achilles, "equally as the *gates of* Pluto, who says one thing and thinks another." "Liars," said Aristotle, "gain this, that they are not believed when they speak (credit is not given to them speaking) the truth." Simplicity and sincerity are most suited (*conveniunt*) to the nature of man.

24.

Ptolemy having conquered (Gr. 692) Demetrius, gained greater glory to himself from his moderation, than from his victory; for he dismissed the friends of Demetrius, not only with their property, but also with valuable gifts, saying that he had not begun the war for the sake of plunder. Not long after, Ptolemy, having engaged with Demetrius a second time, was himself defeated, and, having lost his fleet, fled into Egypt. Demetrius, to requite his kindness (Gr. 627–1), sent back to him his son, his brother, and all his friends, together with their goods.

25.

When Augustus Cæsar was supping with Vedius Pollio (at his house), one of the slaves broke a crystal vessel. Vedius immediately ordered him to be put to death; nor was he to die by a common death, for he ordered him to be thrown into a fish-pond full of lampreys. The boy terrified fled to the feet of Cæsar. The emperor shocked (moved) at the cruel order of Pollio, ordered the boy to be set free, all the crystal vessels to be broken, and the fish-pond to be filled up. "What!" said he, "because your vessel has been broken, shall, therefore, the bowels of a human being be torn in pieces?"

26.

When Pyrrhus, king of Epirus, had made war on the Romans, and he was distant from the Roman army only a few miles (*millibus passuum*), the physician of Pyrrhus came into the camp of Fabricius by night, promising that he would cut off the king by poison, if a reward should be given him proportioned to the magnitude of the service. Fabricius immediately caused him to be carried back to Pyrrhus, saying, it was disgraceful to contend with an enemy by poison, and not by arms. On this (wherefore) the king is reported to have said, "The sun can more easily be turned from his course, than Fabricius from (the path of) honor."

27.

Pisistratus the tyrant conducted himself with the greatest equity in the government of Athens (Athenian government), which he had seized upon unjustly, and, except that he was fond of ruling, no citizen was better than he. If he saw any person walking about idle in the market-place, he called them to him (Gr. 689–1st), and asked why they were idle. If they answered that they had neither cattle nor corn, he gave [them some], and ordered them to go and work (to betake themselves to work). When he appeared (went forth) in public, two or three boys accompanied him, who carried money to be given to the poor.

28.

Gillias of Agrigentum, a man richer in mind than in wealth, was always employed in spending, rather than in getting money. He erected buildings for public purposes (uses), he exhibited (gave) shows to the people, supplied food to the poor, gave dowries to virgins, received strangers in the kindest manner; and, at one time, fed and clothed five hundred horsemen [who had been] driven ashore near his house (Gr. 611) by a storm. In short, whatever Gillias possessed, he seemed to consider as the common patrimony of all [men].

29.

Antisthenes the philosopher was accustomed to exhort his scholars to attend (Gr. 677–3d) diligently to their studies; but few (of them) complied. At last, being in a passion, he sent them all away. Diogenes, however, one of them, being inflamed with a great desire of hearing the philosopher, came often to his school and resolutely stuck to him. Antisthenes threatened that he would break his head (the head of him) with a staff which he was wont to carry; and when he saw that he was not frightened by his threats, he one day did actually beat him.

30.

Diogenes, however, did not go away. "Strike," said he, "if you please, but you will find no staff so hard that it can drive me from your school. I love you, and I desire to hear you; I have made up (taken it into) my mind to suffer (Gr. 677–3d) any thing for the sake of learning." Antisthenes, seeing that he was very desirous of knowledge, admitted him again, and loved (embraced) him with great affection. "Nature," says Tullius, "has implanted in man an insatiable desire of searching for truth, that he may become wiser and better."

31.

Themistocles having conquered the Persians in a naval battle (Gr. 692), said in an assembly at Athens, that he had (Gr. 394) a plan in his mind which would be useful to the state, but that it was necessary it should not be made public. He therefore demanded a person (that some one might be given to him) to whom he might communicate it, and Aristides was appointed (named) for that purpose (thing).

He then told Aristides, that the fleet of the Lacedæmonians, which had been withdrawn to the harbour at Gytheum, might be secretly set *on fire, and thus the [naval]* power of the Lacedæmonians be destroyed (broken).

32.

Aristides having heard this (Gr. 692), returned to the assembly, and told his countrymen that the plan of Themistocles was indeed a very useful [one], but by no means honourable. The Athenians judging that to be unprofitable (not useful) which was not honourable, rejected on the authority of Aristides (Ar. being the author), a plan which they had not even heard. "We are born for (to) justice, nor is right founded on opinion, but on nature. Cicero observes, that justice is the queen of virtues. Let it therefore remain [a principle] with us, that what is dishonourable is never useful."

VOCABULARY.

LATIN AND ENGLISH.

A, ab, prep. *from, by.*
Abaliēno, āre, āvi, ātum, tr. 1. *to alienate.*
Abdĭtus, a, um, pt. *hidden, involved.*
Abdolonymus, i, m. 2. *a man's name.*
Abdōmen, ĭnis, n. 3. *the paunch, the belly.*
Abdūco, ĕre, xi, ctum, tr. 3. *to lead away, to remove.*
Abeo, īre, ii, *seldom* īvi, ĭtum, irr. *to go away, to depart.*
Abhinc, adv. *hence, ago.*
Abhorreo, ēre, ui, — intr. 2. *to shrink, to be averse to, to be unlike.*
Abĭgo, ĕre, ēgi, actum, tr. 3. *to drive away.*
Abjicio, ĕre, jēci, jectum, tr. 3. *to throw away.*
Absens, tis, adj. *absent.*
Absisto, ĕre, stĭti, intr. 3. *to depart from, to desist.*
Absolūtè, adv. *absolutely.*
Absolvo, ĕre, vi, ūtum, tr. 3. *to absolve, to acquit.*
Absterreo, ēre, ui, ĭtum, tr. 2. *to deter, to hinder.*
Abstĭnens, tis, adj. *abstinent, temperate.*
Abstineo, ēre, ui, tentum, tr. & intr. 2. *to keep off, abstain from.*
Abstrăho, ĕre, xi, ctum, tr. 3. *to draw away, to separate.*
Absum, esse, fui, irr. *to be absent, to be wanting.*
Absurdè, adv. *absurdly.*
Absurdus, a, um, adj. *absurd, senseless.*
Abundans, tis, adj. *abounding, rich.*
Abundantia, æ, f. 1. *abundance, plenty.*
Abunde, adv. *abundantly, richly.*
Abundo, āre, āvi, ātum, intr. 1. *to overflow, to abound.*
Ac, conj. *and.*
Academia, æ, f. 1. *the academy.*
Academĭcus, i, m. 2. *an academic.*
Accēdo, ĕre, ssi, ssum, intr. 3. *to advance, to approach.*
Accendo, ĕre, di, sum, tr. 3. *to kindle, to burn.*
Accensus, a, um, pt. *kindled, inflamed.*
Accessus, us, m. 4. *an approach, landing.*
Accĭdo, ĕre, ĭdi, — intr. 3. *to fall down, to happen.*
Accĭpio, ĕre, cēpi, ceptum, tr. 3. *to take, to receive.*

Accĭtus, a, um, pt. *being called, sent for.*

Accŏla, æ, c. 1. *a near inhabitant, a neighbour.*

Accommŏdo, āre, āvi, ātum, tr. 1. *to put upon, to suit, to lend.*

Accusatio, ōnis, f. 3. *accusation.*

Accusātor, ōris, m. 3. *an accuser.*

Accūso, āre, āvi, ātum, tr. 1. *to accuse.*

Acer, & acris, e, adj. *sharp, sour, fierce.*

Acerbe, adv. *bitterly, cruelly.*

Acerbus, a, um, adj. *unripe, sour, sharp, harsh.*

Acervus, i, m. 2. *a heap.*

Achaia, æ, f. 1. *Achaia, a country of Greece.*

Achilles, is, m. 3. *a Grecian hero.*

Acĭdus, a, um, adj. *acid, sour.*

Acies, ēi, f. 5. *a line of soldiers, an army in battle array.*

Acquiro, ĕre, sīvi, sītum, tr. 3. *to acquire.*

Acrĭter, us, acerrĭme, adv. *sharply.*

Acta, ōrum, n. 2. *actions, deeds.*

Actio, ōnis, f. 3. *an action.*

Actus, a, um, part. *done, past, spent.*

Acuminātus, a, um, part. *pointed.*

Acuo, ĕre, ui, ūtum, tr. 3. *to sharpen.*

Acūtus, a, um, adj. *acute, sharp, keen.*

Ad, prep. *to, at, about.*

Adămo, āre, āvi, ātum, tr. 1. *to love.*

Addīco, ĕre, xi, ctum, tr. 3. *to ratify, to adjudge.*

Addo, ĕre, ĭdi, ĭtum, tr. 3. *to add.*

Addūco, ĕre, xi, ctum, tr. 3. *to bring to.*

Adeo, īre, īvi or ii, ĭtum, intr. irr. *to go to, to approach, to visit.*

Adeo, adv. *so, so that, so much.*

Adhæreo, ēre, si, sum, intr. 2. *to stick to, to adhere.*

Adhæresco, ĕre, — — intr. 3. *to stick to, to adhere.*

Adhĭbeo, ēre, ui, ĭtum, tr. 2. *to adopt, to employ, to use, to bring.*

Adhuc, adv. *hitherto, yet, still.*

Adĭmo, ĕre, ēmi, emptum, tr. 3. *to take away, to remove.*

Adipiscor, ipisci, eptus, dep. 3. *to get, to obtain.*

Adĭtus, us, m. 4. *access, passage.*

Adjĭcio, ĕre, jēci, jectum, tr. 3. *to throw to, to add.*

Adjungo, ĕre, xi, ctum, tr. 3. *to join to, to unite.*

Adjūtor, ōris, m. 3. *an assistant.*

Adjutrix, īcis, f. 3. *an assistant.*

Adjŭvo, āre, jūvi, jūtum, tr. 1. *to help, to assist.*

Administro, āre, āvi, ātum, tr. 1. *to manage, to conduct.*

Admiratio, ōnis, f. 3. *wonder, admiration.*

Admīror, āri, ātus, dep. 1. *to wonder at, to admire.*

Admitto, ĕre, mīsi, missum, tr. 3. *to admit.*

Admŏneo, ēre, ui, ĭtum, tr. 2. *to remind, to admonish.*

Adolescens, tis, c. 3. *a youth, a young man* or *woman.*

Adolescentia, æ, f. 1. *youth.*

Adolesco, ĕre, olēvi, *rarely* olui, ultum, intr. 3. *to grow up, to burn.*

Adopto, āre, āvi, ātum, tr. 1. *to adopt.*

Adōro, āre, āvi, ātum, tr. 1. *to adore.*

Adparātus, *see* Apparātus.

Adscisco, ĕre, īvi, ītum, tr. 3. *to take to, to associate.*

Adsto, stāre, stĭti, stĭtum, intr. *to stand by.*

Adsum, esse, fui, irr. *to be present.*

Adŭlans, tis, pt. *flattering.*

Adŭlans, tis, m. 3. *one flattering, a flatterer.*

Adulātor, ōris, m. 3. *a flatterer.*

Adŭlor, āri, ātus, dep. *to flatter*

Adulter, ĕri, m. 2. *an adulterer.*

Adulterīnus, a, um, adj. *false, counterfeit.*
Advĕna, æ, f. 1. *a stranger.*
Advĕnio, īre, vēni, ventum, intr. 4. *to come to, to arrive.*
Adventus, us, m. 4. *advent, approach, arrival.*
Adversarius, ii, m. 2. *adversary, enemy.*
Adversor, āri, ātus, dep. 1. *to oppose.*
Adversus, a, um, adj. *opposite, adverse.*
Adversus, & um, prep. *against, over against.*
Advŏlo, āre, āvi, ātum, intr. *to fly to.*
Aedificium, ii, n. 2, *an edifice.*
Aedifĭco, āre, āvi, ātum, tr. 1. *to build.*
Aedīlis, is, m. 3. *an ædile.*
Aedis, & ædes, is, f. 3. *a building, a temple.*
Aeduus, i, m. 2. *one of the Aedui.*
Aegæ, ārum, f. 1. *Aegæ, the name of a place.*
Aeger, gra, grum, adj. *sick, diseased.*
Aegisthus, i, m. 2. *Aegisthus, a man's name.*
Aegre, ius, gerrĭme, adv. *grievously, with difficulty.*
Aegritūdo, ĭnis, f. 3. *sickness, sorrow.*
Aegrōtus, a, um, adj. *sick, diseased.*
Aegypta, æ, f. 1. *a woman's name.*
Aegyptus, i, f. 2. *Egypt, a country of Africa.*
Aemiliānus, i, m. 2. *a man's name.*
Aemilius, ii, m. 2. *a man's name.*
Aemulatio, ōnis, f. 3. *emulation, competition.*
Aemŭlor, āri, ātus, dep. 1. *to rival, to envy, to imitate.*
Aenēas, æ, m. 1. *Aeneas, son of Anchises.*
Aenĕus, a, um, adj. *made of brass, brazen.*
Aeŏlus, i, m. 2. *the god of the winds.*
Aequālis, e, adj. *equal, contemporary.*
Aequè, adv. *equally.*
Aequĭtas, ātis, f. 3. *equity, justice.*
Aequo, āre, āvi, ātum, tr. 1. *to equal.*
Aequus, a, um, adj. *equal, just, kind.*
Aër, aĕris, m. 3. *the air*, acc. *aëra.*
Aerumna, æ, f. 1. *toil, affliction.*
Aes, æris, intr. 3. *brass, money.*
Aesōpus, i, m. 2. *Aesop.*
Aestas, ātis, f. 3. *summer.*
Aestĭmatio, ōnis, f. 3. *a valuing.*
Aestimātor, ōris, m. 3. *a valuer.*
Aestĭmo, āre, āvi, ātum, tr. 1. *to value, to esteem.*
Aestīvus, a, um, adj. *relating to summer.*
Aestuo, āre, āvi, ātum, intr. 1. *to be heated.*
Aestus, us, m. 4. *the tide.*
Aetas, ātis, f. 3. *age, time.*
Aeternĭtas, ātis, f. 3. *eternity.*
Aether, ĕris, m. 3. *the air.*
Aevum, i, n. 2. *an age, a life.*
Afer, fri, m. 2. *an African.*
Affabilĭtas, ātis, f. 3. *courtesy, kindness.*
Affectatio, ōnis, f. 3. *affection.*
Affectio, ōnis, f. 3. *disposition.*
Affectus, ûs, m. 4. *an affection, a disposition.*
Affĕro, afferre, attŭli, allātum, irr, *to bring to.*
Affĭcio, ĕre, ēci, ectum, tr. 3. *to affect, to move.*
Affīgo, ĕre, xi, xum, tr. 3. *to fix, fasten; affigĕre crŭci, to crucify.*
Affirmo, āre, āvi, ātum, tr. 1. *to affirm, to assert.*
Affluens, tis, adj. *flowing, abounding.*
Afrĭca, æ, f. 1. *Africa.*
Africānus, i, m. 2. *Africanus, a surname.*

Agamemnon, ŏnis, m. 3. *king of Mycenæ.*
Ager, agri, m. 2. *a field, land.*
Agesilaus, i, m. 2. *a Spartan king.*
Aggrĕdior, di, essus, dep. 3. *to go up to, to attack.*
Aggrĕgo, āre, āvi, ātum, tr. 1. *to join.*
Agĭlis, e, adj. *active, nimble.*
Agis, ĭdis, m. 3. *a Spartan king.*
Agĭto, āre, āvi, ātum, tr. 1. *to exercise, to speak of.*
Agmen, ĭnis, n. 3. *an army (on the march).*
Agnosco, ĕre, nōvi, nĭtum, tr. 3. *to recognize, to acknowledge.*
Agnus, i, m. 2. *a lamb.*
Ago, ĕre, ēgi, actum, tr. 3. *to drive, to lead, to do, to treat;* actum est, *it is all over.*
Agrestis, e, adj. *relating to the country, rude.*
Agricŏla, æ, m. 1. *a husbandman.*
Agricŏla, æ, m. 1. *Agricola, a Roman general.*
Agricultūra, æ, f. 1. *agriculture, husbandry.*
Agrigentīnus, a, um, adj. *of Agrigentum.*
Agrigentum, i, intr. 2. *a town of Sicily.*
Aio, def. *I say.*
Ala, æ, f. 1. *a wing, a squadron.*
Albānus, a, um, adj. *of Alba, Alban.*
Alcibiădes, is, m. 3. *Alcibiades.*
Aleātor, ōris, m. 3. *a dice-player, a gamester.*
Alexander, dri, m. 2. *Alexander the Great.*
Alexandria, æ, f. 1. *a city of Egypt.*
Algeo, ēre, si, — intr. 2. *to be very chill, to be cold, to starve.*
Algor, ōris, m. 3. *cold.*
Alias, adv. *at another time;* alias, — alias, *at one time, — at another time.*
Alicubi, adv. *somewhere.*
Aliēnus, a, um, adj. *belonging to another, another's, foreign, free from.*
Alimentum, i, n. 2. *nourishment, food.*
Alio, adv. *to another place.*
Aliquando, adv. *sometimes, once.*
Aliquantus, a, um, adj. *some, considerable.*
Alĭquis, qua, quod *or* quid, pron. *some person* or *thing, some.*
Alĭquo, adv. *to some place.*
Alĭquot, adj. indec. *some.*
Aliquoties, adv. *several times.*
Alĭter, adv. *otherwise.*
Aliunde, adv. *from another place;* aliunde alio, *from one place to another.*
Alius, a, ud, pron. *another.*
Allĭcio, ĕre, exi, ectum, tr. 3. *to attract, to allure.*
Allŏquor, qui, cūtus, *or* quūtus, dep. 3. *to speak to, to address.*
Alo, ĕre, ui, altum, *or* alĭtum, tr. 3. *to feed, to nourish.*
Alpes, ium, m. pl. 3. *the Alps.*
Alter, ĕra, ĕrum, adj. *another the other, second.*
Altus, a, um, adj. *high, deep.*
Alvus, i, f. 2. *the belly.*
Amabĭlis, e, adj. *lovely, amiable.*
Amans, tis, adj. *loving.* Sub. *a lover.*
Ambio, īre, īvi, ītum, tr. 4. *to surround, encircle.*
Ambitio, ōnis, f. 3. *ambition.*
Ambĭtus, us, m. 4. *a going around, a circuit.*
Ambo, æ, o, adj. pl. *both.*
Ambŭlo, āre, āvi, ātum, tr. 1. *to walk.*
Amīce, adv. *friendly.*
Amicio, īre, ui, *or* xi, ctum, tr. 4. *to clothe.*
Amicitia, æ, f. 1. *friendship.*
Amicŭlum, i, n. 2. *a cloak.*
Amīcus, i, m. 2. *a friend.*
Amitto, ĕre, īsi, issum, tr. 3. *to send away, to lose.*

Amnis, is, m. 3. *a river.*
Amo, āre, āvi, ātum, tr. 1. *to love.*
Amor, ōris, m. 3. *love.*
Amŏveo, ēre, ōvi, ōtum, tr. 2. *to remove.*
Amplector, ti, xus, dep. 3. *to twist around, to embrace.*
Amplitūdo, ĭnis, f. 3. *greatness, high station.*
Amplius, adv. *more.*
Amplus, a, um, adj. *large, much, great.*
An, adv. & conj. *whether? or.*
Ancŏra, æ, f. 1. *an anchor.*
Ancus, i (Martius), m. 2. *one of the Roman kings.*
Androgeos, ei, m. 2. *a man's name.*
Ango, ĕre, xi, — tr. 3. *to strangle, to vex, to grieve.*
Angor, ōris, m. 3. *pain, anguish.*
Angustia, æ, f. 1. *a strait, narrowness.*
Angustus, a, um, adj. *narrow, strait.*
Anĭma, æ, f. 1. *breath, life, the soul.*
Animadversio, ōnis, f. 3. *an observation, a reproof.*
Animadverto, ĕre, ti, sum, tr. 3. *to perceive, to consider.*
Anĭmal, ālis, intr. 3. *an animal.*
Anĭmans, tis, f. *sometimes* m. & n. 3. *an animal.*
Anĭmus, i, m. 2. *the mind, the soul, courage.*
Annālis, is, m. 3. *the history of a year*, pl. *annals.*
Annon, adv. *whether or not.*
Annŭlus, i, m. 2. *a ring.*
Annus, i, m. 2. *a year.*
Ante, prep. *before.*
Ante, adv. *before, previously.*
Antea, adv. *before, formerly.*
Anteactus, a, um, pt. *done before.*
Antecēdo, ĕre, cessi, cessum, tr. 3. *to go before, to excel.*
Antecello, ĕre, —, —, intr. *to excel, surpass.*
Anteeo, īre, ii, *seldom* īvi, ĭtum, intr. irr. *to go before, to excel.*
Antefĕro, ferre, tŭli, lātum, tr. irr. *to carry before, to prefer.*
Antegredior, di, gressus, dep. 3. *to go before.*
Antepōno, ĕre, sui, situm, tr. 3. *to set before, to prefer.*
Antĕquam, adv. *before that.*
Anticyra, æ, f. 1. *Anticyra, a city of Phocis.*
Antigŏnus, i, m. 2. *a man's name.*
Antiochus, i, m. 2. *a Syrian king.*
Antipăter, tri, m. 2. *Antipater, one of Alexander's generals.*
Antiquĭtas, ātis, f. 3. *antiquity.*
Antīquus, a, um, adj. *old, ancient.*
Antisthĕnes, is, m. 3. *a cynic philosopher.*
Antonius, ii, m. 2. *Antony.*
Anystis, is, m. 3. *Anystis, a man's name.*
Anxius, a, um, adj. *thoughtful, anxious.*
Aperio, īre, ui, tum, tr. 4. *to open, to explain.*
Apertè, adv. *openly.*
Apertus, a, um, adj. *open, wide.*
Apis, is, f. 3. *a bee.*
Apollo, ĭnis, m. 3. *Apollo, the god of music,* &c.
Apolloniātes, is, m. 3. *a native of Apollonia.*
Apollonius, ii, m. 2. *a man's name.*
Apparātus, us, m. 4. *splendour.*
Appareo, ēre, ui, itum, intr. 2. *to appear.*
Appello, āre, āvi, ātum, tr. 1. *to call to, to name.*
Appĕtens, tis, adj. *desirous, eager for.*
Appetītus, ûs, m. 4. *appetite, desire.*
Appĕto, ĕre, īvi, ītum, tr. 3. *to desire, to catch at, strive after.*
Applĭco, āre, āvi, ātum, *or* ui, ĭtum, tr. 1. *to apply.*
Approbatio, ōnis, f. 3. *approbation.*

Apprŏbo, āre, āvi, ātum, tr. 1. *to approve.*
Appropinquo, āre, āvi, ātum, tr. 1. *to draw nigh, to approach.*
Aprīlis, is, m. 3. *the month of April.*
Aptus, a, um, adj. *fit, suitable, proper.*
Apud, prep. *at, near.*
Apulia, æ, f. 1. *Apulia, a province of Italy.*
Aqua, æ, f. 1. *water.*
Ara, æ, f. 1. *an altar.*
Arabs, ăbis, m. 3. *an Arab.*
Arātor, ōris, m. 3. *a ploughman.*
Aratrum, i, n. 2. *a plough.*
Arbĭtror, āri, ātus, dep. 1. *to judge, to think.*
Arbor, & arbos, ŏris, f. 3. *a tree.*
Arca, æ, f. 1. *a chest, a coffer.*
Arcadius, a, um, adj. *belonging to Arcadia, Arcadian.*
Arceo, ēre, cui, ctum, tr. 2. *to keep off, drive away.*
Arcesilaus, i, m. 2. *a man's name.*
Arcesso, ĕre, īvi, ītum, tr. 3. *to call, to summon.*
Archytas, æ, m. 1. *Archytas, a man's name.*
Arcus, us, m. 4. *a bow, a rainbow.*
Ardeo, ēre, si, sum, intr. 2. *to burn.*
Ardor, ōris, m. 3. *eagerness, ardour.*
Arduus, a, um, adj. *high, steep, difficult.*
Area, æ, f. 1. *a threshing-floor, a field.*
Aresco, ĕre, intr. 3. *to become dry.*
Arganthonius, ii, m. 2. *Arganthonius, a man's name.*
Argentum, i, n. 2. *silver.*
Argilla, æ, f. 1. *white clay.*
Argumentum, i, n. 2. *an argument.*
Arguo, ĕre, ui, ūtum, tr. 3. *to show, to accuse.*
Arĭdus, a, um, adj. *dry.*
Arimĭnum, i, n. 2. *Ariminum, a town in Italy.*
Ariovistus, i, m. 2. *a German king.*
Aristīdes, is, m. 3. *Aristides, an Athenian.*
Aristippus, i, m. 2. *a Grecian philosopher.*
Aristotĕles, is, m. 3. *a Grecian philosopher.*
Arma, ōrum, n. 2. *arms.*
Armenius, ii, m. 2. *an Armenian.*
Armo, āre, āvi, ātum, tr. 1. *to arm, to equip.*
Aro, āre, āvi, ātum, tr. 1. *t plough.*
Arrŏgans, tis, adj. *arrogant, proud.*
Arrogantia, æ, f. 1. *arrogance, pride, insolence.*
Ars, tis, f. 3. *an art, skill.*
Artĭfex, ĭcis, c. 3. *an artist.*
Artus, us, m. 4. *a joint, a limb.*
Aruns, untis, m. 3. *the son of Tarquin.*
Arvum, i, n. 2. *a ploughed field, a field.*
Arx, cis, f. 3. *a fortress, a citadel.*
Ascendo, ĕre, di, sum, tr. 3. *to ascend, to climb.*
Asia. æ, f. 1. *Asia.*
Asiaticus, i, m. 2. *a surname of Scipio.*
Asĭna, æ, m. 1. *a man's name.*
Aspectus, us, m. 4. *aspect, appearance.*
Asper, ĕra, ĕrum, adj. *rough, cruel.*
Aspĭcio, ĕre, exi, ectum, tr. 3. *to look to, to see.*
Assentatio, ōnis, f. 3. *assent, flattery.*
Assentātor, ōris, m. 3. *a flatterer.*
Assentior, īri, sus, dep. 4. *to assent, to agree.*
Assĕquor, qui, cūtus, *or* quūtus, dep. 3. *to overtake, to obtain.*
Assiduus, a, um, adj. *assiduous, constant.*
Assimŭlo, āre, āvi, ātum, tr. 1. *to make like, to compare.*
Assuefacio, ĕre, fēci, factum, tr. 3 *to accustom.*

Assuetūdo, ĭnis, f. 3. *custom, use.*
Astrum, i, n. 2. *a star.*
At, conj. *but.*
Athēnæ, ārum, f. 1. *Athens, the capital of Attica.*
Atheniensis, is, m. 3. *an Athenian.*
Atilius, ii, m. 2. *a man's name.*
Atque, conj. *and.*
Atrox, cis, adj. *atrocious.*
Attentus, a, um, adj. *attentive.*
Attĭcus, i, m. 2. *a man's name.*
Attineo, ēre, ui, — tr. 2. *to hold back, to belong.*
Attingo, ĕre, tigi, tactum, tr. 3. *to reach, arrive at.*
Auctor & Autor, ōris, m. 3, *author, ratifier;* auctor fiĕri, *to confirm.*
Auctorĭtas, ātis, f. 3. *authority.*
Aucupo, āre, āvi, ātum, tr. 1. *to listen to.*
Audacia, æ, f. 1. *boldness, courage.*
Audacter, (cius, cessĭme), adv. *boldly.*
Audax, cis, adj. *bold.*
Audeo, ēre, sus, intr. p. *to be bold, to dare.*
Audio, īre, īvi, ītum, tr. 4. *to hear.*
Audītus, ûs, m. 4. *the sense of hearing.*
Aufĕro, ferre, abstŭli, ablātum, tr. irr. *to take away.*
Augeo, ēre, xi, ctum, tr. 2. *to increase.*
Augur, ŭris, m. 3. *an augur.*
Augurium, ii, n. 2. *an augury.*
Augustus, i, m. 2. *a man's name.*
Aula, æ, f. 1. *a court, a hall.*
Aurelius, ii, m. 2. *a Roman commander.*
Aureus, a, um, adj. *made of gold, golden.*
Auris, is, f. 3. *the ear.*
Aurum, i, n. 2. *gold.*
Auspĭcor, āri, ātus, dep. 1. *to take the auspices, to begin.*
Aut, conj. *or, either.*
Autem, conj. *but, however.*
Auxilium, ii, n. 2. *assistance, help.*
Avaritia, æ, f. 1. *avarice, covetousness.*
Avārus, a, um, adj. *covetous, greedy.*
Avārus, i, m. 2. *a covetous man.*
Aveo, ēre, — — tr. 2. *to desire, to covet.*
Avernus, i, m. 2. *Avernus, a lake in Campania, hell.*
Avernus, a, um, adj. *belonging to Avernus, infernal.*
Averto, ĕre, ti, sum, tr. 3. *to turn away.*
Avis, is, f. 3. *a bird, a fowl.*
Avŏlo, āre, āvi, ātum, intr. 1. *to fly away, escape.*
Avuncŭlus, i, m. 2. *an uncle.*
Avus, i, m. 2. *a grandfather.*

B.

Babylon, ōnis, f. 3. *Babylon, the capital of Chaldæa.*
Babylonia, æ, f. 1. *Babylonia, the country around Babylon.*
Bacca, æ, f. 1. *a berry.*
Baccha, æ, f. 1. *a priestess of Bacchus.*
Bactriānus, a, um, adj. *of Bactriana.*
Baculum, i, n. 2. *a staff.*
Baianus, a, um, adj. *of Baiæ.*
Balbus, i, m. 2. *a man's name.*
Barbărus, a, um, adj. *barbarous, wild.*
Beāte, adv. *happily.*
Beātus, a, um, adj. *happy, blessed.*
Bebius, ii, m. 2. *a man's name.*
Belgæ, ārum, m. 1. *the Belgians.*
Bello, āre, āvi, ātum, intr. 1. *to war.*
Bellua, æ, f. 1. *a large beast.*
Bellum, i, n. 2. *war.*
Bene, adv. 2. *well.*
Benefăcio, ĕre, fēci, factum, tr. 3. *to do good.*

Benefactum, i, n. 2. *a good deed, a favour.*
Beneficentia, æ, f. 1. *beneficence, kindness.*
Beneficium, ii, n. 2. *a benefit, a favour.*
Benefĭcus, a, um, adj. *beneficent, kind.*
Benefĭo, fĭĕri, factus, irr. *to be well done.*
Benevŏle, adv. *kindly.*
Benevolentia, æ, f. 1. *benevolence, good-will.*
Benigne, adv. *bountifully, liberally.*
Benignĭtas, ātis, f. 3. *kindness, generosity.*
Benignus, a, um, adj. *kind, courteous.*
Bestia, æ, f. 1. *a wild beast.*
Bestiŏla, æ, f. 1. *a small animal.*
Bibliothēca, æ, f. 1. *a library.*
Bĭbo, ĕre, bĭbi, bibĭtum, tr. 3. *to drink.*
Bibŭlus, i, m. 2. *a man's name.*
Biduum, i, n. 2. *the space of two days.*
Bīni, æ, a, adj. *two by two, two* (at a time).
Bis, adv. *twice.*
Biturĭges, um, m. 3. *a people of Gaul.*
Blanditia, æ, f. 1. *a compliment, flattery.*
Blandus, a, um, adj. *gentle, kind.*
Bocchus, i, m. 2. *a king of Mauritania.*
Bonĭtas, ātis, f. 3. *goodness.*
Bononia, æ, f. 1. *Bononia, a town in Italy.*
Bonum, i, n. 2. *a good thing, a blessing.*
Bonus, a, um, adj. *good.*
Bos, bovis, c. 3. *an ox* or *cow.*
Brachium, ii, n. 2. *an arm.*
Brevis, e, adj. *short.*
Brevĭtas, ātis, f. 3. *shortness, brevity.*
Brevĭter, (ius, issĭme), adv. *briefly.*
Britannia, æ, f. 1. *Britain.*
Britannus, i, m. 2. *a Briton.*
Brixellum, i, n. 2. *Brixellum, a town in Italy.*
Brundusium, ii, n. 2. *a city of Italy.*
Brutus, i, m. 2. *one of the first Roman consuls.*

C.

Cado, ĕre, cecĭdi, cāsum, intr. 3. *to fall.*
Cadūcus, a, um, adj. *ready to fall, frail.*
Cæcus, a, um, adj. *blind, dark.*
Cædes, is, f. 3. *slaughter, murder.*
Cædo, ĕre, cecīdi, cæsum, tr. 3. *to cut, to kill.*
Cæsar, ăris, m. 3. *Cæsar, a man's name.*
(Cæter, *seldom used,*) ĕra, ĕrum, adj. *the other, the rest.*
Calamĭtas, ātis, f. 3. *a calamity, a misfortune.*
Calamitōsus, a, um, adj. *calamitous, miserable.*
Calcar, āris, n. 3. *a spur.*
Calco, āre, āvi, ātum, tr. 1. *to trample upon, to kick.*
Caleo, ēre, ui, — intr. 2. *to be warm, to be hot.*
Calĭdus, a, um, adj. *warm, fiery, angry, enraged.*
Calĭgo, ĭnis, f. 3. *darkness.*
Calĭgŭla, æ, m. 1. *a Roman emperor.*
Calleo, ēre, ui, — intr. 2. *to grow callous.*
Callidĭtas, ātis, f. 3. *skilfulness, cunning.*
Callĭdus, a, um, adj. *skilful, expert.*
Calor, ōris, m. 3. *heat.*
Calpurnius, ii, m. 2. *a man's name.*
Calumnia, æ, f. 1. *calumny, slander.*
Campus, i, m. 2. *a plain, a field.*

Candor, ōris, m. 3. *whiteness.*
Candĭdus, a, um, adj. *white, bright.*
Canis, is, c. 3. *a dog* or *bitch.*
Canistius, ii, m. 2. *Canistius, a man's name.*
Capesso, ĕre, īvi, ītum, tr. 3. *to take in hand, to begin.*
Capio, ĕre, cepi, captum, tr. 3. *to take, to seize.*
Capitālis, e, adj. *capital, hurtful.*
Capitolium, ii, n. 2. *the Capitol.*
Cappadocia, æ, f. 1. *Cappadocia.*
Capreæ, ārum, 1. pl. *Caprea, an island.*
Captīvus, i, m. 2. *a captive.*
Captus, a, um, pt. *taken, seized, affected, deprived of; one taken, a captive.*
Capua, æ, f. 1. *the city Capua.*
Caput, ĭtis, n. 3. *the head.*
Carbo, ōnis, m. 3. *a Roman consul.*
Carcer, ĕris, m. 3. *a prison.*
Care, adv. *dearly, at a great price.*
Careo, ēre, ui, ĭtum, intr. 2. *to want, to be free from.*
Carĭtas, ātis, f. 3. *dearth, love, affection.*
Carmen, ĭnis, n. 3. *a verse, a song.*
Caro, carnis, f. 3. *flesh.*
Carpo, ĕre, psi, ptum, tr. 3. *to blame.*
Carthāgo, inis, f. 3. *Carthage.*
Cārus, a, um, adj. *dear, beloved.*
Castè, adv. *chastely, devoutly.*
Castellum, i, n. 2. *a fort.*
Castigatio, ōnis, f. 3. *chastisement, reproof.*
Castigātor, ōris, m. 3. *a chastiser, a corrector.*
Castor, ŏris, m. 3. *Castor, one of the sons of Leda.*
Castra, ōrum, n. pl. 2. *a camp.*
Castus, a, um, adj. *chaste, religious.*
Casus, ûs, m. 4. *a fall, an accident.*
Catēna, æ, f. 1. *a chain.*
Catilīna, æ, m. 1. *Catiline, a Roman.*
Cato, ōnis, m. 3. *Cato, a Roman.*
Causa, æ, f. 1. *a cause, a reason, a motive.*
Caute, adv. *cautiously, prudently.*
Caveo, ēre, cāvi, cautum, tr. 2. *to beware of, to avoid.*
Cavo, āre, āvi, ātum, tr. 1. *to make hollow.*
Cecrops, pis, m. 3. *the first king of Attica.*
Cedo, ĕre, cessi, cessum, tr. 3. *to give place, to yield.*
Celebrĭtas, ātis, f. 3. *a throng, a numerous attendance.*
Celebro, āre, āvi, ātum, tr. 1. *to celebrate.*
Celerĭtas, ātis, f. 3. *rapidity, quickness.*
Celerĭter, adv. (ius, errĭme), *quick,* comp. *quicker, sooner.*
Cella, æ, f. 1. *a chapel.*
Celo, āre, āvi, ātum, tr. 1. *to hide, to conceal.*
Celsus, a, um, adj. *erect, high, lofty.*
Censeo, ēre, ui, um, tr. 2. *to think, to judge.*
Censor, ōris, m. 3. *a censor.*
Census, ûs, m. 4. *a valuation of one's estate,* &c., *a census.*
Centēni, æ, a, adj. *a hundred to each.*
Centesĭmus, a, um, adj. *hundredth.*
Centum, adj. ind. *a hundred.*
Centurio, ōnis, m. 3. *a centurion.*
Cēres, ĕris, f. 3. *Ceres, the goddess of corn.*
Cereus, a, um, adj. *made of wax, waxen.*
Cerno, ĕre, crēvi, crētum, tr. 3. *to see clearly.*
Certāmen, ĭnis, n. 3. *a contest, a dispute.*
Certe, adv. *certainly, at least.*
Certo, āre, āvi, ātum, tr. 1. *to contend, to fight.*

Certus, a, um, adj. *certain, sure, confidential, trusty.*
Cervix, ĭcis, f. 3. *the hinder part of the neck, the neck.*
Cespes, ĭtis, m. 3. *a turf, a sod.*
Cesso, āre, āvi, ātum, intr. 1. *to cease, to loiter.*
Cetĕrus (Cætĕrus), a, um, adj. *other.*
Ceu, adv. *as it were, even, as.*
Chamæleon, ontis & ŏnis, m. 3. *a chameleon.*
Charĭtas, ātis, f. 3. *see* Caritas.
Charta, æ, f. 1. *paper.*
Chius, ii, f. 2. *Chios, an island.*
Chrysippus, i, m. 2. *a Stoic philosopher.*
Chrysogŏnus, i, m. *a man's name.*
Cibus, i, m. 2. *food, meat.*
Cicĕro, ōnis, m. 3. *M. T. Cicero, a Roman orator.*
Cimbrĭcus, a, um, adj. *Cimbrian.*
Cimmerius, ii, m. 2. *a Cimmerian.*
Cimon, ōnis, m. 3. *a man's name.*
Cingo, ĕre, xi, ctum, tr. 3. *to gird, to surround.*
Cingonius, ii, m. 2. *a man's name.*
Cinna, æ, m. 1. *Cinna, a Roman consul.*
Circum, prep. *around, about.*
Circumfluo, ĕre, xi, xum, tr. 3. *to flow about, to abound.*
Circumfodio, ĕre, fōdi, fossum, tr. 3. *to dig around.*
Circumfusus, a, um, pt. *surrounded.*
Circumsto, stāre, stĕti, — tr. 1. *to stand around.*
Circumvĕnio, īre, vēni, ventum, tr. 4. *to surround.*
Citerior, us, adj. comp. *hither, on this side.*
Cithăra, æ, f. 1. *a harp.*
Cito, adv. *quickly, soon.*
Cĭto, āre, āvi, ātum, tr. 1. *to cite, call, summon.*
Civīlis, e, adj. *belonging to citizens, civil.*
Civis, is, c. 3. *a citizen.*
Civĭtas, ātis, f. 3. *a state, a city.*
Clam, adv. *secretly, privately.*
Clămor, ōris, m. 3. *clamor, noise, a shout.*
Clarĭtas, ātis, f. 3. *clearness.*
Clarus, a, um, adj. *clear, illustrious, distinguished.*
Classis, is, f. 3. *a fleet.*
Claudius, ii, m. 2. *a man's name.*
Claudo, ĕre, si, sum, tr. 3. *to shut, to close.*
Cleanthes, is, m. 3. *a man's name.*
Cleanthus, i, m. 2. *Cleanthus, a man's name.*
Clementia, æ, f. 1. *courtesy, mercy.*
Clinia, æ, m. 1. *a man's name.*
Clodius, ii, m. 2. *a celebrated Roman.*
Clœlia, æ, f. 1. *a Roman maiden.*
Cluentius, ii, m. *a man's name.*
Clypeus, i, m. & um, i, n. 2. *a shield.*
Coacervatio, ōnis, f. 3. *a heaping together.*
Cocles, is, m. 3. *a man's name.*
Cœlestis, e, adj. *relating to heaven, heavenly.*
Cœlius, ii, m. 2. *a man's name.*
Cœlum, i, n. Pl. i, ōrum, m. 2. *heaven, the sky.*
Cœno, āre, āvi, ātum, intr. 1. *to sup.*
Cœnum, i, n. 2. *dirt, filth.*
Cœpi, cœpisse, def. *to begin.*
Coërceo, ēre, ui, ĭtum, tr. 2. *to restrain, to check.*
Cœtus, ûs, m. 4. *a crowd, a company.*
Cogitatio, ōnis, f. 3. *a thinking, a reflection.*
Cogĭtāto, adv. *designedly.*
Cogĭto, āre, āvi, ātum, tr. 1. *to think, to reflect.*
Cognātus, a, um, adj. *kindred, congenial.*
Cognitio, ōnis, f. 3. *knowledge, an inquiry.*
Cognominātus, a, um, pt. *surnamed.*
Cognomĭnis, e, adj. *of the same name.*

Cognosco, ĕre, nōvi, nĭtum, tr. 3. *to know, to understand.*

Cogo, ĕre, coēgi, coactum, tr. 3. *to force.*

Cohĭbeo, ēre, ui, ĭtum, tr. 2. *to hold, to restrain.*

Cŏhors, tis, f. 3. *a cohort.*

Cohortor, āri, ātus, dep. 1. *to exhort, to encourage.*

Collēga, æ, m. 1. *a colleague.*

Collĭgo, āre, āvi, ātum, tr. 1. *to bind.*

Collĭgo, ĕre, lēgi, lectum, tr. 3. *to collect.*

Collĭno, ĕre, īvi & ēvi, ĭtum, tr. 3. *to besmear, to daub.*

Collis, is, m. 3. a *hill.*

Collŏco, āre, āvi, ātum, tr. 1. *to place.*

Colloquium, ii, n. 2. *a conference.*

Colluceo, ēre, luxi, — intr. 2. *to shine, to blaze.*

Collum, i, n. 2. *the neck.*

Colo, ĕre, colui, cultum, tr. 3. *to till, to cultivate, to worship.*

Colōnæ, ārum, f. pl. 1. *Colonæ.*

Colōnus, i, m. 2. *a colonist, a farmer.*

Cŏlor, ōris, m. 3. *color.*

Cŏmans, tis, adj. *long-haired.*

Comes, ĭtis, c. 3. *a companion.*

Comĭtas, ātis, f. 3. *affability, courtesy.*

Comĭter, adv. *agreeably, politely, courteously.*

Comitia, ōrum, n. pl. 2. *the comitia, an election.*

Comĭtor, āri, ātus, dep. 1. *to accompany.*

Commeātus, us, m. 4. *provisions.*

Commemoratio, ōnis, f. 3. *remembrance.*

Commemŏro, āre, āvi, ātum, tr. 1. *to mention, to talk of.*

Commendo, āre, āvi, ātum, tr. 1. *to recommend.*

Commercium, ii. n. 2. *commerce, intercourse.*

Commentarium, ii. n. 2. *a register.*

Commentatio, ōnis, f. 3. *meditation.*

Commereor, ēri, ĭtus, dep. 2. *to deserve.*

Committo, ĕre, mīsi, missum, tr. 3. *to commit, to cause.*

Commŏde, adv. *conveniently.*

Commŏdo, āre, āvi, ātum, tr. 1. *to accommodate, to lend.*

Commŏdum, i, n. 2. *convenience, advantage.*

Commŏdus, a, um, adj. *convenient, suitable.*

Commŏneo, ēre, ui, ĭtum, tr. 2. *to warn, to remind.*

Commŏror, āri, ātus, dep. 1. *to abide, to hinder.*

Commŏveo, ēre, ōvi, ōtum, tr. 2. *to move, to disturb.*

Communio, īre, īvi, ītum, tr. 4. *to fortify.*

Commūnis, e, adj. *common.*

Communĭtas, ātis, f. 3. *community, fellowship.*

Commūto, āre, āvi, ātum, tr. 1. *to change.*

Compăro, āre, āvi, ātum, tr. 1. *to prepare, to compare.*

Compello, ĕre, pŭli, pulsum, tr. 3. *to compel.*

Compenso, āre, āvi, ātum, tr. 1. *to compensate.*

Complector, ti, xus, dep. 3. *to embrace.*

Compleo, ĕre, ēvi, ētum, tr. 2. *to fill up, to finish.*

Complūres, a & ia, adj. pl. *many.*

Compōno, ĕre, ŏsui, ŏsĭtum, tr. 3. *to arrange, to compose.*

Compos, ŏtis, adj. *master of.*

Compositio, ōnis, f. 3. *a composition.*

Comprendo, ĕre, di, sum, tr. 3. *to take hold of, to comprise.*

Conātus, ûs, m. 4. *an endeavour, an attempt.*

Concēdo, ĕre, cessi, cessum, tr. 3. *to depart, to yield, to grant.*

Concelebro, āre, āvi, ātum, tr. 1. *to celebrate.*

Concessus, us, m. 4. *consent.*
Concilio, āre, āvi, ātum, tr. 1. *to conciliate, to procure.*
Concio, ōnis, f. 3. *an assembly, a speech, harangue.*
Concipio, ĕre, cēpi, ceptum, tr. 3. *to conceive.*
Conclāmo, āre, āvi, ātum, intr. 1. *to cry out.*
Concludo, ĕre, si, sum, tr. 3. *to shut up, to conclude, to form.*
Concordia, æ, f. 1. *concord, agreement.*
Concordia, æ, f. 1. *Concord, the name of a deity.*
Concupisco, ĕre, īvi, ītum, tr. 3. *to desire greatly, to covet.*
Concurro, ĕre, ri, sum, intr. 3. *to rush together, to engage (in battle).*
Condemno, āre, āvi, ātum, tr. 1. *to accuse, to condemn.*
Condimentum, i, n. 2. *sauce, seasoning.*
Conditio, ōnis, f. 3. *a condition.*
Condo, ĕre, dĭdi, dĭtum, tr. 3. *to place together, to build, to hide.*
Confabŭlor, āri, ātus, dep. 1. *to talk.*
Confĕro, ferre, tŭli, lātum, tr. irr. *to bring together, to compare;* conferre se, *to hasten.*
Confĭcio, ĕre, ēci, ectum, tr. 3. *to finish, to waste.*
Confīdo, ĕre, sus, intr. p. *to trust.*
Confiteor, fitēri, fessus, dep. 2. *to confess.*
Conflīgo, ĕre, xi, ctum, tr. 3. *to fight, engage in battle.*
Confluo, ĕre, xi, xum, intr. 3. *to flow together.*
Conformo, āre, āvi, ātum, tr. 1. *to form, to fashion.*
Confŭgio, ĕre, fūgi, fugĭtum, intr. 3. *to flee to, to take refuge.*
Congredior, di, gressus, dep. 3. *to engage in battle.*
Congruo, ĕre, ui, — intr. 3. *to agree.*
Conjicio, ĕre, jēci, jectum, tr. 3. *to throw, to hurl.*
Conjunctissĭme, adv. sup. *very closely, in the greatest intimacy.*
Conjunctus, a, um, pt. *joined together, united.*
Conjungo, ĕre, xi, ctum, tr. 3. *to join.*
Conjuratio, ōnis, f. 3. *a conspiracy.*
Conjūro, āre, āvi, ātum, tr. 1. *to conspire, to enter into a conspiracy.*
Conjux, ŭgis, c. 3. *a husband* or *wife.*
Connecto, ĕre, xui, xum, tr. 3. *to tie, to fasten.*
Conniveo, ēre, nivi *or* nixi, intr. 2. *to wink, to shut the eyes.*
Conor, āri, ātus, dep. 1. *to endeavour.*
Conquĕror, quĕri, questus, dep. 3. *to complain.*
Conquiesco, ĕre, ēvi, ētum, intr. 3. *to be quiet.*
Conquiro, ĕre, sīvi, sītum, tr. 3. *to search for.*
Conscientia, æ, f. 1. *consciousness.*
Conscisco, ĕre, īvi, ītum, tr. 3. *to commit, to procure.*
Conscius, a, um, adj. *conscious.*
Conscrībo, ĕre, psi, ptum, tr. 3. *to write, to enrol.*
Conscriptus, a, um, adj. *conscript, chosen;* conscripti patres, *conscript fathers, assembled fathers,* the form used in addressing the Roman senate.
Consensio, ōnis, f. 3. *consent, agreement.*
Consensus, ûs, m. 4. *consent, an agreement.*
Consentaneus, a, um, adj. *agreeable.*
Consentio, īre, si, sum, tr. 4. *to consent, to agree.*
Consĕquor, qui, cūtus *or* quūtus, dep. 3. *to follow, to obtain, overtake.*
Conservo, āre, āvi, ātum, tr. 1. *to preserve.*

Consĭdeo, ēre, ēdi, essum, intr. 2. *to sit together.*

Considerāte, adv. *with consideration, cautiously.*

Considĕro, āre, āvi, ātum, tr. 1. *to consider.*

Consīdo, ĕre, sēdi, sessum, intr. 3. *to sit together, to settle, encamp.*

Consilium, ii, n. 2. *counsel, advice.*

Consisto, ĕre, stĭti, stĭtum, intr. 3. *to stop, to stand, to consist of.*

Consocio, āre, āvi, ātum, tr. 1. *to unite.*

Consolatio, ōnis, f. 3. *consolation, comfort.*

Consōlor, āri, ātus, dep. 1. *to console.*

Consors, tis, m. 3. *a partner.*

Conspectus, ûs, m. 4. *a sight, a view.*

Conspicio, ĕre, spexi, spectum, tr. 3. *to see.*

Conspicuus, a, um, adj. *conspicuous, superb.*

Constans, tis, adj. *steady, constant.*

Constanter, adv. *constantly, steadily.*

Constantia, æ, f. 1. *constancy, firmness.*

Constat, impers. (consto), 1. *it is agreed, it is evident.*

Constituo, ĕre, ui, ūtum, tr. 3. *to place, to determine.*

Consto, āre, stĭti, stĭtum, & stātum, intr. 1. *to stand together, to cost, to consist.*

Consuesco, ĕre, ēvi, ētum, intr. 3. *to be accustomed.*

Consuetūdo, ĭnis, f. 3. *a custom, a habit.*

Consuētus, a, um, pt. *accustomed.*

Consul, ŭlis, m. 3. *a consul.*

Consulāris, e, adj. *belonging to a consul, consular.*

Consulātus, us, m. 4, *consulship.*

Consŭlo, ĕrĕ, ui, tum, tr. 3. *to consult.*

Consulto, adv. *designedly, on purpose.*

Consūmo, ĕre, psi, ptum, tr. 3. *to consume, to spend.*

Contemno, ĕre, psi, ptum, tr. 3. *to despise.*

Contendo, ĕre, di, tum, tr. 3. *to strive for, insist upon, contend.*

Contentio, ōnis, f. 3. *contention.*

Contentus, a, um, adj. *content.*

Contĕro, ĕre, trīvi, trītum, tr. 3. *to waste.*

Contineo, ēre, tinui, tentum, tr. 2. *to hold, to contain.*

Contingo, ĕre, tĭgi, tactum, tr. 3. *to touch, to happen.*

Continuo, adv. *forthwith, instantly.*

Contra, prep. *against.*

Contradīco, ĕre, xi, ctum, tr. 3. *to contradict, to refuse.*

Contrăho, ĕre, xi, ctum, tr. 3. *to draw together, to contract, to get (money).*

Contrarius, a, um, adj. *contrary;* e contrario, *on the contrary.*

Contremisco, ĕre, intr. 3. *to tremble.*

Controversia, æ, f. 1. *controversy.*

Contubernium, ii, n. 2. *a tent, companionship.*

Contumelia, æ, f. 1. *an affront, a reproach.*

Conturbo, āre, āvi, ātum, tr. 1. *to trouble, to disturb.*

Convalesco, ĕre, ui, — intr. 3. *to recover health.*

Conveniens, tis, adj. *suitable, proper.*

Convenienter, adv. *conveniently.*

Convĕnio, īre, vēni, ventum, intr. 4. *to assemble, to meet, to agree, to suit.*

Convĕnit, imp. *it is meet, or suitable.*

Conventum, i, n. 2. *an agreement, a compact.*

Conventus, ûs, m. 4. *an assembly, a meeting.*

Converto, ĕre, ti, sum, tr. 3. *to turn, to convert, to apply.*

Convictus, us, m. 4. *society, fellowship.*

Convīva, æ, c. 1. *a guest.*

Copia, æ, f. 1. *plenty.* Pl. *forces.*
Copŭlo, āre, āvi, ātum, tr. 1. *to couple, unite.*
Cor, cordis, n. 3. *the heart.*
Cōram, prep. *before, in presence of*
Corcyra, æ, f. 1. *Corcyra, an island.*
Corinthius, a, um, adj. *Corinthian.*
Corinthus, i, f. 2. *Corinth, a city of Greece.*
Cornelia, æ, f. 1. *a woman's name.*
Cornelius, ii, m. 2. *Cornelius, one of the Cornelian gens.*
Cornu, n. 4. indecl. sing. (pl. cornua), *a horn, a wing of an army.*
Corōna, æ, f. 1. *a crown, a circle, an audience.*
Corpus, ŏris, n. 3. *a body.*
Correctio, ōnis, f. 3. *a correction, an amendment.*
Corrĭgo, ĕre, exi, ectum, tr. 3. *to correct, to amend.*
Corrumpo, ĕre, rūpi, ruptum, tr. 3. *to corrupt, to spoil, to destroy.*
Corruo, ĕre, rui, rūtum, intr. 3. *to fall, to fall into, to go to ruin.*
Corruptēla, æ, f. 1. *corruption, a bribe.*
Corruptus, a, um, pt. *corrupted;* adj. *corrupt.*
Corsi, ōrum, m. pl. 2. *the Corsicans.*
Cortex, icis, f. 3. *bark, rind.*
Corvus, i, m. 2. *a raven, a crow.*
Cras, adv. *to-morrow.*
Crassus, i, m. 2. *a man's name.*
Crastĭnus, a, um, adj. *of to-morrow.*
Credibĭlis, e, adj. *credible.*
Credo, ĕre, ĭdi, ĭtum, tr. 3. *to believe, to trust.*
Credulĭtas, ātis, f. 3. *credulity.*
Crĕmo, āre, āvi, ātum, tr. 1. *to burn, to consume.*
Creo, āre, āvi, ātum, tr. 1. *to create, to beget, to appoint.*
Cresco, ĕre, crēvi, crētum, intr. 3. *to increase, to grow.*
Crēta, æ, f. 1. *Crete, an island.*
Crimen, ĭnis, n. 3. *a charge, a crime.*
Criminatio, ōnis, f. 3. *an accusation.*
Crimĭnor, āri, ātus, dep. 1. *to accuse.*
Crinis, is, m. 3. *the hair.*
Critias, æ, m. 1. *Critias, one of the thirty tyrants.*
Crœsus, i, m. 2. *Crœsus, king of Lydia.*
Crotoniātes, æ, m. 1. *an inhabitant of Crotona.*
Cruciātus, us, m. 4. *torture.*
Crucio, āre, āvi, ātum, tr. 1. *to torment, to vex.*
Crudēlis, e, adj. *cruel.*
Crudelĭtas, ātis, f. 3. *cruelty.*
Cruor, ōris, m. 3. *blood, gore.*
Crus, cruris, n. 3. *the leg.*
Crux, crucis, f. 3. *a cross, torture.*
Crystallīnus, a, um, adj. *of crystal.*
Cubĭtum, i, n. 2. *a cubit.*
Cujus, a, um, adj. *whose? whereof?*
Cūlex, ĭcis, m. 3. *a gnat.*
Culpa, æ, f. 1. *a fault.*
Culpo, āre, āvi, ātum, tr. 1. *to blame.*
Cultio, ōnis, f. 3. *culture.*
Cultor, ōris, m. 3. *a husbandman, a tiller.*
Cultrum, i, n. 2. *a knife.*
Cultus, us, m. 4. *culture.*
Cum, prep. *with, along with.*
Cumulātus, a, um, adj. & pt. *complete, completed.*
Cunctatio, ōnis, f. 3. *delay.*
Cunctus, a, um, adj. *all, whole.*
Cupidĭtas, ātis, f. 3. *desire, covetousness.*
Cupīdo, ĭnis, f. *sometimes* m. 3. *desire, lust.*
Cupĭdus, a, um, adj. *desirous, covetous.*
Cupiens, tis, adj. & pt. *desirous.*
Cupio, ĕre, īvi, ītum, tr. 3. *to desire, to covet.*
Cur, adv. *why?*
Cura, æ, f. 1. *care.*
Curia, æ, f. 1. *the senate-house.*
Curiatii, ōrum, m. 2. *the three Alban brothers.*
Curiatius, ii, m. 2. *a man's name.*
Curio, ōnis, m. 3. *a man's name.*

Curius, ii, m. 2. *a man's name.*
Curo, āre, āvi, ātum, tr. 1. *to take care, to attend to, to cause.*
Curricŭlum, i, n. 2. *a race-course.*
Curro, ĕre, cucurri, cursum, tr. 3. *to run.*
Currus, us, m. 4. *a chariot.*
Cursor, ōris, m. 3. *a runner, a courier.*
Cursus, us, m. 4. *a course, current.*
Custodia, æ, f. 1. *a guarding, a charge.*
Custōdio, īre, īvi, ītum, tr. 4. *to guard, to keep.*
Custos, ōdis, c. 3. *a keeper, a guardian.*
Cyprus, i, f. 2. *the island Cyprus.*
Cyrus, i, m. 2. *Cyrus, king of Persia.*

D.

Damascus, i, m. 2. *Damascus.*
Damno, āre, āvi, ātum, tr. 1. *to condemn.*
Damnum, i, n. 2. *loss, damage.*
Damœtas, æ, m. 1. *Damœtas.*
(Daps, *seldom used*), dapis, f. 3. *food, a feast.*
Darius, ii, m. 2. *Darius, king of Persia.*
Datămes, is, m. 3. *Datames, a man's name.*
Dătus, a, um, pt. *given, dated.*
De, prep. *of, concerning.*
Dea, æ, f. 1. *a goddess.*
Debeo, ēre, ui, ĭtum, tr. 2. *to owe.*
Decēdo, ĕre, cessi, cessum, intr. 3. *to depart, to die.*
Decem, adj. indec. *ten.*
Decens, tis, adj. *comely, beautiful.*
Decerno, ĕre, crēvi, crētum, tr. 3. *to think, to decree, to contend.*
Decerpo, ĕre, psi, ptum, tr. 3. *to gather.*
Decet, imp. *it becomes.*
Decĭmus, a, um, adj. *the tenth.*
Decipio, ĕre, cēpi, ceptum, tr. 3. *to deceive.*

Declāro, āre, āvi, ātum, tr. 1. *to declare.*
Declīno, āre, āvi, ātum, tr. 1. *to bend* or *turn, to leave.*
Decŏro, āre, āvi, ātum, tr. 1. *to decorate, to adorn.*
Decōrus, a, um, adj. *comely, becoming, honourable.*
Decrētum, i, n. 2. *a decree.*
Decumbo, ĕre, cubui, cubĭtum, intr. 3. *to lie down.*
Decurro, ĕre, curri, cursum, intr. 3. *to run down.*
Decus, ŏris, n. 3. *an ornament, grace, honour.*
Dedĕcet, imp. *it is unbecoming.*
Dedĕcus, ŏris, n. 3. *disgrace, dishonour.*
Deditio, ōnis, f. 3. *a surrender.*
Dedo, ĕre, ĭdi, ĭtum, tr. 3. *to submit, to devote one's self, to give up.*
Dedūco, ĕre, xi, ctum, tr. 3. *to bring down, to remove.*
Defectus, us, m. 4. *a failing, an eclipse (of the sun).*
Defendo, ĕre, di, sum, tr. 3. *to defend, to protect.*
Defensio, ōnis, f. 3. *a defence.*
Defensor, ōris, m. 3. *a defender.*
Defĕro, ferre, tŭli, lātum, tr. irr. *to bestow.*
Defĭcio, ĕre, fēci, fectum, tr. 3. *to fail, to stop.*
Defluo, ĕre, xi, xum, intr. 3. *to flow away, escape.*
Deformis, e, adj. *deformed, ugly.*
Deformitas, atis, f. 3. *deformity.*
Degĕner, ĕris, adj. *degenerate, base.*
Dego, ĕre, ēgi, — tr. 3. *to lead, to spend.*
Deinceps, adv. *successively, henceforth.*
Deinde, adv. *then, after that.*
Deiotarus, i, m. 2. *a man's name.*
Dejicio, ĕre, jēci, jectum, tr. 3. *to throw down.*
Delectat, imp. *it delights.*
Delectatio, ōnis, f. 3. *delight, pleasure.*

Delecto, āre, āvi, ātum, tr. 1. *to delight, to allure.*

Delectus, a, um, pt. *chosen, select.*

Delectus, ûs, m. 4. *an election, a choice, a levy.*

Deleo, ēre, ēvi, ētum, tr. 2. *to blot out, to destroy.*

Delibĕro, āre, āvi, ātum, tr. 1. *to consult, to deliberate.*

Deliciæ, ārum, f. pl. 1. *delight, darling.*

Delictum, i, n. 2. *a fault, a crime, an offence.*

Delĭgo, ĕre, ēgi, ectum, tr. 3. *to pick out, to choose.*

Delinquo, ĕre, līqui, lictum, intr. 3. *to fail in duty, to offend.*

Deliquesco, ĕre, licui, — intr. 3. *to melt, to grow soft.*

Deliratio, ōnis, f. 3. *dotage, madness.*

Delīro, āre, āvi, ātum, intr. 1. *to dote, to rave.*

Delphi, ōrum, m. pl. 2. *a city of Phocis, famous for its oracle.*

Delphinus, i, m. 2. *a dolphin.*

Demens, tis, adj. *mad.*

Demeto, ĕre, messui, messum, tr. 3. *to reap.*

Demetrius, ii, m. 2. *Demetrius, a man's name.*

Demĭgro, āre, āvi, ātum, intr. 1. *to depart.*

Demitto, ĕre, īsi, issum, tr. 3. *to send down.*

Democrĭtus, i, m. 2. *Democritus.*

Demolior, īri, ītus, dep. 4. *to demolish, to pull down.*

Demosthĕnes, is, m. 3. *Demosthenes, a Grecian orator.*

Demum, adv. *at length, at last.*

Dēni, æ, a, adj. pl. *ten each.*

Denĭque, adv. *at last, finally.*

Densitas, atis, f. 3. *density, closeness.*

Dentātus, i, m. 2. *a man's name.*

Denuo, adv. *anew, again.*

Denuncio, āre, āvi, ātum, tr. 1. *to denounce, to foretell.*

Depecŭlor, ari, atus, dep. 1. *to plunder.*

Deperdo, ĕre, dĭdi, dĭtum, tr. 3. *to destroy, to lose.*

Deplōro, āre, āvi, ātum, tr. 1. *to deplore.*

Depōno, ĕre, sui, sĭtum, tr. 3. *to lay down.*

Deporto, āre, āvi, ātum, tr. 1. *to carry away, to banish.*

Depravātus, a, um, pt. *vitiated, depraved.*

Derŏgo, āre, āvi, ātum, tr. 1. *to take away.*

Descendo, ĕre, di, sum, intr. 3. *to descend.*

Descensus, ûs, m. 4. *a descent.*

Descisco, ĕre, īvi or ii, ītum, tr. 3. *to depart from.*

Descrībo, ĕre, psi, ptum, tr. 3. *to write down, to copy.*

Desĕro, ĕre, ui, tum, tr. 3. *to desert, to forsake.*

Desiderium, ii, n. 2. *desire, love.*

Desidĕro, āre, āvi, ātum, tr. 1. *to long for, to desire.*

Desidia, æ, f. 1. *sloth, idleness.*

Desidiōsus, a, um, adj. *slothful, idle.*

Designatus, a, um, pt. *appointed elect.*

Desīno, ĕre, īvi & ii, ĭtum, intr. 3. *to cease, to leave off.*

Desisto, ĕre, stĭti, stĭtum, intr. 3. *to leave off, to desist.*

Desperatio, ōnis, f. 3. *despair.*

Despēro, āre, āvi, ātum, tr. 1. *to despair.*

Despĭcio, ĕre, exi, ectum, tr. 3. *to look down, to despise.*

Despondeo, ēre, di, sum, tr. 2. *to promise in marriage, to betroth.*

Destĭno, āre, āvi, ātum, tr. 1. *to tie, to determine, to appoint.*

Desum, esse, fui, irr. *to be wanting.*

Detego, ĕre, texi, tectum, tr. 3. *to uncover, detect, manifest.*

Deterior, us, adj. *worse, inferior.*

Deterreo, ēre, ui, ĭtum, tr. 2. *to deter.*
Detestabĭlis, e, adj. *detestable.*
Detestor, āri, ātus, dep. 1. *to detest, to abhor.*
Detineo, ēre, ui, tentum, tr. 2. *to detain.*
Detrăho, ĕre, xi, ctum, tr. 3. *to draw down, to detract, to take away, remove.*
Deus, i, m. 2. *God.*
Devincio, īre, xi, ctum, tr. 4. *to attach, bind to.*
Devinco, ĕre, vīci, victum, tr. 3. *to conquer.*
Devius, a, um, adj. *devious, out of the way.*
Devŏlo, āre, āvi, ātum, intr. 1. *to fly down, to fly away.*
Devŏro, āre, āvi, ātum, tr. 1. *to devour.*
Dexter, tra, trum, adj. *right, on the right hand.*
Dextra, æ, f. 1. *the right hand.*
Diāna, æ, f. 1. *the goddess of hunting.*
Diadēma, ătis, n. 3. *a diadem, a crown.*
Dicæarchus, i, m. 2. *a man's name.*
Dico, ĕre, xi, ctum, tr. 3. *to tell, to say.*
Dictātor, ōris, m. 3. *dictator.*
Dictum, i, n. 2. *a word, a saying.*
Dies, ēi, m. *or* f. Pl. *always* m. *a day, time.*
Diffĕro, ferre, distŭli, dilātum, irr. *to put off, to differ.*
Diffĭcĭlis, e, adj. *difficult, hard.*
Diffĭcĭle, adv. *with difficulty, hardly.*
Difficultas, ātis, f. 3. *difficulty.*
Dignè, (ius, issĭme,) adv. *worthily, in a manner worthy of.*
Dignĭtas, ātis, f. 3. *dignity.*
Dignus, a, um, adj. *worthy.*
Dilābor, bi, psus, dep. 3. *to slip away.*
Dilacĕro, āre, āvi, ātum, tr. 1. *to tear in pieces.*
Dilatio, ōnis, f. 3. *a putting off a delay.*
Dilĭgens, tis, adj. *diligent, loving.*
Diligenter, adv. *diligently.*
Diligentia, æ, f. 1. *diligence.*
Dilĭgo, ĕre, exi, ectum, tr. 3. *to love, to esteem.*
Dilūceo, ēre, xi, — intr. 2. *to shine.*
Dimĭco, āre, āvi, ātum, intr. 1. *to fight.*
Dimidium, ii, n. 2. *the half.*
Diminuo, ĕre, ui, ūtum, tr. 3. *to break, to break in pieces.*
Diogĕnes, is, m. 3. *a Cynic philosopher.*
Dion, ōnis, m. 3. *a man's name.*
Dionysius, ii, m. 2. *a man's name.*
Diripio, ĕre, ripui, reptum, tr. 3. *to plunder.*
Diruo, ĕre, ui, ūtum, tr. 3. *to pull down, destroy.*
Discēdo, ĕre, cessi, cessum, intr. 3. *to depart, to go away.*
Disciplīna, æ, f. 1. *discipline, instruction.*
Discipŭlus, i, m. 2. *a scholar.*
Disco, ĕre, didĭci, — tr. 3. *to learn.*
Discordia, æ, f. 1. *discord.*
Discrimen, ĭnis, n. 3. *distinction, difference, danger.*
Discrucio, āre, āvi, ātum, tr. 1. *to torture, distract.*
Disertus, a, um, adj. *eloquent.*
Disjicio, ĕre, jēci, jectum, tr. 3. *to disperse.*
Dispello, ĕre, pŭli, pulsum, tr. 3. *to dispel.*
Dispertio, īre, īvi, ītum, tr. 4. *to divide, distribute.*
Dispĭcio, ĕre, exi, ectum, tr. 3. *to look about, to consider.*
Displĭceo, ēre, ui, ĭtum, tr. 2. *to displease.*
Disputatio, ōnis, f. 3. *a discourse.*
Dispŭto, āre, āvi, ātum, tr. 1. *to reason, to dispute.*
Dissensio, ōnis, f. 3. *dissension, discord.*
Dissentio, ire, sensi, sensum, tr. 4. *to think differently, disagree.*

Dissĕro, ĕre, ui, tum, tr. 3. *to discourse, to debate.*
Dissidium, ii, n. 2. *a disagreement.*
Dissimŭlo, āre, āvi, ātum, tr. 1. *to disguise, conceal.*
Dissolvo, ĕre, solvi, solūtum, tr. 3. *to break down, to destroy.*
Dissuadeo, ēre, si, sum, tr. 2. *to dissuade.*
Distans, tis, adj. *distant, different.*
Distraho, ĕre, xi, ctum, tr. 3. *to divide, to end (a controversy).*
Ditis, e, (ior, issĭmus), adj. *rich.*
Diu, adv. *a long time.*
Diurnus, a, um, adj. *daily.*
Diutīnus, a, um, adj. *long, lasting.*
Diversorium, ii, n. 2. *an inn, a lodging.*
Diversus, a, um, adj. *diverse, various.*
Dives, ĭtis, adj. *rich.*
Divĭdo, ĕre, īsi, īsum, tr. 3. *to divide.*
Divīnus, a, um, adj. *divine, heavenly.*
Divitiăcus, i, m. 2. *a Gallic general.*
Divitiæ, ārum, f. 1. *riches.*
Do, dăre, dĕdi, dătum, tr. 1. *to give.*
Doceo, ēre, ui, tum, tr. 2. *to teach.*
Docĭlis, e, adj. *easily taught, docile.*
Doctor, ōris, m. 3. *a teacher.*
Doctrīna, æ, f. 1. *learning.*
Doctus, a, um, adj. *learned, skilful.*
Documentum, i, n. 2. *an example, warning, proof.*
Dolabella, æ, m. 1. *a man's name.*
Doleo, ēre, ui, ĭtum, intr. 2. *to be in pain, to grieve.*
Dolor, ōris, m. 3. *pain, grief.*
Dŏlus, i, m. 2. *a stratagem.*
Domestĭcus, a, um, adj. *domestic.*
Domicilium, ii, n. 2. *a dwelling place.*
Domĭna, æ, f. 1. *a mistress.*
Dominātus, ûs, m. 4. *authority, power.*
Domĭnor, āri, ātus, dep. 1. *to rule, to domineer.*
Domĭnus, i, m. 2. *a lord, a master.*
Dŏmo, āre, ui, ĭtum, tr. 1. *to subdue.*
Domus, ûs & i, f. 4. & 2. *a house.*
Donec, adv. *until, as long as.*
Dono, āre, āvi, ātum, tr. 1. *to bestow freely, to present.*
Dōnum, i, n. 2. *a gift, a present.*
Dormio, īre, īvi, ītum, intr. 4. *to sleep.*
Dos, dotis, f. 3. *a dowry, a portion.*
Drachma, æ, f. 1. *a drachm.*
Drăco, ōnis, m. 3. *a snake.*
Dubĭto, āre, āvi, ātum, tr. 1. *to doubt, to hesitate.*
Dubius, a, um, adj. *doubtful, uncertain.*
Ducēni, æ, a, adj. *two hundred to each.*
Ducenti, æ, a, adj. *two hundred.*
Duco, ĕre, xi, ctum, tr. 3. *to lead, to draw, to take* or *carry.*
Dulcēdo, ĭnis, f. 3. *sweetness.*
Dulcis, e, adj. *sweet.*
Duillius, ii, m. 2. *a man's name.*
Dum, adv. *while, whilst, until.*
Dummŏdo, adv. *provided.*
Dumnorix, ĭgis, m. 3. *one of the Ædui.*
Duo, æ, o, adj. *two.*
Duodĕcim, adj. *twelve.*
Duodeviginti, num. adj. indec. *eighteen.*
Duplex, duplĭcis, adj. *double.*
Duro, āre, āvi, ātum, tr. & intr. 1. *to harden, to endure, to last.*
Dūrus, a, um, adj. *hard.*
Dux, ducis, c. 3. *a leader, a general.*

E.

E, prep. *out of, from.*
Ebriĕtas, ātis, f. 3. *drunkenness.*
Ebrius, a, um, adj. *drunk.*
Ecquid, adv. interrog. *whether?*
Ecquis, —, ecquid, interrog. pr. *any one, any thing.*
Edax, ācis, adj. *eating much, consuming.*

Edīco, ĕre, xi, ctum, tr. 3. *to declare, proclaim.*
Edictum, i, n. 2. *an edict, a decree.*
Edisco, ĕre, didĭci, — tr. 3. *to learn by heart* or *thoroughly.*
Edĭtus, a, um, pt. *raised;* adj. *lofty.*
Edo, ĕre, edĭdi, edĭtum, tr. 3. *to give out, publish.*
Edo, edĕre & esse, ēdi, ēsum, tr. 3. *to eat.*
Edormio, īre, īvi, ītum, intr. 4. *to sleep soundly.*
Edŭco, āre, āvi, ātum, tr. 1. *to educate, bring up.*
Edūco, ĕre, xi, ctum, tr. 3. *to lead out from.*
Effectus, us, m. 4. *an effect, result, proof.*
Effĕro, efferre, extŭli, elātum, irr. *to carry out, to save.*
Efficio, ĕre, fēci, fectum, tr. 3. *to effect, to render.*
Effodio, ĕre, fodi, fossum, tr. 3. *to dig out, to mine.*
Effœtus, a, um, adj. *barren, worn out.*
Effŭgio, ĕre, fūgi, fugĭtum, tr. 3. *to escape, to elude.*
Effusio, ōnis, f. 3. *a pouring out, prodigality.*
Egēnus, a, um, adj. *needy, destitute.*
Egeo, ēre, ui, — intr. 2. *to need, to be in want.*
Egestas, ātis, f. 3. *want, poverty.*
Ego, mei, pron. *I.*
Egŏmet, meimet, pron. *I myself.*
Egredior, di, gressus, dep. 3. *to go out, to go beyond.*
Egregie, adv. *excellently, nobly.*
Egregius, a, um, adj. *excellent, noble.*
Ejicio, ĕre, jēci, jectum, tr. 3. *to cast out, banish.*
Ejusmodi, adv. *of such a kind.*
Eleganter, adv. *elegantly, nicely.*
Elephantus, i, m. 2. *an elephant.*
Elicio, ĕre, elicui or elexi, — tr. 3. *to draw out, to entice.*
Elĭgo, ĕre, lēgi, lectum, tr. 3. *to choose, to select.*
Elis, ĭdis & ĭdos, f. 3. *Elis, a town in Greece.*
Elŏquens, tis, adj. *eloquent.*
Eloquentia, æ, f. 1. *eloquence.*
Elŏquor, qui, cutus, dep. 3. *to speak.*
Elysius, ii, m. 2. *a man's name.*
Emano, āre, āvi, ātum, intr. 1. *to flow out, to get abroad.*
Emax, ācis, adj. *fond of buying.*
Emendo, āre, āvi, ātum, tr. 1. *to amend.*
Emĭnens, tis, adj. *eminent, high.*
Emitto, ĕre, īsi, issum, tr. 3. *to send out, to let fall.*
Emo, ĕre, ēmi, emptum, tr. 3. *to buy.*
Emollio, īre, ii, ītum, tr. 4. *to soften, to effeminate.*
Emolumentum, i. n. 2. *profit, advantage.*
Emŏrior, i, tuus, dep. 3. *to die.*
Emporetĭcus, a, um, adj. *coarse.*
Enim, conj. *for, indeed.*
Ennius, ii, m. 2. *Ennius, a Roman poet.*
Ensis, is, m. 3. *a sword.*
Enumĕro, āre, āvi, ātum, tr. 1. *to enumerate, to reckon up.*
Enuncio, āre, āvi, ātum, tr. 1. *to give utterance, to speak out.*
Eo, īre, īvi, ĭtum, irr. *to go.*
Eo, adv. *thither, to that extent.*
Epaminondas, æ, m. 1. *a Theban general.*
Ephesius, a, um, adj. *Ephesian.*
Epicrates, is, m. 3. *a man's name.*
Epicureus, i, m. 2. *an Epicurean.*
Epicūrus, i, m. 2. *Epicurus, a Grecian philosopher.*
Epīrus, i, f. 2. *a province of Greece.*
Epistŏla, æ, f. 1. *a letter, an epistle.*
Epulæ, ārum, f. pl. 1. *food, dainties.*
Equester & Equestris, e, adj. *equestrian.*
Equĭdem, adv. *indeed.*
Equitas, ātis, f. 3. *equity.*
Equitātus, us, m. 4. *cavalry.*

Eques, ĭtis, m. 3. *a horseman, a knight.*
Equus, i, m. 2. *a horse.*
Erga, prep. *towards.*
Erĭgo, ĕre, rexi, rectum, tr. 3. *to raise, to exalt.*
Erĭpio, ĕre, ui, eptum, tr. 3. *to take away by force.*
Erŏgo, āre, āvi, ātum, tr. 1. *to spend.*
Errātum, i, n. 2. *an error, a fault.*
Erro, āre, āvi, ātum, tr. 1. *to wander, to mistake.*
Error, ōris, m. 3. *an error, a mistake.*
Erudio, īre, īvi, ītum, tr. 4. *to polish, train up.*
Erudītus, a, um, adj. *taught, learned.*
Esca, æ, f. 1. *food, a bait.*
Esurio, īre, —, ītum, intr. 4. *to desire to eat, to be hungry.*
Et, conj. *and, also.*
Etiam, conj. *also, even.*
Etiamsi, conj. *even if, although.*
Etrusci, ōrum, m. 2. *the Etrusci, Tuscans.*
Etsi, conj. *although.*
Eumenes, is, m. 3. *a man's name.*
Eunuchus, i, m. 4. *a eunuch.*
Euphrātes, is, m. 3. *the river Euphrates.*
Eurōpa, æ, f. 1. *Europe.*
Evādo, ĕre, si, sum, intr. 3. *to go out, to escape, to become.*
Evĕnio, īre, vēni, ventum, intr. 4. *to come out, to happen.*
Eventus, us, m. 4. *event, issue.*
Everto, ĕre, ti, sum, tr. 3. *to overturn, to destroy.*
Evilesco, ĕre, lui, incep. 3. *to be undervalued.*
Ex, prep. *out of, from.*
Exardesco, ĕre, arsi, arsum, intr. 3. *to inflame.*
Exaudio, īre, īvi, ītum, tr. 4. *to hear.*
Excēdo, ĕre, cessi, cessum, intr. 3. *to go out, to depart, to exceed.*
Excellens, tis, adj. *excellent.*
Excellentia, æ, f. 1. *excellence.*
Excello, ĕre, ui, — intr. 3. *to excel, to surpass.*
Exceptio, ōnis, f. 3. *an exception.*
Excīdo, ĕre, di, sum, tr. 3. *to cut off, to destroy.*
Excĭpio, ĕre, cēpi, ceptum, tr. 3. *to receive.*
Excĭto, āre, āvi, ātum, tr. 1. *to rouse, to excite, call up.*
Exclāmo, āre, āvi, ātum, tr. 1. *to exclaim, cry out.*
Exclūdo, ĕre, si, sum, tr. 3. *to shut out, to exclude.*
Excrucio, āre, āvi, ātum, tr. 1. *to torment, to vex.*
Excusatio, ōnis, f. 3. *an excuse, a defence.*
Excūso, āre, āvi, ātum, tr. 1. *to excuse.*
Exĕdo, ĕre, ēdi, ēsum, tr. 3. *to eat up, to consume.*
Exemplar, āris, n. 3. *a copy, an example.*
Exemplum, i, n. 3. *an example, a plan, a copy.*
Exeo, īre, ii, *seldom* īvi, ĭtum, intr. irr. *to go out.*
Exerceo, ēre, ui, ĭtum, tr. 2. *to exercise.*
Exercitatio, ōnis, f. 3. *practice.*
Exercitus, us, m. 4. *an army.*
Exhaurio, īre, si, stum, tr. 4. *to exhaust, to bring out.*
Exhĭbeo, ēre, ui, ĭtum, tr. 2. *to hold out, to exhibit.*
Exhorresco, ĕre, intr. 3. *to be shocked.*
Exĭgo, ĕre, ēgi, actum, tr. 3. *to exact, to demand.*
Exiguus, a, um, adj. *small, scanty.*
Eximius, a, um, adj. *excellent, distinguished.*
Existimatio, ōnis, f. 3. *a supposition, reputation.*
Existĭmo, āre, āvi, ātum, tr. 1. *to judge, to think.*
Exitium, ii, n. 2. *destruction.*
Exĭtus, us, m. 4. *issue, event.*
Exorior, īri, ortus, dep. 4. *to arise.*

Exōsus, a, um, adj. *hating.*
Expectatio, ōnis, f. 3. *expectation, hope.*
Expecto, āre, āvi, ātum, tr. 1. *to look for, to expect.*
Expedio, īre, īvi, ītum, intr. 4. *to get free;*—expedit, *it is expedient, it is profitable.*
Expeditio, ōnis, f. 3. *an expedition.*
Expello, ĕre, ŭli, ulsum, tr. 3. *to drive out, to expel.*
Expergiscor, gisci, rectus, dep. 3. *to awake.*
Experior, īri, tus, dep. 4. *to try, to experience.*
Expers, tis, adj. *having no part in, free from.*
Expĕto, ĕre, īvi, ītum, tr. 3. *to desire greatly, to covet.*
Explāno, āre, āvi, ātum, tr. 1. *to explain.*
Expleo, ēre, ēvi, ētum, tr. 2. *to fill up, to complete.*
Explĭco, āre, ui, ĭtum, & āvi, ātum, tr. 1. *to unfold, to explain.*
Explorātor, ōris, m. 3. *an inspector.*
Explōro, āre, āvi, ātum, tr. 1. *to search diligently, to explore, to inspect.*
Expōno, ĕre, sui, sĭtum, tr. 3. *to expose.*
Exportatio, ōnis, f. 3. *an exportation.*
Expugno, āre, āvi, ātum, tr. 1. *to take by assault.*
Exscindo, ĕre, ĭdi, issum, tr. 3. *to cut off, to destroy.*
Exsecror, āri, ātus, dep. 1. *to curse, to execrate.*
Exsĕquor, qui, cūtus *or* quūtus, dep. 3. *to follow after, to perform.*
Exsilio, ire, ui, — intr. 4. *to leap up, bound, to palpitate.*
Exsilium (exilium), ii, n. 2. *exile.*
Exsŭlo, āre, āvi, ātum, intr. 1. *to be an exile.*
Exsurgo, ĕre, rexi, rectum, intr. 3. *to arise.*
Extemplo, adv. *immediately.*
Externus, a, um, adj. *external, outward.*
Extinguo, ĕre, xi, ctum, tr. 3. *to put out, to extinguish.*
Exto, āre, tĭti, tĭtum, intr. 1. *to stand out, to exist.*
Extra, prep. *without, out of.*
Extraho, ĕre, xi, ctum, tr. 3. *to draw out, to extract.*
Extrēmus, a, um, adj. sup. *extreme, last, at the end of.*
Extruo, ĕre, xi, ctum, tr. 3. *to erect, to build.*
Exul & exsul, ŭlis, c. 3. *an exile.*
Exuo, ĕre, ui, ūtum, tr. 3. *to put off, lay aside.*

F.

Faba, æ, f. 1. *a bean.*
Fabius, ii, m. 2. *a man's name.*
Fabricius, ii, m. 2. *a noble Roman.*
Fabŭla, æ, f. 1. *a fable, a story.*
Fabŭlor, āri, ātus, dep. 1. *to speak, to talk.*
Facies, ēi, f. 5. *the face.*
Facĭle, adv. *easily.*
Facĭlis, e, adj. *easy.*
Facilĭtas, ātis, f. 3. *facility, ease, gentleness.*
Facĭnus, ŏris, n. 3. *an action, a crime.*
Facio, ĕre, fēci, factum, tr. 3. *to do, to make.*
Factum, i, n. 2. *an action, a deed.*
Facultas, ātis, f. 3. *power, ability.*
Fallax, ācis, adj. *deceitful, treacherous.*
Fallo, ĕre, fefelli, falsum, tr. 3. *to deceive.*
Falso, adv. *falsely.*
Falsus, a, um, adj. *false.*
Fama, æ, f. 1. *fame.*
Fames, is, f. 3. *famine, hunger.*
Familia, æ, f. 1. *a family.*
Familiāris, e, adj. *of the same family, familiar.*

Familiāris, is, m. 3. *an intimate friend.*
Familiarĭtas, ātis, f. 3. *friendship, familiarity.*
Famulātus, us, m. 4. *bondage, slavery.*
Fannius, ii, m. 2. *Fannius, a man's name.*
Fānum, i, n. 2. *a temple.*
Fas, indec. *right.*
Fascicŭlus, i, m. 2. *a packet, a parcel.*
Fascĭno, āre, āvi, ātum, tr. 1. *to fascinate, bewitch.*
Fascis, is, f. 3. *a bundle,* pl. *the fasces.*
Fastidio, īre, īvi *or* ii, ītum, intr. *to be disgusted.*
Fastidium, ii, n. 2. *pride, haughtiness, dislike.*
Fastus, ûs, m. 4. *haughtiness, pride.*
Fateor, ēri, fassus, dep. 2. *to confess, to acknowledge.*
Fatum, i, n. 2. *fate, destiny.*
Fautor, ōris, m. 3. *a favourer, a friend.*
Faventia, æ, f. 1. *Faventia, a town in Italy.*
Faveo, ēre, favi, fautum, tr. 2. *to favour.*
Favor, ōris, m. 3. *favour, good-will.*
Febris, is, f. 3. *a fever.*
Felicĭtas, ātis, f. 3. *felicity, happiness.*
Felicĭter, adv. *happily.*
Felix, īcis, adj. *happy.*
Femĭna, æ, f. 1. *a woman.*
Fera, f. 1. *a wild beast.*
Ferax, ācis, adj. *fruitful, fertile.*
Fere, adv. *almost, commonly.*
Ferīnus, a, um, adj. *of wild beasts, cruel.*
Ferme, adv. *almost.*
Fero, ferre, tŭli, lātum, tr. irr. *to bear, to carry, to suffer.*
Ferocia, æ, f. 1. *ferocity.*
Ferox, ōcis, adj. *insolent, fierce.*
Ferrum, i. n. 2. *iron, a sword.*
Fertĭlis, e, adj. *fertile, fruitful.*
Ferus, a, um, adj. *wild, cruel.*
Festīno, āre, āvi, ātum, tr. 1. *to make haste.*
Festus, a, um, adj. *festive, holy*
Fidēlis, e, adj. *faithful.*
Fides, ĕi, f. 5. *faith, a promise.*
Fidus, a, um, adj. *faithful, trusty.*
Figo, ĕre, xi, xum, tr. 3. *to fix.*
Filia, æ, f. 1. *a daughter.*
Filiōla, æ, f. 1. dim. *a little daughter.*
Filius, ii, m. 2. *a son.*
Filix, ĭcis, f. 3. *fern.*
Fingo, ĕre, finxi, fictum, tr. 3. *to form, to fashion, to feign.*
Finio, īre, īvi, ītum, tr. 4. *to finish.*
Finis, is, m. & f. 3. *the end, a limit.*
Fio, fiĕri, factus, irr. *to be made, to become;* fit, *it happens.*
Firmĭtas, ātis, f. 3. *firmness, steadiness.*
Firmo, āre, āvi, ātum, tr. 1. *to strengthen, establish.*
Firmus, a, um, adj. *firm, strong.*
Fistulōsus, a, um, adj. *hollow.*
Flabellum, i, n. 2. *a fan.*
Flagitium, ii, n. 2. *a base action, infamy.*
Flagĭto, āre, āvi, ātum, tr. 1. *to demand.*
Flaminius, ii, m. 2. *a Roman general.*
Flamma, æ, m. 1. *a man's name.*
Flavus, a, um, adj. *yellow.*
Flecto, ĕre, xi, xum, tr. 3. *to bend, to turn.*
Fleo, ēre, ēvi, ētum, tr. 2. *to weep.*
Floccus, i, m. 2. *a lock of wool.*
Florens, tis, adj. *flourishing.*
Floreo, ĕre, ui, — intr. 2. *to flourish.*
Fluctus, us, m. 4. *a wave.*
Fluo, ĕre, xi, xum, intr. 3. *to flow, to run.*
Flumen, ĭnis, n. 3. *a river.*
Fluvius, ii, m. 2. *a river.*
Fodio, ĕre, fodi, fossum, tr. 3. *to dig, to bore.*
Fœdus, a, um, adj. *filthy, base.*

Fœdus, ĕris, n. 3. *a league, a treaty.*
Fœneratio, ōnis, f. 3. *a lending of money, usury.*
Fons, fontis, f. 3. *a fountain.*
(For, *not used*), fāri, fātus, dep. 1. *to speak.*
Forem, fore, def. irr. *I should be.* Gr. 222–5.
Foris, adv. *without, abroad.*
Forma, æ, f. 1. *a form, shape, beauty.*
Formiānum, i, n. 2. *a villa of Cicero.*
Formīca, æ, f. 1. *an ant.*
Formo, āre, āvi, ātum, tr. 1. *to form.*
Forsan, Forsĭtan, Fortasse, } adv. *perhaps.*
Forte, adv. *by chance.*
Fortis, e, adj. *brave.*
Fortĭter, adv. *bravely.*
Fortitūdo, ĭnis, f. 3. *bravery.*
Fortuĭto, adv. *accidentally.*
Fortuĭtus, a, um, adj. *accidental.*
Fortūna, æ, f. 1. *fortune.*
Fortunātus, a, um, adj. *fortunate, happy.*
Fŏrum, i, n. 2. *the forum.*
Fossa, æ, f. 1. *a ditch.*
Fræнum, i, n. 2. *a bridle, a bit.* Pl. *i* and *a.*
Fragĭlis, e, adj. *brittle, frail.*
Fragilĭtas, ātis, f. 3. *brittleness, frailty.*
Fragmentum, i, n. 2. *a fragment.*
Fragor, ōris, m. 3. *a crash, a noise.*
Frango, ĕre, frēgi, fractum, tr. 3. *to break.*
Frater, tris, m. 3. *a brother.*
Fraus, dis, f. 3. *fraud, deceit.*
Frĕmo, ĕre, ui, ĭtum, intr. 3. *to be enraged.*
Frēnum, i. n. 2. *a bridle.*
Frĕquens, tis, adj. *full, crowded.*
Frequenter, adv. *frequently.*
Frequento, āre, āvi, ātum, tr. 1. *to frequent, to people.*
Fretus, a, um, adj. *trusting to, relying on.*
Frīgus, ŏris, n. 3. *cold.*
Frons, tis, f. 3. *forehead.*
Fructuōsus, a, um, adj. *fruitful, productive.*
Fructus, ûs, m, 4. *fruit.*
Frugalĭtas, ātis, f. 3. *frugality.*
Frugi, adj. ind. *thrifty, frugal.*
(Frux, *not used,*) frugis, f. 3. *corn, grain.*
Frumentarius, a, um, adj. *of corn;* res frumentaria, *provisions.*
Frumentum, i, n. 2. *corn, grain.*
Fruor, i, ctus & ĭtus, dep. 3. *to enjoy*
Frustra, adv. *in vain.*
Frustum, i, n. 2. *a piece.*
Fufetius, ii, m. 2. *a man's name.*
Fŭga, æ, f. 1. *flight.*
Fugio, ĕre, fūgi, ĭtum, tr. 3. *to fly, to escape.*
Fugitīvus, i, m. 2. *a fugitive.*
Fugĭto, āre, āvi, ātum, tr. 1. *to fly eagerly, to shun.*
Fugo, āre, āvi, ātum, tr. 1. *to put to flight, to rout.*
Fulgur, ŭris, n. 3. *lightning.*
Fulmen, ĭnis, n. 3. *a flash of lightning.*
Fulvius, ii, m. 2. *a man's name.*
Fulvus, a, um, adj. *yellow, tawny.*
Fundamentum, i, n. 2. *a foundation.*
Fundĭtus, adv. *from the very bottom, entirely.*
Fundo, ĕre, fūdi, fūsum, tr. 3. *to pour out, to rout.*
Fundus, i, m. 2. *a farm, an estate.*
Fungor, i, ctus, dep. 3. *to discharge an office, to execute.*
Fūnus, ĕris, n. 3. *a funeral.*
Furca, æ, f. 1. *a fork.*
Furibundus, a, um, adj. *raging.*
Fŭro, ĕre, — intr. 3. *to rage.*
Furor, ōris, m. 3. *fury, madness.*
Furranius, ii, m. 2. *a man's name.*
Futĭlis, e, adj. *foolish, shallow.*
Futilĭtas, ātis, f. 3. *foolishness, silliness.*
Futūrus, a, um, adj. *about to be, future.*

G.

Gades, ium, f. 3. *Cadiz, an island and town of Spain.*
Gæsum, i, n. 2. *a dart.*
Galea, æ, f. 1. *a helmet.*
Gallia, æ, f. 1. *Gaul.*
Gallus, i, m. 2. *a Gaul.*
Gaudeo, ēre, gavīsus, intr. p. *to rejoice.*
Gaudium, ii, n. 2. *joy, gladness.*
Gelu, n. indec. *frost.*
Gemĭno, āre, āvi, ātum, tr. 1. *to double.*
Gemma, ătis, n. 3. *a gem, a jewel.*
Genĕro, āre, āvi, ātum, tr. 1. *to beget, to produce.*
Generōsus, a, um, adj. *noble, generous.*
Gens, tis, f. 3. *a tribe, a nation.*
Genu, n. indec. *the knee.*
Genus, ĕris, n. 3. *a race, a kind, descent.*
Germania, æ, f. 1. *Germany.*
Germanus, a, um, adj. *german, of the same father, genuine, true.*
Germanus, i, m. 2. *a German.*
Gero, ĕre, ssi, stum, tr. 3. *to bear, to carry, to conduct.*
Gerundium, ii, n. 2. *a gerund.*
Gesto, āre, āvi, ātum, tr. 1. *to bear, to carry.*
Gestum, i, n. 2. *an exploit.*
Gestus, a, um, pt. *done, carried on;* res gestæ, *a history.*
Gestus, ûs, m. 4. *gesture, behaviour.*
Gigas, antis, m. 3. *a giant.*
Gigno, ĕre, genui, genĭtum, tr. 3. *to beget, to produce.*
Gillias, æ, m. 1. *a man's name.*
Glacies, ēi, f. 5. *ice.*
Gladius, ii, m. 2. *a sword.*
Gloria, æ, f. 1. *glory.*
Glorior, āri, ātus, dep. 1. *to glory, to boast.*
Gloriōsus, a, um, adj. *glorious, illustrious.*
Gnavĭter, adv. *strenuously, actively.*
Gracchus, i, m. 2. *a Roman general.*
Gradus, us, m. 4. *a step, a pace.*
Græcia, æ, f. 1. *Greece.*
Græcus, a, um, adj. *of Greece, Grecian.*
Grandævus, a, um, adj. *old, advanced in life.*
Grandis, e, adj. *great, large, grand.*
Granum, i, n. 2. *a grain.*
Gratia, æ, f. 1. *grace, a favour.* Pl. *thanks;* adv. *for the sake of.*
Gratifĭcor, āri, ātus, dep. 1. *to gratify, to oblige.*
Gratŭlor, āri, ātus, dep. 1. *to congratulate, to rejoice.*
Gratus, a, um, adj. *grateful, agreeable.*
Gravis, e, adj. *heavy, difficult, wise.*
Gravĭtas, ātis, f. 3. *heaviness, severity.*
Gravĭter, adv. *heavily, seriously.*
Gregarius, a, um, adj. *belonging to the herd, common.*
Grex, gregis, m. seldom f. *a flock, a herd.*
Guberno, āre, āvi, ātum, tr. 1. *to govern.*
Gutta, æ, f. 1. *a drop.*
Gyges, is, m. 3. *a king of Lydia.*
Gymnicus, a, um, adj. *gymnastic.*

H.

Habeo, ēre, ui, ĭtum, tr. 2. *to have.*
Habĭlis, e, adj. *fit, able.*
Habĭto, āre, āvi, ātum, tr. 1. *to dwell, to inhabit.*
Hæredĭtas, ātis, f. 3. *an inheritance.*
Hæreo, ēre, hæsi, hæsum, intr. 3. *to hesitate.*
Hæres, ēdis, c. 3. *an heir* or *heiress.*
Hamus, i, m. 2. *a hook.*
Hannibal, is, m. 3. *a Carthaginian general.*
Harpăgus, i, m. 2. *a man's name.*
Haruspex, ĭcis, m. 3. *a soothsayer.*
Hasdrubal, is, m. 3. *Hasdrubal, a Carthaginian general.*

Hasta, æ, f. 1. *a spear.*
Haud, adv. *not.*
Haurio, īre, hausi, haustum, tr. 4. *to draw (as water.)*
Hector, ŏris, m. 3. *Hector, son of Priam.*
Helĕna, æ, f. 1. *Helen, wife of Menelaus.*
Hellespontus, i, m. 2. *the Hellespont.*
Helvetius, ii, m. 2. *a Helvetian.*
Hephæstion, ōnis, m. 3. *a man's name.*
Herba, æ, f. 1. *an herb, a plant.*
Hercŭles, is, m. 3. *Hercules.*
Herculeus, a, um. adj. *of Hercules, Herculean.*
Heri, adv. *yesterday.*
Herma, æ, f. 1. *a statue of Mercury.*
Herus, i, m. 2. *a master.*
Hesiŏdus, i, m. 2. *Hesiod, a Grecian poet.*
Hesternus, a, um, adj. *of yesterday, yesterday's.*
Hiberna, ōrum, n. pl. 2. *winter-quarters.*
Hibernia, æ, f. 1. *Hibernia, Ireland.*
Hic, hæc, hoc, pron. *this.* Pl. *these.*
Hic, adv. *here.*
Hiems (hyems), is, f. 3. *winter.*
Hilăris, e, adj. *cheerful, gay.*
Hilarĭtas, ātis, f. 3. *cheerfulness, gaiety.*
Hilum, i, m. 2. *the black of a bean, nothing.*
Hirundo, ĭnis, f. 3. *a swallow.*
Hispania, æ, f. 1. *Spain.*
Historia, æ, f. 1. *history.*
Historĭcus, i, m. 2. *a historian.*
Histrio, ōnis, m. 3. *a player.*
Hodie, adv. *to-day.*
Hodiernus, a, um, adj. *of to-day.*
Homērus, i, m. 2. *Homer.*
Homo, ĭnis, c. 3. *a man* or *woman, a fellow.*
Honestas, ātis, f. 3. *honour, honesty.*
Honeste, adv. *honourably.*
Honestus, a, um, adj. *honourable, honest.*
Honor, & honos, ōris, m. 3. *honour.*
Honorātus, a, um, adj. *honourable.*
Honōro, āre, āvi, ātum, tr. 1. *to honour.*
Hora, æ, f. 1. *an hour.*
Horatius, ii, m. 2. *Horace, a man's name.*
Horreo, ēre, ui, —, intr. 2. *to shiver, to tremble.*
Horrĭdus, a, um, adj. *rough.*
Hortensius, ii, m. 2. *a man's name.*
Hortor, āri, ātus, dep. 1. *to exhort, to encourage.*
Hortŭlus, i, m. 2. dim. *a little garden.*
Hospes, pĭtis, c. 3. *a guest, a stranger.*
Hospitium, ii, n. 2. *a place of entertainment, friendship.*
Hostilius, ii, m. 2. *a man's name.*
Hostis, is, c. 3. *an enemy.*
Huc, adv. *hither.*
Hujuscemŏdi, adv. *of this nature, to this effect.*
Humanĭtas, ātis, f. 3. *humanity, kindness.*
Humānus, a, um, adj. *human.*
Humĕrus, i, m. 2. *the shoulder.*
Hūmor, ōris, m. 3. *a liquid, water.*
Humus, i, f. 2. *the ground, land.*
Hyems, is, f. 3. *winter.*
Hypănes, is, m. 3. *the name of a river.*
Hystaspes, is, m. 3. *the father of Darius.*

I.

Iberus, i, m. 2. *the river Iberus (Ebro).*
Ibi, adv. *there.*
Ictus, ûs, m. 4. *a blow, a stroke.*
Idcirco, adv. *therefore, for this reason, because.*
Idem, eădem, idem, pron. *the same.*
Ideo, adv. *accordingly.*
Idoneus, a, um, adj. *fit, proper.*
Idus, ûs, m. 4. *the Ides.*
Ignavia, æ, f. 1. *laziness, inactivity.*

Ignarus, a, um, adj. *ignorant.*
Ignavus, a, um, adj. *indolent.*
Igniculus, i, m. 2. *a spark.*
Ignis, is, m. 3. *fire.*
Ignōro, āre, āvi, ātum, tr. 1. *to be ignorant of.*
Ignosco, ĕre, ōvi, ōtum, tr. 3. *to pardon.*
Ignōtus, a, um, adj. *unknown.*
Iliăcus, a, um, adj. *of Troy, Trojan.*
Iliensis, e, adj. *belonging to Ilium, the people of Ilium.*
Ilion, ōnis, n. 3. *Ilium, Troy.*
Illæsus, a, um, pt. *unhurt.*
Ille, illa, illud, pron. *he, she, it; that;* pl. *they, those.*
Illecĕbra, æ, f. 1. *an enticement, an allurement.*
Illic, adv. *there.*
Illĭco, adv. *straightway.*
Illo, Illuc, } adv. *thither, to that place.*
Illustris, e, adj. *clear, illustrious.*
Imāgo, ĭnis, f. 3. *an image.*
Imbecillĭtas, ātis, f. 3. *weakness.*
Imbecillus, a, um, adj. *weak, feeble.*
Imber, bris, m. 3. *rain.*
Imbuo, ĕre, ui, ūtum, tr. 3. *to moisten, to imbue.*
Imĭtor, āri, ātus, dep. 1. *to imitate.*
Immānis, e, adj. *cruel, savage, huge.*
Immedicabĭlis, e, adj. *incurable.*
Immĕmor, ŏris, adj. *unmindful, forgetful.*
Immigro, āre, āvi, ātum, intr. 1. *to enter.*
Immĭneo, ēre, ui, — intr. 2. *to overhang.*
Immoderatè, (ius, issĭme,) adv. *without restraint, excessively.*
Immŏlo, āre, āvi, ātum, tr. 1. *to sacrifice.*
Immortālis, e, adj. *immortal.*
Immortalĭtas, ātis, f. 3. *immortality.*
Immūto, āre, āvi, ātum, tr. 1. *to change.*
Impedio, īre, īvi, ītum, tr. 4. *to hinder, prevent.*
Impello, ĕre, pŭli, pulsum, tr. 3. *to urge, to impel.*
Impendeo, ēre, — — intr. 2. *to overhang, to be near.*
Impendo, ĕre, di, sum, tr. 3. *to spend money, to bestow.*
Impensus, a, um, adj. *considerable, great.*
Imperātor, ōris, m. 3. *a commander.*
Imperatorius, a, um, adj. *of a commander.*
Imperĭto, āre, āvi, ātum, tr. 1. *to rule, to have the supremacy.*
Imperītus, a, um, adj. *unskilful, ignorant.*
Imperium, ii, n. 2. *command, power.*
Impĕro, āre, āvi, ātum, tr. 1. *to command, to rule.*
Impertio, īre, īvi, ītum, tr. 4. *to impart, to bestow.*
Impĕtro, āre, āvi, ātum, tr. 1. *to accomplish, to obtain.*
Impĕtus, ûs, m. 4. *an attack, violence.*
Impiĕtas, ātis, f. 3. *impiety.*
Impius, a, um, adj. *impious, wicked.*
Impleo, ēre, ēvi, ētum, tr. 2. *to fill.*
Implicĭtus, a, um, pt. *being attacked.*
Implĭco, āre, āvi, ātum, & ui, ĭtum, tr. 1. *to implicate, to involve.*
Implōro, āre, āvi, ātum, tr. 1. *to beg, to implore.*
Impŏno, ere, sui, sĭtum, tr. 3. *to place upon, lay, thrust.*
Impos, ŏtis, adj. *unable, without power.*
Imprŏbo, āre, āvi, ātum, tr. 1. *to disapprove, to dislike.*
Imprŏbus, a, um, adj. *wicked, dishonest.*
Imprudenter, adv. *imprudently.*
Impunĭtas, ātis, f. 3. *impunity.*
In, prep. *in, into.*
Inānis, e, adj. *empty, unsatisfied.*
Inarātus, a, um, adj. *unploughed.*
Incendium, ii, n. 2. *a fire, a burning.*
Incensus, a, um, pt. *incensed.*

Inceptum, i, n. 2. *an undertaking.*
Incertus, a, um, adj. *uncertain.*
Incĭdo, ĕre, ĭdi, āsum, intr. 3. *to fall into, to happen.*
Incĭpio, ĕre, cēpi, ceptum, tr. 3. *to begin.*
Incĭto, āre, āvi, ātum, tr. 1. *to incite, to impel.*
Inclamatus, a, um, pt. *being called.*
Inclinatio, ōnis, f. 3. *inclination, partiality.*
Inclūdo, ĕre, si, sum, tr. 3. *to shut up, to enclose.*
Incognĭtus, a, um, adj. *unknown.*
Incolo, ĕre, ui, — tr. 3. *to inhabit.*
Incommŏdum, i, n. 2. *an inconvenience, a loss.*
Incommŏdus, a, um, adj. *inconvenient.*
Inconditus, a, um, adj. *disorderly.*
Inconsiderāte, adv. *inconsiderately.*
Inconstantia, æ, f. 1. *inconstancy.*
Incorruptus, a, um, adj. *uncorrupted, pure.*
Incredibĭlis, e, adj. *incredible.*
Incredulĭtas, ātis, f. 3. *incredulity, unbelief.*
Incumbo, ĕre, cubui, cubitum, intr. 3. *to apply, to pay attention.*
Incuria, æ, f. 1. *negligence, carelessness.*
Incurro, ĕre, curri, & cucurri, cursum, tr. 3. *to run against, to attack.*
Incūso, āre, āvi, ātum, tr. 1. *to blame, to accuse.*
Incŭtio, ĕre, ssi, ssum, tr. 3. *to strike upon.*
Indāgo, āre, āvi, ātum, tr. 1. *to track* or *trace* (*as a dog*).
Inde, adv. *from thence.*
Indecōre, adv. *unhandsomely.*
Indicium, ii, n. 2. *a discovery.*
Indĭco, āre, āvi, ātum, tr. 1. *to show, to declare.*
Indīco, cĕre, xi, ctum, tr. 3. *to denounce, to publish.*
Indĭgens, tis, adj. *poor, indigent.*
Indĭgeo, ēre, ui, — intr. 2. *to want.*
Indignor, āri, ātus, dep. 1. *to be indignant.*
Indignus, a, um, adj. *unworthy.*
Indĭgus, a, um, adj. *needy.*
Indoctus, a, um, adj. *untaught, ignorant.*
Indūco, ĕre, xi, ctum, tr. 3. *to lead, to persuade.*
Indulgentia, æ, f. 1. *indulgence.*
Indulgeo, ēre, si, tum, tr. 2. *to indulge, to gratify.*
Induo, ĕre, ui, ūtum, tr. 3. *to put on, to array.*
Industria, æ, f. 1. *industry.*
Inedia, æ, f. 1. *want of food, hunger.*
Ineo, īre, ii, *seldom* īvi, ĭtum, irr *to go into, to enter, to begin.*
Ineptia, æ, f. 1. *silliness, foolishness.*
Ineptus, a, um, adj. *silly, foolish.*
Iners, tis, adj. *slothful, lazy.*
Inertia, æ, f. 1. *unskilfulness, laziness.*
Inexplebĭlis, e, adj. *insatiable.*
Infamia, æ, f. 1. *infamy.*
Infans, tis, c. 3. *an infant.*
Infectus, a, um, adj. *not done, undone.*
Infelicĭtas, ātis, f. 3. *misfortune.*
Infelix, īcis, adj. *unhappy, cursed.*
Infĕri, ōrum, m. 2. *the infernal gods.*
Inferior, us, adj. comp. of infĕrus, *inferior.*
Infĕro, ferre, tŭli, lātum, irr. *to bring into, to introduce, to carry forward.*
Infĕrus, a, um, adj, *below, low.*
Infīdus, a, um, adj. *unfaithful.*
Infĭmus, a, um, adj. sup. *lowest.*
Infirmĭtas, ātis, f. 3. *weakness, feebleness.*
Infirmus, a, um, adj. *weak, infirm.*
Inflammo, āre, āvi, ātum, tr. 1. *to inflame.*
Inflo, āre, āvi, ātum, tr. 1. *to inflate, puff up.*

Influo, ĕre, xi, xum, intr. 3. *to flow into.*

Ingenĕro, āre, āvi, ātum, tr. 1. *to implant.*

Ingenium, ii, n. 2. *natural capacity, genius, wit.*

Ingens, tis, adj. *great.*

Ingenuus, a, um, adj. *native, ingenuous, liberal.*

Ingrātus, a, um, adj. *ungrateful.*

Ingrĕdior, di, ssus, dep. 3. *to go into, to enter.*

Inhoneste, adv. *dishonestly.*

Inimīcus, a, um, adj. *unfriendly, hostile.*

Inimīcus, i, m. 2. *a private enemy, an enemy.*

Inīquus, a, um, adj. *unequal, hostile.*

Initium, ii, n. 2. *a beginning.*

Injicio, ĕre, jēci, jectum, tr. 3. *to cast* or *put upon.*

Injucundus, a, um, adj. *unpleasing.*

Injuria, æ, f. 1. *an injury, injustice.*

Injussu, m. 4. (used only in the abl. sing.) *without command.*

Injustè, adv. *unjustly.*

Injustitia, æ, f. 1. *injustice.*

Injustus, a, um, adj. *unjust.*

Innascor, sci, ātus, dep. 3. *to be born in, to grow in.*

Innatus, a, um, pt. & adj. *innate.*

Innŏcens, tis, adj. *innocent.*

Innocentia, æ, f. 1. *innocence.*

Innocuus, a, um, adj. *harmless.*

Innumĕrus, a, um, adj. *innumerable, countless.*

Inopia, æ, f. 1. *want.*

Inops, ŏpis, adj. *poor, needy.*

Inquam, def. *I say.*

Inquĭno, āre, āvi, ātum, tr. 1. *to pollute, to defile.*

Inquisitio, ōnis, f. 3. *an inquiry.*

Insania, æ, f. 1. *madness.*

Insanio, īre, īvi, ītum, intr. 4. *to be mad, to be insane.*

Insānus, a, um, adj. *insane, mad, raging.*

Insatiabĭlis, e, adj. *insatiable.*

Inscientia, æ, f. 1. *want of knowledge, ignorance.*

Inscitia, æ, f. 1. *ignorance.*

Insculptus, a, um, pt. *engraven.*

Insequor, qui, cūtus, dep. 3. *to pursue.*

Insidiæ, ārum, f. 1. *an ambush, treachery.*

Insĭdo, ĕre, sedi, sessum, tr. 3. *to settle upon, to take post upon.*

Insigne, is, n. 3. *an ornament.*

Insignis, e, adj. *adorned, magnificent.*

Insimŭlo, āre, āvi, ātum, tr. 1. *to feign, to accuse.*

Insipiens, tis, adj. *unwise, foolish.*

Insons, tis, adj. *innocent, harmless.*

Inspĭcio, ĕre, exi, ectum, tr. 3. *to look upon, to view.*

Insterno, ĕre, strāvi, strātum, tr. 3. *to strow upon, to cover over.*

Instituo, ĕre, ui, ūtum, tr. 3. *to appoint, to ordain.*

Institūtum, i, n. 2. *a custom, a decree.*

Instrumentum, i, n. 2. *an instrument, an implement.*

Instruo, ĕre, xi, ctum, tr. 3. *to form a line, to draw up (an army).*

Insuētus, a, um, adj. *not accustomed.*

Insŭla, æ, f. 1. *an island.*

Insum, esse, fui, irr. *to be in.*

Intactus, a, um, adj. *untouched, entire.*

Intĕger, gra, grum, adj. *whole, entire, untouched.*

Integrĭtas, ātis, f. 3. *integrity.*

Intelligentia, æ, f. 1. *understanding, intelligence.*

Intellĭgo, ĕre, exi, ectum, tr. 3. *to understand.*

Intempĕrans, tis, adj. *intemperate, disorderly.*

Intemperantia, æ, f. 1. *intemperance.*

Intentus, a, um, adj. *intent.*

Inter, prep. *between, among.*

Interceptus, a, um, pt. *intercepted, being.*
Interdīco, ĕre, xi, ctum, tr. 3. *to forbid, to interdict.*
Interdum, adv. *sometimes.*
Interea, adv. *in the mean time.*
Intereo, īre, ii, *seldom* īvi, ĭtum, intr. irr. *to perish, to die.*
Interest, imp. *it concerns.*
Interfector, ōris, m. 3. *a slayer.*
Interficio, ĕre, feci, fectum, tr. *to slay, to destroy.*
Interfluo, ĕre, xi, — intr. 3. *to flow through* or *between.*
Intĕrim, adv. *in the mean time.*
Interjaceo, ēre, intr. *to lie between.*
Interjectus, a, um, pt. *thrown between, having intervened.*
Intermissio, ōnis, f. 3. *a ceasing, a respite.*
Internosco, ĕre, ōvi, ōtum, tr. 3. *to distinguish.*
Interpello, āre, āvi, ātum, tr. 1. *to interrupt.*
Interrŏgo, āre, āvi, ātum, tr. 1. *to ask.*
Intersum, esse, fui, intr. irr. *to be present.*
Intervĕnio, īre, vēni, ventum, intr. & tr. 4. *to come in the meantime, to intervene.*
Intĭmus, a, um, adj. *innermost.*
Intolerabĭlis, e, adj. *intolerable.*
Intra, prep. *within.*
Intro, āre, āvi, ātum, tr. 1. *to enter.*
Introeo, īre, ivi, *or* ii, ĭtum, intr. irr. *to go in.*
Intueor, ēri, ĭtus, dep. 2. *to look upon, to behold.*
Intumesco, ĕre, ui, — intr. 3. *to swell, to be puffed up.*
Inultus, a, um, adj. *unrevenged, unpunished.*
Inutĭlis, e, adj. *useless.*
Invādo, ĕre, si, sum, tr. 3. *to invade.*
Invalesco, ĕre, ui, — intr. 3. *to grow strong, to be in health.*
Invectio, ōnis, f. 3. *a bringing in, an importation.*
Invĕho, ĕre, xi, ctum, tr. 3. *to carry in.*
Invĕnio, īre, vēni, ventum, tr. 4. *to find out, to invent.*
Inventio, ōnis, f. 3. *a finding out, an invention.*
Inventrix, īcis, f. 3. *an inventress.*
Inverto, ĕre, ti, sum, tr. 3. *to turn in.*
Investigatio, ōnis, f. 3. *investigation.*
Investīgo, āre, āvi, ātum, tr. 1. *to trace, to investigate.*
Invĭcem, adv. *in turn, in return.*
Invictus, a, um, adj. *unconquered.*
Invĭdeo, ēre, vīdi, vīsum, tr. 2. *to envy, to hate.*
Invidia, æ, f. 1. *envy.*
Invigĭlo, āre, āvi, ātum, tr. 1. *to watch diligently, to attend to.*
Invītus, a, um, adj. *unwilling.*
Ionĭcus, a, um, adj. *of Ionia, Ionian.*
Ipse, ipsa, ipsum, pron. *he himself, she herself, itself;* pl. *they themselves.*
Ira, æ, f. 1. *anger.*
Iracundia, æ, f. 1. *irascibility, passion.*
Iracundus, a, um, adj. *passionate, angry.*
Irascor, sci, — dep. 3. *to be angry.*
Irātus, a, um, adj. *angry.*
Irrevocabĭlis, e, adj. *not to be recalled, irrevocable.*
Irrīdeo, ēre, si, sum, tr. 2. *to laugh at, to mock.*
Irrĭgo, āre, āvi, ātum, tr. 1. *to irrigate, to water.*
Irritamentum, i, intr. 2. *an incitement.*
Irrĭtus, a, um, adj. *of no effect, vain.*
Irrumpo, ĕre, rupi, ruptum, intr. 3. *to rush in.*
Is, ea, id, pron. *he, she, it, that;* pl. *they, those.*
Isocrătes, is, m. 3. *a Greek orator.*
Iste, ista, istud, pron. *he, she, that;* pl. *those.*
Ister, tri, m. 2. *the river Ister.*
Isthic, hæc, hoc, *or* huc, pron. *the self-same, this.*

Istic, adv. *in that place, there, then.*
Ita, adv. *so, even so, thus.*
Italia, æ, f. 1. *Italy.*
Italĭcus, i. m. *an Italian.*
Ităque, adv. *therefore, and so.*
Iter, itinĕris, n. 3. *a journey, a way.*
Itĕrum, adv. *again, a second time.*
Itĭdem, adv. *also, in like manner.*

J.

Jaceo, ēre, ui, — intr. 2. *to lie.*
Jacto, āre, āvi, ātum, tr. 1. *to throw, to toss to and fro.*
Jactūra, æ, f. 1. *a loss, damage.*
Jacŭlum, i, n. 2. *a javelin, a dart.*
Jam, adv. *now, immediately.*
Jampridem, adv. *long ago, long since.*
Janicŭlum, i, n. 2. *one of the seven hills of Rome.*
Janua, æ, f. 1. *a gate.*
Jason, ŏnis, m. 3. *Jason, a king of Thessaly.*
Jejūnus, a, um, adj. *fasting, hungry.*
Jocus, i, m. 2 *a joke, a jest*; pl. *i, & a.*
Jovianus, i, m. 2, *Jovian, a man's name.*
Jubeo, ēre, ssi, ssum, tr. 2. *to order, to command.*
Jucunde, adv. *pleasantly, cheerfully.*
Jucundĭtas, ātis, f. 3. *pleasantness, mirth.*
Jucundus, a, um, adj. *pleasant, agreeable.*
Judæa, æ, f. 1. *Judea, a country in Asia.*
Judex, ĭcis, c. 3. *a judge.*
Judicium, ii, n. 2. *judgment.*
Judĭco, āre, āvi, ātum, tr. 1. *to judge.*
Jugĕrum, i, n. 2. *an acre.*
Jugum, i, n. 2. *a yoke.*
Jugurtha, æ, m. 1. *Jugurtha, a man's name.*
Julianus, i, m. 2. *Julian, a man's name.*
Julius, ii, m. 2. *the month of July.*
Julius, ii, m. 2. *a man's name.*
Jumentum, i, n. 2. *a beast of burden,* Pl. *cattle.*
Jungo, ĕre, xi, ctum, tr. 3. *to join.*
Jūno, ōnis, f. 3. *Juno, the queen of the gods.*
Jupiter, Jovis, m. 3. *Jupiter, king of the gods.*
Jure, adv. *rightly, by right.*
Juro, āre, āvi, ātum, tr. 1. *to swear.*
Jus, juris, n. 3. *right, law.*
Juste, adv. *justly.*
Justitia, æ, f. 1. *justice.*
Justus, a, um, adj. *just.*
Juvat, it, āre, imp. *it delights, it pleases.*
Juvenālis, is, m. 3. *Juvenal, a Roman poet.*
Juvenīlis, e, adj. *youthful.*
Juvĕnis, is, c. 3. *a young man* or *woman.*
Juventa, æ, f. 1. *youth, the time of youth.*
Juventus, ūtis, f. 3. *youth.*
Jŭvo, āre, jūvi, (*seldom* jūtum,) tr. 1. *to help, to assist.*
Juxta, prep. & adv. *nigh to, even, alike.*

K.

Kalendæ, ārum, f. pl. 1. *the Kalends.*

L.

Labiēnus, i, m. 2. *a Roman general.*
Labor, ōris, m. 3. *labour.*
Labor, labi, lapsus, dep. 3. *to slide, to fall.*
Labōro, āre, āvi, ātum, tr. & intr. 1. *to labour, to be in distress.*
Lacedæmon, ŏnis, f. 3. *Lacedemon, the capital of Laconia.*

Lacedæmonius, a, um, adj. *Lacedemonian.*
Lacesso, ĕre, īvi, ītum, tr. 3. *to provoke, to annoy.*
Lacrĭmo, āre, āvi, ātum, intr. 1. *to weep.*
Lacryma, æ, f. 1. *a tear.*
Lædo, ĕre, si, sum, tr. 3. *to strike, to hurt.*
Lætitia, æ, f. 1. *joy, gladness.*
Lætor, āri, ātus, dep. 1. *to rejoice.*
Lætus, a, um, adj. *glad, joyful.*
Lævīnus, i, m. 2. *a Roman consul.*
Lævor, ōris, m. 3. *smoothness.*
Lamentatio, ōnis, f. 3. *lamentation.*
Laneus, a, um, adj. *woollen, of wool.*
Lanificium, ii, n. 2. *spinning wool.*
Laodicēa, æ, f. 1. *Laodicea, a city of Asia.*
Lapis, ĭdis, m. 3. *a stone.*
Larcius, ii, m. 2. *a man's name.*
Largior, īri, ītus, dep. 4. *to give liberally, to lavish.*
Largus, a, um, adj. *large, plentiful.*
Lascivia, æ, f. 1. *lasciviousness, wanton joy.*
Late, ius, issime, adv. *widely.*
Lateo, ēre, ui, — intr. 2. *to be concealed, to lie hid.*
Latine, adv. *in Latin.*
Latinus, a, um, adj. *Latin.*
Latitūdo, ĭnis, f. 3. *breadth.*
Latro, ōnis, m. 3. *a robber.*
Latus, a, um, adj. *broad.*
Laudabĭlis, e, adj. *laudable, praiseworthy.*
Laudatio, ōnis, f. 3. *a eulogy.*
Laudātor, ōris, m. 3. *a praiser, a commender.*
Laudo, āre, āvi, ātum, tr. 1. *to praise.*
Laurus, i, f. 2. *a laurel.*
Laus, dis, f. 3. *praise.*
Laxe, ius, issime, adv. *widely, loosely, carelessly.*
Laxo, āre, āvi, ātum, tr. 1. *to loosen, extend.*
Lectĭto, āre, āvi, ātum, tr. 1. *to read often, to peruse.*
Lectum, i, n. 2. *a bed.*
Lectus, a, um (ior, issimus), adj. *choice, select.*
Legātus, i, m. 2. *an ambassador, a lieutenant.*
Legio, ōnis, f. 3. *a legion.*
Lego, ĕre, lēgi, lectum, tr. 3. *to read, to gather.*
Lenio, īre, īvi *or* ii, ītum, tr. 4. *to soften.*
Lenis, e, adj. *smooth, gentle.*
Lenĭter, adv. *softly, gently.*
Lentus, a, um, adj. *pliant, slow.*
Leo, ōnis, m. 3. *a lion.*
Lepus, ŏris, m. 3. *a hare.*
Letilius, ii, m. 2. *a man's name.*
Levis, e, adj. *light, swift, trifling.*
Lēvo, āre, āvi, ātum, tr. 1. *to relieve.*
Lex, legis, f. 3. *a law.*
Libānus, i, m. 2. *Lebanon.*
Libellus, i, m. 2. dim. *a little book, a memorial, a petition.*
Libenter, adv. *willingly, gladly.*
Liber, bri, m. 2. *bark, a book.*
Liber, ĕra, ĕrum, adj. *free.*
Liberālis, e, adj. *liberal, free.*
Liberalĭtas, ātis, f. 3. *civility, liberality.*
Liberalĭter, adv. *liberally, generously.*
Liberātor, ōris, m. 3. *a deliverer.*
Libĕri, ōrum, m. 2. *children.*
Libĕro, āre, āvi, ātum, tr. 1. *to free, to release.*
Libertas, ātis, f. 3. *liberty, freedom.*
Libertus, i, m. 2. *a freedman.*
Libīdo, ĭnis, f. 3. *desire, will, lust.*
Licentia, æ, f. 1. *liberty, licentiousness.*
Licet, ēre, uit, & ĭtum est, imp. *it is lawful, it is in the power of.*
Licet, conj. *although.*
Lictor, ōris, m. 3. *a lictor.*
Liger, ĕris, m. 3. *the Liger* (*Loire*).
Lignum, i, n. 2. *wood.*

Limen, ĭnis, n. 3. *a threshold, a door.*
Lingua, æ, f. 1. *the tongue.*
Liquĭdus, a, um, adj. *liquid, clear, pure.*
Lis, litis, f. 3. *strife, a lawsuit.*
Litĕra, æ, f. 1. *a letter.* Pl. *an epistle, learning.*
Literarius, a, um, adj. *literary, of letters;* ludus literarius, *a school.*
Literātus, a, um, adj. *lettered, literary.*
Littus (lĭtus), ōris, n. 3. *the shore.*
Livius, ii, m. 2. *Livy, a man's name.*
Lŏco, āre, āvi, ātum, tr. 1. *to place, to contract for, to hire out.*
Locuples, ētis, adj. *rich, wealthy.*
Locuplēto, āre, āvi, ātum, tr. 1. *to enrich.*
Locus, i, m. 2. *a place.* Pl. i *or* a.
Longe, adv. *far, far off.*
Longinquĭtas, ātis, f. 3. *distance, remoteness.*
Longitūdo, ĭnis, f. 3. *length.*
Longus, a, um, adj. *long.*
Loquax, ācis, adj. *loquacious.*
Loquor, qui, cūtus, *or* quūtus, dep. 3. *to speak.*
Lubenter, adv. *willingly, with pleasure.*
Luceo, ēre, xi, — intr. 2. *to shine.*
Lucesco, ĕre, intr. incep. 3. *to dawn.*
Lucĭfer, ĕri, m. 2. *the morning star.*
Lucilius, ii, m. 2. *a man's name.*
Lucius, ii, m. 2. *Lucius, a philosopher,*
Lucretia, æ, f. 1. *Lucretia, wife of Collatinus.*
Lucrum, i, n. 2. *gain.*
Luctus, ûs, m. 4. *grief.*
Lucus, i, m. 2. *a grove, a wood.*
Ludibrium, ii, n. 2. *a mockery, a sport.*
Ludo, ĕre, si, sum, tr. 3. *to play, to sport.*
Ludus, i, m. 2. *play, sport.*
Lugeo, ēre, luxi, luctum, intr. 2. *to mourn.*
Lumen, ĭnis, n. 3. *light.*
Luna, æ, f. 1. *the moon.*
Luo, ĕre, i, ĭtum, tr. 3. *to pay, to expiate.*
Lusor, ōris, m. 3. *a sporter, a gamester.*
Lusus, ûs, m. 4. *a play, a sport.*
Lux, lucis, f. 3. *light.*
Luxuria, æ, f. 1. } *luxury.*
Luxuries, ēi, f. 5. }
Luxurio, āre, āvi, ātum, intr. 1. *to be luxurious, to be wanton.*
Luxus, ûs, m. 4. *riot, excess.*
Lycurgus, i, m. 2. *Lycurgus.*
Lydus, i, m. 2. *a man's name.*
Lysander, dri, m. 2. *Lysander.*
Lysimăchus, i, m. 2. *Lysimachus, a man's name.*

M.

Macedo, ŏnis, m. 3. *a Macedonian.*
Macies, ēi, f. 5. *leanness.*
Mæcēnas, ātis, m. 3. *Mæcenas, a Roman.*
Magis, adv. *more.*
Magister, tri, m. 2. *a master.*
Magistrātus, ûs, m. 4. *a magistrate, magistracy.*
Magnanĭmus, a, um, adj. *magnanimous, brave.*
Magnes, ētis, m. 3. *the loadstone.*
Magnifĭcus, a, um, adj. *magnificent, splendid.*
Magnitūdo, ĭnis, f. 3. *greatness.*
Magnopĕre, adv. *greatly.*
Magnus, a, um, adj. *great.*
Mago, ōnis, m. 3. *Mago, a brother of Hannibal.*
Majestas, ātis, f. 3. *greatness, majesty, treason.*
Major, us, adj. comp. *greater;* major nātu, *older.*
Majōres, um, pl. m. 3. *ancestors.*
Mala, æ, f. 1. *the cheek.*
Male, adv. *badly, wickedly.*

Maledīco, ĕre, xi, ctum, tr. 3. *to rail at, abuse.*
Maleficium, ii, n. 2. *a wicked action, mischief.*
Malevolentia, æ, f. 1. *ill-will, malice.*
Malitia, æ, f. 1. *malice, wickedness.*
Malo, le, ui, irr. *to be more willing, to prefer.*
Malum, i, n. 2. *an evil, a mischief.*
Malus, a, um, adj. *bad, wicked.*
Mancipium, ii, n. *a slave.*
Mando, āre, āvi, ātum, tr. 1. *to commit to one's charge, to command.*
Maneo, ēre, si, sum, intr. & tr. 2. *to stay, to wait for, remain.*
Manlius, ii, m. 2. *a man's name.*
Māno, āre, āvi, ātum, intr. 1. *to flow, drop.*
Mansuetūdo, ĭnis, f. 1. *good nature, clemency.*
Mantĭca, æ, f. 1. *a wallet, a bag.*
Mantinea, æ, f. 1. *a city of Arcadia.*
Mantua, æ, f. 1. *Mantua, a city in Italy.*
Manumitto, ĕre, mĭsi, missum, tr. 3. *to manumit, set free.*
Manus, ûs, f. 4. *the hand, a band.*
Marăces, is, m. 3. *a man's name.*
Marathon, ōnis, m. 3. *Marathon.*
Marcellīnus, i, m. 2. *a man's name.*
Marcellus, i, m. 2. *Marcellus.*
Marcius (Ancus), ii, m. 2. *a Roman king.*
Marcus, i, m. 2. *a man's name.*
Mardonius, ii, m. 2. *a Persian general.*
Măre, is, n. 3. *the sea.*
Margarīta, æ, f. 1. *a pearl.*
Marius, ii, m. 2. *Marius, a Roman general.*
Marmor, ŏris, m. 3. *marble.*
Mars, tis, m. 3. *Mars, the god of war.*
Marsus, a, um, adj. *Marsian.*
Marsyas, æ, m. 1. *a man's name, a river in Phrygia.*
Masinissa, æ, m. 1. *a king of Numidia.*
Massa, æ, m. 1. *a man's name.*
Massagĕtæ, ārum, pl. m. 1. *a people of Scythia.*
Mater, tris, f. 3. *a mother.*
Materia, æ, & Materies, ēi, f. 1. & 5. *material, wood, timber.*
Mathematĭcus, i, m. 2. *a mathematician, an astrologer.*
Matūre, adv. *speedily, early.*
Matūro, āre, āvi, ātum, intr. 1. *to make haste.*
Matūrus, a, um, adj. *mature, ripe.*
Matutīnus, a, um, adj. *early in the morning.*
Maurus, i, m. 2. *a Moor.*
Maxĭme, adv. sup. *very much.*
Maximus, a, um, adj. sup. *very great, greatest.*
Medicamentum, i, n. 2. *a potion.*
Medicīna, æ, f. 1. *medicine, a cure.*
Medĭcus, i, m. 2. *a physician.*
Mediocris, e, adj. *ordinary.*
Meditatio, ōnis, f. 3. *meditation, study.*
Medĭtor, āri, ātus, dep. 1. *to meditate, to practise.*
Medius, a, um, adj. *middle.*
Megăra, æ, f. 1. *the name of a city.*
Melior, us, adj. comp. *better.*
Melius, adv. comp. *better.*
Mellifĭco, āre, āvi, ātum, tr. 1. *to make honey.*
Membrāna, æ, f. 1. *a membrane.*
Membrum, i, n. 2. *a member, a limb.*
Memĭni, isse, def. *to remember.*
Memor, ŏris, adj. *mindful.*
Memoria, æ, f. 1. *memory, recollection.*
Memŏro, āre, āvi, ātum, tr. 1. *to relate, to tell.*
Mendacium, ii, n. 2. *a lie.*
Mendax, ācis, adj. *lying, deceitful.* Sub. *a liar.*
Menelāus, i, m. 2. *Menelaus, brother of Agamemnon.*
Menismĭni, ōrum, m. 2. *the Menismini.*
Mens, tis, f. 3. *the mind.*

Mensa, æ, f. 1. *a table.*
Mensis, is, m. 3. *a month.*
Mensura, æ, f. 1. *a measure.*
Mentio, ōnis, f. 3. *mention.*
Mentior, īri, ītus, dep. 4. *to lie.*
Mercator, ōris, m. 3. *a merchant.*
Merces, ēdis, f. 3. *a reward, hire.*
Mercor, āri, ātus, tr. dep. 1. *to buy.*
Mercurius, ii, m. 2. *Mercury.*
Mereo, ēre, ui, ĭtum, tr. 2. *to earn, to deserve.*
Mereor, ēri, ĭtus, dep. 2. *to deserve.*
Meridiānus, a, um, adj. *of mid-day, meridian.*
Merĭto, adv. *deservedly.*
Merĭtum, i, n. 2. *a reward, merit.*
Meta, æ, f. 1. *a goal, a limit.*
Metellus, i, m. 2. *Metellus, a man's name.*
Metuo, ĕre, i, — tr. 3. *to fear, to be afraid.*
Metus, ûs, m. 4. *fear,*
Meus, a, um, pron. *my,* or *mine.*
Micipsa, æ, m. 1, *a king of Numidia.*
Migro, are, āvi, ātum, intr. 1. *to remove, to depart from.*
Miles, ĭtis, m. 3. *a soldier.*
Milesius, a, um, adj. *a Milesian.*
Militāris, e, adj. *military, of a soldier.*
Militia, æ, f. 1. *warfare, military service;* militiæ, *abroad.*
Mille, n. ind. *a thousand;* Pl. millia, ium, &c.
Milo, ōnis, m. 3. *Milo, a famous athlete of Croton.*
Miltiades, is, m. 3. Miltiădes.
Mĭna, æ, f. 1. *a threat,* more commonly minæ ārum, pl.
Mina, æ, f. 1. *a pound.*
Minerva, æ, f. 1. *Minerva, the goddess of wisdom, &c.*
Minĭme, adv. *least, very little.*
Minĭmus, a, um, adj. *least, very little.*
Minor, us, adj. *less.*
Minor, āri, ātus, dep. 1. *to threaten.*
Mīnos, ōis, m. 3. *Minos, a celebrated lawgiver.*
Minuo, ĕre, i, ūtum, tr. 3. *to lessen, to diminish.*
Minus, adv. *less.*
Miracŭlum, i, n. 2. *a miracle.*
Miror, āri, ātus, dep. 1. *to wonder, to admire.*
Mirus, a, um, adj. *wonderful.*
Misceo, ēre, scui, stum, *or* xtum, tr. 2. *to mix.*
Miser, era, ĕrum, adj. *wretched, miserable.*
Miserabĭlis, e, adj. *miserable.*
Misereor, ēri, ertus, *or* erĭtus, dep. 2. *to pity.*
Miseresco, ĕre, — — tr. 3. *to pity.*
Misĕret, ēre, uit, & ertum est, imp. *it pities.*
Miseria, æ, f. 1. *misery.*
Misericordia, æ, f. 1. *pity.*
Misericors, dis, adj. *merciful.*
Mithridātes, is, m. 3. *King of Pontus.*
Mitĭgo, āre, āvi, ātum, tr. 1. *to tame, to mitigate.*
Mitto, ĕre, mīsi, missum, tr. 3. *to send.*
Mobĭlis, e, adj. *moveable, fickle.*
Moderātè, adv. *moderately, with moderation.*
Moderatio, ōnis, f. 3. *moderation.*
Modĕror, āri, ātus, dep. 1. *to moderate, to govern.*
Modestia, æ, f. 1. *moderation, modesty.*
Modo, adv. *just now, only.*
Modus, i, m. 2. *a measure, a manner, moderation.*
Mœnia, ium, n. pl. 3. *walls.*
Mœreo, ēre and Mœreor, ēri, intr. 2. *to mourn, to lament, to be sad.*
Mœror, ōris, m. 3. *grief, sorrow.*
Mœstitia, æ, f. 1. *sadness, gloom.*
Mœstus, a, um, adj. *sad, sorrowful.*
Moleste, adv. *grievously, painfully.*
Molestia, æ, f. 1. *trouble, uneasiness.*
Molestus, a, um, adj. *disagreeable.*

Molior, īri, ītus, dep. 4. *to contrive, to prepare.*
Mollio, īre, īvi, ītum, tr. 4. *to soften.*
Mollis, e, adj. *soft.*
Moneo, ēre, ui, ītum, tr. 2. *to advise, to admonish.*
Monĭtor, ōris, m. 3. *an adviser.*
Monĭtum, i, n. 2. *an advice.*
Mons, montis, m. 3. *a mountain.*
Monstro, āre, āvi, ātum, tr. 1. *to show, point out.*
Montanus, i, m. 2. *a mountaineer.*
Monumentum, i, n. 2. *a monument.*
Mora, æ, f. 1. *delay.*
Morātus, a, um, adj. *of good morals.*
Morbus, i, m. 2. *a disease.*
Morior, i, tuus, dep. 3. *to die.*
Mŏror, āri, ātus, dep. 1. *to delay.*
Mors, tis, f. 3. *death.*
Mortālis, e, adj. *mortal.*
Mortalĭtas, ātis, f. 3. *mortality.*
Mos, moris, m. 3. *a manner, a custom.*
Motus, ûs, m. 4. *a motion.*
Moveo, ēre, ōvi, ōtum, tr. 2. *to move.*
Mox, adv. *by and bye, presently.*
Muciānus, i, m. 2. *a man's name.*
Mulier, ĕris, f. 3. *a woman.*
Multitūdo, ĭnis, f. 3. *a multitude.*
Multo, āre, āvi, ātum, tr. *to fine, to punish.*
Multo, adv. *by much, much.*
Multus, a, um, adj. *much.*
Mūlus, i, m. 2. *a mule.*
Mummius, ii, m. 2. *a man's name.*
Mundus, i, m. 2. *the world.*
Munifĭcus, a, um, adj. *munificent.*
Munio, īre, īvi, ītum, tr. 4. *to fortify, to defend.*
Munus, ĕris, n. 3. *a gift, an office.*
Muræna, æ, f. 1. *a lamprey*
Murus, i, m. 2. *a wall.*
Musa, æ, f. 1. *a Muse.*
Mutatio, ōnis, f. 3. *change.*
Mutius, ii, m. 2. *Mutius, a Roman.*
Muto, āre, āvi, ātum, tr. 1. *to change.*
Mutus, a, um, adj. *mute, silent.*
Mutuus, a, um, adj. *lent,* or *borrowed, mutual.*

N.

Næ, adv. *assuredly, truly.*
Nam, conj. *for.*
Nanciscor, nancisci, nactus, dep. 3. *to get, to obtain.*
Nantuātes, um, m. pl. 3. *a people of Gaul.*
Narratio, ōnis, f. 3. *a narrative.*
Narro, āre, āvi, ātum, tr. 1. *to tell, to relate.*
Nascor, nasci, natus, dep. 3. *to be born.*
Natālis, e, adj. *relating to one's birth, native.*
Natio, ōnis, f. 3. *a nation.*
Nato, āre, āvi, ātum, tr. 1. *to swim*
Natūra, æ, f. 1. *nature.*
Naturālis, e, adj. *natural.*
Natus, a, um, adj. *born, descended.*
Naucrates, is, m. 3. *a man's name.*
Naucum, i, n. 2. *a trifle;* nauci, *of no value.*
Naufragium, ii, n. 2. *a shipwreck.*
Navālis, e, adj. *naval.*
Navigatio, ōnis, f. 3. *a sailing, navigation.*
Navĭgo, āre, āvi, ātum, tr. 1. *to sail.*
Navis, is, f. 3. *a ship.*
Ne, conj. *lest, that not, not.*
Ne, an enclitic particle, used to ask a question, and always subjoined to another word.
Neapolitānus, a, um, adj. *Neapolitan.*
Nebŭlo, ōnis, m. 3. *a rascal, a worthless fellow.*
Nec, conj. *nor, neither.*
Necessarius, a, um, adj. *necessary.*
Necessarius, ii, m. 2. *an intimate friend.*
Necesse, adj. indec. *necessary.*
Necessĭtas, ātis, f. 3. *necessity.*

Necessitūdo, ĭnis, f. 3. *friendship.*
Necne, conj. *or not.*
Nĕco, āre, āvi, or ui, ātum, tr. 1. *to kill.*
Nefas, n. ind. (used only in the nom. acc. and voc.) *an unlawful thing, wickedness.*
Negligens, tis, adj. *negligent, careless.*
Negligentia, æ, f. 1. *negligence.*
Neglĭgo, ĕre, exi, ectum, tr. 3. *to neglect, to despise.*
Nego, āre, āvi, ātum, tr. 1. *to deny, to refuse.*
Negotium, ii, n. 2. *a business, an employment.*
Nemo, ĭnis, c. 3. *nobody.*
Neptis, is, f. 3. *a grand-daughter.*
Nequam, adj. ind. *worthless, wicked.*
Neque, conj. *neither, nor.*
Nequeo, īre, īvi, & ii, ītum, irr. *not to be able, to be unable.*
Nequicquam, adv. *in vain.*
Nequis, qua, quod, *or* quid, pron. *lest any one, no one.*
Nequitia, æ, f. 1. *worthlessness, wickedness.*
Nĕro, ōnis, m. 3. *a Romam emperor.*
Nerva, æ, m. 1. *a Roman emperor.*
Nervus, i, m. 2. *a nerve, a sinew.*
Nescio, īre, īvi, ītum, tr. 4. *not to know, to be ignorant.*
Nescius, a, um, adj. *ignorant.*
Neuter, tra, trum, adj. *neither of the two.*
Neutĭquam, adv. *by no means.*
Nex, necis, f. 3. *death (by violence).*
Nicānor, ōris, m. 3. *a man's name.*
Nidifĭco, āre, āvi, ātum, tr. 1. *to make a nest.*
Nigresco, ĕre, intr. 3. *to grow black.*
Nihil, n, ind. (used only in the nom. acc. & voc.) *nothing.*
Nihĭlum, i, n. 2. *nothing.*
Nil, *contracted for nihil.*
Nilus, i, m. 2. *the Nile, a river of Egypt.*
Nimis, adv. *too much, or too little.*
Nimium, adv. *too much, exceedingly.*
Nimius, a, um, adj. *too great, excessive.*
Nīnus, i, m. 2. *Ninus, the builder of Nineveh.*
Nisi, conj. *if not, unless.*
Nitor, niti, nisus, *or* nixus, dep. 3. *to strive, to attempt.*
Nitrōsus, a, um, adj. *nitrous.*
Nix, nīvis, f. 3. *snow.*
Nobilis, e, adj. *well-known, famous, noble.*
Nobilĭtas, ātis, f. 3. *renown, nobility.*
Nocens, tis, adj. *hurtful.*
Noceo, ēre, ui, ĭtum, tr. 2. *to hurt.*
Noctu, adv. *in the night.*
Nodōsus, a, um, adj. *full of knots, knotty.*
Nolo, le, ui, irr. *to be unwilling.*
Nomen, ĭnis, n. 3. *a name.*
Nominātim, adv. *by name.*
Nomĭno, āre, āvi, ātum, 1, *to name.*
Non, adv. *not.*
Nonaginta, num. adj. indec. *ninety.*
Nondum, adv. *not yet.*
Nonne, adv. *not? if—not.*
Nonnullus, a, um, adj. *some;* Pl. *some persons.*
Nonnunquam, adv. *sometimes.*
Nosco, ĕre, vi, tum, tr. 3. *to learn, to become acquainted with.*
Noster, tra, trum, pron. *our, ours.*
Notitia, æ, f. 1. *knowledge.*
Novendiālis, e, adj. *of nine days.*
Nôvi, *I know; Perf. of* nosco.
Novissĭmus, a, um, adj. sup. *latest, last.*
Novĭtas, ātis, f. 3. *newness.*
Novus, a, um, adj. *new.*
Nox, ctis, f. 3. *night.*
Noxius, a, um, adj. *hurtful, guilty.*
Nubes, is, f. 3. *a cloud.*
Nūbo, ĕre, psi, ptum, tr. *to marry, (spoken of a woman.)*
Nudus, a, um, adj. *naked, bare.*
Nullus, a, um, adj. *none, no.*

Num, adv. *whether or not? whether.*
Numa, æ, m. 1, *Numa, the second king of Rome.*
Numantinus, a, um, adj. *of Numantia, Numantine.*
Numen, ĭnis, n. 3. *a nod, the will of the gods, a deity.*
Numĕro, āre, āvi, ātum, a. 1. *to number, to pay.*
Numĕrus, i, m. 2. *a number.*
Numidia, æ, f. 1. *Numidia.*
Nummus, i, m. 2. *a piece of money, money.*
Numquis—numquid, interrog. pr. = num quis.
Nunc, adv. *now.*
Nuncio, āre, āvi, ātum, tr. 1. *to announce, to tell, to carry tidings.*
Nuncius, ii, m. 2. *a messenger.*
Nuncŭpo, āre, āvi, ātum, tr. 1. *to call, to name.*
Nunquam, adv. *never.*
Nuper, adv. *lately.*
Nusquam, adv. *nowhere.*

O.

O, int. *O!*
Oaxis (Oaxes), is. m. 3. *a river of Crete.*
Ob, prep. *for, on account of.*
Obambŭlans, tis, pt. *walking about.*
Obdūco, ĕre, xi, ctum, tr. 3, *to lead against, to cover.*
Obēdio, īre, īvi, ītum, tr. 4. *to obey.*
Objicio, ĕre, jēci, jectum, tr. 3, *to throw before.*
Objurgo, āre, āvi, ātum, tr. 1. *to chide, to reprove.*
Oblĭgo, āre, āvi, ātum, tr. 1. *to tie round, to bind.*
Obliquus, a, um, adj. *oblique, crooked.*
Oblivio, ōnis, f. 3. *forgetfulness.*
Obliviscor, ivisci, ītus, dep. 3. *to forget.*
Obnoxius, a, um, adj. *liable, exposed to.*
Obnūbo, ĕre, psi, ptum, tr. 3. *to veil.*
Obrēpo, ĕre, psi, ptum, tr. 3. *to creep upon.*
Obruo, ĕre, ui, ūtum, tr. 3. *to cover, to overwhelm.*
Obscūrus, a, um, adj. *obscure, dark.*
Obsecro, āre, āvi, ātum, tr. 1. *to beseech.*
Obsequium, ii, n. 2. *compliance, obsequiousness.*
Obsĕquor, qui, cūtus, *or* quūtus, dep. 3. *to comply with, to obey.*
Observo, āre, āvi, ātum, tr. 1. *to observe.*
Obses, ĭdis, c. 3, *a hostage.*
Obsideo, ēre, sēdi, sessum, tr. 2, *to besiege.*
Obsisto, ĕre, stĭti, (*rarely* stĭtum,) tr. 3. *to stop, to hinder.*
Obsto, āre, stĭti, stātum, tr. 1. *to stand in the way, to oppose.*
Obstupesco, ĕre, ui, —, intr. 3. *to be amazed.*
Obsum, esse, fui, irr. *to hurt.*
Obtempĕro, āre, āvi, ātum, tr. 1. *to comply with, to obey.*
Obtineo, ēre, tinui, tentum, tr. 2. *to hold, to obtain.*
Obtrectatio, ōnis, f. 3. *an envying, a detracting.*
Obvenio, īre, vēni, ventum, intr. 4. *to meet.*
Obviam, adv. *in the way, toward, against;* īre obviam, *to meet.*
Obvolvo, ĕre, vi, ūtum, tr. 3. *to muffle up.*
Occīdo, ĕre, di, sum, tr. 3. *to kill.*
Occĭdo, ĕre, cĭdi, cāsum, intr. 3. *to fall, to die.*
Occŭlo, ĕre, ui, tum, tr. 3. *to hide, to conceal.*
Occumbo, ĕre, cubui, cubĭtum, intr. 3. *to fall, to die.*
Occŭpo, āre, āvi, ātum, tr. 1. *to occupy, to take possession of.*

Occurro, ĕre, curri, *or* cucurri, cursum, tr. 3. *to run against, to meet.*
Oceănus, i, m. 2, *the ocean.*
Octavius, ii, m. 2. *a man's name.*
Octo, adj. num. indec. *eight.*
Octogesĭmus, a, um, adj. *the eightieth.*
Octoginta, adj. ind. *eighty.*
Ocŭlus, i, m. 2. *the eye.*
Odi, odisse, def. *to hate.*
Odium, ii, n. *hatred.*
Offendo, ĕre, di, sum, tr. 3. *to strike against, to offend.*
Offensio, ōnis, f. 3. *misfortune, offence.*
Offĕro, offerre, obtŭli, oblātum, irr. *to bring before, to offer.*
Offĭcio, ĕre, fēci, fectum, tr. 3. *to hinder, to obstruct.*
Officiōsus, a, um, adj. *dutiful, attentive.*
Officium, ii, n. 2. *an office, a duty.*
Oleo, ēre, ui, ĭtum, intr. 2. *to emit a smell.*
Olīva, æ, f. 1. *the olive.*
Olympia, æ, f. 1. *Olympia, a plain of Elis, in Greece.*
Olympias, ădis, f. 3. *Olympiad.*
Olympius, a, um, adj. *Olympian.*
Omitto, ĕre, si, ssum, tr. 3. *to neglect, to omit.*
Omnīno, adv. *wholly, altogether.*
Omnis, e, adj. *all, every.*
Onĕro, āre, āvi, ātum, tr. 1. *to load.*
Onus, ĕris, n. 3. *a burden, a load.*
Opĕra, æ, f. 1. *work, endeavour, pains.*
Operōsus, a, um, adj. *laborious, active, difficult.*
Opĭfex, ĭcis, m. 3. *a workman.*
Opimius, ii, m. 2. *a Roman consul.*
Opinio, ōnis, f. 3. *an opinion, a belief.*
Opīnor, āri, ātus, dep. 1. *to help, to assist.*
Opis, *Gen.* opem, ope, f. 3. *power, help;* pl. opes, um, &c., *riches.*
Opitulor, āri, ātus, dep. 1. *to help, to assist.*
Oportet, ēre, uit, imp. *it behoves, it is fit.*
Oppianĭcus, i, m. 2. *a man's name.*
Oppĭdum, i, n. 2, *a town.*
Opportūnus, a, um, adj. *suitable, convenient.*
Opprĭmo, ĕre, essi, essum, tr. 3. *to press against, to oppress, to bury*
Opprobrium, ii, n. 2. *a reproach.*
Oppugnatio, ōnis, f. 3. *an attack.*
Optabĭlis, e, adj. *desirable.*
Optĭme, adv. *very well.*
Optĭmus. a, um, adj. *very good, best.*
Opto, āre, āvi, ātum, tr. 1. *to wish, to desire.*
Opŭlens, tis, adj. *rich, wealthy.*
Opulentia, æ, f. 1. *riches, wealth.*
Opulentus, a, um, adj. *rich, wealthy.*
Opus, ĕris, n. 3. *work, labour.*
Opus, n. ind. *need.*
Opus, adj. ind. *needful, expedient.*
Oracŭlum, i, n. 2. *an oracle.*
Oratio, ōnis, f. 3. *an oration, a speech.*
Orātor, ōris, m. 3. *an orator, a negotiator.*
Oratorĭcè, adv. *oratorically.*
Orbis, is, m. 3. *a circle, the world.*
Orbo, āre, āvi, ātum, tr. 1. *to deprive.*
Ordino, āre, āvi, ātum, tr. 1. *to arrange, put in order.*
Ordo, ĭnis, m. 3. *order.*
Orestes, is, m. 3. *Orestes, a man's name.*
Oriens, tis, m. 3. *the rising sun, the east.*
Orior, īri, tus, dep. 3. *to rise, to arise.*
Ornamentum, i, n. 2. *an ornament, grace.*
Ornātus, ûs, m. 4. *an ornament, a dress.*
Orno, āre, āvi, ātum, tr. 1. *to adorn, to dress.*

Oro, āre, āvi, ātum, tr. 1. *to speak, to beg.*
Orphĭcus, a, um, adj. *Orphic, of Orpheus.*
Os, oris, n. 3. *the mouth, face, countenance.*
Oscŭlum, i, n. 2. *a kiss.*
Ostendo, ĕre, di, sum, tr. 3. *to show, to declare.*
Ostentatio, ōnis, f. 3. *ostentation, vanity.*
Ostento, āre, āvi, ātum, tr. *to show.*
Otho, ōnis, m. 3. *Otho, a Roman surname,*
Otiōsus, a, um, adj. *idle.*
Otium, ii, n. 2. *idleness, leisure.*
Ovidius, ii, m. 2. *Ovid, a Latin poet.*
Ovis, is, f. 3. *a sheep.*

P.

Pabŭlum, i, n. 2. *fodder.*
Pactum, i, n. 2. *a bargain, an agreement.*
Pădus, i, m. 2. *the river Po.*
Pæne, adv. *almost, nearly.*
Pagus, i, m. 2. *a canton.*
Pāla, æ, f. 1. *a stone (of a ring.)*
Pālam, adv. *openly.*
Pālans, tis, pt. *wandering.*
Palla, æ, f. 1. *a palla,* or *robe.*
Pallium, ii, n. 2. *a robe.*
Palma, æ, f. 1. *the palm of the hand.*
Palpebra, æ, f. 1. *an eyelid.*
Pālus, ūdis, f. 3. *a marsh.*
Pamphĭlus, i, m. 2. *a man's name.*
Panætius, ii, m. 2. *a man's name.*
Pānis, is, m. 3. *bread.*
Par, paris, adj. *equal, like.*
Parce, adv. *sparingly.*
Parco, ĕre, peperci, parsum, *seldom* parsi, parsĭtum, tr. 3. *to spare.*
Parens, tis, c. 3. *a parent.*
Pareo, ēre, ui, ĭtum, tr. 2. *to appear, to obey.*
Paries, ĕtis, m. 3. *the wall of a house, a house.*
Pario, ĕre, pepĕri, partum, *or* parĭtum, tr. 3. *to bring forth, to produce, to procure.*
Paris, ĭdis, m. 3. *Paris, the son of Priam.*
Parĭter, adv. *in like manner, equally.*
Parma, æ, f. 1. *Parma, a city in Italy.*
Parmenio, ōnis, m. 3. *one of Alexander's generals.*
Paro, āre, āvi, ātum, tr. 1. *to prepare, to acquire.*
Pars, tis, f. 3. *a part.*
Parsimonia, æ, f. 1. *frugality, parsimony.*
Parthus, i, m. 2. *a Parthian.*
Partĭceps, ĭpis, adj. *sharing, privy to.*
Partim, adv. *partly.*
Parum, adv. *little, too little.*
Parvŭlus, a, um, adj. *very little, very small.*
Parvus, a, um, adj. *little, small.*
Pasco, ĕre, vi, stum, tr. 3. *to feed.*
Passus, ûs, m. 4. *a pace.*
Patefăcio, ĕre, fēci, factum, tr. 3. *to open, to clear.*
Pateo, ēre, ui, — intr. 2. *to be open.*
Pater, tris, m. 3. *a father.*
Pater-familias, pātris-familias, m. 3 & 1, *the father of a family.*
Paternus, a, um, adj. *paternal, of a father.*
Patiens, tis, adj. *capable of enduring, patient.*
Patienter, adv. *patiently.*
Patientia, æ, f. 1. *patience.*
Patior, i, passus, dep. 3. *to bear, to suffer.*
Patria, æ, f. 1. *one's native country.*
Patrimonium, ii, n. 2. *patrimony.*
Patro, āre, āvi, ātum, tr. 1. *to bring to an end.*
Patronus, i, m. 2. *a patron.*

Patruus, i, m. 2. *an uncle by the father's side, an uncle.*
Pauci, æ, a, *seldom* us, a, um, adj. *few.*
Paulo, adv. *by a little, a little.*
Paululum, adv. *a little, very little.*
Paululus, a, um, adj. *a very little.*
Paulum, adv. *a little.*
Paulus, i, m. 2. *Paulus, a man's name.*
Pauper, ĕris, adj. *poor.*
Paupertas, ātis, f. 3. *poverty.*
Pausanias, æ, m. 1. *Pausanias.*
Pavor, ōris, m. 3. *great fear.*
Pax, pācis, f. 3. *peace.*
Peccātum, i, n. 2. *a fault, a sin.*
Pecco, āre, āvi, ātum, tr. 1. *to sin, to offend. to blunder.*
Pectus, ŏris, n. 3. *the breast, the mind.*
Pecūlor, āri, ātus, dep. 1. *to rob, to plunder.*
Pecunia, æ, f. 1. *money.*
(Pecus *seldom used,*) ŭdis, f. 3. *a beast, a sheep;* Pl. *cattle.*
Pedes, ĭtis, m. 3. *a foot soldier.*
Pejero, āre, āvi, ātum, tr. 1. *to violate an oath.*
Pejor, us, adj. *worse.*
Pellæus, a, um, adj. *belonging to Pella, Pellæan.*
Pellis, is, f. 3. *a skin.*
Pello, ĕre, pepŭli, pulsum, tr. 3. *to drive.*
Pendeo, ēre, pependi, pensum, intr. 2. *to hang.*
Pendo, ĕre, pependi, pensum, tr. 3. *to weigh, to value, to esteem.*
Penes, prep. *in the power of.*
Penetro, āre, āvi, ātum, tr. 1. *to penetrate.*
Penĭtus, adv. *entirely, far.*
Pensīlis, e, adj. *hanging.*
Penso, āre, āvi, ātum, tr. 1. *to weigh.*
Pensum, i, n. 2. *concern, care, regard.*
Penuria, æ, f. 1. *want, scarcity.*
Per, prep. *by, through.*
Perăgo, ĕre, ēgi, actum, tr. 3. *to finish;* pass., *to be over.*
Percĭpio, ĕre, cēpi, ceptum, tr. 3. *to perceive, to learn, to gather (fruit), to enjoy.*
Percontor, āri, ātus, dep. 1. *to inquire, to examine.*
Percrebesco, ĕre, brui, & bui, —, intr. 3. *to spread abroad, to become known.*
Perculsus, a, um, pt. *being struck.*
Percunctor, āri, ātus, dep. 1. *to question.*
Percutio, ĕre, cussi, cussum, tr. 3. *to strike;* percutĕre secūri, *to behead.*
Perdiccas, æ, m. 1. *a general of Alexander.*
Perdisco, ĕre, didĭci, —, *to learn thoroughly, to commit to memory.*
Perdo, ĕre, dĭdi, dĭtum, tr. 3. *to destroy, to lose.*
Perdŏmo, āre, ui, ĭtum, tr. 1. *to subdue, to conquer.*
Peregrīnus, i, m. 2. *a foreigner.*
Pereo, īre, ii, *seldom* īvi, ĭtum, intr. irr. *to perish, to be lost, to die.*
Perfecte, adv. *perfectly.*
Perfectio, ōnis, f. 3. *perfection.*
Perfectus, a, um, adj. *perfect, entire.*
Perfĕro, ferre, tŭli, lātum, tr. irr. *to suffer.*
Perfĭcio, ĕre, fēci, fectum, tr. 3. *to finish, to execute.*
Perfidia, æ, f. 1. *treachery, perfidy.*
Perfĭdus, a, um, adj. *perfidious.*
Perfŏro, āre, āvi, ātum, tr. 1. *to pierce through.*
Perfruor, ui, uctus, *or* uĭtus, dep. 3. *to enjoy very much.*
Perfŭgio, gĕre, fūgi, fugĭtum, intr. 3. *to fly for shelter.*
Perfugium, ii, n. 2. *a refuge.*
Pergamum, i, n. 2. *Pergămus, the citadel of Troy.*
Pergo, ĕre, exi, ectum, tr. 3. *to go forward, to proceed.*
Perhumanĭter, adv. *very kindly.*
Periculōsus, a, um. adj. *dangerous.*

Periculum, i, n. 2. *danger.*
Perinde, adv. *just the same, eqnally.*
Perītus, a, um, adj. *skilled, accustomed.*
Permaneo, ēre, si, sum, n. 2. *to remain, to continue.*
Permansio, ōnis, f. 3. *a remaining.*
Permeo, āre, āvi, ātum, tr. 1. *to flow through.*
Permitto, ĕre, īsi, issum, tr. 3. *to send away, to allow.*
Permoveo, ēre, vi, tum, tr. 2. *to move.*
Permultus, a, um, adj. *very many.*
Permutatio, ōnis, f. 3. *a changing, an altering.*
Perniciōsus, a, um, adj. *destructiue, hurtful.*
Pernix, īcis, adj. *swift, nimble.*
Pernocto, āre, āvi, ātum, intr. 1. *to pass the night.*
Perpĕram, adv. *rashly, amiss.*
Perpetior, pĕti, pessus, dep. 3. *to suffer.*
Perpetuo, adv. *perpetually.*
Perpetuus, a, um, adj. *perpetual, continual.*
Perquam, adj. *very.*
Persæ, ārum, m. pl. 1. *Persians.*
Persæpe, adv. *very often.*
Perscrībo, ĕre, psi, ptum, tr. 3. *to describe.*
Persĕquor, qui, cūtus, *or* quūtus, dep. 3, *to follow close, to pursue.*
Persevēro, āre, āvi, ātum, tr. 1. to *persevere.*
Persĭcus, a, um, adj. *Persian.*
Persis, ĭdis, m. 3. *Persia.*
Persōna, æ, f. 1. *a person, a mask.*
Perspĭcio, ĕre, exi, ectum, tr. 3. *to see plainly, to understand.*
Perspicuus, a, um, adj. *clear, manifest.*
Persuādeo, ēre, si, sum, tr. 2. to *persuade.*
Pertimesco, ere, timui, — tr. 3. *to fear, to dread.*
Pertinacia, æ, f. 1. *obstinacy, pertinacity.*
Pertinacĭter, adv. *resolutely.*
Pertinax, ācis, m. 3. *a man's name.*
Pertineo, ēre, ui, tentum, intr. 2. *to pertain, to tend.*
Perturbatio, ōnis, f. 3. *a confusion, a disturbance.*
Perturbo, āre, āvi, ātum, tr. 1. *to disturb greatly, to embroil.*
Pervĕnio, īre, vēni, ventum, n. 4. *to come to, to arrive at.*
Pes, pedis, m. 3. *a foot.*
Pessīmus, a, um, adj. *very bad, worst.*
Pessundo, āre, dēdi, datum, tr. 1. *to ruin, to destroy.*
Pestĭfer, ĕra, ĕrum, adj. *pestiferous, ruinous.*
Pestis, is, f. 3. *a pest, a plague.*
Peto, ĕre, īvi, ītum, tr. 3. *to ask, to seek, to go to.*
Petŭlans, tis, adj. *petulant.*
Phæthon, ōntis, m. 3. *Phæthon.*
Phalăris, ĭdis, m. 3. *Phalaris, a tyrant of Agrigentum.*
Phalĕra, æ, f. 1. *horse trappings.*
Pharus, i, f. 2. *Pharus, an island opposite to the mouth of the Nile.*
Philippus, i, m. 2. *Philip.*
Philocrates, is, m. 3. *Philocrates.*
Philonīdes, is, m. 3. *Philonides, a man's name.*
Philosophia, æ, f. 1. *philosophy.*
Philosŏphor, āri, ātus, dep. 1. *to philosophize.*
Philosŏphus, i, m. 2. *a philosopher.*
Philotimus, i, m. 2. *a man's name.*
Pictūra, æ, f. 1. *a painting, a picture.*
Pie, adv. *piously.*
Pierĭdes, um, f. 3. *the Muses.*
Piĕtas, ātis, f. 3. *piety, affection.*
Piget, ēre, uit, *or* ĭtum est, imp. *it grieves.*
Piger, gra, grum, adj. *slow, dull.*
Pīla, æ, f. 1. *a ball.*
Pīlum, i, n. 2. *a javelin, heavy dart.*
Pinguesco, ĕre, — — n. 3. *to grow fat.*

Pinguis, e, adj. *fat.*
Piscīna, æ, f. 1. *a fish pond.*
Piscis, is, m. 3. *a fish.*
Pisistrătus, i, m. 2. *Pisistratus, a tyrant of Athens.*
Piso, ōnis, m. 3. *a man's name.*
Pius, a, um, adj. *pious, affectionate.*
Placabĭlis, e, adj. *easy to be pacified, placable,*
Placabilĭtas, ātis, f. 3. *gentleness, placability.*
Placātè, adv. *peaceable, with patience.*
Placentia, æ, f. 1. *Placentia, a city of Italy.*
Placeo, ēre, ui, ĭtum, tr. 2. *to please.*
Placet, ēre, uit, imp. *it pleases.*
Placĭde, adv. *gently, mildly.*
Placĭdus, a, um, adj. *gentle, mild.*
Plăco, āre, āvi, ātum, tr. 1. *to appease.*
Plāne, adv. *plainly, evidently.*
Planitia, æ, f. 1. & planities, ei, 5. f. *a plain.*
Platănus, i, f. 2. *the plane tree.*
Plato, ōnis, m. 3. *Plato, a Grecian philosopher.*
Plebs, plēbis, c. 3. *the common people.*
Plecto, ĕre, xui, & xi, xum, tr. *to twist, to plait, to punish.*
Plenus, a, um, adj. *full.*
Plerīque, æque, āque, adj. *the most, many.*
Plerumque, adv. *for the most part, commonly.*
Ploro, āre, āvi, ātum, tr. 1. *to weep, to lament.*
Plurĭmum, adv. *very much, most.*
Plurĭmus, a, um, adj. *very much, most.*
Plus, pluris, adj. *more;* pl. plures, a.
Plŭto, ōnis, m. 3. *God of the infernal regions.*
Pocŭlum, i, n. 2. *a goblet, a cup.*
Podagra, æ, f. 1. *the gout in the feet.*
Poēma, ātis, n. 3. *a poem.*
Pœna, æ, f. 1. *a compensation, punishment.*
Pœnĭtet, ēre, uit, imp. *it repents.*
Pœnus, i, m. 2. *a Carthaginian.*
Poēta, æ, m. 1. *a poet.*
Polio, īre, īvi, ītum, tr. 4. *to smooth, to polish.*
Polite, adv. *politely, elegantly.*
Pollux, ūcis, m. 3. *Pollux.*
Polliceor, ēri, ĭtus, dep. 2. *to offer, to promise.*
Pollio, ōnis, m. 3. *a man's name.*
Pŏlus, i, m. 2. *the pole, the sky.*
Pomœrium, ii, n. 2. *the pomœrium, an open space on both sides of the walls of a town.*
Pompeius, i, m. 2. *Pompey, a Roman general.*
Pomponius, ii, m. 2. *a man's name.*
Pondus, ĕris, n. 3. *weight.*
Pōno, ĕre, pŏsui, pŏsĭtum, tr. 3. *to put, to place.*
Pons, tis, m. 3. *a bridge.*
Populāris, e, adj. *of the people, popular.*
Popŭlus, i, m. 2. *a people.*
Porcia, æ, f. 1. *a woman's name.*
Porcius, a, um, adj. *Porcian, of Porcius.*
Porcus, i, m. 2. *a hog, a sow.*
Porrīgo, īnis, f. 3. *scab, mange.*
Porta, æ, f. 1. *a gate, a door.*
Porto, āre, āvi, ātum, tr. 1. *to carry.*
Portus, us, m. 4. *a harbor.*
Posco, ĕre, poposci, — tr. 3. *to ask, to demand.*
Possessio, ōnis, f. 3. *a possession.*
Possĭdeo, ēre, ēdi, essum, tr. 2. *to possess.*
Possum, posse, potui, irr. *to be able.*
Post, prep. *after, behind.*
Postea, adv. *afterwards.*
Posteaquam, adv. *after, after that.*
Posterĭtas, ātis, f. 3. *posterity.*
Postĕrus, a, um, adj. *coming after, following.*
Posthac, adv. *hereafter.*
Postis, is, f. 3. *a post.*

Postpōno, ĕre, ŏsui, ŏsĭtum, tr. 3. *to set behind, to esteem less.*
Postquam, adv. *after, afterwards.*
Postrĭdie, adv. *the day after.*
Postŭlo, āre, āvi, ātum, tr. 1. *to ask, to demand.*
Potentia, æ, f. 1. *power, force.*
Potestas, ātis, f. 3. *ability, power.*
Potio, ōnis, f. 3. *drinking, a draught.*
Potior, īri, ītus, dep. 4. *to be master of, to obtain.*
Potior, us (comp. of potis), adj. *better.*
Potissĭmum, adv. *chiefly, especially.*
Potius, adv. *rather, better.*
Poto, āre, āvi, ātum, *or* potum, tr. 1. *to drink.*
Potus, ūs, m. 4. *drink.*
Præ, prep. *before, for, on account of;* after the comparative, *than.*
Præbeo, ēre, ui, ĭtum, tr. 2. *to afford.*
Præcēdo, ĕre, cessi, cessum, tr. 3. *to go before, to excel.*
Præceptor, ōris, m. 3. *an instructor, a master.*
Præceptum, i, n. 2. *an order, a precept.*
Præcĭpio, ĕre, cēpi, ceptum, tr. 3. *to take before, to order.*
Præcipĭto, āre, āvi, ātum, tr. 1. *to throw headlong, to precipitate.*
Præcipuus, a, um, adj. *chief.*
Præclāre, adv. *very clearly, nobly.*
Præclārus, a, um, adj. *very clear, illustrious.*
Præco, ōnis, m. 3. *a herald.*
Præda, æ, f. 1. *prey.*
Prædĭco, āre, āvi, ātum, tr. 1. *to publish, to proclaim.*
Præditus, a, um, adj. *endued with.*
Præfectus, i, m. 2. *a prefect, a chief officer.*
Præfĕro, ferre, tŭli, lātum, tr. irr. *to carry before, to prefer.*
Prælectio, ōnis, f. 3. *a lesson.*
Prælium, ii, n. 2. *a battle.*
Præmeditatio, ōnis, f. 3. *premeditation.*
Præmitto, ĕre, mīsi, missum, tr. 3. *to send before.*
Præmium, ii, n. 2. *a reward.*
Præopto, āre, āvi, ātum, tr. 1. *to wish rather.*
Præparatio, ōnis, f. 3. *a preparation.*
Præpăro, āre, āvi, ātum, tr. 1. *to prepare.*
Præpondĕro, āre, āvi, ātum, tr. 1. *to outweigh, to prefer.*
Præpōno, ĕre, ŏsui, ŏsitum, tr. 3. *to set before, prefer.*
Præscrībo, ĕre, psi, ptum, tr. 3. *to write before, to prescribe.*
Præsens, tis, adj. *present, favourable.*
Præsentia, æ, f. 1. *presence.*
Præsertim, adv. *especially.*
Præsĭdeo, ēre, ēdi, — intr. 2. *to preside, to rule.*
Præsidium, ii, n. 2. *a guard, a garrison.*
Præstabĭlis, e, adj. *excellent.*
Præstans, tis, adj. *excellent.*
Præstantia, æ, f. 1. *excellence.*
Præstituo, ĕre, ui, ūtum, tr. 3. *to determine, to fix.*
Præsto, adv. *ready, at hand.*
Præsto, āre, ĭti, ĭtum *or* ātum, tr. 1. *to stand before, to excel, to perform;* præstat, *it is better.*
Præsum, esse, fui, intr. irr. *to be set over, to rule over.*
Præter, prep. *beside, except.*
Prætereo, īre, ii, *seldom* īvi, ĭtum, tr. & intr. irr. *to pass over, to omit;* præteritus, *past.*
Prætermitto, ĕre, īsi, issum, tr. 3. *to omit, to pass over.*
Præterquam, adv. *except.*
Prætor, ōris, m. 3. *prætor, commander, judge.*
Præveho, ĕre, vexi, vectum, tr. 3. *to be carried,* or *to flow by,* or *in front of.*
Prævenio, īre, vēni, ventum, tr. & intr. 4. *to come before (another), to anticipate, get the start of, to be the first to do* or *make.*

Prandeo, ēre, di, sum, tr. 2. *to dine.*
Pratum, i, n. 2. *a meadow.*
Pravĭtas, ātis, f. 3. *crookedness, wickedness.*
Pravus, a, um, adj. *crooked, wicked, mean.*
Preci, em, e, f. 3. *a prayer, an entreaty ;* pl. preces, um, &c.
Precor, āri, ātus, dep. 1. *to pray.*
Prĕmo, ĕre, pressi, pressum, tr. 3. *to press.*
Pretiosus, a, um, adj. *precious.*
Pretium, ii, n. 2. *a price, a reward.*
Pridie, adv. *the day before.*
Primo, adv. *at first, in the first place.*
Primum, adv. *first of all.*
Primus, a, um, adj. *first.*
Princeps, ĭpis, c. 3. *a prince* or *princess.*
Principātus, us, m. 4. *mastery, reign.*
Principium, ii, n. 2. *a beginning.*
Prior, us, adj. *former, preferable.*
Pristĭnus, a, um, adj. *former, ancient.*
Prius, adv. *sooner, before.*
Priusquam, adv. *before.*
Privātim, adv. *privately.*
Privatio, ōnis, f. 3. *privation.*
Privātus, a, um, adj. *private.*
Prīvo, āre, āvi, ātum, tr. 1. *to deprive.*
Prīvus, a, um, adj. *private, peculiar.*
Pro, prep. *for, as, instead of.*
Probatio, ōnis, f. 3. *proof, evidence.*
Probe, adv. *well.*
Probĭtas, ātis, f. 3. *goodness, honesty.*
Probo, āre, āvi, ātum, tr. 1. *to approve, to prove.*
Probrum, i, n. 2. *a disgrace.*
Probus, a, um, adj. *honest, good.*
Procēdo, ĕre, cessi, cessum, tr. 3. *to proceed, to advance.*
Proclīvis, e, adj. *inclined, prone.*
Procrastinatio, ōnis, f. 3. *a delaying, procrastination.*
Procreo, āre, āvi, ātum, tr. 1. *to beget, to produce.*
Procul, adv. *far, far off.*
Procurro, ĕre, ri, sum, intr. *to extend, reach forth.*
Prodeo, īre, ii, ĭtum, intr. irr. *to go forth.*
Prodigium, ii, n. 2. *a prodigy.*
Prodĭgo, ĕre, ēgi, — tr. 3. *to drive forth, to lavish.*
Prodĭgus, a, um, adj. *prodigal, lavish.*
Proditio, ōnis, f. 3. *treachery.*
Prodo, ĕre, ĭdi, ĭtum, tr. 3. *to discover, to hand down, to betray.*
Prodūco, ĕre, xi, ctum, tr. 3. *to bring out, to produce.*
Prœlium, ii, n. 2. *See* prælium.
Profānus, a, um, adj. *profane.*
Profecto, adv. *truly.*
Profestus, a, um, adj. *not holy, common.*
Profĭcio, ĕre, fēci, fectum, tr. 3. *to profit, to do good.*
Proficiscor, ficisci, fectus, dep. 3. *to set out, to proceed.*
Profundo, ĕre, fūdi, fūsum, tr. 3. *to pour forth.*
Progredior, di, gressus, dep. 3. *to advance, go forward.*
Prohĭbeo, ēre, ui, ĭtum, tr. 2. *to keep off, to prohibit.*
Proinde, adv. *in like manner, just.*
Projectus, a, um, pt. *cast forth, abject.*
Projicio, ĕre, jēci, jectum, tr. 3. *to cast* or *throw forth, to squander, to waste.*
Promissum, i, n. 2. *a promise.*
Promitto, ĕre, īsi, issum, tr. 3. *to promise.*
Promoveo, ēre, mōvi, mōtum, tr. 2. *to move forward.*
Promptu, m. 4. (used only in the abl.) *in readiness.*
Promptus, a, um, adj. *ready, prompt.*

Pronus, a, um, adj. *prone, headlong.*
Prope, adv. *near, hard by.*
Propensus, a, um, adj. *inclined, prone.*
Propěro, āre, āvi, ātum, tr. & intr. 1. *to hasten.*
Propinquĭtas, ātis, f. 3. *nearness, kindred.*
Propinquus, a, um, adj. *near, adjoining.*
Propior, us, adj. comp. *nearer.*
Propōno, ěre, ŏsui, ŏsĭtum, tr. 3. *to propose, to offer, to set forth, to display.*
Proposĭtum, i, n. 2. *a purpose.*
Proprius, a, um, adj. *proper, peculiar.*
Propter, prep. *for, because of.*
Propterea, adv. *because;* propterea quod, *because (that).*
Propulso, āre, āvi, ātum, tr. 1. *to drive away.*
Prōra, æ, f. 1. *the prow.*
Prorsus, adv. *straightway, certainly, truly.*
Prosěquor, qui, cūtus *or* quūtus, dep. 3. *to follow after, to pursue.*
Prospe, & Prospěrus, a, um, adj. *prosperous.*
Prospicio, ěre, pexi, pectum, tr. 3. *to look forward to.*
Prosum, esse, fui, intr. irr. *to do good, to avail.*
Protēgo, ěre, xi, ctum, tr. 3. *to protect.*
Prout, adv. *as, according as.*
Providentia, æ, f. 1. *providence.*
Provĭdeo, ēre, vīdi, vīsum, tr. 2. *to foresee, to provide.*
Provincia, æ, f. 1. *a province.*
Proxĭme, adv. *next, very near.*
Proxĭmus, a, um, adj. *nearest, next, last;* sub. *a neighbour.*
Prudens, tis, adj. *wise, prudent.*
Prudenter, adv. *prudently, wisely.*
Prudentia, æ, f. 1. *prudence, wisdom.*
Prussias, æ, m. 1. *Prussias, king of Bithynia.*
Ptolemæus, i, m. 2. *Ptolemy.*
Pubesco, ěre, incep. 3. *to bud, to bloom, to grow to maturity.*
Publĭcè, adv. *publicly, at the public expense.*
Publĭcus, a, um, adj. *public.*
Publius, ii, m. 2. *Publius, a man's name.*
Pudens, tis, adj. *modest.*
Pudet, ēre, uit, & ĭtum est, imp. *it ashames.*
Pudor, ōris, m. 3. *shame, modesty.*
Puer, ěri, m. 2. *a boy.*
Puerīlis, e, adj. *of a boy, puerile, boyish.*
Pueritia, æ, f. 1. *boyhood.*
Pugna, æ, f. 1. *a battle.*
Pugno, āre, āvi, ātum, tr. 1. *to fight, differ.*
Pulcher, chra, chrum, adj. *fair, beautiful.*
Pulchre, adv. *beautifully.*
Pulchritūdo, ĭnis, f. 3. *beauty.*
Pulsus, a, um, pt. *driven.*
Pumilio, ōnis, m. 3. *a dwarf.*
Punctum, i, n. 2. *a point.*
Punĭcus, a, um, adj. *Punic, Carthaginian.*
Punio, īre, īvi, ītum, tr. 4. *to punish.*
Pupula, æ, f. 1. *the pupil of the eye, the eye.*
Purpŭra, æ, f. 1. *purple.*
Purpureus, a, um, adj. *purple.*
Purus, a, um, adj. *pure.*
Puteōli, ōrum, m. 2. *the city Puteoli.*
Puto, āre, āvi, ātum, tr. 1. *to prune, to think.*
Putresco, ěre, — — intr. 3. *to become rotten* or *putrid.*
Pylădes, is, m. 3. *Pylades, a man's name.*
Pyrrhus, i, m. 2. *a man's name.*
Pythagŏras, æ, m. 1. *Pythagoras, a Grecian philosopher.*
Pythagoreus, a, um, adj. *Pythagorean.*

Pythagoreus, i, m. 2. *a Pythagorean.*

Pythius, a, um, adj. *Pythian.*

Q.

Qua, adv. *where.*

Quadragesimus, a, um, adj. *fortieth.*

Quadraginta, adj. ind. *forty.*

Quadrimātus, a, um, adj. *four years old.*

Quadringenti, æ, a, adj. *four hundred.*

Quærĭto, āre, āvi, ātum, tr. 1. *to search diligently, to inquire.*

Quæro, ĕre, sīvi, sītum, tr. 3. *to seek for, to ask.*

Quæsītum, i, n. 2. *a question, a demand, a thing gotten.*

Quæso, def. *I pray.*

Quæstor, ōris, m. 3. *a quæstor.*

Qualis, e, adj. *of what kind, such as.*

Quam, conj. *how, than, as.*

Quamdiu, adv. *how long, as long as;* after tamdiu, *as.*

Quamobrem, adv. *wherefore, why.*

Quamprīmum, adv. *as soon as possible.*

Quamvis, adv. *however.*

Quando, adv. *when.*

Quanquam, conj. *although.*

Quantopĕre, adv. *how greatly.*

Quantum, adv. *as much as, how much.*

Quantus, a, um, adj. *how great, as much as.*

Quare, adv. *wherefore, why.*

Quartus, a, um, adj. *fourth.*

Quasi, conj. *as if, as it were.*

Quater, adv. *four times.*

Quaterni, æ, a, adj. *four each, by fours.*

Quatio, ĕre, (quassi), quassum, tr. 3. *to shake.*

Quatriduum, i, n. 2. *the space of four days.*

Quatuor, adj. indec. *four.*

Que, conj. (always annexed to another word) *and, also.*

Quemadmŏdum, adv. *in what manner, how.*

Queo, īre, quīvi, def. irr. *to be able.*

Querēla, æ, f. 1. *a complaint.*

Queror, ri, questus, dep. 3. *to complain.*

Questus, ûs, m. 4. *a complaint.*

Qui, quæ, quod, rel. pron. *who, which, that.*

Qui, adv. *how? why?*

Quia, conj. *because.*

Quicunque, quæcunque, quodcunque, pron. *whosoever, whatsoever.*

Quidam, quædam, quoddam, *or* quiddam, pron. *a certain one, some one.*

Quidem, conj. *indeed, truly, even.*

Quies, ētis, f. 3. *rest, ease.*

Quiesco, ĕre, ēvi, ētum, n. 3. *to rest, to repose.*

Quiēte, adv. *quietly, peaceably.*

Quiētus, a, um, adj. *quiet.*

Quin, adv. & conj. *why not? but, yet.*

Quinctius, ii. m. 2. *a man's name.*

Quindecim, adj. indec. *fifteen.*

Quingenti, æ, a, adj. *five hundred.*

Quinquagēni, æ, a, adj. *fifty to each.*

Quinquaginta, adj. indec. *fifty.*

Quinque, adj. ind. *five.*

Quintus, i, m. 2. *a man's name.*

Quippe, conj. *because, for.*

Quirītes, ium, m. 3. *Quirites, Romans.*

Quis, quæ, quod, *or* quid, pron. *who, which, what? any.*

Quisnam, quænam, quodnam, *or* quidnam, pr. indef, *who, what.*

Quisquam, quæquam, quodquam, *or* quidquam, pron. *any one.*

Quisque, quæque, quodque, *or* quidque, pron. *every one.*

Quisquis, — quidquid, *or* quicquid, pron. *whosoever, any one.*

Quivis, quævis, quodvis, *or* quidvis, pron. *any one, whosoever.*

Quo, conj. *that, in order that.*
Quo, adv. *whither.*
Quoad, adv. *till, until.*
Quocunque, adv. *whithersoever.*
Quod, conj. *that, because.*
Quomĭnus, adv. *that not, from.*
Quomŏdo, adv. *how.*
Quōnam, adv. *whither? to what place?*
Quondam, adv. *formerly.*
Quoniam, adv. *since, seeing that.*
Quoque, conj. *also, too, even.*
Quot, adj. ind. *how many.*
Quotidie, adv. *daily.*
Quoties, adv. *how often.*
Quotusquisque, aquæque, umquodque, pron. *what one amongst many.*
Quousque, adv. *how long?*
Quum, conj. *when, whilst, since, although.*

R.

Rabies, ēi, f. 5. *madness, fury.*
Rāmus, i, m. 2. *a branch, a bough.*
Rāna, æ, f. 1. *a frog.*
Rapĭdus, a, um, adj. *rapid.*
Rapio, ĕre, ui, tum, tr. 3. *to take (by force), to seize.*
Raptus, a, um, pt. *taken, seized.*
Raro, adv. *rarely, seldom.*
Rarus, a, um, adj. *thin, rare.*
Raster & Rastrum, tri, n. 2. *a mattock, a rake.*
Rătes, is, f. 3. *a raft.*
Ratio, ōnis, f. 3. *reason, an account.*
Ratiuncŭla, æ, f. 1. *a trifling argument* or *reason.*
Ravenna, æ, f. 1. *the name of a city.*
Recēdo, ĕre, cessi, cessum, intr. 3. *to go away, retire.*
Receptacŭlum, i, n. 2. *a receptacle, a refuge.*
Recipio, ĕre, cēpi, ceptum, tr. 3. *to receive, to recover.*
Recordatio, ōnis, f. 3. *a remembrance.*

13*

Recordor, āri, ātus, dep. 1. *to remember.*
Recreo, āre, āvi, ātum, tr. 1. *to recreate, revive, to recover.*
Recte, adv. *rightly, properly.*
Rectum, i, n. 2. *rectitude, honesty.*
Rectus, a, um, adj. *straight, proper.*
Recupĕro, āre, āvi, ātum, tr. 1. *to recover.*
Recurro, ĕre, ri, sum, n. 3. *to run back, to recur.*
Recūso, āre, āvi, ātum, tr. 1. *to refuse.*
Reddo, ĕre, ĭdi, ĭtum, tr. 3. *to give back, to restore.*
Redeo, īre, ii, *seldom* īvi, ĭtum, intr. irr. *to return.*
Redĭgo, ĕre, ĕgi, actum, tr. 3. *to bring back, to reduce.*
Redĭmo, ĕre, ēmi, emptum, tr. 3. *to redeem, to ransom.*
Redintĕgro, āre, āvi, ātum, tr. 1. *to renew.*
Redĭtus, ûs, m. 4. *a return.*
Redundo, āre, āvi, ātum, n. 1. *to overflow, to abound.*
Redūco, ĕre, xi, ctum, tr. 1. *to bring back, to restore.*
Refello, ĕre, felli, —, tr. 3. *to refute.*
Refĕro, ferre, tŭli, lātum, tr. irr. *to bring back, to relate, to return, to requite.*
Refert, imp. *it concerns.*
Refĭcio, ĕre, ēci, ectum, tr. 3. *to repair, to recover.*
Refugio, ĕre, i, ĭtum, intr. 3. *to fly back, to take refuge.*
Regīna, æ, f. 1. *a queen.*
Regio, ōnis, f. 3. *a region.*
Regius, a, um, adj. *kingly, royal.*
Regno, āre, āvi, ātum, tr. 1. *to reign, to rule.*
Regnum, i, n. 2. *a kingdom.*
Rego, ĕre, xi, ctum, tr. 3. *to rule.*
Regredior, di, gressus, dep. 3. *to go back, return.*
Regŭla, æ, f. 1. *a rule.*

Regŭlus, i, m. 2. *a prince, a petty king.*

Regŭlus, i, m. 2. *a Roman general.*

Rejicio, ĕre, jēci, jectum, tr. 3. *to reject.*

Religio, ōnis, f. 3. *religion.*

Religiōsus, a, um, adj. *religious, sacred.*

Relinquo, ĕre, līqui, lictum, tr. 3. *to leave, to forsake.*

Reliquiæ, ārum, f. 1. *remains, leavings.*

Relĭquus, a, um, adj. *the rest.*

Reluctor, āri, ātus, dep. 1. *to struggle against, to oppose.*

Remedium, ii, n. 2. *a remedy, a cure.*

Rēmi, ōrum, m. 2. *the Remi, a tribe of the Gauls.*

Reminiscor, isci, — dep. 3. *to remember.*

Remitto, ĕre, mīsi, missum, tr. 3. *to send back, to relax;* intr. *to abate.*

Remōtus, a, um, adj. *remote, distant.*

Remŏveo, ēre, ōvi, ōtum, tr. 2. *to remove.*

Remunĕro, āre, āvi, ātum, tr. 1. *to reward.*

Rēmus, i, m. 2. *Remus, the brother of Romulus.*

Renuncio, āre, āvi, ātum, tr. 1. *to bring back word, to announce.*

Reor, rēri, ratus, dep. 2. *to think.*

Rependo, ĕre, di, sum, tr. 3. *to repay.*

Repente, adv. *suddenly.*

Repentīnus, a. um, adj. *sudden.*

Repĕrio, īre, ĕri, ertum, tr. 4. *to find, to discover.*

Repertor, ōris, m. 3. *a finder, an inventor.*

Repĕto, ĕre, īvi, ītum, tr. 3. *to ask, to demand;* repetĕre rem, *to demand redress.*

Repōno, ēre, ŏsui, ŏsitum, tr. 3. *to replace.*

Reposco, ĕre, poposci, —, tr. 3. *to ask again, to demand.*

Reprehendo, ĕre, di, sum, tr. 3. *to reprove, to blame.*

Reprehensio, ōnis, f. 3. *censure.*

Repŭdio, āre, āvi, ātum, tr. 1. *to reject, to refuse.*

Repugno, āre, āvi, ātum, tr. 1. *to resist, to oppose.*

Repŭto, āre, āvi, ātum, tr. 1. *to think again, to consider.*

Requiesco, ēre, ēvi, ētum, n. 3. *to rest, to oppose.*

Requīro, ĕre, sīvi, sītum, tr. 3. *to seek for.*

Res, rei, f. 5. *a thing, an estate.*

Rescisco, ĕre, īvi, ītum, tr. 3. *to come to know, to understand.*

Rescribo, ĕre, psi, ptum, tr. 3. *to write back.*

Reservo, āre, āvi, ātum, tr. 1. *to keep, to reserve.*

Resisto, ĕre, stĭti, stĭtum, intr. & tr. 3. *to stand still, to resist.*

Respĭcio, ĕre, exi, ectum, tr. 3. *to look back, to regard.*

Respondeo, ēre, di, sum, tr. 2. *to answer.*

Responsum, i, n. 2. *an answer.*

Respublĭca, reipublĭcæ, f. 5. & 1. *a republic, a commonwealth.*

Restauro, āre, āvi, ātum, tr. 1. *to restore, rebuild.*

Restis, is, f. 3. *a halter, a rope.*

Restituo, ĕre, ui, ūtum, tr. 3. *to restore.*

Resto, āre, stĭti, stātum, intr. 1. *to stay, to remain.*

Reticeo, ēre, ui, — tr. 2. *to conceal.*

Retĭneo, ēre, inui, entum, tr. 2. *to hold back, to detain.*

Retro, adv. *backwards.*

Reus, i, m. 2. *a person accused, a culprit.*

Revēra, adv. *actually, in truth.*

Reverenter, adv. *reverently.*

Reverentia, æ, f. 1. *respect, reverence.*

Revereor, ēri, ĭtus, dep. 2. *to respect, to reverence.*
Revertor, ti, sus, dep. 3. *to return.*
Revŏco, āre, āvi, ātum, tr. 1. *to recall.*
Rex, regis, m. 3. *a king.*
Rhēnus, i, m. 2. *the Rhine.*
Rhētor, ŏris, m. 3. *a rhetorician.*
Rhodus, i, f. 2. *Rhodes, an island off the south-west corner of Asia Minor.*
Rideo, ēre, si, sum, tr. 2. *to laugh.*
Ridicŭlus, a, um, adj. *ridiculous.*
Rigeo, ēre, ui, — intr. 2. *to be stiff, to be benumbed.*
Rĭgo, āre, āvi, ātum, tr. 1. *to water.*
Risus, ûs, m. 4. *a laughing, a laugh.*
Ritus, ûs, m. 4. *a rite, a fashion.*
Rixa, æ, f. 1. *a quarrel.*
Rōbur, ŏris, n. 3. *strength.*
Rogo, āre, āvi, ātum, tr. 1. *to ask.*
Rŏgus, i, m. 2. *a funeral pile.*
Roma, æ, f. 1. *Rome, the capital of Italy.*
Romāni, orum, m. 2. *the Romans.*
Romānus, a, um, adj. *Roman.*
Romŭlus, i, m. 2. *Romulus, the founder of Rome.*
Roscius, ii, m. 2. *a celebrated actor.*
Rubens, tis, pt. *being red;* adj. *red.*
Rubeo, ēre, — intr. 2. *to be red, to blush.*
Rŭdis, e, adj. *rude, unskilled, unacquainted with.*
Rūfus, i, m. 2. *a man's name.*
Ruina, æ, f. 1. *ruin.*
Rumor, ōris, m. 3. *rumor, report.*
Ruo, ĕre, i, ĭtum, tr. & intr. 3. *to throw down, to fall.*
Rursus, adv. *again.*
Rus, ruris, n. 3. *the country.*

S.

Sabīnus, a, um, adj. *belonging to the Sabines (a people of Italy), Sabine;* Sabina, *a Sabine woman.*
Sacer, cra, crum, adj. *sacred.*
Sacerdos, ōtis, c. 3. *a priest,* or *priestess.*
Sacrilĕgus, a, um, adj. *sacriligious.*
Sacrum, i, n. 2. *a sacrifice, a festival.*
Sæpe, adv. *often.*
Săgax, ācis, adj. *sagacious.*
Saguntum, i, n. 2. *a town in Spain.*
Salii, ōrum, m. pl. 2. *the Salii, priests of Mars.*
Saltem, adv. *at least.*
Salto, āre, āvi, ātum, intr. 1. *to dance.*
Salūber and Salūbris, bre, adj. *healthy.*
Salus, ūtis, f. 3. *safety, health.*
Salūto, āre, āvi, ātum, tr. 1. *to salute.*
Salvus, a, um, adj. *safe.*
Samnis, ītis, m. 3. *a Samnite.*
Samothrax, ācis, m. 3. *a Samothracian.*
Sancio, īre, xi, ctum, *or* cīvi, cītum, tr. 4. *to consecrate, to ratify.*
Sanctè (ius, issĭme), adv. *sacredly, religiously.*
Sanctus, a, um, adj. *sacred, holy.*
Sanguis, ĭnis, m. 3. *blood.*
Sanus, a, um, adj. *sound, sane.*
Sapiens, tis, adj. *wise.*
Sapiens, tis, m. 3. *a wise man.*
Sapienter, adv. *wisely.*
Sapientia, æ, f. 1. *wisdom.*
Sapio, ĕre, ui, — intr. 3. *to taste, to be wise.*
Sapor, ōris, m. 3. *taste, a relish.*
Sardinia, æ, f. 1. *Sardinia, an island in the Mediterranean.*
Sat, Satis, } adv. *enough.*
Satăgo, ĕre, ēgi, — intr. 3. *to be busy.*
Satietas, ātis, f. 3. *satiety.*
Satio, āre, āvi, ātum, tr. 1. *to satiate, to satisfy.*
Satisfăcio, ĕre, fēci, factum, tr. 3. *to satisfy.*

Satrius, ii, m. 2. *a man's name.*
Saturnus, i, m. 2. *the god Saturn.*
Saxum, i, n. 2. *a large stone, a rock.*
Scabies, ēi, f. 5. *a scab, a mange.*
Scaldis, is, m. 3. *the river Scheldt.*
Scateo, ēre, ui, — intr. 2. *to abound.*
Scelerātus, a, um, adj. *wicked.*
Scelus, ĕris, n. 3. *wickedness.*
Scena, æ, f. 1. *the stage.*
Schōla, æ, f. 1. *a school.*
Sciens, tis, adj. *knowing, skilful.*
Scientia, æ, f. 1. *knowledge.*
Scilĭcet, adv. *in fact, to wit.*
Scindo, ĕre, scidi, scissum, tr. 3. *to divide.*
Scio, īre, īvi, ītum, tr. 4. *to know.*
Scipio, ōnis, m. 3. *Scipio, a Roman general.*
Scisco, ĕre, scīvi, scītum, tr. 3. *to enact.*
Scribo, ĕre, psi, ptum, tr. 3. *to write.*
Scriptum, i, n. 2. *a writing.*
Scutum, i, n. 2. *a shield.*
Scythia, æ, f. 1. *Scythia.*
Scythĭcus, a, um, adj. *Scythian.*
Secerno, ĕre, crēvi, crētum, tr. 3. *to separate, to distinguish.*
Sĕco, āre, ui, tum, tr. 1. *to cut.*
Secreto, adv. *in secret, privately.*
Sector, āri, ātus, dep. 1. *to follow, to attend.*
Secŭlum, i, n. 2. *an age.*
Secundum, prep. *according to.*
Secundus, a, um, adj. *second, prosperous.*
Secūrè, adv. *securely, in safety.*
Secūris, is, f. 3. *an axe.*
Secūrus, a, um, adj. *secure, careless.*
Secus, adv. *otherwise.*
Sed, conj. *but.*
Sedĕcim, adj. indec. *sixteen.*
Sedeo, sedēre, sēdi, sessum, intr. 2. *to sit.*
Sedes, is, f. 3. *a seat.*
Seditio, ōnis, f. 3. *sedition.*
Sedo, āre, āvi, ātum, tr. 1. *to allay, to mitigate.*
Sedūco, ĕre, xi, ctum, tr. 3. *to lead aside, to seduce.*
Segnis, e, adj. *dull, lazy.*
Segnitia, æ, f. 1. *or* Segnities, ēi, f. 5. *dulness, sloth.*
Segrĕgo, āre, āvi, ātum, tr. 1. *to divide.*
Sejungo, ĕre, xi, ctum, tr. 3. *to separate.*
Seleucus, i, m. 2. *a king of Syria.*
Semel, adv. *once.*
Semen, ĭnis, n. 3. *seed.*
Semĭno, āre, āvi, ātum, tr. 1. *to plant, to sow.*
Semirămis, is, f. 3. *the wife of Ninus.*
Semīta, æ, f. 1. *a footpath.*
Semper, adv. *always.*
Sempiternus, a, um, adj. *everlasting.*
Sempronius, ii, m. 2. *a man's name.*
Senatorius, a, um, adj. *of a senator, senatorian.*
Senātus, ûs, m. 4. *a senate.*
Senātus consultum, i, n. 2. *a decree of the senate.*
Senecta, æ, f. 1. *old age.*
Senectus, ūtis, f. 3. *old age.*
Senex, senis, adj. *old.*
Sēni, æ, a, adj. *six each.*
Senīlis, e, adj. *belonging to old age.*
Senior, ōris, adj. comp. *older.*
Sensus, ûs, m. 4. *sense, judgment.*
Sententia, æ, f. 1. *an opinion, a sentence.*
Sentīna, æ, f. 1. *filthy water, dregs, refuse, rabble.*
Sentio, īre, si, sum, tr. 4. *to think, to feel.*
Sepio, īre, sepsi, septum, tr. 4. *to inclose, protect.*
Sepōno, ĕre, sui, sĭtum, tr. 3. *to set aside.*
Septem, adj. indec. *seven.*
Septēni, æ, a, adj. *seven each.*

Septentrio, ōnis, m. 3. *the north.*
Septĭmus, a, um, adj. *seventh.*
Septuagenarius, a, um, adj. *of seventy.*
Septuaginta, adj. indec. *seventy.*
Sepulchrum, i, n. 2. *a grave, a sepulchre.*
Sequanus, i, m. 2. *one of the Sequani.*
Sequor, qui, cūtus, *or* quūtus, dep. 3. *to follow.*
Serēnus, a, um, adj. *serene, clear.*
Sermo, ōnis, m. 3. *speech, conversation, language.*
Sero, ius, adv. *late, too late.*
Sero, ĕre, sēvi, sătum, tr. 3. *to sow, to plant.*
Serpens, tis, m. 3. *a serpent.*
Serus, a, um, adj. *late.*
Servio, īre, īvi, ītum, tr. 4. *to serve, to obey.*
Servitium, ii, n. 2. *the slaves* (of a household).
Servĭtus, ūtis, f. 3. *slavery, bondage.*
Servius, ii, m. 2. *Servius, a man's name.*
Servo, āre, āvi, ātum, tr. 1. *to preserve, to save, to retain.*
Servus, i, m. 2. *a slave, a servant.*
Seu, conj. *or.*
Severĭtas, ātis, f. 3. *severity, rigour.*
Sevērus, a, um, adj. *severe.*
Sex, adj. indec. *six.*
Sexaginta, adj. indec. *sixty.*
Sexcentesĭmus, a, um, adj. *six hundredth.*
Sexcenti, æ, a, adj. *six hundred.*
Sextus, a, um, adj. *sixth.*
Sextus, i, m. 2. *a man's name.*
Si, conj. *if.*
Sic, adv. *so, thus.*
Sicarius, ii, m. 2. *an assassin.*
Sicilia, æ, f. 1. *Sicily.*
Sicŭlus, i, m. 2. *a Sicilian.*
Sicyon, ōnis, f. 3. *Sicyon, a city of the Morea.*
Sido, ĕre, sīdi, —, intr. 3. *to sink down.*
Sidus, ĕris, n. 3. *a constellation, a star.*
Signifĭco, āre, āvi, ātum, tr. 1. *to signify, to express.*
Signum, i, n. 2. *a sign, a signal, a statue.*
Silentium, ii, n. 2. *silence.*
Silex, ĭcis, m. *or* f. 3. *a flint-stone.*
Silius, ii, m. 2. *a man's name.*
Silvestris, e, adj. *of the wood, wild.*
Simia, æ, f. 1. *an ape.*
Simĭlis, e, adj. *like.*
Similitūdo, ĭnis, f. 3. *likeness.*
Simonĭdes, is, m. 3. *Simonides, a Grecian poet.*
Simplex, ĭcis, adj. *simple.*
Simplicĭtas, ātis, f. 3. *simplicity.*
Simplicĭter, adv. *simply, openly, with frankness.*
Simul, adv. *together, at the same time.*
Simulatio, ōnis, f. 3. *a pretence, a dissembling.*
Simŭlo, āre, āvi, ātum, tr. *to pretend.*
Sine, prep. *without.*
Singulāris, e, adj. *singular, remarkable.*
Singŭlus, a, um, (more commonly used in the plural,) *single, one by one, each.*
Sinister, tra, trum, adj. *left.*
Sino, ĕre, sīvi, sĭtum, tr. 3. *to permit, to allow, to place.*
Sīnus, us, m. 4. *a gulf, a bay.*
Sisygambus, i, m. 2. *a man's name.*
Sitio, īre, īvi, ītum, tr. 4. *to be thirsty, to thirst.*
Sitis, is, f. 3. *thirst.*
Sĭtus, a, um, pt. (*sino*), *situated.*
Sĭtus, us, m. 4. *situation.*
Sive, conj. *or, either, whether;* sive—sive, *whether—or.*
Sobrius, a, um, adj. *sober.*
Sociĕtas, ātis, f. 3. *partnership, a society.*
Socius, ii, m. 2. *a companion, an ally.*

Socordia, æ, f. 1. *want of thought, indolence.*

Socrătes, is, m. 3. *Socrates, a Grecian philosopher.*

Sol, solis, m. 3. *the sun.*

Solatium, ii, n. 2. *comfort, consolation.*

Soleo, ēre, ĭtus, n. p. *to be wont.*

Solicitūdo, ĭnis (and soll.), f. 3. *solicitude.*

Solĭdus, a, um, adj. *solid, firm.*

Solitūdo, ĭnis, f. 3. *solitude.*

Sollennis, e, adj. *solemn.*

Sollertia (solertia), æ, f. 1. *skill, acuteness.*

Sollicĭto, āre, āvi, ātum, tr. 1. *to solicit, to trouble.*

Sollicĭtus, a, um, adj. *solicitous, anxious.*

Solum, i, n. 2. *the ground, the soil.*

Solum, adv. *only, alone.*

Solus, a, um, adj. *alone, only.*

Solvo, ĕre, vi, ūtum, tr. 3. *to loose, to pay.*

Somnium, ii, n. 2. *a dream.*

Somnus, i, m. 2. *sleep.*

Sonĭtus, ûs, m. 4. *a sound.*

Sopio, īre, īvi *or* ii, ītum, tr. 4. *to lull to sleep.*

Soracte, is, n. 3. *Soracte, a mountain in Etruria.*

Sorbeo, ēre, psi, ptum, tr. 2. *to suck.*

Sordes, is, f. 3. *squalor, a mourning garment.*

Soror, ōris, f. 3. *a sister.*

Sors, tis, f. 3. *lot, chance.*

Sortior, īri, ītus, dep. 4. *to cast lots.*

Sparta, æ, f. 1. *Sparta, a city of Greece.*

Spatium, ii, n. 2. *a race-ground, a space of ground,* or *of time.*

Species, ēi, f. 5. *a form, a figure.*

Speciōse, adv. *speciously.*

Speciōsus, a, um, adj. *beautiful.*

Spectacŭlum, i, n. 2. *a spectacle.*

Specto, āre, āvi, ātum, tr. 1. *to behold, to look to, to try, to prove.*

Speculātor, ōris, m. 3. *a beholder, a spy.*

Specŭlum, i, n. 2. *a mirror.*

Sperno, ĕre, sprēvi, sprētum, tr. 3. *to despise.*

Spero, āre, āvi, ātum, tr. 1. *to hope.*

Spes, spei, f. 5. *hope.*

Spicŭlum, i, n. 2. *an arrow, a dart.*

Spirĭtus, ûs, m. 4. *breath, the soul.*

Spīro, āre, āvi, ātum, intr. 1. *to blow.*

Spolio, āre, āvi, ātum, tr. 1. *to rob, to plunder.*

Spolium, ii, n. 2. *spoil.*

Sponsus, i, m. 2. *a (betrothed) lover.*

Spontis, sponte, f. 3. (used only in the gen. and abl.) *of one's own accord.*

Squalĭdus, a, um, adj. *squalid, unsightly.*

Staberius, ii, m. 2. *a man's name.*

Stadium, ii, n. 2. *a race-course, a stadium.*

Statim, adv. *immediately.*

Statīvus, a, um, adj. *stationary, standing.*

Statua, æ, f. 1. *a statue.*

Statuo, ĕre, ui, ūtum, tr. 3. *to set up, to resolve.*

Stătus, ûs, m. 4. *state, condition.*

Stella, æ, f. 1. *a star.*

Sterĭlis, e, adj. *barren.*

Sterno, ĕre, strāvi, stratum, tr. 3. *to strow, to stretch out, extend.*

Stimŭlo, āre, āvi, ātum, tr. 1. *to stimulate, to incite.*

Stipātus, a, um, pt. *surrounded.*

Stirps, is, f. 3. *a young tree, a shoot.*

Sto, stāre, stĕti, stătum, intr. 1. *to stand.*

Stoĭci, ōrum, m. 2. *the Stoics, a sect of Grecian philosophers.*

Stolĭdus, a, um, adj. *foolish.*

Stomăchor, ări, ātus, dep. 1. *to be angry, to be irritated.*
Stomăchus, i, m. 2. *the stomach, passion.*
Strātum, i, n. 2. *a horse cloth.*
Strātus, a, um, part. *extended, stretched.*
Strenuus, a, um, adj. *strenuous, active.*
Stringo, ĕre, nxi, strictum, tr. 3. *to draw* (a sword).
Studeo, ēre, ui, — tr. 2. *to study, to attend to.*
Studiōse, adv. *diligently, carefully.*
Studiōsus, a, um, adj. *fond.*
Studium, ii, n. 2. *study, diligence.*
Stultitia, æ, f. 1. *folly, silliness.*
Stultus, a, um, adj. *foolish.*
Stultus, i, m. 2. *a fool.*
Suadeo, ēre, si, sum, tr. 2. *to advise.*
Suapte, Gr. 121, Obs. 4.
Suāvis, e, adj. *sweet.*
Suavĭtas, ātis, f. 3. *sweetness.*
Sub, prep. *under, at, about.*
Subdūco, ĕre, xi, ctum, tr. 3. *to withdraw.*
Subĭgo, ĕre, ēgi, actum, tr. 3. *to bring under, to conquer.*
Subimpudens, tis, adj. *somewhat impudent.*
Subĭto, adv. *suddenly.*
Subĭtus, a, um, adj. *sudden.*
Subjectus, a, um, pt. *subjected, stooping.*
Subjicio, ĕre, jēci, jectum, tr. 3. *to subject.*
Sublātus, a, um, pt. of tollo, *taken away.*
Sublicius, a, um, *resting on piles, sublician;* Sublicius pons, *the Sublician bridge.*
Sublīme, adv. *on high.*
Submisse, adv. *lowly, humbly.*
Submoveo, ēre, vi, tum, tr. 2. *to remove, to banish.*
Subrīdens, tis, pt. *smiling.*
Subruo, ĕre, ui, ŭtum, tr. 3. *to undermine.*
Subsĕquor, qui, cūtus, dep. 3. *to follow* (close).
Subsidium, ii, n. 2. *help, assistance.*
Subvenio, īre, i, tum, tr. 4. *to assist.*
Succēdo, ĕre, cessi, cessum, tr. 3. *to approach, to succeed.*
Succenseo, ēre, sui, sum, tr. 2. *to be angry with.*
Succumbo, ĕre, cubui, cubĭtum, tr. 3. *to yield, to give way.*
Succurro, ĕre, curri, cursum, tr. 3. *to succour, to help.*
Succus, i, m. 2. *moisture, juice.*
Suēvi, ōrum, m. pl. 2. *the Suevi.*
Suffes, ētis, m. 3. *a chief magistrate of the Carthaginians.*
Suffĭcio, ĕre, ēci, ectum, intr. & tr. 3. *to substitute, to suffice.*
Suffragium, ii, n. 2. *a vote.*
Suffundo, ĕre, fūdi, fūsum, tr. 3. *to pour upon, to spread over.*
Suggĕro, ĕre, essi, estum, tr. 3. *to raise up, to suggest.*
Sui, *gen.* pron. *of himself, of herself, of itself.*
Sulla, æ, m. 1. *a Roman general.*
Sum, esse, fui, irr. *to be.*
Summa, æ, f. 1. *the sum* or *aggregate of any thing.*
Summissus, a, um, pt. *lowered, let down.*
Summus, a, um, adj. *highest, greatest;* summum bonum, *the chief good.*
Sumo, ĕre, psi, ptum, tr. 3. *to take.*
Sumptifăcio, ĕre, fēci, factum, tr. 3. *to spend.*
Sumtus (sumptus), ûs, m. 4. *expense, allowance.*
Superbia, æ, f. 1. *pride.*
Superbus, i, m. 2. *a surname of Tarquin.*
Superbus, a, um, adj. *proud, haughty.*
Superior, us, adj. *higher, superior.*
Supĕro, āre, āvi, ātum, tr. 1. *to surpass, to overcome.*

Superstes, ĭtis, adj. *surviving, remaining.*
Superstitio, ōnis, f. 3. *superstition.*
Superstitiōsus, a, um, adj. *superstitious.*
Supĕrus, a, um, adj. *high, above, preceding.*
Supervacuus, a, um, adj. *superfluous.*
Supervĕnio, īre, vēni, ventum, tr. 4. *to come upon unexpectedly, to surprise.*
Suppedĭto, āre, āvi, ātum, tr. & intr. 1. *to supply, to suffice.*
Suppĕto, ĕre, īvi, ītum, intr. 3. *to suffice, to be sufficient.*
Supplicatio, ōnis, f. 3. *thanksgiving.*
Supplicium, ii, n. 2. *punishment.*
Supra, prep. *above.*
Suprēmus, a, um, adj. *highest, last.*
Surgo, ĕre, rexi, rectum, tr. 3. *to raise up, to rise.*
Surrĭpio, ĕre, ipui, eptum, tr. 3. *to take secretly, to steal.*
Suscĭpio, ĕre, ēpi, eptum, tr. 3. *to undertake.*
Suspectus, a, um, pt. *suspected.*
Suspendo, ĕre, di, sum, tr. 3. *to hang up, to suspend.*
Suspicio, ĕre, spexi, ctum, tr. 3. *to look up to.*
Suspicio, ōnis, f. 3. *suspicion.*
Suspĭcor, āri, ātus, dep. 1. *to suspect.*
Sustĭneo, ēre, tinui, tentum, tr. 2. *to hold up, to sustain.*
Sustollo, ĕre, — —, tr. 3. *to dispatch, to destroy.*
Suus, a, um, pron. *his own, her own, its own, their own.*
Sylla, æ, m. 1. *Sylla, a Roman general.*
Sylva (silva), æ, f. 1. *a wood.*
Syphax, ācis, m. 3. *Syphax, king of Numidia.*
Syracūsæ, ārum, f. 1. *Syracuse, a city of Sicily.*

T.

Tabŭla, æ, f. 1. *a board, a table.*
Taceo, ēre, ui, ĭtum, intr. 2. *to be silent.*
Taciturnĭtas, ātis, f. 3. *silence.*
Taciturnus, a, um, adj. *silent.*
Tacĭtus, a, um, adj. *silent.*
Tædet, ēre, uit, & ĭtum est, imp. *it wearies, it irks.*
Tædium, ii, n. 2. *weariness.*
Tăges, is, m. 3. *Tages, an Etrurian divinity.*
Talentum, i, n. 2. *a talent.*
Talis, e, adj. *such, such like.*
Tam, adv. *so, so much.*
Tamdiu, adv. *so long.*
Tamen, adv. & conj. *nevertheless, yet.*
Tandem, adv. *at length.*
Tango, ĕre, tetĭgi, tactum, tr. 3. *to touch;* tactus, de cœlo, *struck with lightning.*
Tanquam, adv. *as well as, as if.*
Tantălus, i, m. 2. *Tantalus, a king of Phrygia.*
Tanto, adv. *by so much, so much.*
Tantopĕre, adv. *so much.*
Tantŭlus, a, um, adj. *so little, never so little.*
Tantum, adv. *so much, only.*
Tantummŏdo, adv. *only.*
Tantus, a, um, adj. *so great, so many.*
Tardè (ius, issime), adv. *slowly. late;* tardius, *too late.*
Tardĭtas, ātis, f. 3. *slowness.*
Tardo, āre, āvi, ātum, tr. 1. *to delay, hinder.*
Tarentīnus, a, um, adj. *of Tarentum, Tarentine.*
Tarentīnus, i, m. 2. *a Tarentine.*
Tarentum, i, n. 2. *Tarentum, a city in the south of Italy.*
Tarquinius, ii, m. 2. *Tarquinius, the last king of Rome.*
Taurus, i, m. 2. *a bull.*
Tectum, i, n. 2. *a roof, a house.*
Tegumentum, i, n. 2. *a covering.*

Telesinus, i, m. 2. *a man's name.*
Tellus, ūris, f. 3. *the goddess of the earth, the earth.*
Tēlum, i. n. 2. *a dart, a weapon.*
Temĕre, adv. *rashly.*
Temerĭtas, ātis, f. 3. *rashness.*
Temno, ĕre, — — tr. 3. *to despise.*
Temperantia, æ, f. 1. *moderation, temperance.*
Tempĕro, āre, āvi, ātum, tr. 1. *to moderate, to govern.*
Tempestas, ātis, f. 3. *time, a season, a storm.*
Tempestivĭtas, ātis, f. 3. *a season.*
Templum, i, n. 2. *a consecrated place, a temple.*
Tenax, ācis, adj. *holding fast, tenacious.*
Tendo, ĕre, tetendi, sum, & tum, tr. 3. *to stretch out, to go to, to encamp.*
Tenĕbræ, ārum, f. 1. *darkness.*
Teneo, ēre, ui, tum, tr. 2. *to hold.*
Tener, ĕra, ĕrum, adj. *tender.*
Tento, āre, āvi, ātum, tr. 1. *to feel, to try.*
Tentorium, ii, n. 2. *a tent.*
Tenuis, e, adj. *thin, slender.*
Tenuĭtas, ātis, f. 3. *fineness.*
Tenuo, āre, āvi, ātum, tr. 1. *to make thin, to diminish.*
Tepĭdus, a, um, adj. *warm, tepid.*
Terentia, æ, f. 1. *a woman's name.*
Tergum, i, n. 2. *the back;* a tergo, *from behind.*
Termĭno, āre, āvi, ātum, tr. 1. *to limit, to bound.*
Terra, æ, f. 1. *the earth.*
Terreo, ēre, ui, ĭtum, tr. 2. *to terrify, to frighten.*
Terribĭlis, e, adj. *terrible, dreadful.*
Terror, ōris, m. 3. *terror, alarm.*
Testamentum, i, n. 2. *a will, a testament.*
Testis, is, c. 3. *a witness.*
Testor, āri, ātus, dep. 1. *to call to witness.*
Teter, tra, trum, adj. *foul, cruel.*
Tetrĭcus, a, um, adj. *rude, rough, sullen.*
Teucri, ōrum, m. pl. 2. *Trojans.*
Thales, is, m. 3. *one of the seven wise men of Greece.*
Theatrum, i, n. 2. *a theatre.*
Thēbæ, ārum, f. pl. 1. *Thebes.*
Thebanus, i, m. 2. *a Theban.*
Themistŏcles, is, m. 3. *Themistocles, an Athenian statesman.*
Theodōrus, i, m. 2. *Theodorus, a Grecian philosopher.*
Theophrastus, i, m. 2. *a Greek philosopher.*
Thessalonica, æ, f. 1. *a city of Greece.*
Thrasybūlus, i, m. 2. *the liberator of Athens.*
Thucydĭdes, is, m. 3. *a Greek historian.*
Thursīnus, i, m. 2. *a surname of Augustus.*
Tibĕris (Tiber), is, m. 3. *the Tiber.*
Tiberius, ii, m. 2. *Tiberius, a Roman emperor.*
Ticīnum, i, n. 2. *a city of Gaul.*
Tifāta, ōrum, n. pl. 2. *a mountain ridge near Capua.*
Tigrānes, is, m. 3. *Tigranes.*
Tigris, is, m. 3. *a tiger.*
Timeo, ēre, ui, —, tr. 2. *to fear, to dread.*
Timĭde, adv. *timorously.*
Timĭdus, a, um, adj. *fearful, timorous.*
Timoleon, ontis, m. 3. *a man's name.*
Timor, ōris, m. 3. *fear.*
Tītus, i, m. 2. *a man's name.*
Toga, æ, f. 1. *a gown.*
Togŭla, æ, f. 1. dim. *a little gown* or *toga.*
Tolerabĭlis, e, adj. *tolerable.*
Tollo, ĕre, sustŭli, sublātum, tr. 3. *to raise, to lift up, to take away, to destroy.*
Tonitru, n. 4. indec. in the singular, *thunder.*
Totĭdem, adj. indec *as many.*

Totus, a, um, adj. *whole.*
Tracto, āre, āvi, ātum, tr. 1. *to treat.*
Trado, ĕre, ĭdi, ĭtum, tr. 3. *to give, to deliver up.*
Tradūco, ĕre, xi, ctum, tr. 3. *to bring over, to transport.*
Traho, ĕre, xi, ctum, tr. 3. *to draw, to lead.*
Trajānus, i, m. 2. *Trajan, a Roman emperor.*
Trajĭcio, ĕre, ēci, ectum, tr. 3. *to throw over, to transport.*
Tranquille, adv. *quietly, calmly.*
Tranquillĭtas, ātis, f. 3. *stillness, calmness.*
Tranquillus, a, um, adj. *calm, still.*
Trans, prep. *over, beyond, on the other side.*
Transeo, īre, ii, *seldom* īvi, ĭtum, intr. irr. *to go* or *pass over.*
Transfĕro, ferre, tuli, lātum, tr. irr. *to transfer.*
Transfŭga, æ, m. 1. *a deserter.*
Transĭgo, ĕre, ēgi, actum, tr. 3. *to transact, to conclude, to come to terms.*
Transnāto, āre, āvi, ātum, tr. 1. *to swim over.*
Transversus, a, um, adj. *transverse, across.*
Trebonius, ii, m. 2. *a man's name.*
Trecenti, æ, a, adj. *three hundred.*
Trĕmo, ĕre, ui, —, intr. 3. *to tremble, to shake.*
Trepĭdo, āre, āvi, ātum, intr. 1. *to be in a hurry, to tremble.*
Tres, adj. *three.*
Tribūnus, i, m. 2. *a tribune.*
Tribuo, ĕre, ui, ūtum, tr. 3. *to give, to bestow.*
Tricēni, æ, a, adj. *thirty to each.*
Trigemĭni, ōrum, m. pl. 2. *three brothers born at one birth.*
Triginta, adj. ind. *thirty.*
Tristis, e, adj. *sad, gloomy.*
Triumpho, āre, āvi, ātum, intr. 1. *to triumph.*
Triumphus, i, m. 2. *a triumph.*
Troas, ădis, f. 3. *Troas.*
Truncus, i, m. 2. *a trunk* (of a tree).
Trux, trucis, adj. *fierce, cruel.*
Tu, tui, pron. *thou, you.*
Tuba, æ, f. 1. *a trumpet.*
Tueor, uēri, ūtus, & uĭtus, dep. 2. *to see, to defend.*
Tullia, æ, f. 1. *the wife of Tarquin.*
Tullius, ii, m. 2. *one of the Roman kings.*
Tullus, i, m. 2. *a man's name.*
Tum, adv. *then, at that time;* conj. *and, so, also.*
Tumultuor, āri, ātus, dep. 1. *to make a tumult* or *uproar.*
Tumŭlus, i, m. 2. *a hill, a mound.*
Tunc, adv. *then, at that time.*
Tundo, ĕre, tutŭdi, tūsum *or* tunsum, tr. 3. *to beat, to hammer.*
Turba, æ, f. 1. *a crowd.*
Turbulentus, a, um, adj. *disturbed, muddy.*
Turdus, i, m. 2. *a thrush.*
Turpis, e, adj. *base, shameful, unsightly.*
Turpĭter, adv. *basely.*
Turpĭtūdo, ĭnis, f. 3. *baseness, disgrace.*
Turris, is, f. 3. *a tower.*
Tusculānus, a, um, adj. *belonging to Tusculum, a city of Italy.*
Tūtè (ius, issĭme), adv. *safely, safe.*
Tutēla, æ, f. 1. *a defence, protection.*
Tuto, adv. *safely.*
Tūtus, a, um, adj. *safe.*
Tuus, a, um, pron. *thy, thine.*
Tyndărus, i, m. 2. *a king of Sparta.*
Tyrannus, i, m. 2. *a tyrant.*
Tyrrhēnus, i, m. 2. *a man's name.*

U.

Uber, ĕris, adj. *fruitful.*
Ubertas, ātis, f. 3. *abundance.*
Ubi, adv. *where, when.*
Ubicunque, adv. *wheresoever*
Ubĭnam? adv. *where?*
Ubīque, adv. *every where.*

Udus, a, um, adj. *wet, moist.*

Ulciscor, ulcisci, ultus, dep. 3. *to punish, to avenge.*

Ullus, a, um, adj. *any.*

Ulterior, us, adj. comp. *further, more distant.*

Ultĭmus, a, um, adj. sup. *furthest, last.*

Ultio, ōnis, f. 3. *revenge.*

Ultra, prep. *beyond;* adv. *farther.*

Ulysses, is, m. 3. *Ulysses, a king of Ithaca.*

Umbra, æ, f. 1. *a shadow, a shade.*

Una, adv. *together.*

Unda, æ, f. 1. *a wave.*

Unde, adv. *whence.*

Undecĭmus, a, um, adj. *the eleventh.*

Undĭque, adv. *on every side.*

Unguis, is, m. 3. *a nail, a claw.*

Unguo, ĕre, xi, ctum, tr. 3. *to anoint.*

Unĭcus, a, um, adj. *one alone, only.*

Universus, a, um, adj. *whole, universal.*

Unquam, adv. *ever.*

Unus, a, um, adj. *one.*

Unusquisque, unaquæque, unumquodque *or* unumquidque, pron. *every one.*

Urbānus, a, um, adj. *belonging to a city, polite, civil.*

Urbs, urbis, f. 3. *a city.*

Uro, ĕre, ussi, ustum, tr. 3. *to burn.*

Usque, adv. *as far as, even.*

Usūra, æ, f. 1. *use, usury.*

Usus, ûs, m. 4. *use.*

Ut, conj. *that;* adv. *as, when.*

Uter, tra, trum, adj. *whether,* or *which of the two.*

Utercunque, tracunque, trumcunque, — pr. *whichever of the two.*

Uterque, traque, trumque, pr. *both, each.*

Utervis, travis, trumvis, pr. *either.*

Utĭlis, e, adj. *useful, fit.*

Utilĭtas, ātis, f. 3. *usefulness.*

Utĭnam, conj. *I wish that.*

Utor, uti, usus, dep. 3. *to use, to enjoy.*

Utpŏte, adv. *as, seeing that.*

Utrum, adv. *whether?*

Uxor, ōris, f. 3. *a wife.*

V.

Vaco, āre, āvi, ātum, intr. & tr. 1. *to be free from, to be at leisure.*

Vacuus, a, um, adj. *void, empty.*

Valde, adv. *very much, greatly.*

Valeo, ēre, ui, ĭtum, intr. 2. *to be in health, to be strong, to avail.*

Valerius, ii, m. 2. *a man's name.*

Valetūdo, ĭnis, f. 3. *health.*

Vallum, i, n. 2. *a rampart.*

Vanus, a, um, adj. *vain, empty*

Varius, a, um, adj. *various.*

Varro, ōnis, m. 3. *a man's name.*

Vas, vasis, n. 3. *a vessel;* pl. vasa, ōrum, n. 2.

Vasto, āre, āvi, ātum, *to ravage, lay waste.*

Vastus, a, um, adj. *vast, large, waste.*

Vates, is, c. 3. *a prophet, a poet.*

Vatinius, ii, m. 2. *a man's name.*

Ve, *or,* an enclitic particle always subjoined to another word.

Vectīgal, ālis, n. 3. *a tribute, a tax, revenue.*

Vedius, ii, m. 2. *a man's name.*

Vehementer, adv. *vehemently, eagerly.*

Vehicŭlum, i, n. 2. *a carriage.*

Veho, ĕre, vexi, vectum, tr. 3. *to carry.*

Veiens, entis, m. 3. *a Vejentian, one of the Vejentes.*

Vel, conj. *or, either.*

Vellus, ĕris, n. 3. *a fleece.*

Velo, āre, āvi, ātum, tr. 1. *to cover, to veil.*

Velocĭtas, ātis, f. 3. *velocity, swiftness.*

Velox, ōcis, adj. *swift, nimble.*

Vĕlut, velŭti, conj. *as, as if, like as.*

Venditatio, ōnis, f. 3. *a boasting, a vaunting.*
Vendĭtor, ōris, m. 3. *a seller.*
Vendo, ĕre, ĭdi, ĭtum, tr. 3. *to sell.*
Venēnum, i, n. 2. *poison.*
Veneo, īre, ii, — intr. 4. *to be sold.*
Venĕror, āri, ātus, dep. 1. *to adore, to worship.*
Venĕti, ōrum, m. pl. 2. *the Veneti.*
Venia, æ, f. 1. *leave, pardon.*
Venio, īre, vēni, ventum, tr. 4. *to come.*
Venor, āri, ātus, dep. 1. *to hunt.*
Venter, tris, m. 3. *the belly.*
Ventĭto, āre, āvī, ātum, intr. 1. *to come often.*
Ventŭlus, i, m. 2. dim. *a little wind, a small breeze.*
Venundo, ăre, dĕdi, dătum, tr. 1. *to sell.*
Vēnus, ĕris, f. 3. *Venus.*
Verbĕro, āre, āvi, ātum, tr. 1. *to beat, to scourge.*
Verbum, i, n. 2. *a word, diction.*
Vere, adv. *truly, verily.*
Verecundia, æ, f. 1. *modesty, bashfulness.*
Verecundus, a, um, adj. *modest, bashful.*
Vereor, ēri, ĭtus, dep. 2. *to respect, to fear.*
Vergo, ĕre, — intr. 3. *to incline, tend to.*
Verĭtas, ātis, f. 3. *truth.*
Vero, adv. *truly, indeed;* conj. *but.*
Verres, is, m. 3. *Verres, a man's name.*
Versor, āri, ātus, dep. 1. *to be employed, to stay with one.*
Versus, adv. *toward.*
Versus, ûs, m. 4. *a line, a verse.*
Verto, ĕre, ti, sum, tr. 3. *to turn.*
Verum, i, n. 2. *the truth.*
Verum, conj. *but, but yet.*
Veruntamen, adv. *yet, nevertheless.*
Verus, a, um, adj. *true.*
Vescor, vesci, — dep. 3. *to eat, to feed upon.*
Vespasiānus, i, m. 2. *Vespasian, a Roman emperor.*
Vesper, & us, i, m. 2. *the evening,* and
Vesper, ĕris, m. 3. *the evening, the evening star, the west.*
Vester, tra, trum, pron. *your,* or *yours.*
Vestibŭlum, i, n. 2. *a vestibule, porch.*
Vestigium, ii, n. 2. *mark, trace, vestige.*
Vestio, īre, īvi, ītum, tr. 4. *to clothe.*
Vestis, is, f. 3. *a garment.*
Vestītus, ûs, m. 4. *clothing, dress.*
Veto, āre, ui, ĭtum, tr. 3. *to forbid.*
Vetus, ĕris, adj. *old, ancient.*
Vetustas, ātis, f. 3. *antiquity, age.*
Vexillum, i, n. 2. *a standard.*
Vexo, āre, āvi, ātum, tr. 1. *to harass.*
Via, æ, f. 1. *a way.*
Viatĭcum, i, n. 2. *provisions for a journey.*
Viātor, ōris, m. 3. *a traveller.*
Vibius, ii, m. 2. *a man's name.*
Vibullus, i, m. 2. *a man's name.*
Vicēni, æ, a, adj. *twenty to each.*
Vicīnus, a, um, adj. *neighbouring, contiguous.*
Vicīnus, i, m. 2. *a neighbour.*
Vicis, is, f. 3. *change, lot, misfortune.*
Victĭma, æ, f. 1. *a victim.*
Victor, ōris, m. 3. *a conqueror.*
Victoria, æ, f. 1. *a victory.*
Victus, ûs, m. 4. *food, sustenance.*
Vĭdeo, ēre, vīdi, vīsum, tr. 2. *to see;* pass. *to seem.*
Vigilia, æ, f. 1. *a watch* (of the night), *a sentry, wakefulness, studies.*
Vigĭlo, āre, āvi, ātum, tr. 1. *to watch, to be vigilant.*
Viginti, adj. indec. *twenty.*
Vīlis, e, adj. *mean.*
Villa, æ, f. 1. *a villa.*
Villĭcus, i, m. 2. *a steward.*
Vincio, īre, xi, ctum, tr. 4. *to bind.*
Vinco, ĕre, vīci, victum, tr. 3. *to conquer.*

Vincŭlum, i, n. 2. *a bond, a chain.*
Vindex, ĭcis, m. 3. *an avenger.*
Vindicta, æ, f. 1. *revenge, vengeance.*
Vinum, i, n. 2. *wine.*
Violentia, æ, f. 1. *violence.*
Viŏlo, āre, āvi, ātum, tr. 1. *to hurt, to violate.*
Vir, viri, m. 2. *a man, a husband.*
Virgilius, ii, m. 2. *Virgil, a Latin poet.*
Virgo, ĭnis, f. 3. *a virgin.*
Virĭtim, adv. *man by man, to each man.*
Virtus, ūtis, f. 3. *virtue.*
Vis, vis, f. 3. *force, strength, power, quantity;* pl. vires, ium, &c.
Viscus, ĕris, n. 3. *the viscera, bowels, entrails, vitals.*
Viso, ĕre, visi, — tr. 3. *to go to see, to visit.*
Vita, æ, f. 1. *life.*
Vītis, is, f. 3. *a vine.*
Vitium, ii, n. 2, *a fault, vice.*
Vito, āre, āvi, ātum, tr. 1. *to shun, to avoid.*
Vitupĕro, āre, āvi, ātum, *to blame, to disparage.*
Vivax, ācis, adj. *long lived, lively.*
Vivo, ĕre, vixi, victum, intr. 3. *to live.*
Vīvus, a, um, adj. *alive.*
Vix, adv. *scarcely.*
Vocifĕro, āre, āvi, ātum, intr. *to cry out.*
Voco, āre, āvi, ātum, tr. 1. *to call.*
Volo, āre, āvi, ātum, intr. 1. *to fly.*
Volo, velle, volui, irr. *to be willing, to wish.*
Volscæ, ārum, f. pl. 1. *Volscæ, a city of the Volsci.*
Volsci, ōrum, m. pl. 2. *the Volsci, a people of Italy.*
Volumnia, æ, f. 1. *a woman's name.*
Voluntarius, a, um, adj. *voluntary, willing.*
Voluntas, ātis, f. 3. *will, inclination, desire.*
Voluptas, ātis, f. 3. *pleasure.*
Volvo, ĕre, vi, ūtum, tr. 3. *to roll, to turn round, bring about.*
Vōtum, i, n. 2. *a vow, promise.*
Voveo, ēre, vi, tum, tr. 2. *to vow.*
Vox, vocis, f. 3. *a voice, a word.*
Vulgāris, e, adj. *vulgar, common.*
Vulgus, i, n. sometimes m. 2. *the common people, the mob.*
Vulnus, ĕris, n. 3. *a wound.*
Vultus, ūs, m. 4. *the countenance.*

X.

Xenophon, ontis, m. 3. *Xenophon, a Greek historian.*
Xerxes, is, m. 3. *Xerxes, a king of Persia.*

Z.

Zāma, æ, f. 1. *the name of a town.*
Zēno, ōnis, m. 3. *Zeno, a Stoic philosopher.*
Zephyrus, i, m. 2. *a zephyr.*

VOCABULARY.

ENGLISH—LATIN.

NOTE.—This Vocabulary contains only the English words in the Exercises in which the Latin words are not given; and the Latin words corresponding to them, are those only to be used in these Exercises. These Latin words are given with their declension, conjugation, meaning, &c., in the preceding Latin-English Vocabulary, and for convenient reference, declinable words are put here in the nominative case, and verbs in the first person singular present indicative—the form to be looked for in every dictionary. When more words than one, with different shades of meaning, are given opposite an English word, the student will, of course, exercise his judgment, as to which of them is the proper word to be used in each particular case. This often calls for nice discrimination and close thinking; and it is the scope afforded, in these exercises, for such mental effort, that renders them peculiarly important.

N. B.—In this Vocabulary, proper names which are the same in Latin as in English are omitted, as they can be found at once in the preceding Vocabulary.

A.

Able (to be able), v. *possum*, *queo*.
Abolish, v. *tollo*, *subruo*.
Abound, v. *abundo*.
About, prep. (to) *ad*, (concerning) *de*.
Absent (to be), v. *absum*.
Absent, adj. *absens*.
Absolutely, adv. *absolutè*, *planè*.
Absurdly, adv. *absurde*.
Academy, n. *Academia*.
Acceptableness, n. *gratia*.
Accompany, v. *comitor*.
Accomplish, v. *conficio*, *efficio*, *gero*.
Accomplished, (highest,) adj. *summus*.
According to, prep. *secundum*.
Accordingly, adv. *itaque*, *ideo*.
Account (on account of), prep. *ab*, *ob*, *propter*; adv. *causâ*; on no account, *nullo modo*.
Accursed, adj. *infelix*.
Accusation, n. *accusatio*.
Accuse, v. *accuso*, *incuso*, *insimulo*, *arguo*.
Accustom, v. *assuefacio*; to be accustomed, *soleo*.
Accustomed, adj. *assuetus*.
Achieve, v. *perficio*.
Acid, adj. *acidus*.
Acknowledge, v. *agnosco*.
Acquainted (to become acquainted with, i. e. to learn), v. *cognosco*.
Acquire, v. *pario*, *adipiscor*, *augeo*, *acquiro*, *paro*.
Acquit, v. *absolvo*.
Across, adj. *transversus*.
Act, v. *ago*, *facio*.
Action, n. *factum*, *res gesta*.
Active, adj. *strenuus*.
Actually, adv. *reverâ*.
Adapt, v. *accommodo*.
Adapted, adj. *idoneus*.
Add, v. *addo*, *adjungo*.
Address, v. *appello*.
Adjoining, adj. *propinquus*.
Admiration, n. *admiratio*.
Admire, v. *miror*, *admiror*;—(praise), *laudo*.
Admit, v. *admitto*, *concedo*.
Admonish, v. *moneo*, *admoneo*.
Adorn, v. *orno*.
Advance, v. *progredior*.
Advantage (means), n. *instrumentum*;—(benefit), *commodum*.
Advantageous, adj. *utilis*;—(fruitful), *uber*.
Adversity, n. *res aspera*.
Advice, n. *consilium*.

Advise, v. *moneo.*
Ædile, n. *ædilis.*
Æsop, n. *Æsopus.*
Affability, n. *affabilitas.*
Affair, n. *res;* private affairs, *res familiaris.*
Affectation, n. *affectatio.*
Affected (seized), pt. *captus.*
Affection, n. *amor, benevolentia, fides,*
After, adv. *post, posteaquam;* after that, *postquam.*
Afterwards, adv. *postea.*
Again, adv. *iterum, rursus.*
Against, prep. *adversum, contra.*
Age, n. (time of life) *œtas;* (period) *seculum;* old age, *senectus.*
Agree, v. *consentio;* it was agreed, *convenit.*
Agriculture, n. *agricultura.*
Aid, v. *subvenio.*
Aid, n. *auxilium.*
Alienate, v. *abalieno.*
All, adj. *omnis, totus, universus.*
Allow, v. (grant) *do,* (acknowledge) *fateor;* to be allowed, *licet,* impers.
Ally, n. *socius.*
Alone, adj. *solus, unus.*
Also, adv. *item;* conjunc. *etiam, quoque.*
Always, adv. *semper.*
Am, v. *sum.*
Amazed (to be), v. *obstupesco.*
Ambassador, n. *legatus.*
Amidst, prep. *inter.*
Among, prep. *inter, in, apud, intra.*
Amusement, n. *ludus.*
Ancestors, n. *majores.*
And, conj. *et, ac, atque, que,* enclitic.
Ancient, adj. *antiquus, pristinus.*
Anger, n. *ira, iracundia;* to be angry with, v. *irascor.*
Animal, n. *animal;* small animal or beast, *bestiola.*
Animate, v. *excito.*
Annals, n. *annales,* pl.
Another, adj. *alius, alter,* (Gr. 276.)
Another's, of another, adj. *alienus.*
Answer, v. *respondeo.*
Answer, n. *responsum.*
Antiquity, n. *antiquitas.*
Antony, n. *Antonius.*
Any, adj. *ullus;* any one, *quis, aliquis;* any thing, *aliquid, quiddam, quidvis.*
Appear, v. *appareo,* (go forth) *prodeo,* (seem) *videor.*
Appearance, n. *aspectus.*
Appease, v. *placo.*
Apply, v. *incumbo.*
Approach, n. *adventus.*
Approbation, n. *approbatio.*
April, n. *Aprilis.*
Are, v. *sum.*
Arise, v. *exorior, nascor,* (set out) *proficiscor.*
Aristotle, n. *Aristoteles.*
Arm, v. *armo.*
Armed, pt. & adj. *armatus.*
Armenians, n. *Armenii.*
Armour, arms, n. *arma,* pl.
Army, *exercitus;* (in line) *acies;* (on the march) *agmen.*
Arrive, v. *venio, pervenio.*
Art, n. *ars.*
Artist, n. *opifex.*
As, conj. *ut;* adv. *ut, uti, prout, quemadmŏdum,* (since) *quoniam;* as if, as it were, *velut, quasi, ceu, tanquam;* as—as, *tam—quam;* so—as, *sic—ut;* as—so, *ut—sic;* so much—as, *tantus—quantus;* as soon as, *simul ac;* as many as, *totidem;* prep. *pro;* as to, *ad.*
Ascertain, v. *intelligo.*
Ashamed (to be), v. *pudēre.*
Ask, v. *rogo, peto, posco, quæro, interrogo.*
Assault, n. *impetus.*
Assemble, v. *convenio.*
Assembly, n. *concio, conventus.*
Assign, v. *do.*
Assist, v. *juvo, adjuvo, accommodo.*
Assistance, n. *opĕra, auxilium.*
Assistant, n. *adjutor, adjutrix.*
Assume, v. *suscipio.*
Astonishing, adj. *mirus.*
At, prep. *ad, apud,*—denoting place, the sign of the ablative.
At length, adv. *demum.*
Athenians, adj. & n. *Atheniensis.*
Athens, n. *Athenæ,* pl.
Attach, v. *devincio.*
Attachment, n. *amor,* (desire), *studium.*
Attack, v. *aggredior.*
Attain, v. *pervenio, consequor,* (have) *habeo.*
Attempt, v. *conor.*
Attend, v. *incumbo.*
Attention, n. *cogitatio.*
Attract, v. *duco.*
Audience, n. *corona.*
Augur, n. *augur.*
Authority, n. *auctoritas.*
Avail, v. *valeo, prosum.*
Avarice, n. *avaritia.*
Avaricious, adj. *avārus.*
Avenger, n. *vindex.*
Avert, v. (redeem) *redimo.*
Avoid, v. *vito, fugio.*
Awe, v. (to stand in awe) *horreo.*

B.

Back, n. *tergum;* on his back, *in tergo;* behind, *a tergo.*
Bad, adj. *malus, improbus.*
Baian, adj. *Baiānus.*
Band, n. *manus, agmen.*
Banished, pt. *expulsus.*
Barbarian, n. *barbarus.*
Bark, n. *cortex.*
Battle, n. *pugna, prœlium, bellum.*
Be, v. *sum, fore;* (to exist) *extare;* (to remain) *restare;* to be wanting, deficient, *deesse;* to be present, at hand, *adesse;* between, *interesse;* absent, distant, *abesse;* to be without, free from, *carēre, vacare;* provoked, *exardescĕre;* angry with, in a passion, *irasci;* at stake, in danger, *agi;* allowable, *licēre;* accustomed, *solēre.*
Bear, v. *fero,* (suffer) *patior.*
Beast, n. *bellua.*
Beat, v. *verbero.*
Beautiful, adj. *speciosus.*
Beauty, n. *pulchritudo.*
Because, adv. *quod, quia;* because that, *propterea-quod.*

Become, v. (to be seemly), *decēre;* it becomes, *decet.*
Become, v. (to be), *fio, evado.*
Becoming, adj. *decōrus.*
Bed, n. *lectum.*
Bee, n. *apis.*
Before, adv. *coram, antea, antequam, priusquam.*
Before, prep. *pro, prœ, ante.*
Beg, v. *peto.*
Begin, v. *incipio, cœpi.*
Behead, v. *percutio securi.*
Behind, adv. *a tergo.*
Behold, v. *cernère, vidēre.*
Behoves, v. *oportet.*
Believe (think), *arbitror;* (give credit) *credo.*
Belly, n. *abdōmen.*
Belong, v. *pertineo*—also *sum* with the gen. (Gr. 364.)
Beloved, adj. *carus.*
Beneficence, n. *beneficentia.*
Benevolence, n. *benevolentia.*
Bereave, v. *orbo.*
Berry, n. *bacca.*
Beseech, v. *obsecro.*
Best, adj. *optimus.*
Betake, v. *confero;* to betake one's self, *conferre se.*
Betray, v. *prodo.*
Betrothed lover, n. *sponsus.*
Better, adj. *melior;* adv. *melius.*
Beyond, prep. *prœter, supra.*
Bind, v. *vincio.*
Birth, adj. *nātalis;* birthday, *natālis dies.*
Blacken, v. to grow black, *nigresco.*
Blame, v. *carpo, reprehendo, vitupĕro.*
Blessings, n. *bona,* pl.
Blood, n. *sanguis.*
Blot out, v. *deleo.*
Blunder, v. *erro;* n. *peccatum.*
Blush, v. *rubeo.*
Body, n. *corpus.*
Bond, n. *vinculum.*
Book, n. *liber.*
Born, pt. *natus;* to be born, *nascor.*
Both, adj. *ambo;* on both sides, *utrinque;* both—and, conj. *et—et; tum—quum.*
Bowels, n. *viscera,* pl. (*viscus*).
Boy, n. *puer.*
Brave, adj. *ortis.*
Bravery, n. *virtus.*
Bravely, adv. *fortiter.*
Bread, n. *panis.*
Break, v. *frango, comminuo;* break down, *diruo.*
Break of day, *prima lux.*
Bridge, n. *pons.*
Bridle, n. *frenum.*
Bring, v. *fero, affero, reddo, adduco;* bring up, *instituo;* fetch, *peto;* bring in, *adhibeo;* bring forth, *pario;* to carry, *veho;* to bring out, *exhaurio;* bring back, *refĕro.*
Britain, n. *Britannia.*
Brother, n. *frater;* three brothers born at one birth, *trigemini.*
Brute, n. *bellua, bestia.*
Build, v. *condo, œdifico.*
Building, n. *tectum, œdificium.*
Burn, v. *ardeo.*
Business, n. *negotium.*
But, conj. *sed, verum, autem, nisi;* but also, *sed etiam, verum etiam.*
Buy, v. *emo, mercor.*
By, prep. *a, ab, per;* (of swearing) *per.*

C.

Calends, n. *Kalendœ,* pl.
Call, (name), v. *appello, voco;* (summon) *voco, cito.*
Call to mind, v. *commemoro.*
Call to witness, v. *testor.*
Called (invoked), pt. *inclamatus;* (sent for) *accitus.*
Callous, v. to grow callous, *calleo.*
Calmly, adv. *placidè.*
Camp, n. *castra,* pl.
Can, v. (be able), *possum.*
Capitally, of a capital crime, *capitis.*
Care, n. *cura.*
Care, v. *curo;* (see to, to cause) *acio.*
Carefully, adv. *diligenter.*
Carry, v. *fero, porto, gesto,* (lead) *duco;* carry back, *reduco;* carry off (consume), *consumo;* carry on war, *bello, bellum gero.*
Carthage, n. *Carthago.*
Carthaginian, adj. & n. *Pœnus.*
Catiline, n. *Catilina.*
Cattle, n. *jumentum,* pl. *a.*
Cause, n. *causa.*
Cause, v. (take care), *curo,* (bring on) *incutio.*
Cavalry, n. *equitātus.*
Cease, v. *desino.*
Centurion, n. *centurio.*
Certain, adj. *certus,* (some) *quidam.*
Certainly, adv. *certè;* for certain, *certo.*
Chain, n. *vinculum, ferrum.*
Chance, n. *casus;* adv. by chance, *forte.*
Change, v. *muto, verto.*
Chapel, n. *cella.*
Character, n. *fama, mores,* pl.
Charge, v. (accuse), *arguo.*
Cheek, n. *mala.*
Cheerful, adj. *hilaris.*
Chest, n. *arca.*
Chief, n. *princeps;* chief good, *summum bonum.*
Children, *liberi,* pl. *pueri,* pl.
Choose, v. *eligo;* choose rather, *malo.*
Chosen, pt. *lectus, delectus.*
Cimbrian, adj. *Cimbricus.*
Circuit, n. *ambitus.*
Circumstance, n. *res.*
Citadel, n. *arx.*
Citizen, n. *civis.*
City, n. *urbs, civitas.*
Clear, adj. *clarus.*
Clemency, n. *clementia.*
Cloak, n. *amiculum.*
Close (the eyes), v. *conniveo.*
Clothe, v. *vestio.*
Coarse, adj. *emporeticus.*
Coffer, n. *arca.*
Cohort, n. *cohors.*
Cold, adj. *algidus,* v. to be pinched with cold, *algeo.*
Cold, n. *frigus.*
Colleague, n. *collega.*
Collect, v. *colligo.*

Colonist, n. *colonus.*
Combat, n. *certamen.*
Come, v. *venio, pervenio;* come to, *adeo, advenio;* come up to, overtake, *consequi.*
Comely, adj. *decens.*
Command, v. *impero, imperito, præcipio.*
Command, n. *jussus.*
Commander, n. *imperator, præfectus.*
Commander's, adj. *imperatorius.*
Commence (battle), v. *committo.*
Commend, v. *laudo, probo.*
Commendable, adj. *laudabilis.*
Commit, a fault, *delinquo.*
Common, adj. *communis, vulgaris,* (cheap) *vilis.*
Common people, n. *vulgus, plebs.*
Common soldier, n. *gregarius miles.*
Commonly, adv. *vulgo.*
Commonwealth, n. *respublica.*
Companion, n. *comes, socius.*
Company, n. *societas.*
Compare, v. *comparo, confero.*
Compassion, n. *misericordia.*
Compel, v. *cogo.*
Complain, v. *queror.*
Complete, adj. *cumulatus.*
Comply, v. *obtempero.*
Compose (verses), v. *facio.*
Composed, adj. *tranquillus.*
Conceal, v. *celo.*
Conceive, v. *concipio.*
Concerned (to be), v. *metuo.*
Concerning, prep. *de.*
Concord, n. *concordia.*
Condition, n. *conditio.*
Conduct, v. *tracto;* to conduct one's self, *gerĕre se.*
Conduct, n. *mores,* pl.
Confer, v. *mando.*
Confess, v. *confiteor.*
Confidence, n. *audacia.*
Congenial, adj. *cognatus.*
Congratulate, v. *gratulor.*
Conquer, v. *vinco, devinco, subigo, supero.*
Conquered, pt. *victus.*
Conscience, n. *conscientia.*
Consciousness, n. *conscientia.*
Conscript, adj. *conscriptus.*
Consent, n. *consensus.*
Consequence—of what consequence? *quanti?* v. to be of consequence, to interest, *interesse.*
Consider (view), v. *video,* (to regard) *habeo.*
Consist, v. *consto, consisto, sum.*
Conspiracy, n. *conjuratio.*
Conspire, v. *conjuro.*
Construct, v. *conficio.*
Consul, n. *consul.*
Consulship, n. *consulātus.*
Consult, v. *delibĕro.*
Contain, v. (hold), *capio.*
Contemplate, v. (have in view), *ago;* that it is contemplated, *agi.*
Contemptible, adj. *absurdus.*
Contend, v. *certo, contendo.*
Content, adj. *contentus.*
Contention, n. *æmulatio.*
Continual, adj. *perpetuus.*
Contract, v. (take up), *suscipio.*
Controversy, n. *controversia.*
Conversation, n. *sermo.*
Copy, n. *exemplum.*
Corinth, n. *Corinthus.*
Corn, n. *frumentum.*
Corrected, pt. *correctus.*
Corrupt, v. *corrumpo.*
Council, n. *concilium.*
Counsel, n. *consilium.*
Countenance, n. *vultus.*
Country, n. *rus;* native country, *patria.*
Countryman (fellow citizen), n. *civis.*
Courage, n. *virtus, fortitūdo.*
Course, n. *cursus.*
Court, v. (seek), *peto.*
Courteously, adv. *comiter.*
Courtesy, n. *comitas.*
Cover, v. *obduco.*
Covering, n. *tegumentum.*
Covetous, adj. *avārus.*
Credit, n. *fides.*
Crete, n. *Creta.*
Crime, n. *crimen, scelus, flagitium, probrum, facinus, maleficium.*
Crowded, adj. *frequens.*
Crown, n. *corona.*
Crucify, v. *cruci affigo.*
Cruel, adj. *immanis, crudelis.*
Cruelty, n. *crudelitas.*
Crystal, adj. *crystallinus.*
Culprit, n. *reus.*
Cultivate, v. *colo.*
Culture, n. *cultus, cultio.*
Cupidity, n. *cupiditas.*
Curia, n. (senate house), *curia.*
Custom, n. *mos.*
Cut, v. (cut down), *cædo;* cut off (destroy), *tollo.*

D.

Daily, adj. *diurnus.*
Daily, adv. *quotidie.*
Danger, n. *periculum, discrimen.*
Dangerous, adj. *periculosus, gravis.*
Dare, v. *audeo.*
Daring, adj. (bold), *audax.*
Dart, n. *telum.*
Dated, pt. *datus.*
Daughter, n. *filia;* little daughter, *filiola.*
Day, n. *dies;* day after, adv. *postridie;* day before, *pridie.*
Dear, adj. (beloved), *carus, dulcis.*
Death, n. *mors.*
Deceive, v. *decipio.*
Decision, n. *judicium.*
Declare, v. *declaro, dico.*
Decorous, adj. *decorus.*
Deed, n. (thing), *res.*
Deem, v. *puto.*
Defeat, v. *vinco.*
Defence, n. (armour), *arma,* pl.
Defend, v. *tueor, defendo.*
Deficient (to be), v. *desum.*
Deity, n. *deus.*
Delay, v. *moror.*
Deliberately, with deliberation, adv. *consideratè.*
Delirious (to be), v. *deliro.*
Deliver, v. *libĕro.*
Deliverer, n. *liberator.*
Demand, v. *posco;* to demand restitution, *res repetĕre.*
Deny, v. *nego.*
Depart, v. *demigro.*
Deplore, v. *deploro.*
Descended, pt. (born), *natus.*
Desert, v. *relinquo, desero.*
Desert, n. *solitudo.*

Deserter, n. *transfuga.*
Deserve, v. *mereor.*
Deservedly, adv. *merito.*
Deserving, adj. *dignus;* not deserving, *indignus.*
Design, v. (intend) *destino.*
Design, n. *consilium.*
Desire, to be desirous, v. *cupio, quæro, appeto, volo.*
Desire, n. *cupīdo;* earnest desire, *studium.*
Desirous, adj. *cupidus, appetens, studiosus.*
Desist, v. *cesso.*
Despair, v. *despēro.*
Despair, n. *desperatio.*
Despise, v. *sperno, contemno.*
Destroy, v. *dissolvo, diruo, deleo, tollo.*
Destruction, n. *exitium.*
Detain, v. *teneo, detineo.*
Detained, pt. *retentus.*
Deter, v. *deterreo.*
Determine, v. *statuo, constituo, instituo;* (judge) *judico.*
Devise, v. *reperio.*
Diadem, n. *diadema.*
Diction, n. *verbum.*
Die, v. *morior, emorior, pereo.*
Differ, v. *pugno.*
Different, adj. *diversus.*
Difficult, adj. *difficilis, arduus.*
Difficulty, n. *difficultas;* with great difficulty, *difficillime, ægerrimè.*
Dignified, adj. *gravis, amplus.*
Dignity, n. *dignitas.*
Diligence, n. *diligentia.*
Diligently, adv. *diligenter.*
Diminish, v. *minuo.*
Disaster, n. *incommodum.*
Discern, v. *video, cerno.*
Discernment, n. *intelligentia.*
Discharge, v. (perform), *fungor.*
Disciple, n. *discipulus.*
Discipline, n. *disciplina.*
Disclose, v. *propono.*
Discourse, n. *disputatio, oratio, sermo.*
Disease, n. *morbus.*
Disgrace, n. *dedecus, turpitudo.*
Disgraceful, adj. *turpis.*
Disgraceful, (to be), v. *dedecēre.*
Disguise, v. *dissimulo.*
Disgust, n. *fastidium.*
Dishonourable, adj. *turpis.*
Dismiss, v. *dimitto.*
Disorder, n. *perturbatio.*
Displease, v. *displiceo.*
Disposed, adj. *promptus, paratus.*
Disposition, n. *animus, natura.*
Disputation, n. *contentio.*
Dispute, v. *disputo.*
Disregard, v. *contemno.*
Dissimilar, adj. *dissimilis;* to be dissimilar, v. *abhorreo.*
Dissuade, v. *dissuadeo.*
Distance (from), adv. *procul;* to be distant, v. *abesse.*
Distinguished, adj. *clarus.*
Distress, n. *miseria;* utmost distress, *omnis miseria.*
Disturb, v. *disturbo.*
Divide, v. *divido, segrego;* (distribute) *dispertio.*
Divine, adj. *divinus.*
Do, v. (act, make), *facio, ago, gero;* (an act of duty) *fungor;* do good, *proficio;* do harm, *officio;* do wrong, *pecco;* do before, *anteago.*
Dog, n. *canis.*
Dolt, n. *nequam.*
Dolphin, n. *delphinus.*
Dominion, n. *principatus.*
Done before, pt. *anteactus.*
Doubt, v. *dubito.*
Doubtful, adj. *dubius.*
Dowry, n. *dos.*
Drachm, n. *drachma.*
Drag, v. (draw), *traho, duco.*
Draw, v. (lead) *duco.*
Dread, v. *pertimesco.*
Drink, v. *bibo.*
Dripping, pt. *manans.*
Drive, v. *amoveo;* (away) *abigo;* (out) *expello;* driven ashore, pt. *in littus compulsus.*
Dry, adj. *aridus.*
During, prep. *inter, per.*
Duty, n. *munus, officium.*

E.

Each, adj. pr. *quisque, unusquisque.*
Ear, n. *auris.*
Early, adv. *maturè;* too early, *maturius.*
Earnestly, adv. *studiosè;* more earnestly, *majore studio.*
Earth, n. *terra.*
Ease, n. (leisure) *otium.*
Easily, adv. *facile;* more easily, *facilius;* very easily, *facillime.*
Easy, adj. *facilis;* (leisurely) *otiosus.*
Eclipse, n. *defectus.*
Edifice, n. *ædificium.*
Educate, v. *erudio.*
Education, n. *doctrina.*
Eighteen, adj. *octodecim, duodeviginti.*
Either, adj. pr. *utervis.*
Either, conj. *aut, vel;* either—or, *vel—vel, aut—aut.*
Elder, older, adj. *major natu, senior.*
Elect, v. *eligo.*
Elect, pt. *designatus.*
Elephant, n. *elephas, elephantus.*
Elicit, v. *elicio.*
Eloquence, n. *eloquentia.*
Else (other), adj. *alius;* nothing else, *necquicquam aliud.*
Emanate, v. (get abroad) *emano.*
Embrace, v. *complector.*
Emperor, n. *imperator.*
Empire, n. *imperium.*
Employ (use), *utor;* to be employed, *ago, versor, occupor.*
Enact, v. *sciscor.*
Enclose, v. *claudo.*
Encounter, n. *prœlium.*
Endeavour, v. *conor.*
Endued, pt. *præditus.*
Endure, v. *sustineo, patior.*
Enemy, n. (in war) *hostis;* (one not friendly) *inimicus.*
Engage, v. *confligo, congredior;* to engage in, *facio.*
Engaging, pt. (in a conflict) *procurrens.*
Engraven, pt. *insculptus.*
Enjoy, v. *utor, fruor, habeo;* not enjoy, *careo.*
Enter, v. *introire.*
Entertain, v. *indulgeo.*
Entire, adj. (perfect) *perfectus.*

Entirely, adj. (as a whole) *totus.*
Entreat, v. *peto.*
Enumerate, v. *enumĕro.*
Envy, v. *invideo.*
Envy, n. *invidia.*
Ephesian, adj. *Ephesius.*
Equal, adj. *par.*
Equally, adv. *æquè;* equally as, *æque ac.*
Equal, v. *æquo.*
Equestrian, adj. *equestris.*
Equity, n. *æquitas.*
Erect, v. *extruo.*
Escape, v. (pass away) *defluo;* (get away) *evado, effugio.*
Especially, adv. *maxime.*
Establish, v. *firmo.*
Esteem, v. (value) *facio, puto, æstimo;* I value much, *facio magni;* more, *pluris;* most, *maximi;* I value so much, *tanti;* little, *parvi habeo.*
Etrurians, n. *Hetrusci.*
Eulogy, n. *laudatio.*
Eunuch, n. *eunuchus.*
Even, adv. *quidem, etiam, vero;* even if, *licet.*
Evening, n. *vesper.*
Event, n. *exitus, res.*
Ever, adv. *unquam.*
Every, adj. *omnis;* every one (each), *quisque, unusquisque;* (any one) *quivis;* every day, *quotidie;* every where, *ubique.*
Evident, adj. *perspicuus.*
Evil (thing), n. *malum.*
Exact (demand), v. *exigo.*
Exalt, v. *erigo.*
Exceed (surpass), v. *supĕro.*
Exceedingly, adv. *plurimum.*
Excel (surpass), v. *supĕro, excello, antecello.*
Excellence, n. *virtus.*
Excellency, n. *bonum.*
Excellent, adj. *egregius, præstans, optimus, summus.*
Except, prep. *præter, præterquam.*
Exception, n. *exceptio.*
Excessive, adj. *nimius.*
Excite, v. *commoveo.*
Exclaim, v. *exclāmo.*
Execrate, v. *exsecror.*
Exercise, v. *utor.*
Exhibit, v. *ostento;* (games) *edo.*
Exhort, v. *hortor, cohortor.*
Exile, *exul, exsul;* to be in exile, *exsulo;* to go into exile, *solum vertere;* (banishment) *exilium.*
Exist, v. *sum, fio, existo;* exist in, *insum.*
Expect, v. *expecto.*
Expectation, n. *expectatio.*
Expedition, n. *expeditio.*
Expense, n. *sumtus, sumptus.*
Experience (make trial), v. *experior.*
Experience, n. *usus.*
Explain, v. *explano;* (open up) *aperio.*
Express, v. *dico, significo.*
Expression, n. *sermo.*
Extend, v. *procurro;* (go forth) *exeo.*
Extol, v. *tollo.*
Extortion, n. *res repetundæ,* pl.
Extraordinary, adj. *egregius, eximius.*
Extreme, adj. (very end) *extremus;* at the extremity of life, *in extremo tempore.*
Eye, n. *oculus.*
Eyelid, n. *palpebra.*

F.

Fable, n. *fabula.*
Fact, n. *res;* in fact, *re.*
Fall, n. *casus.*
Fall, v. (in battle) *cado, corruo, occumbo;* (by lot) *obvenio;* (hasten) *curro.*
Falsely, adv. *falso.*
Fail, v. *deficio, labor.*
Faithful, adj. *fidus.*
Fame, n. *fama.*
Family, n. *genus, familia.*
Famine, n. *fames.*
Far, adv. *longe, longe gentium;* far off, *procul.*
Farm, n. *fundus.*
Farther, adj. *ulterior.*
Fasces, n. *fasces,* pl.
Fat, adj. *pinguis.*
Fate, n. *casus;* unhappy fate, *talis casus;* fates, *fata,* pl.
Father, n. *pater;* father's, of a father, adj. *patrius, paternus.*
Father of a family, n. *pater-familias.*
Fault, n. *vitium.*
Favour, n. *beneficium, meritum, gratia.*
Favour, v. *faveo.*
Fear, v. *metuo, timeo, vereor.*
Fear, n. *metus, pavor.*
Fee, n. *merces.*
Feebleness, n. *infirmitas.*
Feed, v. to be the food of, *pasco;* also to give food to.
Fellow, n. (a term of disrespect) *homo;* that fellow, *iste.* (Gr. 118, 3, 3d.)
Festival, n. *sacrum.*
Few, adj. *pauci,* pl.
Fidelity, n. *fides.*
Field, n. *ager.*
Fifty, adj. *quinquaginta.*
Fight, v. *pugno, contendo.*
Fill up, v. *compleo.*
Finally, adv. *denique.*
Find, v. *invenio, reperio;* (understand) *intelligo.*
Fine, v. *mulcto.*
Finish, v. *finio.*
Fire, n. *ignis.*
Fire, v. (inflame) *inflammo;* set on fire, *incendo.*
Firm, adj. *tenax.*
Firmness, n. *constantia.*
First, adj. *primus,* adv. *primum;* at first, *primo.*
Fish, n. *piscis.*
Fish-pond, n. *piscina.*
Fit, adj. *utilis, idoneus, aptus;* not fit, *inutilis.*
Fit, v. *apto, accommodo.*
Five, adj. *quinque.*
Five hundred, adj. *quingenti.*
Flatter, v. *adulor.*
Fleet, n. *classis.*
Flight, n. *fuga.*
Flow, v. *fluo;* flow through, *interfluo.*
Fly, v. *confugio;* fly to, *advolo.*
Folly, n. *stultitia.*
Follow, v. (go after) *sequor;* (follow closely) *subsequor;* (obey) *pareo.*
Fond, adj. *studiosus.*
Food, n. *alimentum.*
Fool, n. *stultus.*
Foolish, adj. *stultus, stolidus.*
Foot, n. *pes.*

For, prep. (instead of) *pro;* (on account of) *propter;* (from, as a cause) *a, ab;* (concerning) *de;* (towards) *erga.*
For, conj. *enim, nam.*
For that purpose, adv. *ideo, idcirco;* for the sake of, *causâ.*
Forbid, v. *prohibeo.*
Force, n. *vis, vires,* pl.
Forces, n. (troops) *copiæ,* pl.
Forego, v. *omitto.*
Foreign, adj. *externus.*
Forget, v. *obliviscor.*
Forgetful, adj. *oblītus.*
Forgetfulness, n. *oblivio.*
Form, v. (to fashion, make) *facio;* (connect, keep together) *connecto;* (join) *conjungo;* (a line of battle) *instruo.*
Former, pr. *ille,* opposed to *hic,* latter.
Formerly, adv. *quondam.*
Formian, adj. *Formiānus.*
Forsake, v. *desĕro.*
Fort, n. *castellum.*
Fortify, v. *munio, communio.*
Fortitude, n. *fortitudo.*
Fortune, n. *fortuna;* good fortune, *felicitas.*
Forum, n. *forum.*
Found (to lay a foundation), v. *constituo.*
Foundation, n. *fundamentum.*
Four, adj. *quatuor.*
Four hundred, adj. *quadringenti.*
Fragment, n. *fragmentum.*
Free, adj. *liber, expers, vacuus, alienus;* to be free from, v. *vacare;* to be without, *carēre;* to set free, *liberare.*
Frequent, v. *frequento.*
Friend, n. *amicus.*
Friendship, n. *amicitia, necessitudo.*
Frighten, v. *terreo.*
Frightened, pt. *territus, deterritus.*
Frog, n. *rana.*
From, prep. *a, ab, abs, de, e, ex;* after verbs of taking away, it is the sign of the dative or ablative, and often has no corresponding Latin word.
From every side, adv. *undique.*
Frugality, n. *frugalitas, parsimonia.*
Fruit, n. *fructus.*
Fugitive, n. *fugitivus.*
Full, adj. *plenus.*
Furious, adj. *iratus.*
Furnish, v. *orno;* to be well furnished or supplied, to abound, *abundo.*
Fury, n. *furor.*
Future, adj. *futurus;* for the future, *in futurum;* future generation, *posteritas.*

G.

Gain, v. *obtineo, consequor, comparo.*
Game, n. *ludus, lusus.*
Garden, n. *hortus, hortulus.*
Gate, n. *porta.*
Gather, v. (fruit) *decerpo;* (perceive) *percipio.*
Gaul, n. *Gallia.*
Gaul, a, n. *Gallus.*
General, n. *imperator, dux.*
Generous, adj. *liberalis.*
Genius, n. *ingenium.*
Gentleness, n. *mansuetudo.*
Get, v. *paro, contraho.*
Giant, n. *gigas.*
Gift, n. *donum.*
Give, v. *do, impono, trado, affero, præbeo;* (declare) *pronuncio;* give way, yield, *cedo.*
Given (of wounds), *illatus.*
Gladness, n. *lætitia,* v. to be glad, *gaudere;* to be very glad, *vehementer gaudēre.*
Glorious, adj. *gloriōsus.*
Glory, n. *gloria, laus.*
Gnat, n. *culex.*
Go, v. *eo, prodeo;* go to, *peto, adeo, contendo;* (set out) *proficiscor;* go down, *descendo;* go over, *transeo;* away, *recedo;* out, *egredior;* go reluctantly, *concedo;* go on, i. e. do, *ago;* what is going on, *quid agitur.*
God, n. *deus, numen;* of God, *divinus.*
Gold, n. *aurum.*
Golden, of gold, adj. *aureus.*
Good, adj. *bonus, rectus;* (useful) *utilis.*
Goods, n. *bona,* pl.
Good nature, n. *facilitas.*
Gore, n. *cruor.*
Govern, v. *guberno.*
Government, n. *imperium, regnum, respublica.*
Gown, n. *toga;* a little gown, *togula.*
Grace, n. (ornament), *ornamentum.*
Grand, adj. *grandis.*
Grand-daughter, n. *neptis.*
Grand-father, n. *avus.*
Grant, v. *do.*
Gratification, n. *delectatio.*
Gravity, n. *gravitas.*
Great, adj. *magnus, ingens;* (exalted) *superus;* greatest, *supremus, summus;* so great, *tantus.*
Greatly, adv. *vehementer.*
Greece, n. *Græcia.*
Greedy, adj. *avidus.*
Greek, adj. and n. *Græcus.*
Grief, n. *dolor, luctus.*
Grievously, adv. *graviter.*
Grieved (to be,) v. *miseresco.*
Ground, n. *ager.*
Guard, n. *custos.*
Guest, n. *hospes.*
Guide, n. *dux.*
Guilt, n. *culpa.*

H.

Habit, n. *consuetudo.*
Half, n. *dimidium;* by half, *dimidio.*
Hand, n. *manus.*
Hang, v. *suspendo.*
Hang over, v. *impendeo.*
Hanging, adj. *pensilis*
Hap, n. (lot), *vicis.*
Happen, v. *evenio, contingo;* it happens, *fit, accidit.*
Happily, adv. *feliciter, beate.*
Happy, adj. *beatus.*
Harangue, v. *cohortor.*
Harass, v. *sollicito.*
Harbour, n. *portus.*
Hard, adj. *durus;* (difficult), *difficilis.*
Harmony, n. *concordia.*

Hasten, v. *propero.*
Hate, v. *odi.*
Hatred, n. *odium.*
Have, v. *habeo;* (keep) *servo.*
He, pr. *hic, is, ille, iste;* (the same) *idem.*
Head, n. *caput.*
Health, n. *valetudo.*
Hear, hear of, v. *audio.*
Hearer (one hearing), pt. *audiens.*
Heart, n. *cor.*
Heat (to be greatly heated), *æstuo.*
Heat, n. *calor.*
Heaven, n. *cœlum.*
Helen, n. *Helena.*
Hellespont, n. *Hellespontus.*
Helmet, n. *galea.*
Hemisphere, n. *orbis.*
Her, pr. *ejus, suus.*
Herald, n. *præco.*
Here, adv. *hic.*
Herself, pr. *ipsa (ipse).*
Hesitate, v. *dubito, hæreo.*
Hide, v. *condo.*
High, adj. *altus;* the higher, *quo altior.* (Gr. 579.)
Highly, adv. *alte;* (very) *valde;* after verbs of valuing, *magni.*
Hill, n. *collis, tumulus.*
Himself, *ipse;* of himself, *sui.*
Hinder, v. *retardo.*
His (her, its), pr. *ejus* (Gr. 121, Obs. 3), *suus;* his own, *suus.*
Historian, n. *historicus.*
History, n. *historia, res gestæ.*
Hither, adv. *huc,* adj. *citerior.*
Hold, v. *teneo.*
Home, n. *domus.*
Honesty, n. *honestas, probitas;* (an honourable thing) *honestum.*
Honour, n. *honor, honestas.*
Honour, v. *honoro.*
Honourable, adj. *honestus.*
Hope, n. *spes.*
Hope, v. *spero;* (wish for) *opto.*
Horse, n. *equus.*
Horseman, n. *eques.*
Hostage, n. *obses.*
Hostile, adj. *hostilis.*
How, adv. *quomodo, qui, quonam modo;* somehow, *nescio quomodo;* how long, *quamdiu, quousque;* how much, *quam, quantopere;* adj. how much, *quantus;* how many, *quot.*
However, adv. *quamvis, tamen, veruntamen.*
Huge, adj. *ingens.*
Human, adj. *humanus.*
Humanity, n. *humanitas.*
Hundred, adj. *centum.*
Hunger, v. to be hungry, *esurio.*
Hunt, v. *venor.*
Hurt, v. *noceo, obsum, lædo.*
Husband, n. *conjux.*
Husbandman, n. *agricola.*

I.

I, pr. *ego;* I myself, *egomet.*
Ides, n. *Idus.*
Idle, adj. *otiosus.*
Idleness, n. *inertia.*
If, conj. *si;* if not, *nisi, ni.*
Ignorant, *ignarus;* to be ignorant, *ignoro.*
Ill, adv. *malè.*
Illness, n. *morbus.*
Illustrious, adj. *præclarus.*
Imitate, v. *imitor, æmulor.*
Immediately, adv. *statim, extemplo, illico.*
Immoderately, adv. *immoderatè.*
Immortal, adj. *immortalis.*
Impart, v. *impertio.*
Impel, v. *impello.*
Impend, v. *impendeo.*
Impious, adj. *impius.*
Implant, v. *ingenero, sino.*
Implement, n. *instrumentum.*
Implore, v. *imploro, postulo, peto.*
Important, adj. so important, *tantus.*
Improper, adj. *alienus.*
Impunity, n. *impunitas.*
In, prep. *in;* sign of ablative; in the mean time, *interea.*
Inactivity, n. (quiet), *quies.*
Inclination, n. *voluntas.*
Inclined, adj. *propensus.*
Including, pt. *complexus.*
Inconstant, adj. *incertus.*
Increase, v. *augeo.*
Incredible, adj. *incredibilis.*
Incumbent (to be), v. *oportere.*
Indeed, adv. *equidem, sane, vero.*
Individual (any one), pr. *quisquam.*
Indolent, adj. *iners.*
Induce, v. *adduco.*
Industry, n. *industria.*
Infant, n. *infans.*
Infer, v. *colligo.*
Inflamed, pt. *accensus;* to be inflamed, v. *exardeo.*
Inflict punishment, v. *animadverto.*
Inform, v. *facio certiorem.*
Inheritance, n. *hæreditas.*
Inimical, adj. *inimicus.*
Injure, v. (hurt), *noceo.*
Injury, n. *injuria.*
Injustice, n. *injustitia, injuria.*
Innate, adj. *innatus.*
Innocence, n. *innocentia.*
Innocent, adj. *innocens, innocuus.*
Inquire, v. *quæro.*
Insatiable, adj. *insatiabilis.*
Insert, v. (put in), *infĕro.*
Insignificant, adj. *nullus.*
Insist upon, v. *contendo.*
Insolence, n. *arrogantia.*
Inspect, v. *exploro.*
Instead of, prep. *pro.*
Instruct, v. *instituo.*
Instructor, n. *magister.*
Integrity, n. *integritas.*
Intellectual faculty, n. *mens.*
Intent, adj. *intentus.*
Intercepted, pt. *interceptus.*
Interest, n. *utilitas.*
Interrupt, v. *interpello.*
Interview, n. *conventus.*
Intimacy, on the greatest intimacy, adv. *conjunctissimè.*
Into, prep. *in.*
Intrust, v. *committo.*
Inventress, n. *inventrix.*
Investigate, v. *investigo, quæro.*
Ireland, n. *Hibernia.*
Is, v. *est* (*sum*).
It, pr. *is;* from it, after a verb of taking away, *ei,* dative (Gr. 502).
Italy, n. *Italia.*
Itself, pr. *ipse.*

J.

Javelin, n. *pilum.*
Jest. n. *jocus.*
Join, v. *jungo, conjungo, consocio.*
Jovian, n. *Jovianus.*
Joy, n. *gaudium, lætitia.*
Judge, n. *judex,* v. *judico.*
Judgment, n. (judicial proceedings), *judicium.*
Juice, n. *succus.*
Julian, n. *Julianus.*
July, n. *Julius.*
Just, adj. *justus.*
Just as if, adv. *sicut si, velut si.*
Justice, n. *justitia.*

K.

Keep, v. *teneo;* (abstain) *abstineo;* keep from, hinder, *prohibeo.*
Kill, v. *occido, interficio.*
Kind, n. *genus.*
Kind, adj. *benignus.*
Kind action, n. *benefactum.*
Kindly, adv. *benigne;* very kindly, *perhumaniter;* most kindly, *benignissimè.*
Kindness, n. *gratia.*
King, n. *rex;* king's, of a king, adj. *regius.*
Kingdom, n. *regnum.*
Knife, n *cultrum.*
Knight, n. *eques.*
Know, v. *scio, nosco, cognosco, intelligo;* know not, *nescio.*
Knowing, pt. *sciens;* not knowing, *ignorans.*
Knowledge, n. *scientia;* skill, *ars.*
Known, pt. *cognitus.*

L.

Labor, n. *labor.*
Labor, v. (to be in difficulty), *laboro.*
Lacedæmonian, adj. *Lacedæmonius.*
Lament, v. *fleo.*
Lamprey, n. *muræna.*
Land, n. *ager.*
Language, n. (speech), *oratio.*
Large, adj. *ingens, grandis, amplus.*
Last, adj. *novissimus, ultimus, postremus;* at last, adv. *tandem.*
Lately, adv. *nuper.*
Latin, adj. *Latinus.*
Latter, pr. *hic,* opposed to *ille,* former.
Law, n. *lex.*
Lawful (it is), v. *licet.*
Lay down, v. *depono.*
Lead, v. *duco.*
Lead forth, v. *educo.*
Leader, n. *dux.*
Leading man (chief), n. *princeps.*
Lean, or lie down, v. *decumbo.*
Leanness, n. *macies.*
Learn, v. *disco.*
Learning, n. *doctrina.*
Least (of the smallest value), adj *minimi, nauci;* (in the least degree), adv. *minime.*
Leave, v. *relinquo;* to be left, remain, *resto.*
Lebanon, n. *Libanus.*
Legion, n. *legio.*
Leisure (to be at), v. *vaco.*
Length, n. *longitudo.*
Less, adj. *minor;* the less, *eo minor;* adv. *minus, brevius.*
Lessen, v. *levo.*
Lest, conj. *ne.*
Letter (epistle), n. *literæ,* pl. *epistola.*
Liar, n. *mendax.*
Libel, v. (attack, abuse) *lædo.*
Liberality, n. *liberalitas.*
Liberty, n. *libertas.*
Licentious joy, n. *lascivia.*
Lictor, n. *lictor.*
Lie, n. *mendacium.*
Lie (to tell a lie), v. *mentior.*
Life, n. *vita;* time of life, *ætas.*
Light, n. *lux.*
Light, adj. *levis.*
Lightning, n. *fulgura.*
Like, adj. *similis.*
Limitation, n. *exceptio.*
Line (of battle), n. *acies.*
Literary, adj. learned, *literatus.*
Little, adj. *parvus, paululus;* of little value, *parvi, minoris, minimi;* n. a little, *aliquantum.*
Little, adv. *parum;* a little before, *sub;* a little ago, *paulo.*
Live, v. *vivo.*
Lodge, v. *ineo contubernium.*
Lofty, adj. *altus.*
Long, adj. *longus;* long duration, *diutinus.*
Long, adv. *diu;* long since, *jampridem;* long after, *multo post.*
Look into (inspect), v. *intueor.*
Look, v. (seek for), *peto.*
Look forward, v. *prospicio.*
Look, n. *vultus.*
Lose, v. *amitto, dimitto, deperdo.*
Loss, n. *incommodum.*
Lost, pt. *amissus.*
Love, n. *amor;* (desire for) *studium, desiderium, cupiditas.*
Love, v. *amo, diligo;* to fall in love with, *amare.*
Lovely, adj. *amabilis.*
Loving, fond of, adj. *amans.*
Low, adj. *inferus, inferior, infimus,* or *imus.*
Lowered, pt. *summissus.*

M.

Macedonian, n. *Macedo.*
Mad, adj. *insanus.*
Magistracy, n. *magistratus.*
Magistrate, n. *magistratus.*
Magnificent, adj. *insignis.*
Magnitude, n. *magnitudo.*
Maiden, n. *virgo.*
Majesty, n. *majestas.*
Make, v. *facio, efficio;* to be made, *fio;* make war, *infero bellum.*
Man, n. *vir, homo;* man by man, *viritim.*
Manifest, v. *ostendo.*
Mankind, n. *homo.*
Manner, n. *modus;* in like manner, *itidem.*
Manners, n. *mores,* pl. (*mos*).
Many, adj. *multus, plurimus, complures;* very many, *permultus;* so many, *tot;* as many, *totidem.*
Market-place, n. *forum.*

Marry, v. spoken of a woman, *nubo;* of a man, *duco uxorem.*
Marsian, adj. *Marsus.*
Master, n. *dominus, magister.*
Master, v. (govern), *rego.*
Match, n. *par;* not a match, *impar.*
Material, n. *materia,* and *materies.*
May (be able), *possum.*
Me, pr. See *ego.*
Mean, adj. (depraved), *pravus;* in the mean time, *interea.*
Mean, v. (wish), *volo.*
Means, n. *instrumentum, ratio.*
Meditating, n. *præmeditatio.*
Meditation, n. *commentatio.*
Memorial, n. *libellus.*
Memory, n. *memoria.*
Mental powers (mind), n. *ingenium.*
Mention, n. *mentio.*
Mercuries (statues of Mercury), n. *Hermæ,* pl.
Merely, adv. *modo.*
Merit, n. *virtus, meritum.*
Messenger, n. *nuncius.*
Middle, adj. *medius.*
Mild, adj. *mitis.*
Mildness, n. *placabilitas.*
Mile, n. *mille passuum.*
Milesian, n. *Milesius.*
Military, adj. *militaris.*
Mind, n. *mens, animus;* to my mind (to me), *mihi.*
Mindful, adj. *memor.*
Mine, v. (to dig out metals), *effodio metalla.*
Miracle, n. *miraculum.*
Miserable, adj. *miser.*
Misfortune, n. *calamitas, casus.*
Missing, pt. *desiderans.*
Mistake, v. *fallo;* to be mistaken (deceived), *fallor.*
Mode (way), n. *ratio.*
Moderately, adv. *moderatè.*
Moderation, n. *moderatio.*
Modest, adj. *pudens.*
Modestly, adv. *modestè.*
Moisture, n. *succus.*
Money, n. *pecunia, nummus, pretium;* a large sum of money, *grandis pecunia.*
Moon, n. *luna.*
Morals, n. *mores,* pl. (*mos*).
More, adj. *plus, plures.*
More, adv. *magis, plus;* the more, *quo plura, eo ampliora.*
Moreover, adv. *porro.*
Morrow, to-morrow, adv. *cras.*
Mortal, adj. *mortalis.*
Most, adv. *maxime.*
Mother, n. *mater.*
Motion, n. *motus.*
Mount, mountain, n. *mons.*
Move, v. *moveo, permoveo.*
Much, adj. *multus;* so much, *tantus;* as much as, *tantus quantus.*
Much, adv. *multum;* by much, *multo;* so much, *tantopere;* very much, *plurimum, valde.*
Muffle, v. *obvolvo.*
Multitude, n. *multitudo.*
Munificent, adj. *munificus.*
My, pr. *meus.*

N.

Nail, n. *unguis.*
Name, n. *nomen;* by name, *nominatim.*
Named, pt. *appellātus.*
Namesake, adj. (of the same name), *cognominis.*
Narrative, n. *narratio, oratio.*
Nation, n. *natio, gens.*
Native country, n. *germana patria.*
Nature, n. *natura;* of nature, kind, *genus.*
Natural, adj. (of nature), *naturālis.*
Naval, adj. *navalis.*
Near, prep. *apud, juxta.*
Near, adv. *prope;* as near as possible, *quam proxime potuit;* near (in attendance), *præsto.*
Necessary, adj. *necesse, necessarius;* to be necessary, v. *oportēre.*
Neglect, v. *negligo.*
Neglected, pt. *neglectus.*
Negligent, adj. *negligens.*
Negotiator, n. *orator.*
Neither, adj. *neuter.*
Neither, conj. *nec, neque;* neither—nor, *nec—nec.*
Never, adv. *nunquam, ne unquam, haud unquam.*
News, n. *res novæ;* what news? *ecquid novi?*
Night, n. *nox;* night and day, *dies noctesque;* by night, *noctu.*
Nine-day, adj. *novendialis.*
Nitrous, adj. *nitrosus.*
No, adj. *nullus.*
No one, nobody, no man, *nemo, nullus;* that no one, *nequis;* no (by nothing), *nihilo;* by no means, *minime, non omnino, nequaquam.*
Noble, adj. *nobilis.*
Nocturnal studies, n. *vigiliæ.*
Nominate, v. *nomino.*
Nor, conj. *nec, neque, neve, non.*
Not, adv. *non, ne, haud* (interrogatively), *nonne;* not yet, not as yet, *nondum;* not indeed, *ne quidem;* not only, *non modo, non solum.*
Nothing, n. *nihil, nil.*
Now, adv. *jam, nunc.*
Number, n. *numerus.*

O.

O, interj. *O.*
O that, interj. *utinam.*
Obey, v. *servio, obtempero.*
Obscure, adj. *obscurus.*
Observe, v. *observo, animadverto, doceo.*
Obstacle (to be an), v. *officio.*
Obstinacy, n. *pertinacia.*
Obtain, v. *adipiscor, potior.*
Ocean, n. *oceanus.*
Occupy, v. *occupo, teneo.*
Occur, v. *incido.*
Of, prep. (concerning) *de,* (from) *a, ab;* sign of the genitive without a corresponding word, and of the accusative after a verb of asking.
Offend, v. *offendo, pecco.*
Offer sacrifice, v. *facio sacrum.*
Office, n. *magistratus.*
Often, adv. *sæpe;* very

often, *persæpe;* oftener, *sæpius;* oftentimes, *aliquoties.*
Old, old man, *senex;* old age, *senectus;* (far advanced in life) *grandævus, senior.*
Olive, n. *oliva.*
Olympian, adj. *Olympius.*
Olympic, adj. *Olympicus.*
On, prep. *in, ad;* on the least, *ad minimum;* on the other hand, *contra, e contrario.*
One, adj. *unus, alius, alter, quidam;* one—another, *alius—alius.*
Only, adv. *solum, tantummodo, tantum;* not only, *non solum.*
Open, v. *aperio;* to be open, *pateo.*
Opened, pt. (being laid open) *patefactus.*
Openly, adv. *palam, plane.*
Opinion, n. *opinio, sententia.*
Opportunity, n. *potestas.*
Oppose, v. *eo obviam, resisto.*
Or, conj. *aut, vel, ve.*
Oration, oratory, n. *oratio.*
Orator, n. *orator.*
Order, v. *jubeo, edico.*
Order, n. *jussus.*
Origin, n. (source) *fons;* (beginning) *initium.*
Orphean, adj. *Orphicus.*
Other, adj. *alius, alter, cæterus, reliquus.*
Otherwise, adv. *aliter.*
Ought, v. *debeo, oportere.*
Our, pr. *noster.*
Out of, prep. *e, ex.*
Out of the way, adj. *devius.*
Outdo, v. *vinco.*
Over, prep. *super, in.*
Over (finished), v. *actum est;* pt. *peractus.*
Overcome, v. *vinco.*
Overwhelm, v. *obruo, occupo.*
Own, v. (confess) *fateor.*
Owner, n. (master) *dominus.*
Ox, n. *bos.*

P.

Pace, n. *passus.*
Pain, n. *dolor.*
Painful, adj. *gravis.*
Palace, n. *regia (domus.)*
Palm, n. *palma.*
Paper, n. *charta.*
Pardon, n. *venia.*
Part, n. *pars.*
Partaker, n. *particeps.*
Parthians, n. *Parthi,* pl.
Partiality, n. *inclinatio.*
Particular, adj. *singuli, quidam.*
Partly, adv. *partim.*
Party, n. *pars.*
Pass, v. (over) *transeo, trajicio;* by (omit), *omitto.*
Passion, n. *libido, cupiditas;* being in a passion, *iratus.*
Passionate, adj. *iracundus.*
Past, pt. *actus, præterritus.*
Patience, n. *patientia.*
Patrimony, n. *patrimonium.*
Peace, n. *pax.*
Peculiar, adj. *proprius.*
People, n. *populus, plebs, multitudo;* of the people, *popularis.*
Perceive, v. *video, cerno, cognosco.*
Perfect, adj. *perfectus;* (matchless) *singularis.*
Perfectly, adv. *perfectè, omnino.*
Perfidious, adj. *perfidus.*
Perform, v. *ago, præsto;* during the performance (of a play), *inter spectandum.*
Perhaps, adv. *forsitan.*
Perish, v. *pereo.*
Permit, v. *sino;* (suffer) *patior.*
Pernicious, adj. *malus.*
Perpetual, adj. *sempiternus.*
Perplex, v. *conturbo.*
Persia, n. *Persis* and *Persæ.*
Persians, n. *Persæ,* pl.
Person, n. *homo.*
Persuade, v. *persuadeo.*
Petulant, adj. *petulans.*
Philip, n. *Philippus.*
Philosopher, n. *philosophus.*
Philosophize, v. *philosophor.*
Philosophy, n. *philosophia.*
Physician, n. *medicus.*
Pinch (with cold), v. *algeo.*
Pity, v. *misereor.*
Place, n. *locus;* places, *loca,* pl.
Place, v. *pono, impono, colloco.*
Plain, n. *campus.*
Plan, n. *consilium.*
Plane-tree, n. *platanus.*
Plant, v. *semino.*
Play, v. *ludo.*
Pleasant, adj. *jucundus; ex sententia, gratus, dulcis.*
Please, v. *delecto, placeo;* if you please, *si tibi placet;* it pleases, *juvat.*
Pleasing, adj. *dulcis, jucundus.*
Pleasure, n. (will) *voluntas;* (enjoyment) *voluptas;* at their pleasure, *suo jure.*
Plough, v. *aro.*
Plunder, v. *diripio.*
Plunder, n. *præda, rapta,* pl.
Poem, n. *carmen.*
Poet, n. *poeta.*
Poison, n. *venenum.*
Pomœrium, n. *Pomœrium.*
Pompey, n. *Pompeius.*
Poor (man), n. *pauper;* adj. *egenus.*
Popular, adj. *popularis.*
Porcian, adj. *Porcius.*
Possess, v. (have) *possideo;* (take possession) *occupo, insideo.*
Post, v. (to place) *constituo.*
Posterity, n. *posteritas, posteri.*
Power, n. *imperium, potestas; opes,* pl.; in one's own power, *in manu.*
Practice, n. *exercitatio.*
Prætor, n. *Prætor.*
Praise, n. *laus.*
Praise, v. *laudo.*
Pray, v. *precor.*
Precept, n. *præceptum.*
Prefer, v. *antepono, præpono, antefero, malo.*
Present, n. (gift) *donum.*
Present (to be), *adsum, intersum, intervenio.*
Preserve, v. *servo, conservo, obtineo.*
Presume, v. (dare) *audeo.*

Pretend, v. *simulo.*
Prevent, v. *impedio.*
Prey, n. *præda;* (things taken), *rapta.*
Price, n. *pretium.*
Prison, n. *carcer.*
Prisoner, n. (one accused) *reus.*
Private, adj. in a private station, *privatus.*
Privation, n. *privatio.*
Probably, adv. *fortasse.*
Procure, v. *comparo.*
Procured, pt. *paratus.*
Prodigy, n. *prodigium.*
Produce (cause), v. *efficio;* to be produced (born), *nascor.*
Profit, v. *prosum.*
Prohibited, pt. *prohibitus.*
Promise, v. *promitto, polliceor.*
Promise, n. *promissum.*
Pronounce, v. (declare) *dico.*
Proof, n. (effect) *effectus.*
Proper, adj. *proprius, idoneus.*
Property, n. *proprium, res, res familiaris;* to demand restitution of property, *res repetere.*
Proportioned (in proportion to), prep. *pro.*
Propose (a law), v. *fero.*
Prosecute, v. *persequor.*
Protection, n. *præsidium.*
Provide, v. *prospicio, curo.*
Provided, conj. *dum, modo, dummodo.*
Providence, n. *providentia.*
Province, n. *provincia.*
Provision, n. *res frumentaria.*
Provoke, v. *lacesso;* to be provoked, *exardesco.*
Prudence, n. *prudentia.*
Prudently, adv. *prudenter.*
Public, adj. *publicus;* in public, *in publicum;* make public, v. *divulgo.*
Publicly (at the public expense), adv. *publicè.*
Publish, v. *edo.*
Punish, v. *punio.*
Punishment, n. *supplicium.*
Pupil (of the eye), n. *pupula.*
Purchase, v. *mercor.*
Pure, v. *sanctus.*
Purpose (intention), n. *studium;* (use) *usus.*
Pursue, v. *sequor, insequor.*
Pursuit (employment), *studium.*
Put, v. *pono;* put upon (as a garment), *injicio, induo;* put off, *exuo;* put to death, *neco;* (give) *do.*
Ptolemy, n. *Ptolemæus.*
Pythagorean, adj. *Pythagoreus.*
Pythian, adj. *Pythius.*

Q.

Quæstor, n. *quæstor.*
Quantity, n. *vis.*
Queen, n. *regina.*
Quicken, v. *incito.*
Quiet, adj. *quietus.*
Quit (go from), v. *exeo.*
Quite, adv. *prorsus.*

R.

Raft, n. *rates.*
Rage, to be in a rage, v. *fremo.*
Raging, adj. *insanus.*
Rain, n. *imber.*
Rainbow, n. *arcus.*
Raised, pt. *sublatus.*
Rank, n. *locus, ordo.*
Rapidity, n. *celeritas.*
Rascal, n. *nebulo.*
Rashly, adv. *temerè.*
Rashness, n. *temeritas.*
Rate (value), v. *æstimo.*
Reach, v. *attingo.*
Read, v. *lego.*
Readily, adv. *facilè.*
Ready (in attendance), adv. *præsto;* to be ready, prepared, *paror.*
Reap, v. *demeto.*
Reason, n. *ratio;* (cause) *causa;* by reason of, *præ;* with reason, justly, *jure.*
Reasoning, n. *ratio.*
Recall, v. *revoco.*
Receive, v. *recipio, accipio.*
Received, pt. *acceptus.*
Receptacle, n. *receptaculum.*
Reckon, v. *æstimo, habeo.*
Recognize, v. *agnosco.*
Recollection, n. *recordatio.*
Recommend, v. *commendo.*
Recover, v. *recreo, recupero;* (receive back) *recipio.*
Reduce, v. *redigo.*
Reflect, v. *reputo.*
Refute, v. *refello.*
Regard, v. (esteem) *habeo.*
Register, n. *commentarium.*
Regulate, v. *rego.*
Reign, v. *impero.*
Reign, n. *imperium.*
Reject, v. *rejicio, repudio.*
Rejoice, v. *gaudeo;* rejoice with, *gratulor.*
Relate, v. *prodo, dico, fero.*
Relieve, v. *subvenio.*
Religious, adj. *religiosus.*
Religiously, adv. *sanctè.*
Relying on, adj. *fretus.*
Remain, v. *maneo.*
Remaining, n. *remansio.*
Remarkable, adj. *insignis.*
Remember, v. *memini, recordor, reminiscor.*
Remembrance, n. *memoria, recordatio, commemoratio.*
Remove, v. *amoveo, removeo.*
Render (make), v. *facio, reddo.*
Renew, v. *redintegro.*
Repent, v. *pœnitēre.*
Report, n. *fama, rumor.*
Report, v. *fero;* it is reported, *fertur.*
Replace, v. *repono.*
Reply, v. *respondeo.*
Republic, n. *respublica.*
Reputation, n. *existimatio.*
Require, v. *desidero.*
Requite, v. *refero.*
Resentment, n. *ira.*
Reserve, v. *reservo.*
Resist, v. *resisto.*
Resolutely, adv. *pertinaciter.*
Resort (come to), v. *venio.*
Respect, v. *diligo.*
Respected, pt. *expectatus.*
Respecting, prep. *de.*
Rest (remaining), adj. *reliquus.*

Restore, v. *reddo, restituo.*
Retentive, adj. *tenax.*
Retreat, v. *regredior.*
Return, v. *redeo, refero, regredior;* in return, in turn, *invicem.*
Reverence, v. *colo, revereor.*
Revile, v. *maledico.*
Reward, n. *præmium.*
Rhetorician, n. *rhetor.*
Rich, adj. *dives, ditis, locuples.*
Riches, n. *divitiæ,* pl.; great riches, *fortuna.*
Ridiculous, adj. *ridiculus.*
Right, n. *jus.*
Right, adj. *rectus, æquus.*
Rightly, adv. *rectè.*
Rind, n. *liber.*
Ring, n. *anulus* (ann.)
Ripe, adj. *maturus.*
River, n. *fluvius, flumen.*
Rob, v. *peculor.*
Robber, n. *latro.*
Robe, n. *pallium.*
Rock, n. *saxum.*
Rod, n. *virga.*
Roman, adj. *Romanus.*
Rome, n. *Roma.*
Rough, adj. *horridus.*
Royal, adj. *regius.*
Rule, v. *domino, imperito.*
Rule, n. *decretum.*
Run, v. *curro.*
Rush, v. *irrumpo.*

S.

Sacrifice, n. *sacrum.*
Sad, adj. *tristis.*
Safe, adj. *salvus, tutus.*
Safely, adv. *tutè.*
Safety, n. *salus.*
Sagacious, adj. *sagax.*
Sagacity, n. *prudentia.*
Sail, v. *navigo.*
Sailor, n. (one sailing) *navigans.*
Sake (for the sake of), *gratiâ, causâ.*
Salute, v. *saluto.*
Same, adj. *idem;* at the same time, adv. *simul.*
Satiety, n. *satietas.*
Satisfaction, n. (pleasure) *voluptas.*
Satisfy, v. *expleo, satisfacio.*
Save, v. *servo.*
Say, v. *dico, fero, loquor, dissero;* I say, *inquam;* they say, *ferunt;* it is said, *fertur, dicitur.*
Saying, n. *dictum.*
Scarcely, adv. *vix.*
Scholar (pupil), n. *discipulus.*
School, n. *schola, ludus literarius.*
Science, n. *scientia, doctrina.*
Scourge, v. *verbero.*
Sea, n. *mare.*
Search, v. *quæro.*
Season, n. *tempestivitas.*
Seat, n. *sedes.*
Second, adj. *secundus, alter;* adv. a second time, *iterum.*
Secretly, adv. *clam.*
Security, n. *præsidium.*
See, v. *video, cerno.*
Seed, n. *semen.*
Seek, v. *quæro, peto;* seek for, *requiro.*
Seem, v. *videor.*
Seize, v. *capio;* seize upon, *occupo.*
Self, pr. *ipse;* I myself, *ego ipse;* we ourselves, *nosmet ipsi.*
Sell, v. *vendo.*
Senate, n. *senatus.*
Senator, n. *senator.*
Senatorian (of a senator), *senatorius.*
Send, v. *mitto;* send for, *arcesso;* send before, *præmitto;* send away, *dimitto;* send back, *remitto.*
Sensation, n. *sensus.*
Sense, n. *sensus.*
Sentiment, n. *sententia.*
Separate, v. *secerno.*
Sequani, n. *Sequani;* of the Sequani, adj. *Sequanus.*
Serpent, n. *serpens.*
Serve, v. *servio.*
Service, n. *opera, utilitas.*
Sesterces, n. *Sestertii* (Gr. 907).
Set, v. (place) *pono;* set out (depart), *proficiscor;* set before *or* forth, *propono.*
Settle down, v. *consido.*
Seventh, adj. *septimus.*
Seventy, adj. *septuaginta;* of seventy, adj. *septuagenarius.*
Severe, adj. *severus, acerbus.*
Severely, adv. *graviter.*
Severity, n. *severitas.*
Shade, n. *umbra;* in the shades below, *apud inferos.*
Shameful, adj. *turpis, fœdus.*
Share (part), n. *pars.*
Sharpen, v. *acuo.*
She, pr. *ea, illa* (is, ille).
Shield, n. *scutum.*
Shocked, pt. *commotus.*
Shore, n. *litus, littus.*
Short, adj. *brevis;* in short, adv. *denique.*
Shout, shouting, n. *clamor.*
Show, v. *ostendo;* (teach) *doceo;* (point out) *monstro.*
Show, n. *spectaculum.*
Shut up, v. *includo;* pt. *inclusus.*
Sicily, n. *Sicilia.*
Sick, adj. *æger, ægro corpore.*
Side (part), n. *pars.*
Sight, n. *conspectus.*
Signal, n. *signum.*
Silence, n. *taciturnitas.*
Silent, adj. *tacitus;* to be silent, *taceo.*
Silver, n. *argentum.*
Similarity, n. *similitudo.*
Simplicity, n. *simplicitas.*
Sin, n. *peccatum.*
Sin, v. *pecco.*
Since, conj. *quippe.*
Sincerity, n. *sinceritas.*
Single (one), adj. *unus.*
Singly, one by one, adj. *singuli.*
Sink, v. (let down) *demitto.*
Sister, n. *soror.*
Sit, v. *sedeo.*
Six, adj. *sex;* sixth, *sextus.*
Six hundred, adj. *sexcenti.*
Skill, n. *sollertia.*
Skilfully, adv. *apte;* most skilfully, *aptissime.*
Sky, n. *cœlum;* to the skies, *ad cœlum.*
Slaughter, n. *cædis.*
Slave, n. *servus, mancipium;* slaves, *servitium.*
Slavery, n. *servĭtus.*
Slay, v. *occīdo, interficio.*

Sleep, n. *somnus.*
Sleep, v. *dormio.*
Sloth, n. *segnitia.*
Slower, adv. *tardius.*
Smiling, pt. *subridens.*
Snake, n. *draco.*
So, adv. *sic;* (in such a manner) *ita;* (to such a degree) *adeo.*
So much, adj. *tantus;* of so much value, *tanti (pretii);* see much; adv. *tantopere, tam;* so long, *tam diu.*
So many, adj. *tot.*
So that, *ut.*
Society, n. *convictus.*
Soft, adj. *mollis.*
Soften, v. *lenio.*
Softly, adv. *leniter.*
Soil, n. *solum;* (ground) *ager.*
Soldier, n. *miles.*
Solemn, adj. *solennis.*
Solicitude, n. *solicitudo.*
Solitude, n. *solitudo.*
Some, adj. *nonnullus, alius, aliquot;* some—others, *alii—alii;* some one, *aliquis;* (there are some who) *sunt qui;* some (quantity), *aliquantus.*
Something, adj. *aliquid.*
Sometime, adv. *aliquandiu.*
Sometimes, adv. *interdum.*
Somewhat, adv. *aliquid.*
Son, n. *filius.*
Soon, as soon as possible, *quamprimum.*
Soonest, adv. *celerrimè.*
Soothsayer, n. *haruspex.*
Sorrow, n. *mœstitia.*
Sorrowful, adj. *mœstus.*
Soul, n. *animus.*
Sow, v. *sero.*
Spain, n. *Hispania.*
Spare, v. *parco.*
Speak, v. *loquor, eloquor, dico;* speak well of, *benedico.*
Spear, n. *hasta.*
Spectacle, n. *spectaculum.*
Speech, n. *oratio;* freedom of speech, *libera oratio.*
Spend (time), v. *ago, dego;* (give away) *erogo.*
Spent, pt. *actus.*
Spinning, n. *lanificium.*
Spoils, n. *spolia,* pl.
Spoken, pt. *dictus.*

Spur, n. *calcur.*
Stadium, n. *stadium.*
Staff, n. *baculum.*
Stage, n. *scena.*
Stand, v. *sto;* stand in the way, oppose, *obsto.*
Standard, n. *vexillum.*
Star, n. *astrum, sidus.*
State, n. *civitas, respublica.*
Station, n. (place) *locus, fortuna.*
Steer, to go towards, *peto.*
Step (to walk), v. *ingredior.*
Stick, v. *adhæreo.*
Stimulate, v. *impello.*
Stoics, n. *Stoici.*
Stone, n. (bezel of a ring) *pala.*
Storm, n. *tempestas.*
Stranger, n. *hospes.*
Stratagem, n. *dolus.*
Strength, n. *vis, vires,* pl. *robur.*
Strike, v. *percutio.*
Strong, adj. *fortis.*
Struck, pt. *perculsus.*
Study, n. *meditatio;* at his studies, *discens.*
Study, v. *edisco.*
Study (consult for), v. *consulo.*
Style (kind of writing), n. *genus.*
Suavity, n. *suavitas.*
Subdue, v. *domo, perdomo, subigo.*
Subject, n. *res.*
Submit (obey), v. *pareo.*
Succeed, v. *succedo.*
Successful, adj. *secundus.*
Successfully, adv. *benè.*
Such, adj. *talis, tantus.*
Such, adv. (so) *tam.*
Sudden, adj. *subitus.*
Suddenly, adv. *subito.*
Suffer, v. *patior, perpetior.*
Suffice, v. *suppeto.*
Sufficient, sufficiently, adv. *satis.*
Suit, v. *convenio.*
Summon, v. *cito.*
Sun, n. *sol.*
Sup, v. *cœno.*
Superb, adj. *conspicuus.*
Superfluous, adj. *supervacuus.*
Superiority, n. *præstantia.*
Support (hold up), v. *sustineo.*
Supply, v. *suppedito.*

Suppose, v. *arbitror, puto, existimo.*
Surface (upper part), *summus;* surface of the water, *summa aqua.*
Surnamed, pt. *cognominatus.*
Surpass, v. *supero, vinco, præsto.*
Surrender, n. *deditio.*
Surrounded, pt. *stipatus.*
Suspect, v. *suspicor.*
Swear, v. *juro.*
Sweet, adj. *dulcis.*
Swerve, v. *discedo.*
Swim, v. *nato;* swim over, *transnato.*
Sword, n. *gladius, ensis.*
Syracuse, n. *Syracusæ,* pl.

T.

Take, v. *capio;* take away, *aufero, tollo;* derogate, *derogo;* take away forcibly, *detraho, extraho;* take amiss, *moleste fero;* to take captive, *capio;* (to hold) *habeo;* take by assault, *expugno;* take care, *caveo;* take into, *induco;* take (to lead), *duco;* taken, *i. e.* having taken, *nactus.*
Talk together, v. *confabulor.*
Tarquin, *Tarquinius.*
Teach, v. *doceo.*
Teacher, n. *doctor, magister.*
Tear, n. *lacrima.*
Tear in pieces, v. *dilacero.*
Tell, v. *dico;* (relate) *narro;* (commemorate) *memini.*
Temperance, n. *temperantia.*
Temple, n. *ædes, templum.*
Ten, adj. *decem.*
Tend, v. (avail) *valeo.*
Tender, adj. *tener.*
Terminate, v. *patro, detraho.*
Terrified, pt. *territus.*
Terrify, v. *terreo.*
Territory, n. *finis, ager.*
Than, conj. *quam.*
That, sign of the accusativo before the infinitive.
That, conj. *ut, quod, quin;* that not, *ne;* in order that, *quo.*

That, dem. pr. *is*, *ille*, *iste*.
That, rel. pr. *qui*; that which, *id quod*.
Theatre, n. *theatrum*.
Theban, adj. *Thebanus*.
Their, pr. *eorum*, *illorum*; (is, ille) *suus*.
Then, conj. *igitur*.
Then, adv. *tum*, *tunc*; (after that) *inde*, *deinde*.
Thence, adv. *inde*.
There, adv. *ibi*.
Therefore, adv. *igitur*, *itaque*, *ideo*.
They, pr. *ii*, *illi*, pl. (is, ille).
Thief, n. *fur*.
Thing, n. *res*, *negotium*.
Think, v. *puto*, *existimo*, *cogito*, *sentio*, *censeo*.
Third, adj. *tertius*.
Thirst, v. (to be thirsty) *sitio*.
Thirty, adj. *triginta*.
This, pr. *hic*.
Thou, pr. *tu*; you, *tu*, *vos*.
Though, conj. *licet*, *si*, *quum* (*cum*), *quamvis*.
Thousand, adj. *mille*, pl. *millia*.
Threats, n. *minæ*, pl.
Threaten, v. *minor*.
Three, adj. *tres*; three hundred, *trecenti*.
Three brothers (born at one birth), *trigemini*.
Throw, v. *jacio*, *conjicio*, *mitto*.
Throw away, v. *abjicio*.
Thunder, n. *tonitru*, *fulmen*.
Thus, adv. *sic*, *adeo*.
Thy, pr. *tuus*.
Tiber, n. *Tiberis*.
Tide, n. *æstus*.
Tiger, n. *tigris*.
Till, adv. *donec*.
Time, n. *tempus*; (season) *ætas*, *hora*, *dies*; at this time, *hoc tempore*; at one time, *uno tempore*; there was no time, *tempus defuit*.
Tired (to be), v. *tædere*.
To, prep. *ad*; (into) *in*; (towards) *erga*.
To-day, adv. *hodie*.
Together with, adv. *simul cum*.
Tolerable, adj. *tolerabilis*.
Tomb, n. *sepulcrum*.
Tongue, n. *lingua*.
Top, adj. *summus*. (Gr. 273.)
Torment, v. *crucio*.
Torture, n. *crux*, *cruciatus*.
Towards, prep. *adversus*.
Tower, n. *turris*.
Town, n. *oppidum*.
Track (as a dog), v. *indago*.
Train, v. *erudio*.
Tranquillity, n. *tranquillitas*.
Transmit, v. *trado*.
Traveller, n. *viator*.
Treachery, n. *proditio*.
Treason, n. *majestas*.
Tree, n. *arbor*; (young trees) *stirps*.
Tribune, n. *tribunus*.
Triumph, v. *triumpho*.
Troops, n. *copiæ*; (garrison) *præsidium*.
Trouble, v. *ango*.
Trouble, n. *molestia*.
True, adj. *verus*.
Truly, adv. *vere*, *profecto*.
Trumpet, n. *tuba*.
Trusty, adj. *certus*.
Truth, n. *veritas*, *verum*.
Try (a cause), v. *judico*.
Turn, v. *verto*, *converto*; turn away, *averto*; turn to and fro, *versor*; turn out, *evenio*.
Tusculan, adj. *Tusculanus*.
Twenty, adj. *viginti*.
Twist around, v. *complector*.
Two, adj. *duo*; two by two, *bini*; two together, *ambo*.
Two hundred, adj. *ducenti*.
Tyrant, n. *tyrannus*.

U.

Unacquainted, adj. *rudis*.
Uncertain, adj. *incertus*; (not clear) *obscūrus*.
Uncle, n. *avunculus*.
Unconquered, adj. *invictus*.
Under, prep. *sub*, *in*.
Undergo, v. *suscipio*.
Understand, v. *intelligo*, *cognosco*.
Undertake, v. *suscipio*, *ago*.
Unfaithful, adj. *infidus*.
Unfortunate, adj. *miser*.
Unhurt, pt. *illæsus*.
Unite, v. *consocio*.
Unjustly, adv. *unjustè*.
Unknown, pt. *ignotus*.
Unless, conj. *nisi*.
Unlike, adj. *dissimilis*.
Unmindful, adj. *immemor*.
Unpleasing, adj. *injucundus*.
Unsatisfied (empty), adj. *inanis*.
Unsightly, adj. *turpis*.
Unskilful, adj. *imperitus*.
Until, adv. *dum*, *donec*.
Untouched, adj. *integer*.
Unwilling, adj. *invitus*; to be unwilling, v. *nolo*.
Unworthy, adj. *indignus*.
Upon, prep. *in*, *super*, *de*.
Us, pr. *nos*; acc. pl. (*ego*).
Use (make use of), v. *utor*, *adhibeo*.
Use, n. *usus*.
Use (to be wont), v. *soleo*; (to be accustomed) *consuesco*.
Useful, adj. *utilis*; very useful, *perutilis*.
Utility, n. *utilitas*.
Utter (give utterance to), v. *enuncio*.

V.

Valor, n. *virtus*.
Valuable, adj. *pretiosus*.
Value, v. *æstimo*; value greatly, *æstimo magni*; more, *pluris*; most, *maximi*.
Vanity, n. *ambitio*.
Vanquished. pt. *victus*.
Various, adj. *varius*.
Vehemently, adv. *vehementer*.
Veil, v. *obnubo*.
Vent (give vent), v. *agito*.
Verse, n. *versus*.
Very (intensive), adv. *vehementer*, *maxime*, *perquam*, *quam*, *ipse*; very highly, *quam magni*.
Vespasian, n. *Vespasianus*.
Vessel, n. *vas*.
Vestige, n. *vestigium*.
Vex, v. *ango*.
Vice, n. *vitium*.
Victor, n. *victor*.
Victorious, adj. *victor*.
Victory, n. *victoria*.
Vigour, n. *vires*, pl.
Villa, n. *villa*.
Violate, v. *violo*.
Virgil, n. *Virgilius*.
Virgin, n. *virgo*.

Virtue, n. *virtus, honestas.*
Visitor, n. *hospes.*
Vitiate, v. *depravo.*
Voice, n. *vox.*
Voluntary, adj. *voluntarius.*
Vote, v. *fero suffragium.*
Voyage (to have a voyage), v. *navigo.*

W.

Wage war, v. *gero bellum.*
Wakefulness, n. *vigilia.*
Walk, v. *ambulo;* walk about, *obambulo.*
Wall, n. *murus;* (of a fort) *mœnia*, pl.; (of a house) *paries.*
Want (need), v. *egeo, indigeo;* to be wanting, *desum.*
Want, n. *egestas.*
War, v. *bello.*
War, n. *bellum;* in war, *militiæ;* of war, adj. *militaris;* art of war, *res militaris.*
Warm, adj. *tepidus.*
Was, imperf. of am (*sum*).
Water, n. *aqua.*
Weakness, n. *infirmitas.*
Wealth, n. *divitiæ*, pl.
Wealthy, adj. *opulentus, opulens.*
Weighty, adj. *gravis.*
Well, adv. *bene, beate;* very well, *optime.*
Were, v. pl. of *was.*
What? pr. *quis, equis, quisnam.*
What, of what consequence adj. *quantus.*
What (= that which), rel. pr. *quod* (*qui*).
Whatever, pr. *quid, quidcunque, quicquid.*
When, adv. *quum* (*cum*), *ubi.*
Where, adv. *ubi, ubinam;* of what nation? *ubinam gentium?* in what part of the world? *ubi terrarum?*
Wherefore, adv. *igitur, quare.*
Whether, interrog. *num, an.*
Which, interrog. pr. *quis.*
Which, rel. pr. *quod* (*qui*).
Which of two, pr. *uter.*
Whichever, pr. *uterque.*
While, whilst, adv. *dum;* (when) *quum* (*cum*).
Whither, adv. *quo, quonam.*
Who, interrog. pr. *quis.*
Who, rel. pr. *qui;* to whom, *quicum.*
Whole, adj. *omnis, totus.*
Why, adv. *cur, quid* (for *propter quid*).
Wicked, adj. *impius, improbus.*
Wickedness, n. *scelus.*
Wide, adj. *latus.*
Wife, n. *uxor.*
Wild, adj. *silvestris;* wild beast, *fera.*
Will, v. *volo;* will not, *nolo.*
Willingly (freely), adv. *libenter;* (gladly) *lubenter.*
Win, v. *concilio.*
Winter-quarters, n. *hiberna.*
Wisdom, n. *sapientia, consilium.*
Wise, adj. *sapiens, gravis, prudens.*
Wish, v. *volo;* wish rather, prefer, *malo;* I wish, O that, conj. *utinam.*
Wit, n. *ingenium.*
With, prep. *cum, in;* sign of ablative.
Withdraw, v. *deduco.*
Within, prep. *intra, in.*
Without, prep. *sine, extra;* to be without, v. *careo.*
Withstand, v. *sustineo.*
Witness, n. *testis.*
Woman, n. *mulier.*
Wonder, v. *miror.*
Wont (to be), v. *soleo.*
Wood (forest), n. *silva;* (timber) *lignum, materies.*
Wool, n. *lana.*
Woollen, adj. *laneus.*
Word, n. *verbum;* in a word, *denique.*
Work, n. *opus, opera.*
Workman, n. *opifex.*
World, n. *orbis, terræ*, pl.
Worse, adj. *pejor.*
Worthily, worthy, adv. (in a manner worthy), *digne.*
Worthy, adj. *dignus, bonus.*
Would be, v. *forem.* (Gr. 222, 5.)
Wound, v. *vulnero.*
Wound, n. *vulnus.*
Write, v. *scribo;* write back, *rescribo.*

Y.

Year, n. *annus.*
Yesterday's, adj. *hesternus.*
Yet, conj. *tamen, veruntamen.*
Yield to, v. *cedo;* (obey) *pareo.*
Yield (give up), v. *succumbo.*
You, pr. sing. *tu;* pl. *vos.*
Young man, n. *adolescens, juvenis.*
Your (of thee), *tui;* (of you) *vestrum;* adj. pr. *tuus, vester.*
Youth, n. *juventus, adolescentia;* time of youth, *juventa;* young man, *juvenis.*

END.

VIEWS OF THE MICROSCOPIC WORLD; designed for General Reading, and as a Hand-book for Classes in Natural Sciences. By Prof' Brocklesby $1 12.

By the aid of a powerful microscope, the author has given us highly instructive accounts of Infusorial Animalcules, Fossil Infusoria, Minute Aquatic Animals, Structure of Wood and Herbs, Crystallization, Parts of Insects, &c., &c.

To those who are necessarily deprived of the aid of a microscope, and even to those who have it, this is a most valuable work. It is clearly and pleasantly written. The sections on the Animalcules, Infusoria, and Crystallization, are very beautifully illustrated with large and expensive plates. The descriptions of the different kinds of these wonderful little animals, many of which multiply by billions in a few hours, are really very instructive. There is no better school library book in the world. It should be read by every man, woman and child.

HUMAN PHYSIOLOGY; designed for Colleges and the Higher Classes in Schools, and for General Reading. By Worthington Hooker, M. D Professor of the Theory and Practice of Medicine in Yale College. Illustrated with nearly 200 engravings. $1 25.

This is an original work, and not a compilation. It presents the subject in a new light, and at the same time embraces all that is valuable for its purpose that could be drawn from the most eminent sources. The highest encomiums are received from all quarters; a few are subjoined.

From CALEB J. HALLOWELL, *Alexandria High School, Va.*

Hooker's Physiology was duly received. We propose to adopt it as a text-book, and shall order in the course of a fortnight.

From the Boston Medical and Surgical Journal.

We can truly say that we believe this volume is of great value, and we hope that the rare merits of the diligent author will be both appreciated and patronized

From B. F. TEWKSBURY, *Lenoxville, Pa.*

I am ready to pronounce it unqualifiedly the most admirable book or work on the human system that has fallen under my notice, and they have not been few. If any one desires a complete and thorough elucidation of the great science discussed, they can nowhere be better satisfied than in the perusal of Dr. Hooker's most excellent work.

AN INTRODUCTORY WORK ON HUMAN PHYSIOLOGY, by Prof Hooker, has just been published, designed for all persons commencing the study Dr. Hooker's works seem to have taken their place decidedly at the head of all treatises on the subject of Physiology. They are rapidly going into seminaries and normal schools in all parts of the country, and the *best* institutions express their "delight at the result." 60 cents.

A COMPARATIVE ENGLISH-GERMAN GRAMMAR; based on the affinity of the two languages. By Prof. Elias Peissner, late of the University of Munich, now of Union College, Schenectady. $1.00

From the New York Churchman.

Of all the German Grammars we have ever examined, this is the most modest and unpretending, and yet it contains a system and a principle which is the life of it, as clear, as practical, as effective for learning grammar as any thing we have ever seen put forth, with so much more pretense of originality and show of philosophy. It will be found, too, we think, that the author has not only presented a new idea of much interest in itself, but has admirably carried it out in the practical lessons and exercises of his work.

From PROF J. FOSTER, *of Schenectady.*

I have examined Prof. Peissner's German Grammar with some attention, have marked with interest the rapid advancement of students here using it as a text-book, and have myself carefully tested it in the instruction of a daughter eleven years of age. The result is a conviction that it is most admirably adapted to secure easy, pleasant, and *real* progress, and that from no other work which has come under my notice can so satisfactory a knowledge of the language be obtained in a given time

WHITLOCK'S GEOMETRY AND SURVEYING, is a work for advanced students, possessing the highest claims upon the attention of Mathematical Teachers. $1 50.

In comparison with other works of the kind, it presents the following advantages:

1. A better connected and more progressive method of geometrizing, calculated to enable the student to go alone.
2. A fuller, more varied, and available practice, by the introduction of more than four hundred exercises, arithmetical, demonstrative, and algebraical, so chosen as to be serviceable rather than amusing, and so arranged as greatly to aid in the acquisition of the theory
3. The bringing together of such a body of geometrical knowledge, theoretical and practical, as every individual on entering into active life demands.
4. *A system of surveying which saves two-thirds of the labor required by the ordinary process.*

This work is well spoken of universally, and is already in use in some of the best Institutions of this country. It is recommended by Prof. Pierce, of Cambridge, Prof. Smith, of Middletown, Prof. Dodd, of Lexington, and many other eminent mathematicians.

From E. M. MORSE, ESQ.

I consider that I have obtained more mathematical knowledge from Whitlock's Geometry than from *all other* text-books combined. Unlike too many treatises of a similar nature, it is eminently calculated to make *mathematicians.*

PROF. J. B. DODD'S MATHEMATICAL SERIES

COMPRISES

AN ELEMENTARY AND PRACTICAL ARITHMETIC	$0 45
HIGH SCHOOL ARITHMETIC	0 84
ELEMENTS OF ALGEBRA	0 84
HIGHER ALGEBRA	1 50
KEY TO ALGEBRA	0 84
ELEMENTS OF GEOMETRY	1 00

These books are believed to be *unrivaled* in the following particulars:

1. The *philosophical accurateness* with which their topics are arranged, so as to show the mutual dependence and relationship of their subjects.
2. The *scientific* correctness and *practical convenience* of their greatly improved nomenclature.
3. The *clear* and *concise* manner in which *principles* are stated and *explanations* are given.
4. *Brevity* and *completeness* of rules.
5. The *distinctness* with which the true connection between Arithmetic and its cognate branches is developed.
6. The excellent and thorough intellectual discipline superinduced.

RECOMMENDATIONS.

From R. T. P. ALLEN, *Superintendent of Kentucky Military Institute.*

Upon a careful examination of a manuscript Treatise on Arithmetic, by Prof. Dodd, I find it greatly superior to all others which have come under my notice, in system, completeness, and nomenclature. The arrangement is natural, the system complete, and the nomenclature greatly improved. *These improvements are not slight; they are fundamental*—eminently worthy the attention of the mathematical teacher, and give a character of unity to the work which at once distinguishes it from all others on this subject.

From C. M. WRIGHT, *Associate Principal of Mount Palatine Academy.*

I have examined Dodd's Arithmetic, and am fully persuaded that it is *superior* to any other with which I am acquainted. I could speak in detail were it necessary, but *all that is required to establish its reputation and introduction, is to have it known by teachers.*

From M. S LITTLEFIELD, *Grand Rapids, Mich*

I have Dodd's Higher Arithmetic, and unhesitatingly pronounce it the best wors for advanced classes I have ever seen.

From E. HINDS, ESQ., *of Newtown Academy.*

I have recently adopted Dodd's High School Arithmetic, and like it much. Having seen that Prof. Dodd is also author of an Algebra, I should like to see that work be ore forming a *new class.*

From H. ELIAS, ESQ., *Palmyra, Mo.*

I have fairly tested Dodd's Algebra, and am much pleased with it. If I like his eometry as well as the Algebra, I shall forthwith introduce it into my school.

From PROF. W. H. DE PUY.

We have introduced Dodd's Algebra into the Genesee Wesleyan Seminary as a permanent text-book.

From R. H. MOORE, *Ill.*

Dodd's Algebra possesses excellencies pertaining to no other work

From REV J. A. MCCANLEY, *Va.*

I am much pleased with Dodd's Algebra, and will introduce it.

From OSCAR HARRIS, *N. J*

I use Professor Dodd's Algebra, and shall continue it as our regular text-boox

From PROF. A. L. HAMILTON, *President of Andrew College.*

I have examined with some care Prof. Dodd's Elements of Geometry, and, so fai as I am capable of judging, I conceive it to be in many respects decidedly the best work of the kind extant. For simplicity, exactness, and completeness, it can have no superior. Like his Arithmetic and Algebra, in many important particulars, his Geometry stands pre-eminent and alone.

A NEW COMMON-SCHOOL ARITHMETIC, by Prof. Dodd, is in press.

The Department of Public Instruction in Canada has repeatedly ordered Prof Dodd's books, as well as many of F. B. & Co.'s other publications, for use in schools

SCHELL'S INTRODUCTORY LESSONS IN ARITHMETIC; designed as an Introduction to the study of any Mental or Written Arithmetic. It contains a large amount of mental questions together with a large number of questions to be performed on the slate, thus combining mental and written exercises for young beginners. This is a very attractive little book, superior to any of its class. It leads the pupil on by the easiest steps possible, and yet insures constant progress. 20 cents.

From GEO. PAYNE QUACKENBOS, *Rector of Henry street Grammar School, N. Y*

It is unnecessary to do more than to ask the attention of teachers to this work, they cannot examine it impartially without being convinced of its superior merits It will, no doubt, become one of the most popular of school-books.

From J. MARKHAM, *Ohio.*

I wish to introduce Schell's little Arithmetic. It is just the thing for beginners Send six dozen

From G. C. MERRIFIELD, *Ind.*

I am highly pleased with Schell's little book, and shall use it.

From D. F. DEWOLF, *Ohio.*

Schell's little book for children is a *beau-ideal* of my own, and of course it suits

From D. G. HEFFRON, *Sup't. Schools, Utica.*

The School Committee have adopted Schell's Arithmetic for our public schools Send us three hundred.

AN INTELLECTUAL AND PRACTICAL ARITHMETIC; or, First Lessons in Arithmetical Analysis. By I. L. Enos, Graduate of the New York State Normal Schools. 25 cents.

The same *clearness* and *conciseness* characterize this admirable book that belong to the works of Prof. Dodd. The natural arrangements of the text, and the logical mode of solving the questions, is a peculiar and important feature belonging to this book alone.

From PROF. C. M. WRIGHT.

I have examined with care and interest Enos' Mental Arithmetic, and shall introduce it at once into the Academy.

From PROFS. D. I. PINCKNEY, S. M. FELLOWS, S. SEARLE, *Rock River Seminary*

We have examined an intellectual Arithmetic, by J. L. Enos, and like it much. We shall immediately use it in our school.

PROF. PALMER'S BOOK-KEEPING; Key and Blanks. 67 cents.

This excellent book is superior to the books generally used, because:

1. It contains a large number of business blanks to be filled by the learner, such as deeds, mortgages, agreements, assignments, &c., &c.
2. Explanations from page to page, from article to article, and to settle principles of law in relation to deeds, mortgages, &c., &c.
3. The exercises are to be *written* out, *after being calculated*. In other works, the pupil is expected to copy, merely.

Palmer's Book-Keeping is used in the New York Public Schools, and extensively in Academies, It is recommended by Horace Webster, LL. D., G. B. Docharty, LL. D., and a large number of *accountants* and teachers.

REV. P. BULLIONS' ENGLISH AND CLASSICAL SERIES,

COMPRISING

PRACTICAL LESSONS IN ENGLISH GRAMMAR AND COMPOSITION	$0 25
PRINCIPLES OF ENGLISH GRAMMAR	0 50
PROGRESSIVE EXERCISES IN ANALYSIS AND PARSING	0 15
INTRODUCTION TO ANALYTICAL GRAMMAR	0 30
NEW, OR ANALYTICAL AND PRACTICAL ENGLISH GRAMMAR	0 63
LATIN LESSONS, WITH EXERCISES IN PARSING. By Geo. Spencer, A. M. Half cloth, enlarged	0 63
BULLIONS' PRINCIPLES OF LATIN GRAMMAR	1 00
BULLIONS' LATIN READER. With an Introduction on the Idioms of the Latin Language. An improved Vocabulary	1 00
BULLIONS' CÆSAR'S COMMENTARIES	1 00
BULLIONS' CICERO'S ORATIONS. With reference both to Bullions', and Andrew's, and Stoddard's Latin Grammar	1 13
BULLIONS' SALLUST	1 00
BULLIONS' GREEK LESSONS FOR BEGINNERS	0 75
BULLIONS' PRINCIPLES OF GREEK GRAMMAR	1 13
BULLIONS' GREEK READER. With Introduction on the Idioms of the Greek Language, and Improved Lexicon	1 75
BULLIONS' LATIN EXERCISES	1 25
COOPER'S VIRGIL	2 00

In this series of books, the three Grammars, English, Latin, and Greek, are all on the same plan. The general arrangement, definitions, rules, &c., are the same, and expressed in the same language, as nearly as the nature of the case would admit To those who study Latin and Greek, much time and labor, it is believed, will be saved by this method, both to teacher and pupil. The analogy and peculiarities of the different languages being kept in view, will show what is common to all, or pecu bar to each; the confusion and difficulty unnecessarily occasioned by the use of elementary works differing widely from each other in language and structure, will be avoided, and the progress of the student rendered much more rapid, easy, and satisfactory.

No series of Grammars, having this object in view, has heretofore been prepared, and the advantages which they offer cannot be obtained in an equal degree by the study of any other Grammars now in use. They form a complete course of elementary books, in which the substance of the *latest* and *best* Grammars in each language has been compressed into a volume of convenient size, beautifully printed on superior paper, neatly and strongly bound, and are put at the lowest prices at which they can be afforded.

The elementary works intended to follow the Grammars—namely, the Latin Reader and the Greek Reader—are also on the SAME PLAN; are prepared with special references to these works, and contain a course of elementary instruction so unique and simple as to furnish great facilities to the student in these languages.

NOTICES.

From PROF. C. S. PENNEL, *Antioch College, Ohio.*

Bullions' books, by their superior arrangement and accuracy, their completeness as a series, and the references from one to the other, supply a want more perfectly than any other books have done. They bear the marks of the *instructor* as well as the scholar. It requires more than learning to make a good school-book.

From J. B. THOMPSON, A. M., *late Rector of the Somerville Classical Institute, N. J.*

I use Bullions' works—all of them—and consider them the best of the kind that have been issued in this or any other language. If they were *universally* used we would not have so many superficial scholars, and the study of the classics would be more likely to serve the end for which it was designed—the strengthening and adorning of the mind.

From A. C. RICHARDS, ESQ., *Clay Co., Ga.*

We think Bullions' Latin Grammar, in the arrangement of its syntax and the conciseness of its rules, the manner of treating prosody, and the conjugations of the verbs, superior to any other. If his Greek Reader is as good as the Latin Reader, we shall introduce it.

It is almost superfluous to publish notices of books so extensively used.

Within the last few months Dr. Bullions' English Grammar has been introduced into the Public, and many of the Private Schools, the Latin School, the English High School, the City Normal School, of the city of Boston; Normal Schools of Bridgewater and Westfield; Marlborough Academy; cities Salem, Newburyport, &c., Mass.; Portsmouth, Concord, and several academies in New Hampshire; and re-adopted in Albany and Troy, New York. They are used in over seventy academies in New York, and in many of the most flourishing institutions in every State of the Union. Also, in the Public Schools of Washington, D. C., and of Canada, in Oregon and Australia. The classical Series has been introduced into several colleges, and it is not too much to say that Bullions' Grammars bid fair to become the Standard Grammars of the country.

THE STUDENTS' SERIES.

BY J. S. DENMAN, A. M.

	Cents.
THE STUDENTS' PRIMER	7
" " SPELLING-BOOK	13
" " FIRST READER	13
" " SECOND "	25
" " THIRD "	40
" " FOURTH "	75
" " FIFTH "	94
" " SPEAKER	91

The Publishers feel justified in claiming that the Students' Series is decidedly *the best* for teaching reading, and spelling that has yet appeared. The plan of teaching includes, in the first steps, an ingenious and original mode of repetition which is very pleasing and encouraging to the pupil. The first books of the series are very instructive, and the later portions consist of fine selections, which are not hackneyed. Prof. Page, late Principal of the New York State Normal School, said of this system: "*It is the best I ever saw* for teaching the first principles of Reading." Such testimony is of the highest value, and none need be afraid to use the books on such a recommendation.

The numerous notices from all parts of the country where these books have been used, cannot be introduced here. They have just gone into the schools of Seneca County, N. Y., without solicitation; and the same is true of many important schools where they have been examined.

From C. B. Crumb, *N. Y.*

The Students' Series is, in my opinion, *the best in use*. I believe a class of young students will learn *twice as much*, with the same labor, as they would from any other system. The books of this Series excel in the purity and attraction of their style I have introduced them.

DR. COMSTOCK'S SERIES OF BOOKS ON THE SCIENCES, viz:

Introduction to Natural Philosophy. For Children	$0 42
System of Natural Philosophy, newly revised and enlarged, including late discoveries	1 00
Elements of Chemistry. Adapted to the present state of the Science	1 00
The Young Botanist. New edition	50
Elements of Botany. Including Vegetable Physiology, and a Description of Common Plants. With Cuts	1 25
Outlines of Physiology, both Comparative and Human. To which is added Outlines of Anatomy, excellent for the general scholar and ladies' schools.	80
New Elements of Geology. Highly Illustrated	1 25
Elements of Mineralogy. Illustrated with numerous Cuts	75
Natural History of Birds. Showing their Comparative Size. A new and valuable feature	50
Natural History of Beasts. Ditto	50
Natural History of Birds and Beasts. Do. Cloth	1 00
Questions and Illustrations to the Philosophy	30

All the above works are fully illustrated by elegant cuts.

The Philosophy has been republished in Scotland, and translated for the use o schools in Prussia. The many valuable additions to the work by its transatlantic editors, Prof. Lees, of Edinburgh, and Prof. Hoblyn, of Oxford, have been embraced by the author in his last revision. The Chemistry has been entirely revised, and contains all the late discoveries, together with methods of analyzing minerals and metals. Portions of the series are in course of publication in London. Such testimony, in addition to the general good testimony of teachers in this country, is sufficient to warrant us in saying that no works on similar subjects can equal them, or have ever been so extensively used. Continual applications are made to the publishers to replace the Philosophy in schools where, for a time, it has given way to other books. The style of Dr. Comstock is so clear, and his arrangement is so excellent, that no writer can be found to excel him for school purposes, and he takes constant pains to include new discoveries, and to consult eminently scientific men.

HON. J. OLNEY'S GEOGRAPHICAL SERIES.

Ppimary Geography; with Colored Maps. 25 cents.

Quarto Geography; with elegant Cuts, Physical Geography Tables, Map of the Atlantic Ocean, &c. 75 cents.

OLNEY'S SCHOOL GEOGRAPHY AND ATLAS. Containing Ancient Geography, Physical Geography, Tables, an entirely new Chart of the World, to show its physical conformation, as adapted to purposes of commerce, and also for the purpose of reviewing classes; also a Chronological Table of Discoveries. $1 12.

OLNEY'S OUTLINE MAPS. Of the World, United States Europe, Asia, Africa, America, and Canada, with Portfolio and Book of Exercises. $6.

All the recent improvements are included in Olney's Quarto and School Geographies. They are not obsolete or out of date, but fully "up to the times." In eleance or completeness they are not surpassed.

Mr. Olney commenced the plan of simplifying the first lesson, and teaching a child by what is familiar, to the exclusion of astronomy. He commenced the plan of having only those things represented on the maps which the pupil was required to learn. He originated the system of classification, and of showing the government, religion, &c., by symbols. He first adopted the system of carrying the pupil over the earth by means of the Atlas. His works first contained cuts, in which the dress architecture, animals, internal improvements, &c., of each country are grouped, so as to be seen at one view. His works first contained the world as known to the Ancients, as an aid to Ancient History, and a Synopsis of Physical Geography, with maps. In short, we have seen no valuable feature in any geography which has not originally appeared in these works; and we think it not too much to claim that, in many respects, most other works are copies of these. We think that a *fair and candid examination* will show that Olney's Atlas is the largest, most systematic, and complete of any yet published, and that the Quarto and Modern School Geographies contain more matter, and that better arranged, than any similar works; and they are desired to test the claims here asserted.

It is impossible to give here more than a fractional part of the recommendations, of the first order, which the publishers have received for the foregoing list of books Enough has been given to show the claims of the books to examination and use.

All these works are made in very neat, durable style, and are sold as low as a moderate remuneration will allow. Copies supplied to teachers for their own use at one-fifth off from the retail price, and postage paid. Large institutions are furnished sample copies without charge.

PRATT, OAKLEY & CO.

21 MURRAY STREET, NEW YORK.

www.ingramcontent.com/pod-product-compliance
Lightning Source LLC
LaVergne TN
LVHW020210110826
845151LV00003B/667

9781425534431